TOWARD A
HUMEAN
TRUE RELIGION

*Andre C. Willis*

# TOWARD A
# HUMEAN
# TRUE RELIGION

## GENUINE THEISM,
## MODERATE HOPE,
## AND PRACTICAL
## MORALITY

The Pennsylvania State University Press
University Park, Pennsylvania

*Library of Congress Cataloging-in-Publication Data*

Willis, Andre C., author.
Toward a Humean true religion : genuine theism,
moderate hope, and practical morality / Andre C. Willis.
pages    cm
Summary: "An examination of David Hume's
philosophy of religion that situates his conception 'true
religion' within the context of his overall science of
human nature, his rejection of popular religion, and his
Ciceronian influence"—Provided by publisher.
Includes bibliographical references and index.
ISBN 978-0-271-06487-1 (cloth : alk. paper)
1. Hume, David, 1711–1776—Religion.
2. Religion—Philosophy.      I. Title.

B1499.R45W55    2014
210.92—dc23
2014024780

FOR MY DAD,

*Herbert C. Willis*

*(1929–2014)*

# CONTENTS

## ACKNOWLEDGMENTS

This book has been long in the making, and it is, in many ways, a testament to the tenacious support of a persistent community of students, colleagues, and friends. I extend gratitude to David C. Lamberth, who threw me an intellectual lifeline during my time at Harvard and then seriously engaged me on many of the ideas here when they were inchoate. John Hare and former colleagues at Yale Divinity School provided invaluable encouragement for my argument in its early stages. Jennifer Herdt, in particular, went out of her way to patiently share her thoughtful insights with me on a draft of this manuscript. Her perceptive advice was indispensable for shaping the argument.

I am also grateful for colleagues in the Department of Religious Studies at Brown University, particularly in the area of religion and critical thought, who have provided me with an intellectually nurturing environment that has helped sharpen my critical tools. Specifically, I want to thank Tal Lewis, Mark Cladis, and Steve Bush for demonstrating exceptional patience and encouragement as scholar-teachers, for pressing me with difficult and sometimes challenging questions, and for giving examples of wholehearted critical engagement. Susan Harvey, Ross Kraemer, and Greg Schopen have extended invaluable encouragement over the past year or so, and Nancy Khalek has been an extraordinary source of sensitive guidance and intellectual inspiration. The practical assistance of Nicole Vadnais and Tina Creamer made academic life much easier and, by default, made me happier. To them I am also thankful.

The supportive wisdom and deep commitment of my personal friends have kept me going, and to them all I owe deep gratitude. I want to especially thank Thomas W. Johnson for doing whatever, whenever; Stephen K. Smith for his generosity of mind and his tender support; Allen Payne for his creative soul and unyielding inspiration; Craig R. Levine for his soulful presence and intellectual grace; Ronald E. Aubert for stability of presence and his exemplary determination; Adam Mansbach for being a wordsmith and a dependable source of connection. My sons, Clark and Coleman, were daily reminders of the importance of completing this project and, along with the care of my mother, Irene, and the strength of my sister, Pam, suffered long with me to complete it. Christina M. Downs has—at the end of this journey—been a crucial interlocutor and an integral source of joy in my life.

Yet, beyond a shadow of a doubt, I am most deeply indebted to Patricia Lorraine Rose for her inimitable support, perceptive comments, and incessant love as I attempted not only to complete this manuscript but also to grow in wisdom. She helped me learn how to love better every single day that I worked on this text. I am lucky to have a steadfast partner who can be an anchor in a sometimes stormy sea, an inspiration in an often turbulent world, and a lovely, smiling face when needed. All that comes through me is marked by her profound giving, love, and commitment. I thank her beyond thanks, and I graciously and gratefully watch our souls soar together.

## ABBREVIATIONS

DCNR     *Dialogues Concerning Natural Religion*, in *Principal Writings on Religion Including "Dialogues Concerning Natural Religion" and "The Natural History of Religion,"* ed., with intro. and notes, by J. C. A. Gaskin, Oxford World's Classics (Oxford: Oxford University Press, 1993). Cited by part and page number; introduction cited by paragraph number.

E     *An Enquiry Concerning Human Understanding,* in *Enquiries Concerning Human Understanding and Concerning the Principles of Morals,* ed. Lewis A. Selby-Bigge and Peter H. Nidditch (Oxford: Clarendon Press, 1975). Cited by section, part, and paragraph number or by section and paragraph number, where applicable.

EMPL     *Essays: Moral, Political, and Literary,* ed. Eugene F. Miller (Indianapolis: Liberty Classics, 1985). Cited by essay and page number.

EPM     *An Enquiry Concerning the Principles of Morals,* in Selby-Bigge and Nidditch, *Enquiries Concerning Human Understanding.* Cited by section and paragraph number or by section, part, and paragraph number, where applicable.

HE     *The History of England: From the Invasion of Julius Caesar to the Revolution in 1688,* 6 vols. (Indianapolis: Liberty Fund, 1983). Cited by volume and page number.

LET     *The Letters of David Hume,* ed. J. Y. T. Greig, 2 vols. (Oxford: Clarendon Press, 1932). Cited by volume, page, and letter number.

LG     *A Letter from a Gentleman to His Friend in Edinburgh,* ed. Ernest Campbell Mossner and John V. Price (Edinburgh: Edinburgh University Press, 1967). Cited by page number.

NHR     *Natural History of Religion,* in Gaskin, *Principal Writings on Religion.* Cited by section and paragraph number.

T     *A Treatise of Human Nature,* ed. Lewis A. Selby-Bigge, 15th ed. (Oxford: Clarendon Press, 1978). Cited by book, part, section, and paragraph number; introduction and appendix cited by paragraph number.

# INTRODUCTION

On June 6, 1764, Sir James Macdonald, Eighth Baronet of Sleat (a peninsula on the Isle of Skye in the Scottish Highlands), penned a letter from Paris. His friend David Hume, in his role of secretary to the British ambassador, was also in Paris. Hume's writings, particularly his *History* of the Stuarts and *Natural History of Religion*, were greatly admired in France, and statesmen, visiting dignitaries, and patrons of high-society literary salons exalted him as if he were an international luminary. In fact, the entire sojourn in France—Hume's fourth, longest visit (twenty-six months)—was marked by adulation from the French reading public. This enlivened and energized Hume. He may also have been relieved by the sentiment expressed in Sir James's correspondence to a friend in England: "poor Hume, who on your side of the water was thought to have too little religion, is here thought to have too much."[1]

What Sir James dubs Hume's "too much" religion is the point of departure for this book. Hume's contribution to religious thought is generally regarded as negative. He is widely read as an infidel, a critic of the Christian faith, and an attacker of popular forms of worship. His reputation as irreligious is well forged among his readers, and his argument against miracles perennially indoctrinates thousands of first-year philosophy students. The offhanded remark of Sir James, however, whose Oxford training and cosmopolitanism earned him the nickname "the Scottish Marcellus," reminds us that our philosophical views are, ultimately, perspectival and that religion is an interpretive concept. To the French, Hume's writings neither confirmed that he was an atheist in the mode of D'Holbach, nor made clear that he desired to destroy the church à la Voltaire. The iconoclastic French atheists therefore took Hume's critique of religion to be relatively mild.

Perhaps Sir James's comment reflected the philosophes' inclination to see Hume's work as open to the possibility that religion could be understood as a social convention and an artifact of culture that affirmed habits of moral excellence, aimed to moderate passion-inspired beliefs, and, as a result, buttressed the stability of the civic order. To them, even mild receptivity to this concept of religion would have been troubling, for religion required submission and thereby diminished human liberty. Hume actually shared most of the philosophes' criticisms against religious belief: he thought popular religion, in its modern sense as a philosophically legitimate system of beliefs, was mostly dangerous, and he was deeply troubled by the conventional categories of dogmatic Christianity (miracles, a supernatural deity with human attributes, etc.).

Hume took history seriously. He acknowledged religion to be a historical activity of humans in community that sometimes had pernicious outcomes and other times had virtuous ones. He may have understood himself as occupying a watershed moment when the classical notion of *religio*, a set of socially beneficial celebrations of the gods, was being replaced by the modern notion of religion, a system of beliefs, practices, and rules warranted by abstract thought. Treating Hume as a transitional figure between the dying legacy of *cultus deorum, pietas*, and *virtus* and the emergence of the idea 'religion' as a set of epistemically true yet speculative claims repositions the relative weight of his antireligious sentiment. Instead of relying on personal animus, this move allows that both historical and discursive forces were central for his invective against religion. The distinction between modern conceptions of religion that sought philosophical legitimation and the classical idea of *religio* that was marked by the capacity to stabilize sociopolitical order was partially reflected in Hume's bifurcated approach. As a modern thinker, he sometimes took religion to be a broad, neutral phenomenon eminently suited for cross-cultural and transhistorical study that had become corrupt in its contemporary popular manifestations. Yet the classical influence on his thought led him, at other times, to consider religion to be a particular virtue that could serve ethical formation in spite of its rampant distortions. This helps us understand why, on the one hand, Hume advanced a derisive critique of popular religious beliefs yet, on the other, he encouraged the virtue of moderate passions in our religious endeavors (as well as our philosophical and political ones). The dynamic oscillations of Hume's thought project—his veritable attempt to expose the severe limitations of abstract thought and false philosophy and, at the same time, his quest to promote the possibilities of reflective imagination and true philosophy—are accentuated by paying close attention to his handling of religion, which follows from his interrogation of modern philosophy.

Hume challenged false philosophy as abstruse thought by showing that its foundational claims for truth were, on its own standards, unjustifiable. He called, instead, for a reflective turn toward nature and common life—what he named "true philosophy"—to gain a clearer sense of the sources of our ideas and beliefs.

Hume's acute sense of the bidirectional historical tendencies (both classical and modern) tugging at his philosophical consciousness along with his temperament as a thinker coalesced in ways that made his thought project unique. His notion 'true philosophy' was as illuminating an ideal as its appearance was elusive. Its sources were uncommon, and its content—humility, greatness of mind, and benevolence—unusual. More exceptionally, true philosophy might, on rare occasion, invite religion to its "proper office," which Hume named "true religion," following the discursive parameters of his day. Hume did not detail what he meant by true religion. We may reasonably presume, however, based on the overall emphasis of his project, that a Humean true religion might preserve the best of classical religion updated, without the epistemic insecurities of modern philosophy summoned by commitments to rational certainty and moral realism. Too thin for converts and too mild for most religious believers, Hume's true religion manifested only rarely and was mostly an ideal form. Perhaps he took true religion to be something like a (classical) virtue warranted by the (modern) conventions of common life. He may have thought of it as true not because it reflected epistemic certainty but because the outcome of its beliefs could marshal Europe into an age of peace and (true) Enlightenment. That this was very unlikely (as Hume admitted) does not nullify the possibility that a constructive project based on Hume's grappling with religion might be of contemporary use for the philosophy of religion.

Most philosophers of religion hold the view that when it came to religion, Hume was simply a devastating critic. Scholars who take this position, however, cannot deny the warm references to true religion in his thought. Is true religion a throw-away category in Hume—empty or insincere—a mere fig leaf hiding his irreligion? Or is it a bit more—an inchoate suggestion about how we might properly conceive religion? The following argument assesses Hume's philosophy of religion with an eye toward its generative value for contemporary religious thought. I am neither agnostic on the question of Hume's sincerity in his endorsement of true religion nor silent on whether he uses it as a fig leaf. On my reading, it seems that the category 'true religion' fits neatly into Hume's philosophical schema and is a requirement of his bifurcated approach to religion. Further, I demonstrate that it was crucially deployed in the discursive tradition of which Hume was a part. If we can support the idea that true religion is a sincere, genuine category of Hume's thought that signified a nonconventional form of religion, then reconceiving this idea in Hume's work might support generative work in the contemporary study of religion. In other words, to the question, "Can the rarely interrogated constructive components of Hume's philosophy of religion, his sense of religion properly conceived, be of any use for contemporary discourse in religious studies?," this book answers "Yes."

Since Hume's lush writing offers little explicit positive content for his notion of 'true religion,' the reader must decode his suggestions for insights regarding religion's 'proper office.' To make some provisional claims about what a rare form of religion might look like if it reflected a Humean attitude, we might cobble together disparate aspects of his work. Relieved of its claims for metaphysical legitimacy, released from morality derived from fear of divine authority, and unrestricted by a fixed set of worship practices, religion appears quite bare in Hume's work. Yet in this very austerity we might find a way to reconceive of religion as a socially beneficial convention thoroughly grounded in history and community with little interest in competing with science in the quest for epistemic truth. Broadly speaking, this approach correlates with contemporary work in religious studies that refuses to treat religion as a system of beliefs or a transhistorical essence. The speculative argument that follows submits that based on the broad contours of his project, this fertile conception of religion might be constituted by a genuine theism, calm passions, and a practical morality. And, thought of this way, it could be of some use to contemporary theories of religion.

Hume's early philosophical writings and his works on religion are, of course, central for any constructive endeavor based on his work. It behooves us, however, to look beyond these formal writings for a more complete sense of what Hume may have meant when he referred to the "proper office" of religion.[2] Hume's numerous letters provide an important angle into his more private, inner thoughts and give us a key to the Humean attitude; they display his congenial and broad intentions as a thinker. Both his fundamental respect for certain forms and practices of religion as well as his critical disposition toward other forms and elements is evident in the letters.[3] Hume's historical writings reflect this same approach: they attack examples of "modern" religion and its empty rituals yet affirm religion when it facilitates the development of virtuous character and practical morality.[4] Hume's overall account of religion might be summed up in this famous statement from one of his essays: "*That the corruption of the best things produces the worst*, is grown into a maxim, and is commonly proved, among other instances, by the pernicious effects of *superstition* and *enthusiasm*, the corruptions of true religion" (*EMPL*, 10.73). To some degree, all genres of his work take on this bifurcated attitude regarding religion. They reflect that Hume conceived of religion in two basic ways: as both a destructive force in human society (vulgar religion) and a constructive force for human society (true religion).

Assessing Hume's dual sense of religion sanctions our keeping track of the extraordinary breadth of his work. To do this in a Humean way we should honor the emblems of Hume's attitude: the direct challenge to abstruse and philosophical reason, the commitment to historicism and perspectivalism, and the investment in outcomes and utility over rational certainty and analytic clarity. Sifting

Hume's trenchant condemnation of 'false religion' through this Humean filter helps us comprehend his criticism and grasp his indirect suggestions for a true religion. Critics might wonder if the Humean approach is too loose to ferret out a consistent dual line of argument such as I have proposed and be worried that the Humean attitude, with its strident critique of reason, is actually a commitment to *irrationalism*. Neither of these concerns troubles me. Hume's critique of rationality is not a mere rejection of reason; it is an assault on the furnishing of reason with metaphysical and normative authority. As a 'true' philosopher, Hume believed that abstract reason was useful in revealing "relations of ideas" (*T*, 1.2.5.20), not "matters of fact" (*T*, 1.3.7.3). He maintained that our behavior was grounded in habits of reflective common life and that these habits were derived from the passions and social conventions mitigated through the psychological concept "sympathy." The Humean approach, then, undermines the content and temperament of those who dogmatically venerate philosophical reason. At the same time, it exhibits firm loyalty to reasonableness and rational scrutiny. The following argument sustains this commitment: it venerates the reasonable and the reflective as well as the social and the passional over the demands of abstract rational thought and dogmatic metaphysical reasoning. Additionally, it is largely sympathetic to Hume and evades persistent criticisms of his arguments and condemnations of his writings. My aim is to interpret Hume's thought in a way that makes the best sense of it to see what we might learn anew. Philosophical subtlety and intellectual prestige, as Hume's approach confirmed, should not be tied to the capacity to debunk arguments and expose gaps in logic. Following Hume's example, we might consider what it means to operate from the idea that good interpretation is an act of compassion requiring intellectual courage and heroic insight, what he called "greatness of mind" (*EPM*, 7.4).

So as not to distort the author's view, sound interpretative work must be based on the full spectrum of available evidence, honest about its intentions, and clear about its limitations. The standard interpretation regarding Hume and religion situates him as *the* Enlightenment secularist and atheist critic of religion. Although partially true, this is too narrow a view of the existing evidence and it reflects something of a general bias against religion. Most important, this reading of Hume renders his writing barren for generative work in religious studies. An interpretation that attends to the overall arc of his thought project and refuses to take a narrow focus positions us to see that Hume was not simply a detractor of popular religion, a moralist devoid of a sense of the use-value for religion, or a philosopher obsessed with causal logic. Again, Hume was certainly a critic of popular religion: it is undeniable that the experience of evangelical Presbyterianism soured him and that he was concerned that his native Scotland would be further embittered by the Kirk. He made unequivocally horrible and reductive statements about Catholicism, besmirched enthusiastic believers of false religion, and attacked all religious sects that increased factionalism in society. At the same time, however, he contended that religion was a persistent and inescapable fact of human history based on (but not original to) human nature; he showed awareness that, as a social convention, religion could be a potential source of happiness for human beings and a possible benefit to the social order; and he did not challenge that religion provided psycho-emotional support for the vast majority of human beings. These aspects of religion may have formed the basis for his mild suggestion 'true religion.'

*Toward a Humean True Religion* attempts to demonstrate that if we take true religion to be constituted by the positive conclusions of Hume's philosophy of understanding, his thoughts on the passions, and his notion of moral utility, then we might discover its worth for contemporary debates in religious studies. More specifically, the thesis here is that we might construct a true religion based on Hume's work, particularly his ideas of basic theism, his sense of the calm passions, and his commitment to character development. I offer my argument as one possible, usable interpretation, not as a definitive conviction about Hume's intentions. I am more strongly committed, however, to the negative claim: we must object to arguments that reduce Hume to simply an atheist or a skeptic. By providing some constituent yet provisional features of a Humean-inspired true religion, it is my hope that we might be able to bring Hume off of the sidelines of philosophical discourse of religion and fruitfully deploy his thought for current debates in theology, religion, and morality.

## Hume and True Religion

That Hume sparingly mentions the term "true religion" in his corpus should not derail our attempt to understand his notion, for Charles Taylor reminds us that Hume "was like the radical Aufklärer" in that issues "of significance were not acknowledged" directly in his texts. A caveat from Isabel Rivers is also instructive. She discloses that the overdeveloped critical frameworks of radical Enlightenment thinkers were unable to support the generative elements of their thought. Further, Donald Livingston argues that Hume valued the silent wisdom that inhered in customs and the tacit knowledge of common life.[5] To fairly consider Hume's suggestion for religion then, we must pay attention to what is explicit in his work as well as that which he states indirectly, all the while being responsible to his overall concerns.

In a preface to the second volume of his *History of England* (which he later excised) Hume stated that true religion was a "rare form" of religion that "regulates men's hearts" and "humanizes their conduct" and that its "proper office" was to "reform Men's lives, to purify their hearts, to inforce all moral duties, and to secure obedience to the laws and civil magistrate."[6] His historical investigations led him to conclude that the disposition for religion in general permeated humankind. In eighteenth-century Scotland most people practiced what Hume thought of as vulgar or false religion (mostly Presbyterian Calvinism). He acknowledged the importance of local customs and recorded the practical results of believers in his historical work. We might think of his approach as melioristic: he paid attention to the outcomes of religious beliefs and aimed to reduce barbaric ones. Accordingly, Hume quietly held that the best way for humans to be religious was through a rare true religion. Our quest to assign Humean content to this idea might begin by rehearsing the distinction between his notions of 'true' and 'false' religion, a bifurcation rooted in, as I mentioned earlier, the constitutive difference between his notions of true and false philosophy and the fact of his historical positioning between the Latin and modern notions of religion. On the first, constitutive point, for Hume, true religion parallels true philosophy. The word "true" here is not a reference to epistemic status, for the "truth" is well beyond the reach of the human mind. Hume had more of a pragmatic notion of the true: he believed the true was that which affirmed common traditions over abstruse reason and suggested a commitment to the moderation of our beliefs and behaviors for the effective functioning of the individual and society. False religion, implicit in false philosophy, was built on abstract metaphysics, contained superstition and enthusiasm, and posited a supernatural deity worthy of worship. It led to social division and political disharmony. These two religious worldviews, the true and the false, represent distinct approaches to balancing the role of custom with autonomous reason in relation to a deity, invest differently in the project of moderation of the passions, and forge distinct concerns in the regulation of our moral behavior. In other words, true religion and false religion differ in their attitudes toward reason, the passions, and morality.[7]

On the second historical point, in Hume's time the modern notion of religion as a system of beliefs seeking epistemic confirmation through speculative reason stood against the fading classical idea of *religio* as a set of public, ritualized ceremonies that enhanced excellence of character in service of (the artificial virtue) justice. These two notions give a historical dimension to Hume's repeated distinctions between false religion (also referred to as popular religion or vulgar religion) and the rare true religion. Cicero powerfully affirmed the social utility and the public customs of *religio*, the authority of the ancestors, and the interests of the state in religious matters. He took *religio* to be a virtue for civic society and its opposite, *superstitio*, to be a vice. In many ways, Hume extended this classical way of thinking about religion. Hume's Ciceronian influence, combined with the few observations he made about religion's proper office, allow us to postulate that the development of character and the stability of the social order would have been central for his true religion had he developed it further. His modern sensibilities endorsed a new philosophical approach and thus a more skeptical theism, deeper individual and protopsychological investment and thus calmer passions, and a morality that was functional for not just preservation of the state but the stability of conventions of everyday common life. Still, Hume neither lauded any conception of religion to the masses nor endorsed his idea 'true religion' as a mode of personal religious practice. True religion was a rare, quiet convention that, at its best, silently contributed to social harmony.

To foreground the distinction between true and false religion in Hume and to prioritize his self-described debt to Cicero is not to radically reread him; rather, it is to locate the foundations of the proper office of religion and reemphasize parts of his work that are often overlooked. This type of constructive interpretation extends Hume's thought in ways that he may not have anticipated. Nevertheless, the fecundity of his work in religion should not be disregarded. If nothing else, Hume's distinctive handling of religion makes it clear that religion is neither reducible to a set of propositional claims about the supernatural nor limited to a set of external practices that elevate a worship-worthy deity. His acceptance of the possibility that general providence (a basic sense of purposiveness in nature) is intelligible exemplifies an approach to theism that takes a middle path between militant atheists and evangelical theists of our day. This approach can be a constructive resource, along with his insights regarding sympathy and his moderate passions, for current debates in religious studies.

For Hume, history confirmed that the general sentiment for religion was an ever-present feature of the human social being (though it was secondary, and monotheism was not universal).[8] From this it follows that we are, as far as Hume was concerned, generally religious in some form or another. The *matter* of human religiousness, then, was actually settled for Hume. He was not at all skeptical about the presence of religion in most human societies: he affirmed that religion was naturally derived from human passions. His critical work challenged the content of the beliefs of popular religion. It asked the question, how should religion function? In other words, Hume's dilemma regarding religion was about the role religion should play so that we derive more benefit than harm from it. False or popular religion was the set of beliefs and practices legitimated by philosophy that reflected enthusiastic reverence for a deity and celebrated miracles. True religion might be understood, then, as an ensemble of natural beliefs that allows us to moderate our passions and develop our character. This rare form of religion makes us more Humean, that is, better able to take life as it comes, aware of our inextricable connection to our neighbors and our society, and appreciative of the mystery of nature. On my account, these are *religious* issues, not *moral* ones, and Hume's use of the terms "true religion" and "true piety," as well as his many mentions of a deity, religious attributes, beliefs, and so on, suggests that he wanted to be an interlocutor in the conversation on religion and not simply in the one on morality.

Hume took historical manifestations of religion to be mainly destructive. Yet religion in general—that is, the idea of religion—was neither simply good nor bad but always an admixture of both. It is quite evident that he firmly rejected revealed religion and its dramatic transformations, the myths and miracles of vulgar religion, faith narratives that supported popular piety, particular worship practices of churches, and the commandments of the Torah. His true religion, then, cannot be taken as religious in the *conventional* sense. His historical work, however, suggests that a worldview that "reforms" and "purifies" has religious value: it strengthens our feelings of connectedness to all, helps virtuous character development, and assists in the moderation of our passions. To be clear: I have no interest in discussing Hume's personal struggles with Presbyterianism, nor am I interested in reading his work through the lens of Christianity. I aim, instead, to give his suggestion for religion's proper office more use-value for debates in religious studies by foregrounding what I take to be its (potentially) generative insights.

Writers that view Hume's positive claims about religion as insincere or ironic challenge the view that his true religion has any *religious* merit. They contend that he is at best inconsistent on the design argument and that his theories of the passions and morality are ethical positions, not religious ones. These readings are valid. Hume's project does not *demand* to be taken on religious terms. This, however, does not foreclose the possibility that taking it on its religious merits and building from them is both warranted by his use of the term "true religion" and potentially useful for contemporary scholars in religious studies. Nor does it exclude us from raising questions about what constitutes the notion "religious merit" recycled by these writers. I hope to show that a broad reconsideration of Hume's overall position on religion can reveal his work to be a resource for popular debates concerning religion and valuable for work in both religious studies and Hume studies. I defend against the somewhat oxymoronic reading that Hume's true religion has no religious merit.

## Contemporary Scholars on Hume

Scholarly work on the Enlightenment era takes Hume's critique of autonomous reason as the basis for his skepticism and construes his discontent with popular religion as grounds for his atheism.[9] These common interpretations overlook

Hume's clearly stated desire to build a science, mask the degree to which Hume despised dogmatism and atheism, and, finally, disguise his method of empirical observation, his sense of subjective dispositions, and his emphasis on probable conclusions. Two very basic examples of this tendency from general studies of the Enlightenment are Peter Gay's insights, which overemphasize Hume's critical project in religion and position him as the poster child for paganism; and Carl Becker's thesis that Enlightenment thinkers were invested in substituting the concept of heaven with the idea of posterity, which misplaces Hume's constructive project in service of that end.[10] Hume was critical of autonomous, objective, and ahistorical reason, yet he was neither a pagan as Gay argues, nor an advocate of posterity as Becker suggests.

Scholars who have made valuable and highly visible contributions in Hume studies for the last twenty years—particularly Peter Millican, Janet Broughton, and Galen Strawson—mention but do not focus on Hume's bifurcated approach to religion. Terence Penelhum and Keith Yandell, two noted scholars that closely attend to Hume's epistemology, do treat his philosophy of religion.[11] Both thinkers read Hume's religious writings filtered through his theory of ideas as articulated in the *Treatise* and first *Enquiry*. Their detailed analyses emphasize his critique of the rational foundations of religion, the contradictions and inconsistencies of his statements on religious belief, how his theory of belief fits or does not fit into his theory of ideas, his use of irony and sense of theism, and the "absence or near-absence of positive psychological considerations" for religion in his work.[12] Penelhum and Yandell have greatly improved our understanding of Hume's philosophy of religion in important ways. Their conclusions, however, pay scant attention to the role of his philosophical writings for the possibility of genuine theism, and they do not discuss the passional grounds of religion. Thus they largely preclude using Hume as a constructive resource for contemporary debates in religion and underestimate the value of his category 'true religion.' Overall, their work reflects a larger trend: to position Hume as generally irreligious.

Two recent contributions, Paul Russell's *The Riddle of Hume's "Treatise": Skepticism, Naturalism, and Irreligion* and Thomas Holden's *Spectres of False Divinity: Hume's Moral Atheism*, follow in the trajectory of work by Penelhum and Yandell in that they directly explore religious dimensions of Hume's thought. These works are immensely valuable. Russell's well-developed argument for Hume's "irreligion" is compelling, but he discusses only Hume's *Treatise* and says little about religion's proper office.[13] Holden's text is also nicely argued and quite persuasive. It attends to the entirety of Hume's corpus and argues for Hume's *moral* atheism. Both books largely overlook Hume's bifurcated approach to religion and confirm the popular philosophical bias to use Hume's arguments as a resource against religion instead of as a means to reconceive it. Perhaps there is a hidden agenda in the common move by philosophers to emphasize Hume's critique of religion and avoid the plethora of possibilities generated by his explicit belief that religion is coterminous with human life. More likely, this approach reflects an outdated way of conceiving religion that largely has been abandoned by scholars in religious studies. What Russell reads as Hume's irreligion is simply Hume's undermining of orthodox Christian deity and Biblical religion. Similarly, Holden reduces moral atheism to Hume's belief that the conventional Christian God and moral world-view are not the sources of our moral norms. It does not follow, from either Russell's or Holden's argument, that Hume was against religion *at all times and in all forms*. Hume was explicit about this. He was against 'vulgar' ways of thinking about religion, shunned the beliefs of popular religion, and challenged the grounds of conventional Christianity. Russell and Holden have illuminated new ways of thinking about Hume's critique of religion. They are not useful resources, however, for the generative work to be done in the philosophy of religion.

To be fair, Yandell, Penelhum, Holden, and Russell do not intend their work to be a resource for constructive work in religious studies. This effort is the domain of religious studies scholars who take religion as a broad and complicated human enterprise always mixed with beauty and terror. At their best, scholars in the study of religion begin with the implicit understanding that religion is not entirely exhausted by the variety of its historical appearances. Thus, they assess various worldviews that have expansive concepts of deities (e.g., Wicca and nontheistic religions such as Buddhism), moral systems independent of theism, and nonceremonial approaches to the world with one eye on history and another on the future. Attending to certain ideas and practices as religious in this way is a means of investigating the wide range of human symbolic activities that some Westerners have denoted as sacred over time and anticipating ways in which these imaginative constructions might shift in content and outcome for the future. Broadly speaking, it is these sorts of interests that often fuel some of the most useful work in the study of religion, and Hume's constructive interventions have been left out of this conversation. This book aspires, in part, to revive his work in light of these interests. My hunch, as I began thinking about Hume in this way, was that reading his work with this kind of investment might yield something useful for discourse in religious studies. Building on the work of Hume scholars, I link Donald Livingston's idea of "general providence," Joseph Godfrey's notion of moderate "fundamental hope," and Annette Baier's sense of Hume's "practical morality," to argue that it does and that these are the likely pillars that constitute religion's "proper office."[14]

J. C. A. Gaskin and Antony Flew have treated Hume's religious thought in detail and in connection with his philosophical investments. They contend that Hume is neither a skeptic nor an atheist yet they allow for an "attenuated deism," a set of "natural beliefs," and a category called "true religion" in his work.[15] Like Penelhum and Yandell (and Russell and Holden), Gaskin and Flew convincingly present Hume's critical disposition regarding religion: he attributed negative value to its historical manifestations; he strongly argued against central tenets of conventional Christianity (namely, miracles and a particular providence); he made powerful criticisms of superstition and enthusiasm; and he showed little regard for the traditional conceptions of the divine. Unlike Penelhum and Yandell, Gaskin and Flew read across Hume's entire corpus (including his *History of England* and his letters) and represent his thought on religion in its diversity. Their presentation of the breadth of Hume's thought regarding religion gives readers a way to loosen the grip of skeptical interpretations that dog Hume's reputation. Still, their obsession with Hume's treatment of the design argument suggests they equate religion with theism and confirms that their interpretive lens for theism is constrained by an orthodox notion of theism that, by definition, fatefully consigns Hume's perspective to irreligion.[16] I rely on many of the insights provided by Flew and Gaskin. Gaskin's tendency, however, to miss the value of Hume's moral thought for his true religion, as well as Flew's phenomenalist reading of Hume, delimit their potential to effectively situate him for constructive work in the philosophy of religion.[17]

Scholarship on Hume that places his commitment to history and nature within his broad framework and takes his philosophical, historical, *and* religious works seriously provides us with the best sense of his mostly implicit suggestion for religion. This is the method deployed by Donald Livingston and Annette Baier, in very different ways. Baier's work venerates the complicated role that the passions and history play in Hume's moral thought, while Livingston's masterful treatment of Hume explicitly confirms Hume's investment in both true philosophy and true religion.[18] Both thinkers show an acute awareness that Hume was not a dogmatic atheist and that he was primarily invested in philosophy (that is, rational reflection) for social effects: to improve conditions of liberty by increasing stability and happiness.[19] Both thinkers pay close attention to Hume's positive description of religion and correctly privilege the view that his intellectual investments were driven by social and religious concerns as well as political considerations and philosophical strategies. The cornerstones for my argument are the basic theism Livingston grants Hume, Baier's acknowledgment that Hume's calm passions serve socioethical interests, and Joseph Godfrey's idea that religious hope can be fundamental hope (what Hume would call a calm passion).

## My Approach to Hume

In the introduction to his first work Hume claimed that he wanted "to establish a science . . . superior in utility to any other of human comprehension" (*T*, xxiii).

From the beginning of his writing career, "utility" was the ultimate aim and driving force of his wide-ranging enterprise.[20] Against the Platonist commitment to escape time and transcend conditions, Hume's goals were practical: he wanted to contribute ideas that enhanced common life and increased social peace. Against false metaphysics and popular religion, he was confident about the history of human propensity for both good and evil, committed to our being ensconced in a complex web of traditions, and invested in the slight possibility that we might improve conditions for generations to come. In some ways, we can say that the classic repose of stoic tranquility was transformed in Hume to a posture of equipoise: that we do our best to live in full contact with the mystery of life and remain open to its challenging vicissitudes without a paralyzing fear.

Hume's positive project was derived from his attention to history, which confirmed that divisiveness and conflict between both individuals and societies were often based on clashing religious beliefs and nature, the set of constantly combative and generative conditions that provided the grounds for, and connected a variety of, historical events. His philosophical response to the human limitations that history revealed neither fully rejected the radicalism of the philosophes (D'Holbach, Voltaire) nor completely embraced the rationalism of the metaphysicians (Descartes). Similarly, his response to the seeming chaos of experience was neither developed completely outside of the discursive framework of the natural religion of the deists (Tindal, Morgan) nor fully independent of the moderate Presbyterianism of his clergy friends (Blair, Carlyle). We might say that Hume's suggestion for religion—neither a prescription nor a dogmatic plan—was endowed by epistemological humility and an affirmation of common sense, a gentle hope that we could better moderate the passions, and a moral commitment to social and civic stability.

In some ways, Hume's historically grounded challenge to autonomous reason, popular religion, and moral rationalism was also leavened by an inordinate intellectual freedom unmatched by his immediate predecessors and his peers. He was neither constrained by an overwhelming commitment to his Christian lineage nor propelled by an irresistible disdain for it. Never completely against the idea of religion, Hume targeted religion *as a species of philosophy*, the vulgar form of religion that provided the illusion of metaphysical certainty and ontological reliability, supplied strict codes for moral conduct, and relied on fantastical hopes and illusory fears. Hume referred to this specific form of religion (most closely known to him as Scottish Presbyterianism) as popular religion, and it, along with enthusiasm and superstition, drew his ire.

I approach Hume as a broad, synthetic thinker informed by a love of wisdom and as a seeker inspired to find a way—that he might suggest to others—to be happy without the need for otherworldly transformation or sovereign authority and without impinging on the happiness of others. Mine is neither a disengaged reading of Hume nor is it an analytic approach: I try to write from inside the lived experience of joy, frustration, and laughter that I have as I read him. He venerated passionate engagement, energetic style, and lively provocation over disengaged reason, analytic argument, and stale professionalism. He aimed to be emotionally persuasive more than he did to be logically sound and seemed not to mind having contradictions in his writing. Hume strove, against the grain, for a kind of humaneness with his pen. The following argument aspires to this sort of Humean style. My encounter with the sum of Hume's project has led me to believe it is a generative venture that inspires curiosity and aims to challenge many assumptions of the popular approaches of its day. I try to celebrate the spirit of his overall commitments and cherish his verbal dance to transform some of the textual possibilities available to him. Hume was comfortable with the complexity of human beings: our proclivity to good as well as our propensity for evil. My Humean approach takes his work as a philosophical and literary model in the way, for example, that he may have understood the work of Cicero and likely the way that Sir James understood him.

Roughly speaking, I read Hume's epistemology as it relates to the question of theism against the logical positivists and phenomenalists who are generally concerned about the truth-value of propositions in Hume. I also take him to be a synthetic thinker about morality and the development of virtuous character against those who read him as a strict Hutchesonian about morals (someone who accepts that morals depend on an a priori moral sensibility). And I understand his theory of the passions to address not only psychological concerns but also social and political ones.[21] Combining these elements, I hope to give a viable interpretation of a (barely stated) suggestion for religion.

## Organization of the Argument

Admittedly, true religion has always been a contested term in religious discourse. Orthodox Christians use the descriptor "true religion" to refer to religious beliefs that depend on revelation. For freethinkers—many who later identified as deists— true religion was a set of religious beliefs derived from rational reflection on our experience of nature. Hume did not accept either of these views. He held little regard for religion based on revelation, interpretations of nature that led to the idea of a God with moral attributes, and a religion of reason that denied the foundational role of the passions in any human enterprise.

My first chapter is a prologue to the overall argument: it traces a particular narrative of true religion from the classical era through the English Enlightenment to Hume's radical revision. My claim is that the traditional method of interpreting religious writers as either skeptics, critics, and atheists on one side and defenders, supporters, and institutionalizers on the other is obfuscating. I suggest a slight shift in framing: to read some as employing a hermeneutic of curiosity regarding religion and others as employing a hermeneutic of credulity.[22] This allows for a richer assessment of thinkers on both sides of the religious question, and it opens our minds to the constructive components of work written by those we tend to label as critics (and summarily dismiss). Beginning with Cicero, I build a narrative of thinkers who deploy a hermeneutic of curiosity regarding religion, from second- and third-century writers Celsus and Porphyry through late medieval contributions of Hugo Grotius and Lord Herbert of Cherbury to Enlightenment figures Matthew Tindal and Thomas Morgan.

The body of my argument is given in the three chapters that follow the first one. Each attends to a feature of the speculative true religion that I am trying to build. Chapter 2 argues that Hume's early philosophical writings presuppose a natural belief in general providence. Without the presupposition of regularity in nature ("secret springs and principles") Hume could not have formulated his theory of ideas. I call this Hume's *basic* theism and argue that it is foundational to his project and a presupposition of any science. I examine the path Hume carves between Cartesian rationalism and Pyrrhonian skepticism to demonstrate that this basic theism can evolve into either the vulgar theism of false religion or the genuine theism of true religion. I rehearse Hume's theory of ideas and his discussion of belief to show that his causal worldview allows for the assertion that our imagination naturally projects an Author of Nature (ultimately unknowable) based on our observation of effects (with unobservable causes). This genuine theism is made intelligible in Norman Kemp Smith's discussion of Hume's theory of belief, which posits the category of natural belief. Thus, I can justifiably posit natural belief in genuine theism as the first leg in the stool of a Humean true religion.

In chapter 3, I discuss the discourse on the passions that Hume inherited and present his general theory of the passions. He explicitly described the category of hope—the opposite of fear—as a direct passion that occurred when "the mind by an *original* instinct tends to unite itself with the good, and to avoid the evil" (*T*, 2.3.9.2). He showed in both the *Enquiry* (1748) and the *Natural History of Religion* (1757) that this hope, always linked to fear, was the driving force behind popular religion, superstition, and enthusiasm, along with their concomitants, miracles and salvation. My intervention is to elucidate Hume's notion of hope in light of Joseph Godfrey's theory of hope. This exposes that Hume's own hopes—"where experiments of this kind are judiciously collected and compared, we may *hope* to establish on them a science" (*T*, intro., 10)—were very calm and moderate. He never exhibited, in his life, letters, or work, personal hopes of the sort that he described as direct passion hopes. He consciously moderated his passions and was generally known to be of a temperate, peaceful, and congenial disposition even in the face of personal misery. This disposition, which Godfrey contends is a type of hope (fundamental hope), might be a useful component of our Humean true religion. It implies a trust in nature, and this particular kind of trust implies a belief that what we have is all we need.[23]

Chapter 4 places Hume's moral thought in the context of his immediate predecessors, that is, between the rationalists and sentimentalists. This sets up my argument, based on Annette Baier's extensive work, for a religious sensibility in Hume's practical morality. Hume's conviction is that sympathy—a psychological mechanism that allows us to share the feelings of another—assists us in the development of virtuous character. Our moral lives are constituted by the exercise of this mechanism that affirms the power of the affective realm to bind us in a common, sociohistorical project for practical morality. The attainment of a feeling of social happiness leads toward approbation and the development of virtuous character. If we take this practical morality as a means of binding humans more closely, it gives us a final dimension for our Humean true religion. This aspect celebrates our natural capacity to form affective solidarity (the common point of view) and acknowledges the social constitution of our moral sentiments.

My concluding chapter discusses the possible usefulness of attending to genuine theism, practical morality, and moderate hope in Hume's work. It highlights the closeness between Thomas Nagel's recent naturalist teleology and Hume's genuine theism, notes how my reading of Hume can be deployed against radical atheists and evangelicals alike, and discusses some general theories of religion amenable to my argument for Hume's true religion. By doing so, it attempts to provide further justification for why we might benefit from having scrutinized Hume's inchoate category 'true religion.' Or, to put it slightly differently, it gives Hume's argument value for thinkers in religious studies. Philosophers have traditionally dismissed Hume's category 'true religion' on the grounds that it is useless as religious worldview, that Hume was insincere in his assertions of it, or that it was simple way to subvert religion. These approaches refuse to appreciate the breadth of religious theories, methods in the study of religion, and diversity within the history of religion. Reflection on religion demonstrates that affection-based worldviews that celebrate nature yet posit no worship content or those that have a broad sense of a deity with no attributes and refuse to stipulate a firm moral code can still be referred to as "religion."

A general theme that runs through my argument is that the field of philosophy of religion is a mode of inquiry that perennially raises the questions of what constitutes religion and how we might talk about it. This reminds us that religion always manifests as a specific set of beliefs, actions, and reflections located in a particular tradition. These traditions are always fluid and malleable; in part, they are shaped by social forces, habits of common life, political contexts, geographical location, and so on. We should, therefore, consistently challenge our presuppositions about religion and keep track of the various commitments that we import to our discussions of it. I hope that readers will use Hume's work as a source for reenergized discourse in the field of religious studies. If our speculative, Humean-influenced true religion is constituted by a humble philosophical theism, a moral commitment to happiness, and a moderate way of hoping, then we have extended the set of tools we have to work with in religious studies. Still, "I am apt, in a cool hour, to suspect, in general, that most of my reasonings will be more useful by furnishing hints and exciting people's curiosity than as containing any principles that will augment the stock of knowledge that must pass to future ages" (*LET*, 1.16.39).

# 1

## RELIGION AND THE TRUE

But if we consider the matter more closely, we shall find, that this interested diligence of the clergy is what every wise legislator will study to prevent; because in every religion, except the true, it is highly pernicious, and it has even a natural tendency to pervert the true, by infusing into it a strong mixture of superstition, folly, and delusion.

—*HE*, 3.135−36

The majority of the literature on David Hume is relatively silent about what he takes the proper office of religion to be. This is understandable given Hume's powerful critique of traditional Christian doctrine and the fact that he neither offered a prescriptive language for religion nor detailed its proper office. Unlike his peers who assumed the natural progress of history (Smith), proposed a Christian vision for society (Locke), or accepted that the universe had a moral dimension (Hutcheson), Hume challenged these ideas and contested the philosophical justification of religion. Still, his work was rich with constructive insights—some inchoate and others implicit—that contemporary thinkers in religious studies might benefit from considering. Taking his Ciceronian influences into account and reading Hume through the lens of our speculative true religion brings these constructive elements into view. From this perspective, Hume's arguments regarding causation, his sense that passions can be moderated, and his commitment to a *practical morality* (*T*, 3.3.6.6) supply content for what Hume might have meant by religion's proper office. This chapter elaborates on the rare form of religion that "regulate[s] the heart[s] of men" and "humanize[s] their conduct" (*DCNR*, 12.12) and attempts to extend Hume's project for religion so that it might be useful for contemporary discourse in the philosophy of religion.

Hume's explicitly stated aim regarding religion was to discern its manifestations in common life, explain its foundations in reason, and narrate its "origin[s]
in human nature" (*NHR*, introd). His actual reflections on religion went a bit
further: they were multidimensional and included penetrating observations as
well as moderate suggestions couched in the terms he inherited: false religion and
true religion.[1] Characteristically, the critical framework of Hume's science easily
conveyed his distaste for false religion: "a species of philosophy" (*E*, 11.27). His
positive project for religion, however, was largely concealed in indirection. Isabel
Rivers offers a crucial reminder: we must "be aware of what is taken for granted,
the unstated moral and theological assumptions" in the work of Radical Enlightenment philosophers.[2] Her point, that the aspirations of some thinkers cannot
find expression in their theoretical framing due to the critical structure of their
work, is an important filter for the following investigation. To effectively consider
what Hume may have meant by religion's proper office, that is, to detect his mild
suggestions for religion so we might build on them, we should generally work
from a positive philosophical temperament and keep in mind the broad aims of
his project.[3]

We expand our understanding of Hume when we acknowledge both the trenchant criticisms and tacit recommendations for religion *across* his writings. To be
sure, Hume's generically voiced project for religion was mostly a critical one
directed against the Evangelical Presbyterianism in which he was raised. Though
his work contained inconsistencies and incongruities, his critical disposition
toward religion did not vary: he dubbed popular forms of Christian practice and
doctrine "false religion" and he loathed them. Hume further derided the theism
of popular religion that stipulated that God had moral attributes and was worship-
worthy; he detested both superstition and enthusiasm due to their reliance on
extreme passions, and he declared that vulgar religion had a corrupting influence
on moral character. These vituperative positions constituted his direct response to
the religious wars of his time and place, problems that deeply troubled him and
ones that he prioritized in his work. Given his strategic choice to make more of a
critical intervention against popular religion instead of a constructive one, he did
not describe religion's proper office with systematic detail. Still, it is fair to presume from his near obsession with religion, his Presbyterian background, his
reading of Cicero, his commitment to moderation and the reflective, true philosophy, as well as his investment in social stability, that the question of the most
effective form of religion remained near to his thinking. Further, Hume's attitude
toward religion was never *simply* a critical one. He offered (indirect) insights for
true religion. We may extract from these (indirect) reflections—and cobble
together substance for his undeveloped idea 'true religion'—by reading between
the multiple overlapping strands of his writings, assessing what is underneath his

sometimes tacit intentions and closely attending to the fertile oppositions he implies between true and false religion. This sanctions our appraisal of what he may have taken, what he did not explicitly state that might be implicitly present in his work. Beginning with two productive premises—that Hume's powerful work left us some positive resources for religion and that we can build a Humean-inspired true religion from these resources—the following argument posits three Humean commitments that, when combined, might serve as the foundation for a speculative true religion.

The riddle of both true and false religion in Hume is, ultimately—as he says in the last paragraph of his most important work on religion, the *Natural History of Religion*—"an enigma." We can, however, holding the earlier-stated objectives in mind, give some provisional content to both forms of religion. Doing so is not to make a claim about Hume's personal religious beliefs or the content of his spiritual life; it is simply to emphasize Hume's positive attitude and the generative aspects of his contribution to religious discourse. This can resuscitate Hume's work as a resource for scholars in the field. Philosophers of religion trained in philosophy have comfortably appropriated Hume's writings for analytic approaches to philosophy, Kantian-influenced thinkers have seized on his work for its critical "errors" in relation to instrumental reason (most often regarding moral judgment), and skeptics have used him as their flag-bearer. Yet philosophers of religion trained in religious studies tend to avoid Hume, deploy him as an archcritic of religion, or treat him solely as a moralist. The irony here is that philosophers in religious studies generally approach the world of ideas in a Humean fashion: they take history seriously; tackle their work with a broad, philosophical temperament; and remain open to the relative insolubility of religious questions even as they seriously reflect on them. To bring these contemporary thinkers closer to their intellectual inheritance, I gesture, in this chapter, toward some possible historical foundations to foreground the larger argument I aim to develop: that we might construct a Humean-inspired true religion with a genuine theism, a moderation of the passions, and a practical morality.

Critics of Hume, in his day and in ours, have largely dismissed the idea 'true religion' in Hume as a "useless rump" with no religious value and little practical significance.[4] I have two replies to this brush-off. First, to insist that Hume's undescribed true religion has no religious value is to construe religious value in narrow, reductionist terms (that is, as false religion). The study of history, which Hume took to be enjoyable, intellectually edifying, and morally enriching (*EMPL*, 6.565), taught him that religion could be more than an amalgamation of ritualistic practices, ecstatic worship of deity, and a set of unyielding moral rules handed down from above. Second, the claim that Hume's true religion has little practical significance obscures more than it clarifies. The connotation here is that practical significance is a function of direct moral precepts, explicit worship practices, or other formal influences. Hume detested this way of both describing and being religious. Thus, reducing religion to the conventional ideas of religious value and practical significance do not comport with his full perspective on the matter.

Hume considered religion, in its various forms, to be historically potent. And history, according to Hume, was unequivocal: it confirmed that religion was a consistent feature of human experience and that its popular manifestations had terrifying effects in the world.[5] Given this, one might expect that Hume would want humans to be completely against the idea of religion and aim to abolish it. In fact, he took the opposite position. He never contended that humans should destroy all forms of religion, for religious sentiment never could be done away with fully. Instead, Hume actually suggested a state religion to counteract religious enthusiasm and ecclesiastical malfeasance (HE, 3.134–35). He wrote, "Look out for a people, entirely destitute of religion: if you find them at all, be assured, that they are but a few degrees removed from brutes" (NHR, 15.9). These sorts of claims illuminate the value of religion for civil society. They are found throughout Hume's corpus and confirm a mild commitment to religion, sometimes for no other reason but to enhance social stability and augment common morality. Hume believed that religion, in its "proper office," served a socioethical function. He stated that his "philosophy" (presumably, also his "philosophy of religion") "if just, can present us only with mild and moderate sentiments" (T, 1.4.7.13) and suggested that true religion should reflectively affirm the stable, humanizing beliefs of common life (NHR, 12.13).[6] His work also affirmed a basic sense of theism: "The universal propensity to believe in invisible, intelligent power, if not an original instinct is at least a general attendant of human nature" (15.5). Our speculative Humean true religion replaces the supernaturalism of popular religion with the fundamental belief in an Author of Nature. It supplants the "monstrous," "Priestly inventions," and "monkish virtues" of vulgar religion (T, 3.2.5.14) with the emphasis on virtuous character. And it displaces the enthusiastic, direct-passion hopes of false religion with a modest hope.

Hume's work persuades us that useful suggestions for theism, morality, and passions do not, by any means, require religion. Yet if we consider religion, as I think Hume does, as a disposition that quietly connects us more deeply to one another and to that which is greater than us while inspiring excellence of character and steady passions that cultivate happiness and social stability, then we can say that this general theism, moderation of the passions, and practical morality, taken cumulatively, might be religious in effect. Our conjecture 'true religion' jettisons enthusiastic beliefs, divine behavioral codes, sacred rituals and texts, and ecstatic worship. In this way it expands the very idea of what it means to be religious. It advances gentle hopes for how religion might quietly contribute to the development of virtuous character and the moderation of the passions, and it holds a fundamental belief in a sense of general providence that neither creates factions nor aspires to universals. Naming these as provisional elements of a Humean true religion allows us to raise questions about the category 'religion' itself, something usually given scant attention in discussions of Hume.

If it is to be usable, a sound constructive project cannot simply materialize out of thin air: it must rely on historical evidence and corroborate with discursive trends. Locating the seeds for our proposal to build a provisional notion 'true religion' from Hume's thought in efforts that precede his work could be helpful. In this regard, Cicero's approach to religion and the discourse after it is of some use. Hume relied on the conventions of religious discourse post-Cicero by deploying the framework 'true' versus 'false' concerning religion and assuming that religion was a unique feature of human nature. At the same time, he challenged some of the inherited binaries (religious and secular, God and nature, self and world, metaphysical and empirical) and questioned the epistemological aspirations of the category 'religion' in modern discourse. Constructing a Humean true religion from the generative fragments of his work illuminates two crucial insights for our larger concern with this discourse that sometimes remain opaque in secondary scholarship of Hume: that he treats 'religion' as a category without a fixed meaning and that he uses the category 'religion' as part and parcel of a strategic enterprise. Hume approaches use of the term 'religion' as a question of cultural politics: he understands that discourse on religion invents and reifies domains (the religious and the nonreligious) that mark boundaries and serve a purpose beyond the academic.[7] Perhaps attending to Hume's underdeveloped sense of religion's proper office can demonstrate how he simultaneously employed and challenged the category 'religion' in ways remarkable for his time.

Although Cicero's deployment of the category *religio* is generally overlooked in Hume's discussion of religion, it is feasible that he was influenced by Cicero's emphasis on stability, moderation, and morality concerning religion. In fact, the foundational qualities of our Humean true religion—genuine theism, moderate hope, and practical morality—are grounded in Cicero's classical idea of civic religion, which he inherited from the Greeks. *Religio*, in this classical view, aimed not for grace, salvation, or immortality but for the cultivation of civic virtue, political stability, and social trust. There are, however, over seventeen hundred years between Cicero and Hume, during which time discourse on religion shifted from the emphasis on civic virtue and public ritual to concerns about the philosophical legitimacy of beliefs in God and miracles. What might we gain by reading the constructive side of his approach to religion as a preservation of parts of the classical idea *religio* fused with insights from modernity filtered through his counter-Enlightenment lens? To answer these questions I turn to the work of Cicero and to three other key nodal points in the discourse on religion in which Hume participates.

Cicero was the towering figure for early eighteenth-century British thinkers. His work was seminal for Hume, who referred to him often as the wisest of the Roman philosophers (*LG*, 23). Often connected in secondary literature due to their similarly deft application of the extended dialogue form to the vexing questions of religion, their comparable classifications of the passions, and their related approaches to morality, Cicero and Hume are regarded as intellectual co-conspirators operating across a vast historical lacuna.[8] Given Hume's explicit devotion to Cicero's style and his unequivocal classical approach to morality, it is relatively easy to expose their similar emphases and common outlooks, which privilege a moderate skepticism, display a commitment to moderation, and emphasize utility. The well-documented Ciceronian stylistic influence on Hume's moral thought (Hume took himself to be a "classical moralist" concerned about self-formation toward excellence) and his theory of the passions (Hume's self-styled Stoicism venerated moderation) invite us to further consideration of Hume's work on religion. Does Hume conceive of religion in a classical mode? Might his idea of religion's proper office be an updated version of Cicero's *religio*? If so, what content or features might his underdeveloped notion 'true religion' contain?

To explain what Hume may have borrowed from Cicero at a significant moment in *modern* discourse, I provide a brief section on the stylistic features (part 1) and content areas (part 2) of Cicero's writing on religion. Following this section, I characterize a key theme of modern discourse on religion: the notion of truth. Shaped by historical factors (the advance of reason and science, a decline in the authority of the church, and the Enlightenment quest for universal truth) and guided by evolving interests (identity politics, economic interests, and psychological needs), fertile, philosophical discourse on religion post-Cicero established new conceptions of truth and knowledge from which the modern idea of religion would sprout. This characterization of modern discourse on religion illustrates the degree to which Hume may have found himself trapped by discursive boundaries. What language was available for a thinker who was neither a deist nor a conventional theist to describe what he considered a genuine theism? What options were available for a moralist who was neither a dogmatic atheist nor a conventional religionist to discuss the potential positive impact of religion on morality? What philosophical position could one occupy if one wanted a hope that elided both superstition and miracles?

Hume inherited a conversation that engaged the idea 'religion' in terms of true and false, and he followed this discursive convention even as he redefined its terms. Religion that appeared in history and appealed to the (illusory) standard of abstract philosophy he dubbed false religion. True religion was the corrective idea for those forms of religion that aspired to be a species of philosophy. It was the counterpoint to arrogant atheism, stubborn superstition, and emphatic enthusiasm. It was also the inverse to forms of religious thought and practice that venerated the sacred as the source of morality, allowed for a divinity that could perform miracles, and originated in extreme passions. Hume implied that true religion, like Cicero's *religio*, venerated stability in the realm of politics, morality, and our passions. It ratified the natural functions of the mind, the reflective customs and habits of common life, and the development of virtuous character.

The remainder of this chapter elaborates the potential influence Cicero may have had on the style and content on Hume's religious thought and then attempts to situate Hume in the milieu of the religious discourse of his day. Hume's implicit suggestion for religion was informed by historical forces such as the growth of institutional religious authority in Scotland, dynamics in Enlightenment philosophy, developments in modern science, the trajectory of discourse on religion, and his own moderate, skeptical, and naturalist vision. Keeping track of the shifting dimensions of discourse on religion as they manifested post-Cicero in the robust, multifaceted political considerations of Porphyry and Celsus, the quest for universal, rational truth in the work of Hugo Grotius and Lord Herbert of Cherbury, and the naturalizing emphasis of Matthew Tindal and Thomas Morgan brings out the remarkable extent to which the early modern conception of religion revolved around themes that Hume both relied on and challenged. Admittedly, there are other stories one could tell about the philosophical conversation on religion and how it bears on true religion (for example, the history of Christian apologists such as Tertullian, Lucretius, Augustine, and Aquinas situates Christianity as the true religion and is a related trajectory in the same discourse). My hope is that the reader will find my choices to be warranted not simply by my aims but by a sound interpretation of the broad trends of the philosophical discourse and the proper temperament for the constructive task that lay ahead.

## Hume's Ciceronian Influence

Upon the whole, I desire to take my catalogue of Virtues from
Cicero's *Offices*, not from the *Whole Duty of Man*. I had, indeed,
the former Book in my Eye in all my Reasonings.
—*LET*, 1.32.13

Hume admitted that he was deeply influenced by the "noble eloquence" (*EMPL*, 12.223) of Marcus Tullius Cicero.[9] To understand the most significant aspects of Cicero's thoughts about religion and illustrate their impact on Hume, I highlight three features of Cicero's rhetorical and stylized approach to *religio* that appear in Hume's work, then I isolate three of Cicero's philosophical positions concerning religion that Hume seems to share. Attending to possible Ciceronian influences can provide classical foundations for Hume's consideration of religion and thicken our understanding of what he could have meant when he contemplated its proper office.

Cicero is generally considered to be one of the most important literary figures of the Roman Republic due to the breadth of his extant corpus; his quest to situate Greek philosophy in the Latin vernacular; his brilliant comprehension of the nexus of religious, social, and political issues of his time; and his rhetorical virtuosity. It is his remarkable political career and energetic role as statesman, however, that figure most prominently into his intellectual legacy and shape his idea of *religio*. Cicero's status as literatus rests on his vocation as a public servant, for even after his forced retirement from politics (46–44 B.C.E.) he conceived of himself as an active public orator in the Roman public sphere. His complex engagement with religion depended on but was not reducible to his public commitments. As Eli Edward Burriss bluntly writes, "The state was the first love of Cicero, and, if religion could serve the state, Cicero was willing to obey the laws of religion."[10] We should take care, however, not to completely collapse Cicero's contributions on religion into his politics. He was well acquainted with the power humans associated with ritual practices (haruspex, augury, prophesy, etc.), and he showed respect for sacrality. He spoke of these things, and others, strategically, under the idea *religio*, likely derived from the root *legere*, "to gather together" or "to arrange."[11] Still, his intentions for religion cannot be fully detached from his political concerns and the sociocultural matters on which they depended: namely, his attempt to reconcile heterogeneous traditions under a Roman cultural identity and his commitment to develop a rhetoric that compellingly extended Hellenistic traditions through the Latin tongue. His use of *religio* had both intellectual and political components, and Cicero was neither reluctant nor alone in using the term in this way. When viewed through the lenses of utility and stability, Cicero's discussions of religion reveal his functional investments in the order of the republic and the virtue of its citizens.

Three stylistic approaches in Cicero's work on religion are noteworthy points of departure for our Humean true religion. First, Cicero employed different genres of writing in his discussion of the multivocal notion *religio*; second, he spoke both affirmatively and critically about religious beliefs; and, third, he rhetorically embraced the traditions of the ancestors. Arguably, Hume's Enlightenment efforts included these same stylistic features. Additionally, three of Cicero's religious and philosophical commitments may have been significant for Hume. Cicero generally embraced a basic theism based on what he took to be our natural predilections. He also suggested *religio* was, at times, an interior disposition that could moderate our passions. And he advised that the development of virtuous character could be enhanced by certain beliefs and practices. Thus, Cicero's deployment of *religio* was strategic and deeply functional. Both he and Hume ultimately aimed for usability and stability in their reflections on religion.

### Three Stylistic Features of Cicero's Approach to Religion

Distinctions between Cicero's and Lucretius's use of *religio* prove that, like our modern idea 'religion,' the classical deployment of the term held different meanings for different users. The complexity and subtlety of its uses and meanings in the Roman Empire, where we locate the nascent Latin heritage of our modern idea of religion, can baffle even the most patient researcher. This is because the word *religio* was elastic. Getting a firm handle on Cicero's different uses of it is difficult given his shifting rhetorical emphases, multifaceted aims, and evolving perspectives. Generally speaking, however, we can say that Cicero took *religio* to be a synthesis of the following: an inner feeling that engendered balanced affections; a set of state-sanctioned rituals and sacraments to the gods (*culto pio*); a communal affirmation of virtuous or moral behavior; and sets of ceremonies that could enhance political and cultural stability. Cicero also used *religio* to connote the opposite of *superstitio*, worship that stressed the powers of magic, emphasized ecstatic worship, and was relatively unpredictable. His use of *religio* was openly a boundary-marking activity; it differentiated acceptable forms from unacceptable ones.

One shared stylistic feature of Cicero's and Hume's engagement with religion is their cross-genre approach to religion. For Cicero, this enabled him to reach a broader audience and delicately nuance certain positions. The use of different formats may also have appealed to the diverse cultural identities that he aimed to assimilate under the Roman banner. If we compare parts of a speech ("*De domo sua*," 57 B.C.E.), a poem ("*De consulatu suo*," 60 B.C.E.), a letter (to Atticus, 61 B.C.E.), and a philosophical work (*De officiis*, 44 B.C.E.), we notice that writing across these different genres from different moments in his career, Cicero consistently made an identical point: that *religio* was foundational for the unity of the state.[12] His practice of using different genres dispersed his convictions across a wider range of human emotions and enhanced the potential for his ideas to reach and compel the variety of listeners and readers that constituted his audience. It also was an implicit acknowledgment that the spectrum of human sensibilities was broad: those who responded to poetry may have found it difficult to be convinced by a speech or vice versa. In each genre Cicero verified a similar point regarding religion: it was deeply connected to political stability and communal well-being.

As a subset within this first feature, his cross-genre approach, we should add that Cicero placed a particular value on the dialogue form to reveal the depths of the complexity of questions regarding the nature of the gods. The masterpiece from late in his career, *De natura deorum* (45 B.C.E.), thoughtfully exposed the potential of rich dialogue to advance compelling and contrasting positions on theological questions. Its dialogic structure demonstrated intellectual agility and displayed a sense of the complicated, interconnected issues in the discussion of religion. Important for Cicero, and later for Hume, was that an author's views on the thorniest religious issues could be disguised behind character-interlocutors. This sort of concealment licensed both Hume and Cicero to press into controversial terrain and avoid culpability for undermining the beliefs of their readers. For Cicero there was an added benefit to this complicated veiling: it allowed him to choose his later positions from a wide palette and avoid being labeled hypocritical. At various moments in his corpus, but most intensely in his mature *Dialogues Concerning Natural Religion*, Hume wrote in this Ciceronian style of dialogue. Generally speaking, both men opted to suspend final judgment on controversial issues raised in their famous dialogues, yet neither thoroughly denounced traditions that sustained order and inspired virtue.

A second stylistic feature of Cicero's approach that also appeared in Hume's writing is the concomitant championing *and* challenging of religion. Cicero's critical and constructive energy regarding religion was evident in his affirmation of public worship to the gods that supported the republic and his dismissal of private sacraments to the gods that distorted social responsibility. The latter were held as perversions, vices, or *superstitio*: sets of communal practices that could not be assimilated into the Roman religion. Cicero both criticized and supported different forms of *religio* to mark boundaries and serve his individual sense of political stability.

Even when he was not attending to specific distinctions between *religio* and *superstitio*, Cicero's rhetoric on religion was two-sided. The degree to which his affirmations of certain religious beliefs and practices were generally qualified by critical remarks (both early in his career and even in his later works) provide evidence that Cicero never disavowed religion completely or entirely and that his support for religion was never without hesitation. His rhetorical strategy, rather, was to embrace certain aspects of *religio* and abandon others.[13] Hume would take a similar bifurcated approach to religion. Given that his overall support for religion was less conspicuous than Cicero's, his readers likely felt more sting from Hume's critical emphasis.

A third stylistic feature of Cicero's approach to religion that Hume's resembled was his backward-looking means of establishing its claims. Cicero legitimated certain religious traditions of the ancestors over others by picking and choosing from a wide assortment of historical manifestations. We might say that he "defined" religion by granting historical continuity to some practices and denying it to others.[14] Deft deployment of this kind of critique and affirmation (per the second feature) of historical practices served to exalt aspects of the Roman past and thereby point the way to a stable future. These rhetorical acts of reverence for ancestral traditions were clever acts of definition and restriction: they limited acceptable religious practices to those which (Cicero believed) ultimately served imperial interests. Hume did not venerate the ancestors in the way that Cicero did. His historical mode of inquiry generally operated along causal lines— the probability of a past event was able to be determined by evidence we currently have for it. Hume's historical writings assess the contemporary status of both true and popular religion by describing their evolution. Thus Hume's backward look intended to locate resources for a stable future where it was a virtue to love the established religion of one's country ("there must be an ecclesiastical order, and a public establishment of religion in every civilized community" [HE, 3.134–35]).

The cross-genre approach to religion and the use of dialogue form, the critical and affirmative modes of engaging religion, and the importance of the history of religion for stability of the political order were formal features that appeared in both Cicero's and Hume's stylized approaches to religion. In addition to these components, there is overlapping content in the areas of theism, morality, and the passions, the areas I posit as the elemental building blocks for our provisional notion of true religion inspired by and linked to Hume's work.

### Three of Cicero's Philosophical Ideas Concerning Religion

Of course, Hume's radical Enlightenment work cannot be separated from its generally anti-Christian, rational emphases on natural religion. At the same time, its classical influence should not be overlooked. In fact, much of Hume's thought was a synthesis of his extensive reading of classical writers. While he made no direct citations for his specific ideas, his work explicitly referenced scores of classical texts and thinkers. On the grounds of his admitted reading of and high regard for Cicero, we can fairly presume that he was influenced by the notion that religion— at its best—could enhance social and political life and contribute to the stability of the passions and the development of excellence of character. Accordingly, three philosophical ideas concerning religion in Cicero's work stand out: his skeptical embrace of general theism, his notion that religion could moderate the passions, and his belief that religion could enhance virtuous character development. I shall briefly treat these in order.

Nowhere in the Ciceronian corpus do we find a flat-out rejection of the idea of an Author of Nature. Neither, however do we find a full-blown description of Cicero's notion of divinity. Cicero's public position on theism evolved throughout his long career, and he generally concealed his personal theistic beliefs, making it difficult to pinpoint his specific position on theism. Caught in the matrix of a contested yet expanding Hellenic worldview, Cicero's attempt to reconcile Roman political identity with the heterogeneous ethnic and fluid cultural identities that constituted the empire led him to shift between articulating a skeptical theism, suspending judgment on theism, and remaining uncommitted on the question of theism.[15] The general direction of Cicero's dynamic rhetoric on theism, which is generally discernible after a patient reading across his wide corpus, is that our minds naturally assumed a deity.[16] He confirmed this in an early speech, "De haruspicum responsis" (57 B.C.E.), when he asked, "who is so witless that, when he gazes up into heaven, he fails to see that gods exist?"[17] Of course, Cicero's nondogmatic approach to the question of theism was deeply considered and informed by an ethic of utility. His commitment to traditional civic religion required that he embrace, at best, or capitulate, at worst, to a basic theism that acknowledged the inescapability of our powerful belief in a natural order governed by a sense of general providence (that divine reason suffused the cosmos).[18]

Second, Cicero's self-styled Stoic commitment to the virtue of moderation was in Hume's "eye" in "all his reasonings."[19] In De officiis (44 B.C.E.) Cicero gave sacred status to the notion that "people should obey calm of soul and be free from every sort of passion" (1.102).This sacrality invited the notion of religion, which Cicero defined in De inventione (84 B.C.E.) as "that which causes men to pay attention to, and to respect with fixed ceremonies, a certain superior nature, which men call divine nature."[20] He believed the habit for religion enhanced our capacity for self-restraint, our "superior nature" that separated us from animals. Thus, against the Platonic emphasis on knowledge-of-self as virtue (which can create detached philosophers unaware of the laws) and the Aristotelian notion of virtue as the mean between two extremes (which might encourage one to transcend the law), the Ciceronian commitment to moderation served the natural laws that reflected innate, collective duties that had been codified as laws of the state. They also linked to our theistic worldview as described in De finibus bonorum et malorum: "A study of the heavens brings in addition a certain sense of moderation when one observes the great order and control that obtains among the gods as well. To look upon the gods' works and their acts creates in us a loftiness of spirit. And we gain a sense of justice when we understand the will, the design and the purpose of the supreme guide and lord to whose nature philosophers tell us that true reason and the highest law are perfectly matched."[21] Cicero's conception of moderation updated Aristotle's. Hume's moderation of the passions would, in some ways, renew Cicero's.

A third idea of Cicero's that also appeared in Hume's work is that attention to the "heavens" or "divine nature" (*religio*, in the previous argument) both enables moderation and assists in the development of virtuous character, a reflection of classical moral philosophy. Cicero's self-styled Stoicism concerned itself with the political and (by default) personal benefits of *religio*. He supported forms of sacred worship and cultic practices that prioritized justice, which he took to be the Stoic form of natural law. If *religio* led to justice it follows that it assisted the human *telos* toward happiness because "the moral life is the happy life."[22] On this logic, one can argue that *religio* supported the development of virtuous behavior and human excellence to encourage stability—a condition for personal happiness. Thus the development of virtuous character, happiness, and proper functioning of the state were moral considerations undergirding Cicero's use of the supple category *religio*. When read in the direct light of this Ciceronian emphasis, Hume's ethics seems to reflect more of a classical approach to morality. Perhaps his 1742 essay "The Stoic" (*EMPL*, 16.146–54), where he reproduced the style of the Ciceronian "rhetorical dialogue" and argued that "the great end of all human industry, is the attainment of happiness" (16.148), is most obvious in this regard. In it Hume seems to imbue the sense of happiness with something of a religious flavor, in the sense that it is driven by something greater than our personal motivations and natural dispositions.[23] In this sense religion may enhance our moral lives, but the quality of our moral lives does not *depend* on religion.

These features of Cicero's style and content in his treatment of religion are present in Hume's philosophical, religious, and historical writings. Secondary scholarship confirms that Cicero influenced Hume more than any other classical writer. His impact on Hume's moral thought and theory of the passions has been well documented. Religion was an area that was crucial for both men. Given these facts, we may fairly presume a Ciceronian influence on Hume's thinking about religion. More details from Hume's work will emerge in the subsequent discussion, but his Ciceronian stylistic foundations are clear: Hume writes about religion across genres and uses the dialogue form; he takes both a critical and affirmative approach to religion (true and false); and he believes the best of religion is historically grounded in the traditions that serve stability.

Content-wise, the three features of Cicero's position on religion were also evident in Hume's. Each chapter of this book offers more details to the categories that tentatively endow our Humean true religion: a basic theism, moderation of the passions, and veneration of character development, respectively. None of these claims regarding style or content are very controversial. The assertion, however, that we might take his general theism, moderation of the passions, and practical morality, cumulatively, as constitutive of the proper office of religion is maybe more so. It challenges the pervasive views that Hume was an atheist, that he was *only* critical of and hostile to religion, and that his religious interests were subsumed in his moral theory. These views have steered philosophers trained in religious studies away from engaging with the more generative components of Hume's religious thought and concealed his mild affirmations of religion. Consider this clarification from Hume's own hand in his response to charges of irreligion in the *Treatise*: "And must not a Man be ridiculous to assert that our Author denies the Principles of Religion, when he looks upon them as equally certain with the Objects of his Senses?" (*LG*, 21). Commonly explained away as ironic and insincere and as a "smoke screen" for Hume's real position, the persistent association of Hume with hostility to religion deadens us to his quiet suggestions for religion and their Ciceronian influences.

Cicero's approach to *religio* provides a classical starting point for thinking about Hume's views of religion and sheds light on what may have been present in Hume's thought that he did not develop. This allows us to construct our Humean true religion on more solid foundations. Of course, Hume did not explicitly define the features of true religion as genuine theism, moderation of the passions, and practical morality. We extend his thought with our speculative construction as a way of preserving its understated fragments.

Cicero's political interests largely guided his reflections on religion that, in effect, authorized imperial power by endorsing a particular bundle of ritual practices over others. Hume had less of an explicit political investment, and his analysis of and mild suggestion for religion developed out of a discourse structured by modern logic. His eighteenth-century deference to the Ciceronian view of religion reflected the "classical revival" of his time, which was in part a strategy of resistance. Modern science and logic strove to provide the category 'religion' with philosophical legitimacy, for this would make it 'true.' Hume resisted the obsession with abstract, normative reason that informed modern discourse by claiming, like Cicero, that the true was best used to connote the most stable, *not* the most logical.

## Philosophical Discourse on Religion: From *Religio* to True Religion

For with what confidence can I venture upon such bold enterprizes, when beside those numberless infirmities peculiar to myself, I find so many which are common to human nature? Can I be sure that in leaving all establish'd opinions

I am following truth; and by what criterion shall I distinguish
her, even if fortune shou'd at last guide me on her foot-steps?
—*T*, 1.4.7.3

My aim in this section is to give a brief account of the theme of the 'true' in philosophical discourse on religion in the West to illuminate how Hume may have
responded to this discourse. Philosophical discourse on religion has largely been
determined by historical developments in science, philosophy, and religion and
deeply impacted by a complicated matrix of cultural, economic, political, and psychic challenges. It is difficult to tease out single threads from the complicated can
of worms that has informed its arc and decipher their precise impact. A general
history of this discourse bears out two facts: the first is that the idea 'religion' has
proven to be flexible and always in process; the second is that modern philosophical discourse on religion has revolved around the theme of the true.

Cicero's visionary management of *religio* highlighted the vast array of political,
cultural, and economic considerations he faced. Establishing a particular form of
worship as epistemically true was not a primary consideration for him. *Religio*, in
his framing, was not a form of knowledge; it was public worship of the gods that
led to the virtue of justice and supported the stability of the Roman Republic. This
form of civic religion based on the Greek notion of religion was destabilized by
the unpredictable interplay of sociopolitical and cultural factors along with the
dynamism of the growing confrontation between Greek and Christian intellectual
traditions. In other words, we can read the classical approach to *religio* as getting
swept up in the quest for institutional religious authority and its discursive claims
for religion to be true. Third-century Christian apologist Tertullian, for example,
strictly marked the "'true religion' of the true god" (*veram religionem veri dei*) as
distinct from the worship of other gods.[24] The true religion would demand the
most authority and be the most powerful.

The insights of Jeremy Schott and Denise Kimber Buell—through their deployment of postcolonialist theory—remind us that, to a large extent, early Christian
discourse was a confrontation of ethnic identities vying for survival. Under these
circumstances, establishing a particular form of ritual practice as true would have
great significance. Framed around the "truth" of doctrine, practice, or *religio*, the
debate between Christian apologists and Greek intellectuals in the second- and
third-century Roman Empire was a will-to-truth driven by sociopolitical circumstances, material interests, cultural concerns, and psychological needs. This, in
part, explains the shift away from Cicero's practical handling of *religio* as a civic
virtue to others who privileged its status as true. For example, the work of third-
century Platonists Celsus and Porphyry argued against the growing "threat" of
marginal Christians in terms of true and false. Fourth-century Christian apolo-

gists Lactantius, Augustine, and Eusebius—in many ways respondents to Celsus and Porphyry—framed Christianity as the true religion (*vera religio*) and contrasted it with the false religion (*falsa religio*) of the empire. Both sides in this debate claimed theirs was the true religion. The legacy of the framing of religion as either true or false reverberates in religious discourse in our late modern moment.

Celsus and Porphyry, two Platonists, and Lactantius and Eusebius, two Christians, marked the early parameters of the third- and fourth-century debate in Rome between Christian apologists and defenders of imperial religion.[25] In the Ciceronian tradition, Celsus and Porphyry valued the ancestral religions (most of them Romanized so that they could be integrated into imperial service) and contended that the best way to be religious was to affirm beliefs that had already proven to serve political stability. Against this valiant defense of the classical conception of *religio* as having a civic function, early Christian thinkers prioritized a particular set of beliefs and practices that venerated Divine Revelation through Jesus Christ as indisputably true.[26] Celsus and Porphyry showed little appreciation for this Christian form of revelation, its concomitant notion of salvation, and the emphasis on miracles of this Jesus sect. Most important, they did not agree that acceptance of Jesus as Son of God was more important than political sustenance and civic stability. They took the "fringe" movement called Christianity to be inherently destabilizing given its public refusal to be subsumed under Roman political hierarchy or absorbed into Roman religious identity. Celsus and Porphyry were religious thinkers concerned with questions of political good and imperial sustenance. For them, the true religion was justified by its historical performance. The starting point for their assessment of sacred beliefs and practices was, did it stabilize the social order? These two men were often read as critics of early Christianity, attackers of the Christian faith, or traditionalists concerning religion.[27] Adolf Harnack reminds us that they were united by a positive view of religion as the natural disposition that tied individuals in sacred, communal worship of the gods in ways that affirmed political order. A hallmark of their thought was the fundamental synthesis of the religious, social, and political. It followed from this that the Romanization of different systems of religious belief was necessary for a common morality. Celsus wrote, "If everyone were to adopt the Christian's attitude, moreover, there would be no rule of law: the legitimate authority would be abandoned; earthly things would return to chaos and come into the hands of the lawless and savage barbarians."[28]

Celsus and Porphyry extended part of the Ciceronian legacy against the onslaught of Christianity. Their goal-line defense of *religio* as public worship of the gods for the sustenance of political order, however, could not withstand the power of the emerging Christian identity that claimed the crown of *the* true religion and came to dominate the discourse on religion.[29] Post-Constantine, Christianity confidently enjoyed imperial authority. Though there were challenges to it, the link between Christianity and the "truth" has not been uncoupled as discourse on religion has evolved in the West. This is important for our constructivist project on David Hume: it shows the discursive boundaries that he inherited and confirms the possibilities for extending his thought through a deeper awareness of these constraints.

The graceful logic of two seventeenth-century figures, Lord Herbert of Cherbury and Hugo Grotius, presents us with a different sense of the idea of religion and its links with the theme of the true. These two early modern architects of thought advanced philosophical discourse on religion as it engaged with the quest for truth mounted by early modern science. Secondary literature depicts Grotius and Lord Herbert as thinkers who anticipated the new method of philosophical inquiry articulated by Bacon, a radical Protestant who tried to make the Reformed tradition more amenable to reason, and Descartes, an early modern humanist responsible for the development of the fields of natural law and natural religion.[30] I focus on another seminal insight of their work: that Christianity was a universal, rational set of beliefs and practices that relied on a particular form of revealed knowledge. These elements made it true.

The collapse of the authority of the papacy was a watershed moment that paved the way for the work of Grotius and Lord Herbert and the evolution of the modern discourse on religion. While the details are too complicated to describe here at length, both discursive trends and nondiscursive conditions propelled religious thought of their era. Three major discursive trends that contributed to the weakening and collapse of church authority from the thirteenth to the sixteenth centuries were the Renaissance fascination with the glories of the classical age, which inspired a cultural look backward (Ficino, Erasmus); the development of more complex theological systems by Scholastic thinkers in the universities, which led to a bolder distinction between faith and reason (Aquinas); and the scientific revolution, which generated new geographies of knowledge and new conceptions of the truth (Galileo, Newton).

Nondiscursive trends that played a significant role in this age were the increase in international trade and travel, the introduction of other cultures, the invention and proliferation of the printing press, and the development of new economic and political conditions (namely, monetary systems that increased the power of the bourgeoisie and led to the development of strong, centralized government). These circumstances not only inspired questions about the sanctity and usefulness of Roman Catholicism (these circumstances led to the Protestant Reformation) but also weakened the authority of the Christian revelation. Poignantly aware of the historical and cultural context, Grotius and Lord Herbert cleverly answered threats against Christianity by venerating it as the highest form of knowledge and (therefore) the greatest form of good. They deftly aided the transfer of the source of Christian power from the dominion of religious hierarchy (that is, the Catholic Church) to the rational basis of Christianity itself, the universal consensus it naturally generated, and the inner feelings it was based on and inspired. They contended that Christianity was authoritative and true not because clerics imposed it but because of the universal embrace stirred by its internally rational principles, which perfectly reflected the conditions and contexts that supported them.

Grotius and Lord Herbert quelled the dogmatic schisms of the theologians, defended Christianity against Islam and Judaism, and relied on the logic of modern science to establish that the Christian revelation was rationally certain. A major part of their intervention in religious discourse was the seminal importance they gave to the theme of the true. Both men claimed that Christianity was, indisputably, the true religion. They argued that its truth was derived from its universal standing as an inward instinct (not from the laws of science or the Biblical insight of clerics) imprinted by Divine Revelation (this ensured that it was not fully antagonistic to the Church). The true, in the work of both men, was inseparable from revelation and attached to the universal. Their quasi-Scholastic arguments cast a shadow that could not be ignored in subsequent discussions.

The Dutch-born Grotius articulated a conception of true religion in his best-known and groundbreaking work, *De jure belli ac pacis* (1625).[31] A poem he composed in Dutch during his imprisonment in Loevenstein on the truth of the Christian religion (1620), however, might be more important in terms of the links between religion and the theme of the true. This poem, translated into Latin and transformed into a treatise on true religion after his escape, initially appeared in 1626 and took its final form in a 1640 fifth edition as "*De veritate religionis christianae.*"[32] It venerated the idea of a universal religion and argued that the "plain consent of all nations" proved Christianity was the true religion. This universal true religion was inextricably bound to revelation (for "none of these things could be known without a revelation") and served the ends of social harmony and political stability (for "truth was indissolubly linked with peace: where there was no peace there could be no truth").[33]

Lord Herbert aimed for a method of discourse that could settle the bickering between various religious factions by appealing to the fundamental beliefs beneath their competing claims. To get to these foundational matters, Lord Herbert took the necessary step of making an inquiry into the epistemic status of the truth itself. In what is considered to be the first metaphysical work by an English philosopher, *De veritate* (1624, written in Latin), his longest and most important book, Herbert set out to "to examine truth itself" against those who merely asserted opinions (Scholastics, reformers, and skeptics).[34] His investigation confirmed what was true was indeed universal, for "whatever is universally asserted is the truth";

further, it relied on a deity, "for what is universal cannot occur without the influence of the Universal Providence which disposes the movements of events."[35] All
of this was derived from our a priori beliefs or "common notions" that our God-
given natural instincts allowed us to apprehend.[36]

With only slight differences in style and emphasis, Grotius and Herbert located
the theme of the true in the idea of revelation from God. Their focus on justificatory
logic required that the true religion satisfy the standards of abstract philosophy. To
defend Christianity on these grounds, they had to recast its ideas of revelation and
divine grace as forms of knowledge. Establishing these foundations of Christianity as rational, revealed, and universal (and therefore true) provided Grotius a
"good faith" to keep alive "the hope of peace" and Herbert a supreme religion
that would "replace all others by including their basic tenets within itself, and by
doing so would obviate the need for religious conflict."[37] Philosophic reason—
always part mystical (supernatural) and part natural for Grotius and Lord Herbert—
had delivered a coherent notion of the universal true religion that comported
with our inner worlds and confirmed that human thought proceeded "from the
efficiency of that reason impressed upon them, which reason is no other than what
we call God."[38]

Though Grotius and Lord Herbert tied Christianity more tightly to the idea of
the true, the increasing obsession with the method of modern science and concomitant commitment to reason as autonomous and universal in the modern
West was largely responsible for pushing philosophical discourse on religion even
more deeply into the center of the matrix of scientific truth and knowledge. The
illusory ideal of the modern subject as fully autonomous and on a quest for truth
as rational certainty through coherence and logical consistency of argument was
reflected in the modern conception of religion as a stable philosophical idea.
Knowledge, on the logic of abstract thought, was justified purely by proper epistemological commitments. A feature of modern thought that sprung from this
way of thinking is the idea that religion was a form of knowledge to be assessed
for its validity on the standard of scientific reason. On the modern concept, the
*genus* religion is a bundle of philosophically legitimate beliefs and justifiable practices about God and the world that simply arrived in different *species*. This theme
is evident in a number of moments in discourse on religion, particularly its
Enlightenment writings that eloquently treat the tension between philosophical
reason and the natural grounds of religion. The work of Matthew Tindal and John
Toland, for example, recruited aspects of this modern concept of religion and
generally offered true religion as the perfectly rational, completely natural, and
thoroughly universal form of Christianity.

The needs of the new self-regulating and self-determining modern subject, the
extensive religious warfare and violent factionalism of the late sixteenth and early

seventeenth centuries, the further weakening of ecclesiastical theology, and the discoveries of modern science inspired English Enlightenment figures to develop the theme of the true in relation to the natural and moral features of discourse on religion. John Locke's argument for toleration reflected the Enlightenment quest for a universal ethic. Its effect was to press religious thinkers to deemphasize the concept of revelation, which had served as the central category for Grotius and Lord Herbert. Further, the logic of science and the demands of philosophical reason illuminated two insurmountable problems regarding the concept of revelation: it was neither rationally verifiable nor fully universal. Enlightenment thinkers, therefore, jettisoned the idea of revelation because, on the terms of their enterprise, it mitigated against the possibility that Christianity could be fully established as true.

Secondary literature on eighteenth-century discourse about religion generally contends that religious writings of the early Enlightenment were largely anti-Christian, anticlerical, and antiscriptural. They emphasize that religious discourse in the Enlightenment—counter to that of Grotius and Herbert—was obsessed with establishing scientific reason as foundational for religion, devoted to describing religion as fully natural, and invested in demonstrating the truth of religion from its reflection of nature.[39] Though the major texts of this era were not monolithic, this is a fair interpretation of an important strand of Enlightenment writing about religion. The writings of Matthew Tindal and Thomas Morgan are exemplary in this regard: they remained circumscribed by the idea of the true but refused any link to revelation. For them, the true religion was contingent on and marshaled the best of our rational, natural, and moral propensities.[40]

Tindal's most well-known work, *Christianity as Old as Creation* (1730), is written in a quasi-dialogue form between himself and a questioner. Inspired by the work of Cicero, the naturalism of Grotius, and the humanism of Lord Herbert, it further deemphasized the importance of revelation for the true religion. Tindal claimed that revelation was anchored in the particulars of time and place and therefore was too restrictive to be universal. This led to the demotion of the role of revelation in his thought, a watershed move for discourse on religion. Tindal and his deistical cohort undermined revelation not only because they wanted to render a trenchant critique of revealed religion but also because they aimed to put forward a thoroughly universal religious vision that venerated nature, tolerance, and happiness without a personal deity. With revelation—the final impediment to this universal true religion—out of the way, the full burden of human happiness would rest completely on the faculty of unaided human reason. This profound confidence in autonomous reason was derived from the observation of nature for, as Tindal wrote, "the Perfection and Happiness of all rational beings, Supreme as well as subordinate, consists in living up to the dictates of their nature."[41] The laws of nature and reason fully replaced God and revelation as the foundations for the true religion and the sources for human happiness.

Tindal's recommendation for religion, having shed the baggage of revelation, is, in many ways, a practical, ethical project. Yet he expresses it in terms of religion, not morality, and thereby confirms his aim to be part of the discourse on religion. He writes, "'true religion' consist[s] in a constant disposition of mind to do all the Good that we can; and therefore render ourselves acceptable to God in answering the End of his Creation." It is our duty to embrace the moral demands dictated to us by the "One true religion of mankind," the "Religion of Nature and Reason written in the hearts of every one of us from the first Creation."[42] The detachment of ethics from religion was left undeveloped in Tindal's work (as well as Morgan's), but we can fairly state that Tindal was primarily invested in providing a religious prescription, not simply a moral one.

Following the example of Tindal, Thomas Morgan also saw God's truth to be evident in the visible, natural world. He too made nature the ultimate standard for religion, deemphasized the role of divine grace, and undermined revelation. Building on the idea 'true religion' promoted by Tindal (particularly in Morgan's most well-known book, *The Moral Philosopher* [1737], written in dialogue form), Morgan presented a historiography that confirmed true religion as the original religion of humankind that had been corrupted at various stages throughout history. I quote him at length here to show his historical thinking, how he used the idea of nature, and his veneration of the true religion:

> The original, *true religion*, therefore, of God and Nature, consisted in the direct, immediate worship of the one true God, by an absolute resignation to, and dependence on him in the practice of all the duties and obligations of moral truth and righteousness. During this state of true religion, men look'd to and depended upon God, as the sole author of nature, of all the properties and power of subordinate beings and agents, and as the one only original, efficient cause of all Things. . . . Men, in this state of innocency and *true religion*, own'd God, not only as the author, contriver and former of nature, but as the preserver, supporter and director of all nature by his continued agency and providential causality. They considered all events good and evil, as the ordination and appointment of God; the one, as the natural and just reward of wisdom and integrity, and the other, as either the necessary exercise and trial of virtue, or as the punishment and cure of folly or sin. This, as I take it, was the original state of philosophy and *true religion*, before the apostasy of angels and men.[43]

Tindal and Morgan connect religion to the theme of the true more than any other theme, including nature or "the natural."[44] Their discussion of true religion, however, has not generated as much attention in secondary scholarship as their handling of natural religion. Natural religion, the idea that the observation of nature suggests a deity, is the theistic feature of their true religion. Yet the true religion is not reducible to natural religion. Christianity, for example, if not polluted by the hierarchy of the priest craft or driven by revelation and superstition, can be dubbed true religion, not natural religion: its truth is eternal and immutable yet hidden from us by those who gain from keeping people ignorant of it. True religion was deployed by Tindal and Morgan to represent the sum total of natural religion and the virtuous acts it inspired.[45]

Both Tindal and Morgan were obsessed with reason and convinced that God left an indelible and immutable imprint on every living organism in the world. That imprint was visible in the uncorrupted and full expression of the nature of the organism. The nature of humans was expressed through the uninterrupted freedom of reason. It follows that reason was natural to human beings: it was the visible stamp of God, and it helped determine what was true. Unaided reason was necessary and sufficient for human happiness as well as the development of the "universal practice of moral truth and righteousness," or the true religion.[46]

In addition to the thinkers I have mentioned here, a myriad of responses to the conversational shifts and changes in discourse on religion appeared. All, however, were ensconced in a larger discursive project that, in the modern West, leaned toward establishing the beliefs of religion as philosophically valid. While the themes of reason, authority, and universalizability were instructive in a discourse that aimed for a true religion, my analysis of it here is partial and limited; simply put, I hope to invite more detailed discussion on the theme of the true in discourse on religion. The intention of my heuristic account is not only to rehearse the larger context for our Humean true religion but also to provide a loose sense of the terms and trends in the discursive territory Hume inherited. As J. B. Schneewind states, "we need to understand the map of religious options on which Hume's readers would have located him. Whether he accepted the common options or not, he would have known them and taken them into account in the presentation of his views."[47] In the face of these options Hume confronted a dual challenge: to stay within the discursive boundaries of philosophical thinking about religion so that he might remain a relevant interlocutor and, at the same time, to help push the discourse on religion past its limits. How might he justify a form of religion distinct from inherited conceptions of the false and the true? How could he compellingly articulate his unconventional sense of religion's proper office?

The English Enlightenment provided the context for Hume's distinctive intervention in religious discourse. While its notions of epistemic truth and its ideas of subjectivity have been radically challenged by structuralists and postmodernists, and religious discourse has become more porous in our late modern era due to the insights of pragmatism and existentialism, I have tried to show that Hume worked in a moment when the true was venerated. His work challenged religious discourse, but it did not escape the framework of the discourse, which had become inseparable from the theme of the true. Even the argumentatively dexterous and intellectually nimble Hume could not abscond from his own philosophical heritage: he worked within the limits of the modern categories available to him, that is—he used the terms "true" and "false" when it came to religion. Yet Hume subverted the conventional use of these terms. To him, our true ideas and beliefs were not those that could be verified by abstruse thought; they were the ideas and beliefs that reflected the general orientations confirmed by habits and reflective common life. These were our most stable ideas. Like Cicero, Hume's intervention for religion was practical, but only on the discursive level: his argument aimed to moderate a discourse on religion that had gotten carried away by abstract philosophy and metaphysics. That is, Hume was discomfited by the modern view that made religion justifiable on the terms of abstract philosophy. He claimed this was an unintelligible and therefore *false* standard of legitimation that supported vulgar and superstitious forms of religion. True philosophy, he suggested, would put abstruse philosophy and metaphysics in its place, and the rare true religion would shift the grounds of religion back to the reflective traditions of common life. These strategic features of his work reflected its larger aims: to decrease religious factionalism and expose the "frailty of human reason" (*NHR*, 15.12).

Hume's thought was informed by the terms and conventions of the discourse on religion that he inherited, but it developed in the midst of a raging debate between religious liberals—the freethinkers, deists, Arians (as well as Socinians, Latitudinarians, and Unitarians)—against the orthodox Methodists, Presbyterians, and Puritans about the form and content of religious belief and practices.[48] Though raised Presbyterian, Hume occupied an intellectual perch on the margins of Christianity. Still, he saw himself as something of a friend to both sides of this debate. His writings show him to be acutely aware of its terms and able to access its arguments, especially the role of nature and reason, the status of miracles, the possibility of religious certainty, religious authority, and the argument from design. Hume was also somewhat of a foe to each side: he despised the deity of false religion—an assumption of the "dissenters" as well as the believers—and he articulated a philosophical approach of true philosophy that proceeded easily without religion (and potentially replaced it). Still, instead of directly attacking either the liberals or the clergy (or arguing that all forms of religion should be destroyed at all times), Hume challenged the source of their arguments: abstract reason. This did not mean, however, that he never imagined the best form of religion. In fact, his argument against abstruse thought implied that religion was a natural disposition of humans that could be marshaled for larger purposes. Its source was our nature, an "inexplicable mystery" in the terms of philosophy (*NHR*, 15.12), and its proper office would highlight social order, virtuous conduct, and calm passions. Like Cicero, Hume was mostly concerned about the functional value of religion, not its epistemic 'truth' value. His modern version of the classical civic religion was subsidized by his critique of Enlightenment notions of autonomous reason, philosophical discomfort with the idea that the natural was the rational, and a deep historicism that worked against the very idea of a "universal." For Hume, reason was not radically independent; it was intricately bound with hopes, fears, customs, and traditions, hallmarks of the imaginative process by which humans derive orientation and meaning in the world. Though his mitigated skepticism suggested it might be futile, he aimed to tweak customs, moderate passions, and shift our sense of moral authority. He never requested that humans should discard religion altogether.

Following Tindal and Morgan, Hume rejected revelation as an adequate source for religious belief; thus, he destroyed the grounds for revealed religion. Yet, unlike Tindal and Morgan, Hume argued that nature, or natural religion—the capacity to derive an understanding of God and the order of the world through rational consideration of the observable evidence in nature—neither honored the myriad inconsistencies experienced in nature nor respected the limits of reason and the reach of the mind. For Hume, the premise that natural religion could prove God's existence or assert God's attributes (i.e., infinite, wise, good) was unsustainable. It relied on a very narrow interpretation of nature as well as a defective theory of how the mind functioned. Hume's version of religion's proper office stood firmly against the notion of natural religion as articulated by the deists.

Hume similarly dismantled the idea of rational religion presented by the freethinkers of his day. The theory of the mind he articulated in his early philosophical works showed the importance of the passions, the imagination, and our habits, as they traced the genesis of our beliefs. Hume contended that philosophy—always generated by the passions (the sources of our beliefs and behaviors)—could lead us to skeptical dead ends if it was not balanced by the customs and conventions of common life. With the foundations of revealed, natural, and rational religion destroyed, on what could true religion rely? For Hume, and this marked a significant shift in the theme of the true in religious discourse, the true had little to do with the standards of philosophical reason, observation of the natural world, or a universal worldview. In fact, these were the foundations of false religion. True religion, described by Hume in a redacted footnote, was a disposition of the human heart that secured "obedience to the Laws & civil Magistrate."[49]

Hume was never more explicit than this about the content of true religion. We can presume that Cicero's discussion of theism, his articulation of the role of the passions, and his description of the development of virtuous character likely influenced Hume's sense of the proper office of religion. These content areas comport with Hume's larger philosophical commitments: they are moderately skeptical, they affirm the reflective natural beliefs of common life, they challenge abstruse reason of false philosophy, they moderate the passions, and they extol a public morality that produces a more stable political order.[50] They also cohere with the three-part division of Hume's *Treatise* (the understanding, the passions, and morality), which I turn to in chapter 2. Hume—like Cicero—did not make hard distinctions between the social, the philosophic, the political, and the religious. For him, religion was natural, linked to the passions, and omnipresent in history. The disposition 'true religion,' however, was practically impossible to locate in history. As the discursive ideal that reflected the knowledge inherent in the stable beliefs of common life, it was to contrast vulgar religion, which operated under the illusion that it was in sync with the logical standards of metaphysics. One example of Hume's explicit narration of this point occurs in an understudied essay, "Of Parties in General," where he writes,

> Most religions of the ancient world arose in the unknown ages of government, when men were as yet barbarous and uninstructed, and the prince, as well as peasant, was disposed to receive, with implicit faith, every pious tale or fiction, which was offered him. The magistrate embraced the religion of the people, and entering cordially into the care of sacred matters, naturally acquired an authority in them, and united the ecclesiastical with the civil power. But the Christian religion arising, while principles directly opposite to it were firmly established in the polite part of the world, who despised the nation that first broached this novelty; no wonder, that, in such circumstances, it was but little countenanced by the civil magistrate, and that the priesthood was allowed to engross all the authority in the new sect. . . . And the same principles of priestly government continuing, after Christianity became the established religion, they have engendered a spirit of persecution, which has ever since been the poison of human society, and the source of the most inveterate factions in every government. Such divisions, therefore, on the part of the people, may justly be esteemed factions of principle; but, on the part of the priests, who are the prime movers, they are really factions of interest. (*EMPL*, 8.13–14)

The following chapters attempt to support and develop the idea that content for a Humean true religion might be taken from the cumulative results of Hume's project on the passions, his work on epistemology, and his contribution to moral thought. To some scholars, the rarefied status of true religion in Hume's project and Hume's ethical tilt raises questions about its value for religion. Others claim that his choice not to give explicit details to this category suggests irrelevance for his overall project. But David Hume took religious discourse—not just moral discourse—very seriously for intellectual and strategic reasons: he was committed to preventing the abuse of religion for political gain and invested in demonstrating the impossibility of grounding our religious beliefs in abstract thought. He valued religion for what it might do: moderate our passions, assist in the development of moral character, and enable loyalty to the state. He was also invested in preserving the reflexive traditions of common life.

This chapter had a twofold aim: to describe the possible Ciceronian links to Hume's thinking about religion and to give a brief account of the development of the theme of the true in discourse on religion. I highlighted significant interventions in this discourse and showed Hume's general response to the conversation he inherited. We now have some broad historical foundations for the argument of this book: that the cumulative achievements of Hume's mild philosophical theism, the aim of his moral rationalism, and the conclusion of his project on the passions provide the best content for our speculative, Humean influenced notion of true religion.

# GENUINE THEISM

If my philosophy, therefore, makes no addition to the arguments for religion, I have at least the satisfaction to think it
takes nothing from them, but that everything remains precisely
as before.
—*T*, 1.4.5.35

Hume framed his arguments about God within a climate of philosophical discourse on religion that generally reinforced the theism of popular Christianity.
His philosophical mission was, in part, to expose the God of popular religion
to be an unstable concept masquerading as religious truth. To Hume, the vulgar theism of this brand of false religion was both impractical and dangerous;
it relied on a method of reasoning that betrayed the principles of understanding and distorted the natural powers of the mind. On his account the idea of a
morally worthy deity was misleading, belief in worship-worthy divinity created factionalism, and the concept of a God with moral attributes was unintelligible. Hume's devastating critique of popular theism relied on a moral stance
(that God was not the source of our moral judgment), a political commitment
to stability of the social order, historical awareness (from which he deduced
that religion was most often destabilizing), and his approach to understanding
the limits of the human mind. The latter interests frame the argument of this
chapter.

An important focal point of Hume's philosophical writings was his description
of the process by which we come to hold beliefs and ideas. These foundations
were important for his later "religious" writings. In the *Natural History of Religion*
(*NHR*) what Hume called "vulgar theism" (as in common, general, or customary
theistic beliefs) was a distortion that arose from the natural tendency of our imag-

ination to form the idea that "the order of the universe proves an omnipotent mind" (*T*, app., 18n). In his first philosophical work he explained that the creative powers of the imagination—guided by associative principles—fashioned ideas of necessary connection, causal power, and regularity that were indispensable for experience. Some of these ideas struck the mind with vivacity, found support in conventions of social life (i.e., popular religion), and became beliefs. Hume's argument, like any observational science, presupposed order and regularity (though he was critical of causal regularity). In fact, modern science—understood as knowledge of prediction—can proceed only if events and objects exist and produce specific effects according to their nature. Perhaps a Humean perspective would add a further stipulation: for science to be possible our minds must function in a way that makes it seem that events and objects exist and produce specific effects according to their very own mysterious natures.

Approaching Hume's work through the lens of our speculative Humean true religion provides warrant for us to consider the presuppositions of Hume's philosophy, at least provisionally, as a kind of "basic theism." Reflecting on his work from this angle allows insight into his underdeveloped notion 'genuine theism' and provides grounds to determine if it might be justifiably positioned within religion's proper office.

## The Author of Nature

The order of the universe proves an omnipotent mind; that is,
a mind whose will is *constantly attended* with the obedience of
every creature and being.
—*T.*, app., 18n

### Basic Theism: The Source of Vulgar Theism and Genuine Theism

Hume's philosophy, like any science, rested on the general assumption of a rudimentary form of causal regularity. It affirmed both our belief in hidden powers in nature (a source for what we take to be the principles of human nature) and our instinctive perception that the universe is ordered and regular. I name this "basic theism" because, on Hume's argument, to assume a constantly dynamic order is to invite the mind to the idea of an Orderer. Another way to say this—and this is accepted in Hume scholarship—is that the presupposition of order and regularity irresistibly orients the mind to the idea of an Author of Nature. For Hume, the source of this basic belief was neither a causal regress nor the ascription of intention in the universe based on observable effects; it was—more simply—common life's suggestion and a propensity of the imagination to regard the universe as purposive.[1] Unlike the later Kantian approach, the Humean style was not preoccupied with establishing conditions for the possibility of its own observational science. For Hume, true philosophy unself-consciously accepted premises that could not be proven. The Humean approach was invested more in questions that spoke to everyday curiosities instead of philosophical quandaries. Thus, what we can say about this assumption—a dispositive propensity—is that it was sustained by habits of the mind and reflective customs of common life. While the disposition to order and regularity made the belief in "invisible, intelligent power" irresistible, this basic theism presupposed by Hume's philosophy had little to do with conventional religion. Hume was adamant that belief in an all-knowing, omnipotent deity with a moral plan for the universe was unintelligible, historically divisive, and morally contentious. My reading basic theism in Hume's philosophy calls the reader's attention to what is presupposed by Hume's philosophy—more than the sum of what was given in experience—and thereby set up his notion of genuine theism for our speculative Humean true religion.

I am mindful that it may be confusing to name a presupposition of Hume's *philosophy*, even provisionally, a basic theism and that some may disagree with this choice, though I have exercised caution by defining it as a disposition rooted in the simple assumptions of order and regularity. It is of use-value in this study because Hume used the terms "vulgar theism" and "genuine theism" as opposites. He explicitly and repeatedly remarked that the vulgar theism of popular religion was a *distortion* of mind. We can fairly presume that the genuine theism of true religion was an *enlargement* of mind. It follows that for each case we ask, what is being distorted or enlarged? I submit that it is the natural disposition to belief in an Author of Nature. This temperament, the willingness to tacitly cosign belief in an Author of Nature, is what I conditionally call "basic theism." On Hume's science of human nature, it is grounded in the assumption of a natural order, essential for any observational science and fundamental for the form of scientific rationality that undergirds Enlightenment thought. Does Hume's philosophical project presuppose this basic theism or does the argument of the *Treatise* foreclose the intelligibility of basic theism? How can basic theism fund the genuine theism of our Humean true religion? I shall begin to pursue these questions through a brief assessment of Hume's iconoclastic intervention in philosophy. After setting aside the deep skeptical reading of Hume by arguing that—on Donald Livingston's phenomenology of common life—Hume was a mitigated skeptic who left room for true philosophy and true religion (with its genuine theism), I posit some sources for belief in basic theism in his philosophy. A Deleuzian reading of Hume's theory of mind and an interpretation of his thoughts on natural belief as understood by Norman Kemp Smith furnish two methods of understanding how basic theism might be understood as both a presupposition for and a consequence of Hume's philosophy of the imagination and common life.

Though my moderate claim for the irresistibility of the belief in an Author of Nature is largely uncontroversial, some might challenge my assertion that theism exists in the *Treatise* on grounds that the work took little or no interest in religion.[2] My approach, however, acknowledges the significant *religious* interest underneath Hume's intense *philosophical* focus. Hume's philosophy was concerned with how we come to hold beliefs, particularly belief in deity; thus it was crucial for theism. In the well-cited section of the *Treatise*, "Of the Immateriality of the Soul," Hume took a direct stand against both Spinozist and Cartesian positions on theism by claiming "anything may be the cause or the effect of anything" (1.4.5.32). Further, he stated—concerning the existence of God—that "existence of any object is no addition to the simple conception of it" (1.3.7, 2) and that our "idea of deity," if it were to be intelligible on the standards of abstruse reason, should rely on an impression like our other ideas (1.3.14.10). These few examples (there are others) stand against the prevailing view that Hume's *religious* writings are the only ones to be consulted for his views on deity. Paul Russell's important work on Hume's *irreligion*, whose conclusion—that Hume was against popular religion—I support, stands against the conventional reading. Russell argues that "the debate concerning our idea of God is implicated and involved in almost every aspect of Hume's project throughout the *Treatise*," and it is "a mistake to assume that Hume's various discussions in the *Treatise* . . . are irrelevant to the question concerning our idea of *God*." Russell concedes "the fact that Hume rarely mentions the term 'God,' and says little directly about the nature and origin of this idea." He stresses that this "should not obscure the importance of all that he has to say as it relates to the divine attributes." In short, Hume did not successfully "castrate" all the religious or "nobler" parts of his *Treatise*. His early philosophical work offered useful insights for and criticisms of theism and discourse on religion.[3]

It is not surprising that the *Treatise* took up the topic of religion to expose the fragile sources of traditional arguments for God.[4] Hume repeatedly stated that the vulgar theism of false religion was dangerous in part because it stood on unstable foundations. At the same time, he adamantly denied the charges of atheism and rejected the label of "deist." Hume's letters (especially the Letter to Mure, 1743), the first *Enquiry* (1748), *Natural History of Religion* (1757), and *Dialogues Concerning Natural Religion* (1779) demonstrated the obvious: that Hume seriously and strategically considered both more and less useful forms of theism. Given his abiding interest in religion and the textual evidence for it, it is fair to presume that he began thinking about theism very early in his literary career. That Hume seriously considered theism does not mean he believed religion to be an automatic remedy for social ills (he did not) or that popular versions of theism were intelligible on his theory of mind (they were not). It is merely a Humean acknowledgment that what he called the "whimsical condition of mankind" (*E*, 12.2.7) was a state in which the mind seemed to naturally go beyond experience to "the assent of the understanding to the proposition *that God exists*" (*LET*, 1.50.21). This basic theism in Hume's philosophy highlighted the mind's assumption of a (hidden) source for what was given to us in experience, our natural presupposition of a (unseen) cause of perceptions, our sense that the principles of human nature had an (invisible) author, the feeling that there was an ultimate cause behind the (secret) powers of nature, and a disposition to teleology (the feeling that an unknowable purpose probably lightly guided nature).

An interesting debate exists in the secondary scholarship as to whether Hume's discussion of necessary connection and causation resulted in him holding the position that causal power was real.[5] This debate bears heavily on discussions of theism in Hume. I try to circumvent its worries and take advantage of its insights by separating ontological concerns from epistemological ones. I restrict my interest in basic theism and my speculation that the proper office of religion might include a genuine theism to the realm of our thoughts and beliefs. I accept Hume's fundamental caveat that "as long as we confine our speculations to the appearances of objects to our senses, without entering into disquisitions concerning their real nature and operations, we are safe from all difficulties" (*T*, app., 35). I do not take this to mean that Hume sought to limit reality *simply* to our ideas. His nondogmatic skepticism left him open to the possibility of mind-independent reality. Still, I have no pretensions to chime in on this debate; I simply take the path of least resistance in describing basic, vulgar, and genuine theism by situating them entirely within the parameters of the mind and the bounds of the imagination. My interest is in the mind's *supposition* of order and causal power and how it invites a mental disposition toward basic theism. This predilection of mind, that "a purpose, an intention, a design, is evident in everything" (*NHR*, 15.1), can inspire either a vulgar theism—the miracle performing, anthropomorphic God of popular Christianity—or genuine theism, the moderate belief in an unobtrusive Author of Nature. I shall return to the debate surrounding Hume's causal realism. What is important here is that Hume's philosophy is built around the idea that the mind assumes regularity and accepts that "*the future resembles the past*" (*T*, 1.3.12.9). This assumption makes the idea of the Author of Nature irresistible to the mind (this is why I call it "basic theism"). Whether causal power is real or the Author of Nature actually exists is a different matter indeed.

Of course, Hume challenged the very notion that we could have a "feeling" without an impression, and he thought any causal chain that linked the future to the past was unintelligible on the existing standards of reason. This suggests that naming Hume's sense of order as a "basic theism" does not quite comport with his scathing denunciations of popular forms of Christianity, his exasperation with both false religion and traditional metaphysics, or his approach to philosophical truth. But Hume's personal animus for traditional theism and his critical disposition toward vulgar religion do not automatically preclude a basic theism either. In fact, one can reconcile the theistic openness of his work with the elements that seem to oppose it: for example, his self-styled skepticism, his moral critique of popular Christianity, and his idea that to "conceive of something adds nothing to our idea of it" remain viable, crucial features of his thought even as we consider the modest sense of theism at its foundations. What I identify as Hume's basic theism leaves room for expressions of doubt, invites moral criticism of anthropomorphic conceptions of God, and is consistent with the idea that the existence of something adds very little to our idea of it. It also supports his unique form of skepticism, an obstacle to which we will later attend. Whether I am pushing him further than he wanted to go remains an interesting question.

HUME'S EARLY SCIENCE OF SELF-UNDERSTANDING

Hume, raised Presbyterian by a single mother, claimed to have "never had entertained any belief in religion since he had begun to read Locke and Clarke" (around his twentieth birthday).[6] These thinkers were seminal for his first philosophical work, now canonical, which was published when he was twenty-eight years old. John Rawls, in his *Lectures on the History of Moral Philosophy*, reminds us that its general content was "projected" when the author was fourteen, "planned" before he turned twenty-one, and largely "composed" before he was twenty-five. Thus it is safe, albeit somewhat cheeky, to note that this text, described as the greatest work of philosophy written in the English language, was conceived by a Scottish "tween" and written on his first major trip beyond his homeland. It is likely, given both the deep religious sentiments of his day and his break from the religious tradition of his family, that the young man's first major effort would attend—even if only in an iconoclastic fashion—to issues pertinent for religion, especially belief in God. Perhaps the "new scene of thought" he referenced in his famous "Letter to a Physician" (*LET*, 1.17.3) would even recast religion and reconceive theism in ways that Locke and Clarke would appreciate.

As he matured, Hume distanced himself from the 1739 *Treatise*. In an autobiographical essay written just months before his death, he claimed, "Never a literary attempt was more unfortunate than my *Treatise*. . . . It fell *deadborn from the press*" (*L*, 4). The description of the *Treatise* as "deadborn" was, in part, literary performance; by then he had breathed life back into it, corrected its errors, and rendered many of its most important arguments clearer in an *Enquiry Concerning Human Understanding* (1748).[7] Revisions notwithstanding, Hume did *not* distance himself from philosophical discourse on religion. The first *Enquiry*, in fact, consisted of twelve sections, two of which were explicitly and harshly critical of popular religion: "Of Miracles" and "Of Providence and Any Future State." These sections, "castrated" from the early *Treatise*, challenged important beliefs of Christian believers. Their analysis rested, however, on the foundations of the critique of religion contained in the first philosophical work.

Despite Hume's expressed disavowal of the *Treatise* and his rebranding of its most important interventions under a new banner, it still holds a unique place in Western thought and is usually given priority when it comes to the study of his philosophy. It is also elemental for his philosophy of religion. What is it about Hume's philosophical first let serve that has allowed it to survive as the cornerstone of his thought in spite of his repudiations of it? What did the young Hume, suffering through his own "disease of the mind" during the planning and composing of the text, articulate here that survived redaction, landed in the first *Enquiry*, and served as foundational for his body of thought? What has brought my interest in basic theism to the doorstep of his inchoate philosophical classic?

The answers to these questions have to do with subtle historical and interpretive factors surrounding Hume's early work.[8] On the larger questions of the survival and canonization of the *Treatise*, perhaps this is a matter of the temperament behind the argument. The text is, in many ways, a radical statement written by a man-child in the Enlightenment Promised Land, convinced that philosophy was in need of an intervention. To him, the grand philosophical systems of the seventeenth century (e.g., Descartes, Leibniz, and Spinoza) were abstruse and built on "weak foundations" (*T*, introd., 1). They employed self-certifying principles to establish timeless and transcendent truths about the nature of the universe and the essence of matter that led to vulgar theism and popular religion. Against these weak foundations the iconoclastic young man searched for firmer and more powerful ones to illuminate the moment of arising and evolution of our ideas, beliefs, and customs. Hume observed that nature, customary associations of the mind, tacit knowledge inherent in the customs of common life, and the passions served to ground our ideas, actions, and beliefs. The *Treatise* was both an original work of philosophy and an analysis of the state of philosophical discourse. It deftly raised questions about the overall aims of philosophical reflection—what made its claims intelligible, what its foundational criteria were, and how it might do something more than the trivial and the disputational. In this regard, the bold, unsullied, youthfulness of the *Treatise* made it stand out. Rejecting the standard positions and well-worn arguments regarding metaphysical reason, moral motivation, and the sources of religious belief, Hume's challenge to philosophical authority seemed, paradoxically, both to undermine and celebrate belief in things that we could neither see nor touch.

To some of his contemporaries, the *Treatise* contained flashes of brilliance. To most it exposed him to be something of a philosophical acolyte trying to address the quandaries that dogged philosophical discourse and preoccupied religious thinkers from the position of an outsider. Acute in his recognition that the "love of wisdom" was stuck in a bind, he poignantly expressed a profound disillusionment early in the text: "We have, therefore, no choice left but betwixt a false reason and none at all. For my part, I know not what ought to be done in the present case" (*T*, 1.4.7.7). The dilemma, as Hume saw it, was either to work within the confines of a philosophical method that strove for rational verification in the mode of Descartes or to abandon this sort of philosophical enterprise and discover a more adequate source for understanding our actions that would render our ideas intelligible. Hume thought the way to enhance our self-understanding and make our ideas clearer was to interrogate their sources. To serve this aim, he inaugurated a self-styled natural "science" in which he was, technically, both participant and observer. As the sole recorder and reporter of his own "scientific" data, he situated himself as an unchallengeable authority on experience. The mostly probable and provisional descriptions that he offered were marked by his unique reflective powers, which crucially relied on and critically undermined the very terms and categories that he interrogated (including the ideas of a self, Designer, and external objects). The flexible ideas 'nature' and 'common life' were the unique cornerstones of his extension of Baconian method.

In effect, the *Treatise* turned out to be something like a hand grenade thrown into the bunker of Enlightenment rationalism. The first *Enquiry* has, in some ways, remained its gentler companion text. The explosive critical elements of the *Treatise* guaranteed, paradoxically, that Hume would never receive a job in the academy *and* that he would be immortalized by it. Its skeptical aspects offended many, but even its moderate constructive elements, particularly the appeal to nature and affirmation of common life—crucial for the basic theism I am discussing—violently shook the tree of philosophical convention. To readers of his day, Hume did not offer an appropriate way out of the philosophical predicament he exposed; he merely illuminated the bear trap in which philosophy was caught. The young thinker unmasked the emptiness of abstruse reason: it could not live up to its claims for rational certainty or moral truth. Philosophers and nonphilosophers alike, "who must act and reason and believe," would remain unable, to Hume, "by their most diligent enquiry, to satisfy themselves concerning the foundation of these operations, or to remove the objections, which may be raised against them" (*E*, 12.2.7).

Some of the seeming gaps in the *Treatise* are filled by pointing out the basic theism that was fundamental to its logic. The *Treatise* reasoned that the functions of the mind were based on passions and that its ideas depended on associations.

Both passions and associations were unstable categories to the rationalists. On the Humean standard, however, passions and associations were stabilized by the assumption of hidden causes, also known as "original qualities of human nature" (*T*, introd., 8) and "powers of nature" (1.4.4.5). The "ultimate principles" and "general rules" of human nature consistently guided the mind to form and associate ideas. Idea formation requires the mind to relate a collection of distinct perceptions, that is, to do something that goes well beyond the scope of immediate experience. Given this, we might say that the formation of ideas and their subsequent association was partially an act of transcending what was given in experience. Another way to state this is to say that ideas were formed by the mind's immediate *collation* of what experience provided. For the Humean, this act of collating perceptions depended on principles of collation itself that were mysteriously given by hidden powers of nature. This means that the principles of human nature that *guided* the mind *transcended* the mind (and possibly nature). Gilles Deleuze, in his fascinating study of Hume, *Empiricism and Subjectivity*, remarked that Hume's empiricism was defined by just this kind of dualism. He contended that in the *Treatise* "an empirical dualism exists between terms and relations, or more exactly between the causes of perceptions and the causes of relations, between the hidden powers of nature and the principles of human nature." Deleuze's idea of a "transcendental empiricism" expands our ability to keep track of the basic theism at the core of Hume's philosophy. He reminds us that our subjectivity, for example, is constituted by, but not reducible to, what is given to us in experience. This means that there is something beyond experience, that Hume is not a strict empiricist, and that—for Deleuze—Hume embraces a form of transcendence. I label the disposition for this sort of transcendence "basic theism." Deleuze explains it as follows: "We cannot make use of the principles of association in order to know the world as an effect of divine activity, and even less to know God as the cause of the world; but we can always think of God negatively as the cause of the principles [of human nature]. It is in this sense that theism is valid."[9]

My claim that Hume's early philosophy has a basic theism—a sense of order and regularity—can be articulated in both strong and weak forms. The stronger statement is that basic theism is a presupposition of Hume's philosophy; the weaker one is that Hume's early philosophy does not foreclose the possibility of basic theism. Neither position demands religious expression nor requires Christian deity. Both rely very minimally if at all on traditional metaphysical arguments for theism, or make any claims about the nature of this "Author." The disposition I want to direct our attention to is a simple and basic belief, a foundational assumption from which Hume launched into his philosophical work. This belief in basic theism makes experience comprehensible due to the fact that it gives the mind mysterious principles to form an identity by associating ideas of the imagination. If the mind is, as Deleuze argues it is for Hume, a mere "assemblage" of "things as they appear," then there must be something beyond it, something that is not given in this assemblage but required by it.[10] Basic theism is the acceptance of this background for the mind: it meets the Humean standard of reasonability and allows the mind to hold fictions of identity, constancy, and uniformity as it composes ideas. This basic belief and the fictions it both relies on and produces have merit for true and false forms of religion. From the perspective of my speculative project for true religion, the value of documenting this assumption in Hume's early philosophy is that it allows us to discuss how basic theism might morph into more of a genuine theism.

The evolution of basic theism to genuine theism mirrors the logic of the evolution of basic theism to vulgar theism. *NHR* explains the latter: the direct passions, fear and hope, modify the disposition basic theism into the vulgar theism of false religion. Thus, it follows that calm passions can modify belief in basic theism into the genuine theism of true religion. Following the path of basic theism to false religion exposes "sick men's dreams" (15.6), yet conjecturing on how basic theism might lead to true religion makes Hume's ideal for religion less opaque. The rare, true religion could, under very exceptional conditions, help to "reform Men's Lives, to purify their Hearts, to inforce all moral Duties, & to secure Obedience to the Laws & civil Magistrate."[11] Note Hume's use of the infinitive form of verbs: "to reform," "to purify," "to inforce," and "to secure." Cumulatively and in significant part, we might say that these are the functions of a Humean true religion.

It is important not to overstep: the fact that Hume "warmly endorses what he calls 'true religion'" and "sometimes speaks approvingly of 'true religion'" does not dismantle his powerful conviction that most of the time our unmediated fears and hopes shape the natural propensity for basic theism into belief in a particular providence or a personal god, the vulgar theistic attitude of false religion.[12] He writes, "Examine the religious principles, which have, in fact, prevailed in the world. You will scarcely be persuaded that they are other than sick men's dreams: or perhaps will regard them more as the playsome whimsies of monkeys in human shape" (*NHR*, 15.6). He seems to at least allow, however, for a less vulgar alternative, a basic or general "universal propensity to believe in invisible, intelligent power, if not an original instinct, being at least a general attendant of human nature" (15.5).

POTENTIAL RESPONSES TO MY ARGUMENT FOR BASIC THEISM

My emphasis on basic theism in Hume's early philosophy is likely to generate four responses. I name them the standard, fideist, moderate, and skeptical readings. The standard interpretation vehemently rejects the designation 'theism' when it is applied to Hume's work. This position begins by reducing the idea of religion to a system of beliefs about God, an error generally made by those who hold conventional conceptions of both theism and religion. Theism, on this view, is conceived as veneration of a worship-worthy, omnipotent, omniscient, and benevolent deity and taken as the substance of religion. From this perspective Hume is considered irreligious due to his frontal assault on popular religion and his trenchant criticisms of traditional metaphysics.[13] It follows that if religion is purely reducible to theism, then Hume's irreligion must be the equivalent of antitheism. This way of reading Hume completely ignores the basic theism in his philosophy and leaves us with a nontheistic and irreligious David Hume.[14]

The standard interpretation is useful: it reaffirms Hume's seminal criticisms of religion and reminds us of the close connections between religion and theism. To completely reduce religion to theism, however, delimits our capacity to consider nontheistic traditions as religious and restricts the possibility that our beliefs in "universal principles" (*T*, 1.1.4.1), "elements and powers of nature" (*T*, 1.4.4.5), and order in the universe (e.g., *T*, app., 18n) might mark a nonconventional, basic theism. Additionally, from this view Hume's claim that the "whole frame of nature bespeaks an intelligent author" (*NHR*, 1.1) is comprehensible only as ironic, deceitful, or cunning. Finally, the standard interpretation diminishes our ability to think creatively about the proper office for religion and truncates the conversation about the role nontraditional theism might play in a speculative, Humean-inspired true religion. In short, the standard position gives us no traction in our quest to use Hume as a generative resource in religious studies.

A second response to the idea that Hume's work contains a basic theism is the fideist view. This position claims that Hume's skepticism concerning reason along with his refusal to explicitly discard theism make his work compatible with those who hold the idea that reason is not warranted to justify religious belief.[15] Fideists ground this contention on the belief that Hume's statement, "our most holy religion is founded on *Faith*, not on reason" (*E*, 10.2.27), was a critique of rationalist theology and an endorsement of an authentic Christian faith. They allow that for Hume, God is unknowable through reason and the universe is ultimately mysterious. On this view, Hume accepts God and God's ineffability on *faith*.

The fideist interpretation is important: it reminds us not to lose sight of the fluidity between skepticism and faith, a binary that is hierarchical, invertible, and codependent (as Derrida taught). The fideist reading also refuses to toss aside Hume's noncritical claims about theism and religion as simply ironic. Hume was neither invested in a Kierkegaardian leap of faith to Christian belief nor willing to cosign any extant religious doctrine such that he would recommend dogmatic commitment to it. He argued that direct-passion hopes and fears—always on a continuum—were the sources of our popular religious beliefs, and he mounted a scathing moral challenge against these false beliefs. His intentions were more humble than the fideists allowed: to observe the machinery of the mind in common life, understand its principles of association of ideas, and illuminate sources of our beliefs and actions. Hume accepted that our natural sense of universal order and regularity was not warranted by either abstruse reason or faith. It is safe to say that he recognized, as Deleuze wrote, that "the subject goes beyond what the mind gives it."[16] Still, Hume did *not* endorse faith as a means to the truth as fideism generally holds; rather, he observed religious practice in common life and described it as grounded in a set of imaginative beliefs. Further, he suggested that Christianity took root because of the psychic relief it provided for human fears and hopes, not because of the faith it inspired.

A more moderate view constitutes the third response to the contention that Hume's work confirms the idea of basic theism. This position holds that Hume's philosophy admits our belief in a genuine sense of order and regularity in the universe due to the mind's functioning as a cause-seeking tool. Best represented in the work of J. C. A. Gaskin and Keith Yandell, it rests on statements such as "our idea, therefore, of necessity and causation arises entirely from the uniformity observable in the operations of nature, where similar objects are constantly conjoined together, and the mind is determined by custom to infer the one from the appearance of the other" (*E*, 8.5). Gaskin locates what he calls an "attenuated deism" in Hume's work. This form of deism is the belief that God is a remote, unknowable Orderer of the universe, unconcerned with human existence. It does not, on Gaskin's argument, recommend itself to any religious vision nor does it inspire morality. It is meaningless for religion. Similarly, Yandell calls Hume's position a "diaphanous theism"—a theistic worldview that is too thin to merit anything positive for religion.[17]

The moderate position as taken up by Gaskin and Yandell is important. It thoughtfully attempts to sort out the theistic dimensions of Hume's claim that our minds are hardwired to think causally. The verdict that Hume's theism (or deism, for Gaskin) is completely irrelevant for human life is, however, overstated. What is curious about this position is its uncritical reliance on conventional approaches to both theism and religion. Gaskin and Yandell rightfully point out that our belief in order and regularity has little relevance for *popular* religion. They miss the crucial role, however, that this belief might play for true religion and true philosophy. Their insight, that Hume's idea of false religion supplied a vulgar theism and led to factionalism, is attenuated by their oversight regarding Hume's basic theism. The very existence of the category 'true religion' in Hume's thought grants some possible religious meaning to his basic theism, which is clearly useful for his philosophy. Unfortunately, Gaskin and Yandell leave these options unconsidered; thus, their slightly modified version of standard theism gives us no greater purchase on Hume's true religion.

True religion and vulgar religion are similarly formed. Hume tells us that vulgar religion is grounded on vulgar theism; it follows that true religion is based on genuine (or true) theism. Vulgar theism is formed by our direct-passion fears and hopes of unknown causes (*NHR*, secs. 1–5). We can presume then that genuine theism is formed by the moderation of our fears and hopes of unknown causes. To put it in a way that privileges a more conventional religious perspective: patient acceptance of the order and regularity of experience—particularly when experience does not seem ordered and regular—is a kind of peacefulness. We can understand this sort of equanimity, a trait normally associated with religious faith, as an effect of true religion. Thus construed, the genuine theism of true religion—the source of which is the basic theism of Hume's philosophy—has religious significance: it points us toward another dimension of the universe, sustains our overall sense of order and relationality, bears on our sense of who we are and what we can do, and opens us to possibilities beyond those that we can conceive. Perhaps Hume would have taken something like this genuine theism as implicit for his true religion. This fundamental belief in general providence, unlike its counterpart in false religion (belief in particular providence), could lead to a sense of equipoise, stability, and humility. These are the practical life outcomes and amenable results of religion when it remained in its proper office.

### Cartesian Rationalism and Pyrrhonian Skepticism

To establish either or both weak and strong forms of my premise—that the *Treatise* does not foreclose a sense of basic theism—we must rescue the text from its skeptical interpreters. The conventional skeptical reading forecloses the possibility of our justifiably holding belief in basic theism. It also nullifies the constructive potential of Hume's descriptive project and denies the tacit knowledge inherent in custom. Further, a thoroughly skeptical reading of the *Treatise* prohibits us from intelligibly attaching meaning to many of our most useful ideas and beliefs. Thus, to read the text simply as a skeptic is automatically to eliminate the possibility that a basic theism might be presupposed by its argument. Against traditional skeptical interpretations, I argue that Hume's philosophy successfully navigated between a critique of Cartesian rationalism and the embrace of Pyrrhonian skepticism. Charting a way between Pyrrhonism and Cartesianism, the *Treatise* shows dexterity and some ambiguity in its approach to skepticism. These nuances are often lost by that slice of interpreters who quickly reduce Hume to a skeptic, and they are overlooked by those who reject his basic theism out of hand.

The *Treatise* acknowledges both Cartesianism and Pyrrhonism as coherent systems of thought and compelling philosophical approaches.[18] Skeptical interpretations situate the text either as full-blown in the Pyrrhonian spirit or as a critical annihilation of the Cartesian approach. There is partial truth to each of these claims. The *Treatise*, however, neither thoroughly embraces nor fully rejects either method; it merely repositions them in relation to experience and belief. For example, against Pyrrhonism, the *Treatise* affirms the inescapability of certain ideas and beliefs; against Cartesianism, it confirms that we have warrant to hold certain ideas and beliefs as projections of our imagination or habits of the mind. For Hume, philosophy that begins with universal doubt (Cartesianism) and philosophy that refuses to assert conclusions (Pyrrhonism) are species of dogmatism. The Cartesians reason demonstratively to timeless conclusions of false philosophy and vulgar religion; they dogmatically resist the power of experience. Pyrrhonism, a brand of excessive skepticism, employs skeptical arguments that ultimately lead to nowhere; they dogmatically resist the power of belief. Hume writes, "the skeptical and dogmatical reasons are of the same kind, tho' contrary in their operation and tendency" (*T*, 1.4.1.12).

## CARTESIANISM

The introduction to the *Treatise* implies that it was partially catalyzed by Cartesianism: "Principles taken upon trust, consequences lamely deduced from them, want of coherence in the parts and of evidence of the whole, these are everywhere to be met with in the systems of the most eminent philosophers, and seem to have drawn disgrace upon philosophy itself" (*T*, introd., 1). This disgrace is multiplied, Hume claims, because the philosophical method of "the most eminent philosophers" (e.g., Descartes) supports the beliefs of popular religion. This is disturbing to Hume, for "the errors in religion are dangerous; those in philosophy only ridiculous" (1.4.7.13).

Hume's dissatisfaction with false metaphysical speculation and the conclusions it inspired for popular religion, namely the innate idea of a supernatural deity and immortal, immaterial souls, led him to work from the "analogy of nature" (*T*, 1.4.6.35) and the observation of experience. This approach challenged seminal aspects of the Cartesian method as it built on Newton's quest (best represented in his 1687 *Principia mathematica*) to find evidence through observation of the physical world to ground scientific and theological principles. Descartes commenced his project with universal doubt from the consciousness of an individual human subject and employed a priori concepts in service of timeless, transcendent ideas. To a large extent, the experimental method of Newton sidestepped this deep doubt. It allowed that nonmaterial forces caused physical effects (Newton held no notion of uniformity or necessary connection) and denied both Cartesian dualism and the immortality of the soul. Still, like Descartes, Newton embraced a conception of God as infinite and eternal. Roughly speaking, Hume cosigned Newton's "experimental method of reasoning." He worked from experience, or the "bottom up," in response to Descartes's "top-down" approach to philosophical "truths." Against Cartesianism he wrote, "If we reason *a priori*, anything may appear able to produce anything" (*E*, 12.3.6) and "Cartesian doubt, therefore, were it ever possible to be attained by any human creature (as it plainly is not) would be entirely incurable" (12.1.3). Hume wanted to subdue the passions for a priori method with his a posteriori technique. Further, he affirmed nature, habits of mind, and the power of common life against metaphysical reasoning. His work privileged experience and belief over abstruse reason and skepticism: he aimed "only to represent the common sense of mankind in more beautiful and more engaging colours" (1.4).

Hume relied on Descartes's privileging of the mind and individual subjectivity, but he directly challenged two prominent conclusions derived from the a priori method that were important for religion: the innate idea of an infinite, omnipotent God and the notion that the soul was immaterial and immortal. Descartes's statement, "true ideas, which are innate in me, of which the first and most important is the idea of God" was contested by Hume: "The *Cartesians*, proceeding upon their principle of innate ideas, have had recourse to a supreme spirit or deity. . . . But the principle of innate ideas being allow'd to be false, it follows that the supposition of a deity can serve us in no stead" (*T*, 1.3.14.10).[19] Note his dissatisfaction is with the idea of God as innate, *not* the belief in order and an Orderer (basic theism). The *Treatise* argues that we gain little usable knowledge when we merely assume the existence of deity at the beginning of our philosophical quest. We learn most about the operations of our mind and discover a more usable conception of deity as we observe humans undergoing repeated experiences "as they appear in the common course of the world, by men's behaviour in company, in affairs, and in their pleasures" (introd., 10).

Descartes, whose views on the soul evolved throughout his career, not only inherited the notion of the soul as immaterial and immortal from the Scholastics but also became an apologist for it with his assertion, in the Sixth Meditation, that the *res cogitans* was indivisible and therefore immaterial and eternal. Hume refuted this conclusion by arguing that it went well beyond the proper purview of philosophy. He wrote, "matter and spirit are at bottom equally unknown and we cannot determine what qualities may inhere in the one or in the other."[20] I take this to mean that the soul cannot bring about the effects that the Cartesians expect (i.e., thought). For "we shall never discover a reason, when any object may or may not be the cause of any other" (*T*, 1.4.5.30). As far as Hume was concerned, the soul was not the source of thought and Descartes's argument for the soul as both immortal and immaterial rested on weak foundations.

Hume's early philosophical works navigated between and responded to a vast array of philosophical strategies and temperaments. Against Cartesian a priori conceptions of deity, he highlighted experience and nature and described our predilection to believe in basic theism as largely derived from hidden powers of nature and teleological principles of mind. In tone and content the *Treatise* asserted probabilistic conclusions in response to the hubris of Cartesian claims. Adroit in his contentions and mostly modest in his conclusions, the Humean flair that manifested in the *Treatise* offered a stylistic challenge to the Cartesian method. More or less, in the presence of strong deistic assertions (Tindal and Morgan), Hume emphasized the skeptical. When the skepticism went extreme (as in atheism and Pyrrhonism), Hume affirmed the propensity for belief. He mitigated abstruse philosophy (Cartesianism) with nature and common life, and to those who read him as dogmatically antireligious he had a basic theism and an inchoate category 'true religion.' Intellectually nimble and philosophically dexterous, the young Hume borrowed from Descartes yet moved beyond him to accept implicit beliefs mediated through custom, which could not satisfy the seminal demands of abstract reason of the Cartesian approach.

## PYRRHONISM

In the unfolding literary drama of Hume's early work, his response to Pyrrhonism further reflected the adeptness of his approach. Concerning Hume's skepticism, Nicholas Capaldi writes that "no issue has engendered more misunderstanding in Hume scholarship than this one."[21] I shall not delve into the full range of skeptical interpretations here. I simply explain that Hume equated Pyrrhonism with an egregious form of skepticism, then he relied on nature, beliefs, and habits as fundamental for experience. Hume generally possessed an affinity for skeptical solutions in epistemology and sensitivity to the Pyrrhonian suspension of judgment. He offered, however, two inseparable arguments against the Pyrrhonian attitude.[22] The first held that one cannot actually act from a thoroughly Pyrrhonian consciousness in common experience; thus, Pyrrhonism was *impossible*. The second argument stipulated that the Pyrrhonian method of hesitation produced no convictions; therefore, Pyrrhonism was *impractical*.

The *Treatise* gives mostly probable conclusions, makes provisional judgments based on observation, and traces the origins of our most significant beliefs. On its argument the complete suspension of judgment is simply not viable for a philosophical thinker. It is, in fact, impossible. Thus, Hume's early work conciliates between belief and skepticism. His "mitigated skepticism" reminds him to be humble in his judgments and "diffident of his philosophical doubts, as well as of his philosophical convictions" (1.4.7.14). Defending himself in his *Letter from a Gentleman* against being labeled a Pyrrhonian, Hume writes,

> As to *Scepticism* with which the author is charged, I must observe, that the doctrine of the *Pyrrhonians* or *Scepticks* have been regarded in all ages as Principles of mere Curiosity, or a Kind of *Jeux d' esprit*, without any Influence on a Man's steady Principles or Conduct in Life. In Reality, a Philosopher who affects to doubt of the Maxims of *common Reason* and even of his *Senses*, declares sufficiently that he is not in earnest, and that he intends not to advance an Opinion which he would recommend as Standards of Judgment and Action. (2)

The second argument Hume renders against the questions of Pyrrhonism is "*that they admit of no answer and produce no conviction*" (*E*, 12.1.14n). Pyrrhonism is highly impractical. The excessively skeptical method, described as the "*intense view of these manifold contradictions and imperfections in human reason,*" consistently challenges the veracity of our ideas, beliefs, and actions and leaves us "ready to reject all belief and reasoning" (*T*, 1.4.7.8). This leads us into a skeptical dead end, useless for the task of describing the origins of our ideas and beliefs. Hume's method *requires* taking a stance—albeit a humble one.

A premise of Hume's philosophy, which might better be described as reflective theorizing about the ground of our *actions*, was that humans held certain ideas and acted on certain beliefs. Hume wondered about the derivation of our ideas and beliefs and attempted to describe their origins through his reflective observations of human behavior. The assumption at the core of his project, that the full suspension of judgment was impossible, disallowed a Pyrrhonian approach. Further, it was impractical for philosophers to suspend judgment if they wanted to participate in the advancement of any human science. The major problem of the Pyrrhonian skeptic—and to Hume this was disastrous—was indecisiveness and wavering, which easily led to paralysis and despair. The cures for this "philosophical melancholy and delirium" caused by the vacillating predicament of Pyrrhonism were the steady, yet largely unpredictable, nature and common life. They assisted us "either by relaxing this bent of mind, or by some avocation, and lively impression of my senses, which obliterate all these chimeras. I dine, I play a game of back-gammon, I converse, and am merry with my friends" (*T*, 1.4.7.9). In other words, "nature breaks the force of all skeptical arguments in time, and keeps them from having any considerable influence on the understanding" (1.4.1.12).

The *Treatise*, however, did not reject skepticism entirely. It argued that a balanced skepticism was both natural and useful: it could help limit our philosophical exploration to topics that met the terms of the particular kind of inquiry in which we were engaged.[23] Hume's confirmation of our belief in basic theism and his reflective approach to common life undermine two potential worries that the skeptical position evokes: nihilism and antihistoricism. In Ciceronian spirit, Hume's mitigated or balanced skepticism did not completely deny the implicit knowledge in our customs, repudiate the justifiability of all our beliefs, or limit us from holding provisional conclusions. It reminded us, however, that just prior to reaching those conclusions we should acknowledge the merits of our earlier doubt and remain humble about our assumptions and decisions. He argued, though "sceptical doubt, both with respect to reason and the senses is a malady, which can never be radically cur'd," it "arises naturally from a profound and intense reflection" (1.4.2.57). Further, it reminds us of the constraints of reason. Hume wrote, "*Modesty* then, and *Humility*, with regard to the Operations of our natural Faculties, is the Result of *Scepticism*; not a universal Doubt, which it is impossible for any Man to support" (*LET*, 1.49.19). He opted for "a more *mitigated* skepticism or *academical* philosophy, which may be both durable and useful, and which may, in part, be the result of this Pyrrhonism, or *excessive* skepticism, when its undistinguished doubts are, in some measure, corrected by common sense and reflection" (*E*, 12.3.1). This moderation of Pyrrhonism enabled philosophical humility and the awareness of the implicit beliefs. It also helped contain reflection within its "proper sphere" and confirmed "a fair confession of ignorance in subjects, that exceed all human capacity" (*T*, app., 36).

To summarize: Cartesian and Pyrrhonian forms of doubt informed Hume's early work. In response to these forms of dogmatism, Hume's descriptive science took a moderate skeptical approach and asserted mostly probable conclusions from and about experience. To counter the thoroughly skeptical interpretations of Hume we might think of him as a true philosopher, comfortably observing and reporting human ideas, beliefs, and behaviors that were unjustifiable on the standards of abstract reason (because of its requirements for necessary connection and universal truth). Hume celebrated—against a particular strand of his philosophical inheritance—the human tendency to exhibit a propensity for beliefs and perform practices in common life that went beyond the given in experience. The consistent reliance on and fundamental affirmation of that which rests behind and vitally informs all experience yet cannot fully be represented by it points us toward our assumptive belief in basic theism. Demonstrative, a priori, and even inductive reason do not verify this belief; only "custom or a certain instinct of our nature" makes it intelligible, though still it "may be fallacious and deceitful" (*E*, 12.2.6).

After scrutinizing the skeptical reading it seems that in both its weak and strong versions my position on belief in basic theism—the source of the genuine theism of our speculative true religion—is not undermined by Hume's mitigated skepticism. Thus, with the skeptical arguments effectively neutralized, I turn to

Hume's theory of mind and then to his thoughts on belief to assess how belief in basic theism might be intelligible on Hume's philosophical schema.

## The Theory of Ideas and Ultimate Causal Power

Thus the observation of human blindness and weakness is
the result of all philosophy, and meets us at every turn, in spite
of our endeavours to elude or avoid it.
—*E*, 4.1.12

Hume's theory of ideas has significant ramifications for his notion of causality, a widely discussed feature of his philosophy. On his argument, the understanding cannot help but function in a way that naturally assumes causation. The sense of purposiveness is built-in to the mind: we tend to assume that observable effects (objects, events) have a source or a purpose (observable or unobservable). It is this constant conjunction that guides our mental machinery to presuppose a very basic theism. This belief has broad implications. For example, belief in basic theism begs the question about whether or not Hume takes ultimate causal power to be *real*. I shall return to this issue below. It also invites us to consider the epistemological elements of Hume's notion of causal power. In short, considerations of basic theism redirect us to Hume's ideas of causation and power and their popular interpretations.

Generally speaking, causation refers to the relation between two (or more) objects or events where one produces the other. Interpretations of Hume's discussion of causality are diverse: some contend that he does not articulate a coherent position on causality, while others offer conflicting interpretations of his stance on the issue. The salience of Hume's position on causation is important for our quest to justify a basic theism in his philosophy, as our theistic ideas are grounded in causalogical or teleological frameworks (Hume did not differentiate between these two approaches in the way Kant would later). Hume challenged the causal realism of popular religion (the view that causal statements are confirmed by the existence of real power in the universe) as well as atheism and its causal antirealism (the denial of the existence of universal power). He reasoned that our causal language was based on a habit of mind derived from experience of constant conjunctions in nature. If ultimate causal power did exist independent of our minds, he figured that we could never fully grasp it. It follows from this that our minds were (naturally) limited when it came to causality and purposiveness: thus, we could neither justifiably reduce causation to simple regularity nor intelligibly elevate it to confirm a worship-worthy deity. How did we come to hold a notion of causation inseparable from basic theism?

## Hume's Theory of Ideas

Because Hume believed that "to explain the ultimate causes of our mental actions is impossible" (*T*, 1.1.7.11), the *Treatise* "pretends only to explain the nature and causes of our perceptions, or impressions and ideas" (1.2.5.26). In other words, it starts with what is given to us in experience, drawing our attention to the genetic conditions for our sense encounter with the "world." There are, of course, some thorny interpretive issues here.[24] My position is that Hume's theory of mind attempts to locate the sources at the root of this sense encounter and trace their development through the mind into our ideas and belief-based actions. Thus, most basically, I take Hume's theory of mind as an attempt to elucidate the process by which our ideas are formed. Stated differently, we might say that Hume's theory of mind describes the manner by which we constitute identity (personal identity, identity and consistency of external objects, the identity of the mind). This natural teleology of the mind depends on, among other things, regularity, order, and succession. Since Hume tells us that *"we are ignorant of those powers and forces, on which this regular course and succession of objects totally depends"* (*E*, 5.45; italics added), this process is a mystery. The formation of our ideas about identity requires that we somehow go beyond what is given in sense experience. Gilles Deleuze grasps the underlying mystery of this "somehow." He interprets the spirit of inventiveness in Hume's work quite poignantly, writing, "through belief and causality the subject *transcends* the given. Literally, the subject goes beyond what the mind gives it: I believe in what I have neither seen nor touched."[25] Deleuze's transcendence, however, remains immanent, that is, fully instantiated in the realm of experience (as far as we can tell), yet he describes it as a form of theism nonetheless: "philosophy has nothing to say on what causes the principles and on the origin of their power. There, it is the place of God."[26]

Does Hume's theory of ideas support or undermine belief in basic theism? We naturally assume that experience is somehow guided by principles and that (what we take to be) constituent elements of nature are ordered and behave relatively consistently. Modern science takes as its starting point what Hume calls the "universal springs and principles" of nature. If, as he claims, the mind is "a kind of theatre, where several perceptions successively make their appearance; pass, re-pass, glide away, and mingle in an infinite variety of postures and situations" (*T*, 1.4.6.4), what kind of building houses this theater, and does its performance have an author? How are these "several perceptions" generated? Why are they successive (or do they just appear as such)? Hume's description of the inner workings of the mind is based on the (potentially illusory) existence of perceptible objects or events, our human capacity to perceive, and our sense of regularity, consistency, and order. These events all are endowed by hidden powers of nature (sense perception) and principles of human nature (association), which—as Deleuze contends—suggests a basic theism. Thus, belief in basic theism is justifiable on Hume's theory of ideas and the implications of this sense of basic theism bear on his thoughts about religion.

The fundamental premise that drives Hume's theory of ideas is twofold: that knowledge is not attainable by independent, rational insight and that we tend to derive our ideas from the basic materials of experience, which are always social, historical, and natural. The conclusion of this theory provides two crucial features of his thought: we actually hold many ideas for which experience turns out *not* to be able to furnish the correlative raw materials, and our complex ideas emanate from the nonrational faculty of the imagination and associative habits that inform it. In some ways, the theory of ideas might better be described as a theory of the inadequacy of our ideas. It confirms the limits of our understanding and removes abstract reason from its lofty perch. Its insights pervade Hume's entire corpus and open him to deeper questions. For example, if reason is neither a priori nor fully furnished through experience, from whence do our ideas and beliefs (for example, our belief in the identity of self, mind, world) come?

To begin to formulate a reply to questions of this sort and to articulate a properly scientific rendering of the origins of our ideas, Hume described the functions of our mental machinery. Building on Locke's argument that the mind was full of ideas of two types, "ideas of perception" and "ideas of sensation," Hume posited that the more precise way to give a technical description of the mind's work was to order perceptions into two kinds, "impressions and ideas," which were distinguishable "in their force and liveliness" (*T*, 1.1.1.1).[27] H. O. Mounce explains this distinction: "When I see an object, I have a vivid impression of it. When the impression ceases, I am left with an idea or image, fainter than the impression, which copies it. In that way, I can think of the impression when I no longer have it."[28] On the view of Mounce's naturalist reading (to which we shall return) Hume's theory rests on some crucial presuppositions. First, it implies trust in the existence of mind-independent, perceivable matter and events. Second, it assumes that perceptions *immediately* furnish the mind, that is, they strike directly on the mind and are not mediated by something external to it. Third, and by default, it affirms mind-independent things operate in what we take to be a causal fashion: they are the source of our impressions. We can state these assumptions, cumulatively, as *mind-independent things exist and they operate with regularity*. According to Jeffrey Bell, Deleuze takes this to mean that "Hume sought, within the given, to account for the constitution of that which is irreducible to the given."[29] Defining "the given" as "virtual multiplicity" of "pre-individual singularities," Deleuze emphasizes Hume's creativity in using the imagination to constitute a subjectivity greater than the given, out of the given. To do so, Hume had to presuppose something beneath the given: hidden powers of nature. We may think of these powers, not reducible to the genetic conditions of actual experience, as a very basic and unconventional form of theism. Hume writes, "A purpose, an intention, a design is evident in everything; and when our comprehension is so far enlarged as to contemplate the first rise of this visible system, we must adopt, with the strongest conviction, the idea of some intelligent cause or author" (*NHR*, 15.1). Our reflective disposition to order, succession, and regularity naturally sanctions the mind to assume something behind sense experience, an Orderer. This presupposition, as well as the entire cohort of background assumptions recruited in the act of perception, is indispensable for Hume's discussion.[30] The theory of ideas then both relies on and ratifies a very basic theism that has no connection to popular or true religion.

Book 1 of the *Treatise* traces the theory of ideas from its fundamental categories, impressions, and ideas, across numerous "divisions of the subject" (*T*, 1.1.2.1). The theory begins with "feelings," "sentiments," "perceptions," and "impressions." From these, it drafts a schema of distinctions made in terms of category pairs: impressions and ideas, beliefs and ideas, and fictions and beliefs. Hume further distinguishes between pairs and within them, including two types of ideas (simple and complex) and two types of impressions (of reflection and of sensation). This variety of categories and subdistinctions comports with the scientific spirit of Hume's day. The quest to systematize sets of categories and create a lexicon such that meaning was internal to a system of thought echoed the strategy of scientific codification. Additionally, the fact that the distinctions between terms of his categories were reducible to internal, subjective feelings that (somehow) remained fairly consistent between individuals mirrored the discourse of science that claimed to operate above subjectivity in such a way that the opinions, desires, and particular experiences of the individual had very little bearing on what the observation revealed. Another way to put this is to say that Hume's "science" disclosed features about human behavior that were (somehow) impacted neither by the will of the subject nor the aims of the observer. Its mode of "cautious observation" and "exact experimentation" aimed for compatibility with the discourse of science by presupposing, as all science does, order and (provisional) regularity in the universe as well as a kind of teleology, the starting points for all science.

Memory and imagination are the co-stars of Hume's theory of ideas. "The ideas of the memory are much more lively and stronger than those of the imagination" (*T*, 1.1.3.1), they strike the mind with vivacity similar to that of an impression and create stable ideas (many of which, if they are enlivened properly, become perceptual beliefs). The imagination has an almost unlimited creative power. It can synthesize ideas and project new complex ones in ways that we cannot fully trace or comprehend. Some of these complex ideas are not directly funded by experience and therefore not derived directly from impressions. They "can be trac'd beyond our senses, and inform us of existences and objects, which we do not see or feel" (1.3.2.3). This claim, and others like it, authorizes the basic theism that this chapter highlights and confirms our background sense of "universal springs and principles."

The establishment of the imagination as the centerpiece of our epistemological inquiries marks a profound shift in the attempt to provide a philosophical justification of our ideas. Hume's theory stifles widely held notions that our complex ideas come from God (Berkeley), that they are innately placed in the mind (Descartes), or that they are *simply* derived from experience (Locke).[31] It contends that they are derived from the creative powers of the imagination in tandem with nature, habit, and reflective common life. Hume reminds us, however, that the imagination does not function randomly, it is guided by principles of association. He felt that his "discovery" of these associative principles—contiguity, succession, and resemblance—was the most important aspect of this theory of ideas. He wrote, "Two objects are connected together in the imagination, not only when the one is immediately resembling, contiguous to, or the cause of the other, but also when there is interposed betwixt them a third object which bears to both of them any of these relations" (*T*, 1.1.4.3).[32] The faculty of the imagination—not self-certifying reason or our unmediated senses—works in a predictable and consistent fashion to shape and combine impressions and synthesize ideas into novel ones. And even though "nothing is more free" than the imagination, it acts in accordance with "universal principles, which render it, in some measure, uniform with itself in all times and all places" (1.1.4.1). Holding at bay the question of whether these universal principles are "real" for Hume, we can confirm that ideas of the imagination (e.g., equality) are derived from impressions, collated and formed by the principles of association, and confirmed in common life. Our most steady ideas are those that connect us to experience more deeply and help us codify it in a stable way. Other ideas, also "offspring of the imagination" (1.3.9.4), may be "fictions" (1.3.9.3). Hume writes, "We can, in our conception, join the head of a man to the body of a horse; but it is not in our power to believe that such an animal has ever really existed" (*E*, 5.2.1). That he dubs certain ideas "fictions" is not a declaration about their truth-value; it is merely a statement about the way they were formed. In fact, depending on the degree of liveliness they inspire and the social influence they generate, certain fictions may evolve into beliefs and become guides for our behavior. We are not to abandon fictions as if they were bugaboos, we are to develop a better sense of their process of formation.[33]

Hume could have taken the idea of an Author of Nature to be a fictive idea. Or he may have considered it a relative idea, one that we can have a sense of only from its constant conjunction with an observable effect. We cannot fully grasp the relative ideas of the existence of external objects, power, and causation in themselves. They are projections of the imagination manifested in our understanding through an object to which they are constantly conjoined. Relative ideas do not rely on a single impression or on the materials provided in sense experience. None of them are, as far as Hume is concerned, fully intelligible on the standards of abstruse rationality. They are either formed improperly and are therefore fictions on Hume's theory of ideas or aids to make other concepts intelligible. It is not important that we categorize the idea of an Author of Nature as either a fictive or a relative idea. We should simply understand that either way, what I label "basic theism" in Hume's philosophical writings can easily be distorted into the deity of false religion detailed in his religious writings.

Hume accepted that the most rudimentary components of experience that furnished his theory of ideas, impressions of sensation, were supplied by order and regularity in nature. The mind's tendency to think causally made the belief in an Orderer an irresistible belief of this presupposed order and regularity (his basic theism). As an enterprise of early modern science, Hume's project was conditioned to take this mild form of basic theism, or the hidden powers of nature, as its starting point, for without the presupposition of our belief in order (and the implied Orderer) operating behind all experience, the theory of ideas could not reach liftoff. It is in this way that we can situate basic theism as an indispensable category of Hume's philosophy. This premise is recognizable in the rare instance when a true philosopher is able to moderate abstruse reason and recognize that the foundations of his thoughts are based on general assumptions that do not meet the standards of philosophical reason, are not given in sense experience, and are not reducible to the terms of experience. Hume's very approach to philosophy, his moderate skepticism, and his theory of mind do not deny—and stated more strongly, presuppose—belief in basic theism. Might we further justify this basic theism, the means by which we organize and frame experience as a *belief* on the grounds of his theory of ideas?[34]

*Causation and Necessary Connection*

As the twentieth-century thinkers Theodore W. Adorno and Max Horkheimer argue, "Enlightenment, understood in the widest sense as the advance of thought, has always aimed at liberating human beings from fear and installing them as masters."[35] The articulated goal of Hume's *Treatise* was to establish an experienced-based method that could be applied across a vast swath of human concerns. There is little doubt that he believed the successful establishment of his "science" would encourage greater self-understanding, namely, reflective awareness of the limitations of our minds, fluency with the role of our passions and sentiments, and sensitivity to our situatedness in history and community. Hume pronounced that his early work might best be qualified as leading us to "mild and moderate sentiments" (*T*, 1.4.7.13). His approach was more humble than the full-blown quest for mastery depicted by Adorno and Horkheimer.

I noted above that some take Hume to hold that causal power is real. Hume's statement that "we can only define power by connexion" (*T*, 1.4.5.31) is a good place to begin a discussion about whether causation is real for Hume. We should not overlook, however, that he acknowledges distinctions in these "connexions." For example, causal power (a relationship between objects [1.1.4.5]) was, by definition, different from mental power (the creative capacity of the mind to excite ideas [1.3.5.2]), dissimilar to the power of riches (to acquire property [2.1.10.3]), different from political power (authority over others [3.2.8.3]), distinct from the power of the passions (producing pain or pleasure [3.1.1.3]), and not equal to the power of nature ("Everything is conducted by springs and principles" [2.2.12.1]). Of course, these different manifestations are connected but not reducible to causal power. Pursuing these distinctions might be an interesting, though somewhat dicey, matter, as Hume has done little untangling for us. I only note—in hopes to inspire efforts to hash out distinctions in his discussion of power—that the differences in types of power, no matter how slight, at least demonstrate that we reduce the complexity of Hume's treatment of power if we default to a single interpretive lens in order to assess it. Doing so has calcified discussions of power in Hume, which are largely overdetermined by the standard approach and common "default" positions that present power in Hume only as causation and necessary connection. This is understandable, yet it undermines our capacity to comprehend distinctions between types of power (political, psychological, passional, natural), ascertain the complex functions of power in history, and describe the nature of power, features that are explicitly covered, in different degrees, in the *Treatise*. Applying different lenses to Hume's reflections about the dissimilar forms of power in the *Treatise* makes it less likely that we will diminish his wide-ranging concerns.

One way to unpack the set of default assumptions deployed in discussions of power in the *Treatise* is to keep Hume's fundamental interests in mind. This prevents us from obscuring the subtleties of his approach, the dichotomies in his arguments, and the spirit that drives his writing. Hume was not simply concerned with challenging theological arguments about divine power (Malebranche, Scholastics), rationalist arguments about causal power (Descartes), skeptical arguments concerning the very existence of power (Pyrrhonism), and arguments about political power (Hobbes); he wanted to interrogate how we perceived power, how our minds came to grasp it, how it functioned practically in our habits and passions, and how it informed us in common life regarding proper governmental authority. Hume was stirred up by what he took to be the weakness of abstract thought and our psychological feelings of powerlessness at a moment when traditional sources of authority were waning in the West. To Hume, Western culture was on the brink of a moment when self-regulating subjects would stand alone in the face of new and mysterious possibilities as liberty, reason, science, and progress—valiant themes of the English Enlightenment—opened up new possibilities. Some of these possibilities, however, were less than ideal, particularly the increase in feelings of loneliness, alienation, and powerlessness. Hume personally understood these psychic and existential challenges: "I am confounded with all these questions, and begin to fancy myself in the most deplorable condition imaginable, inviron'd with the deepest darkness, and utterly depriv'd of the use of every member and faculty." He thought reason impotent in the face of this darkness, "incapable of dispelling these clouds" (T, 1.4.7.9).

THE POWER OF THE MIND AND THE IDEA OF POWER

Hume's description of the power of the mind ("the mind is endow'd with a power of exciting any idea it pleases" [T, 1.2.5.20]) generally followed the Newtonian method, which was preoccupied with delineating what we could legitimately know and how we were able to arrive at this knowledge. Hume was invested in reasonableness, and he made a crucial distinction between rational certainty, which was merely a quality of 'relations of ideas' that told us little about actual experience, and 'matters of fact' that were corroborated in experience (but could not deliver rational certainty). On Hume's account the power of the mind was most evident in the way it associated ideas based on their contiguity, resemblance, and causation. As I have described, like Newton, Hume concentrated on what was *observable* to the scientist and acknowledged the limits of the power of the mind:

> Nothing, at first view, may seem more unbounded than the thought of man, which not only escapes all human *power* and authority, but is not even restrained within the limits of nature and reality. . . . But though our thought seems to possess this unbounded liberty, we shall find, upon a nearer examination, that it is really confined within very narrow limits, and that all this creative *power* of the mind amounts to no more than the

faculty of compounding, transposing, augmenting, or diminishing the materials afforded us by the sense and experience. (*E*, 2.3; italics added)

For Hume all perceptions—the raw materials of experience—were fundamentally distinguishable by the degree of impact they exerted on the mind. Building on Locke's notion that there was no a priori knowledge, Hume posited two categories of perception, ideas and impressions, as the sources of understanding. His theory of mind held that perceptions were historical (present ideas referred to past impressions) and distinguished by power (they "differ only in their strength and vivacity" [*T*, 1.1.7.5]). Additionally, mental formations named "beliefs" generally referred backward to an impression and were also constituted by history and power (belief "is nothing but *a more vivid and intense conception of any idea*" [1.3.10.3]). Finally, the imagination had imagistic, conceptual, and creative power; it was "not restrain'd to the same order and form with the original impressions; while the memory is in a manner ty'd down in that respect, without any *power* of variation" (1.1.3.2; italics added). The machinery of the mind measured power above all else, yet Hume was keen to show the limits of the power of the mind itself.

In addition to restraining the mind to collating, altering, and extending "the materials afforded us by the sense and experience" (*E*, 2.4), Hume reflected further on the terms by which the mind comes to hold the *idea* 'power': "All ideas are deriv'd from, and represent impressions. We never have any impression that contains any power or efficacy. We never therefore have any idea of power." This is Hume's theory of ideas in action conveying that our minds derived the idea 'power' by naturally associating causes with effects in experience (thus it relies on yet is not reducible to causal reasoning). His emphasis here clarifies that power is a determination of our minds: there is no simple impression of it, and it does not reside in objects (*T*, 1.3.14.11–12). He honors the fact, however, that we *talk* about this idea 'power' as if it is mind-independent. Hume reminds us that we come to hold the complex idea of power, and discuss it the way we do in common life, because of the way our mental machinery naturally functions as we live in social space. His point is to show that we make a mistake when we assume that power is mind-independent: we go beyond the limits of the mind.

*Interpretations: Phenomenalism and Meaning-Empiricism.* One of the ways that Hume's discussion of the power of the mind has been described is as his "bundle-theory": the notion that the mind works by collectivizing individual perceptions that it receives. This "bundle-theory" reading has spawned two related interpretive frameworks: *phenomenalism*, the idea that external objects are fully reducible to actual or possible perceptions, and *meaning-empiricism*, the idea that a word has meaning only if it is derived from experience. To phenomenalists, objects are not comprehensible as things-in-themselves; they are merely perceptions internal to the mind. These thinkers often cite Hume's statement that "the mind has never anything present to it but the perceptions, and cannot possibly reach any experience of their connection with objects" (*E*, 12.1.11) as evidence of his phenomenalist commitments.

Some content in Hume's early work supports the phenomenalist interpretation. He writes that the "connexion betwixt external objects . . . [is] a quality, which can only belong to the mind that considers them" (*T*, 1.3.14.26). He also underscores that "the only existences, of which we are certain, are perceptions, which being immediately present to us by consciousness, command our strongest assent, and are the first foundation of all our conclusions" (1.4.2.47). Antony Flew popularized the phenomenalist interpretation of Hume in his 1961 classic *Hume's Philosophy of Belief*, which argued from this phenomenalist foundation that Hume depended on Locke's theory of language. Locke's theory held that ideas were merely images that occurred in the privacy of one's mind and obtained meaning when we attached a word to them.[36] On this reading, standard meaning is reduced to mental images and is fully private and subjective. It follows that power is strictly a phenomenon of the mind.

Georges Dickers, among others, modified the strict phenomenalist reading by working from an expanded idea of experience that included both "sense perception and introspective awareness of our own states of mind."[37] For Dickers, this broader notion of experience was the source of all content for our words and expressions. This interpretation has come to be known as *meaning-empiricism*. Power, in this interpretation, is not only mind-dependent but also meaningless if we cannot find its impression in experience.

Both the phenomenalist and meaning-empiricist interpretations of Hume illuminate an important part of his thesis: that the power of the mind is derived from experience (either totally private, for Flew, or from a bit wider concept of sense perception, for Dickers). Both interpretations rely on solid evidence from the *Treatise* and first *Enquiry* and are plausible renderings of Hume's treatment of the idea 'power.' Because both positions confine the idea 'power' to the mind and immediate sense perception, however, they are difficult sources on which to build a case for basic theism that might be of some use for a Humean true religion. Further, each of these interpretations provides insights, but they obscure the breadth of Hume's wider social and political concerns.

What Flew interprets as an argument for language derived from private logic is accurate about Locke but less so about Hume. Likewise, Dickers's slight expansion of "experience" also works well as a description of Locke's theory of perception due to the fact that Locke argued that perceptions reached inward to secret interstices of the mind. For Hume, however, perception seems to reach outward and have a *social* dimension: the images and words derived from it are dependent on a larger historical consciousness and collective network of habits, passions, and traditions we experience in common life, not simply a private mental sphere and sense perceptions. Hume's theory of ideas has both internal and external dimensions: it is sociohistorical in ways that make it not simply private but also always public, not fully subjective nor completely objective, not only phenomenalist but also physicalist.

To take a specific example, Hume's discussion of external objects does not square with either the phenomenalist or meaning-empiricist interpretation. He writes, "Given an account of all the systems both popular and philosophical, with regard to external existences . . . whatever may be the reader's opinion at this present moment, that an hour hence he will be persuaded there is both an external and internal world" (*T*, 1.4.2.56–57). I read this to mean, paradoxically, that there are no rational justifications for the knowledge we have of objects as separate and distinct from the mind and that we cannot deny their independent and distinctive existence. This supports the sense of basic theism that Hume's project assumes. All we have the power to know about an object (even if it is) external to our minds is how we experience it. This, however, does not mean that the object is fully reducible to our perceptions of it. We might then say, more accurately, that the functions of the mind are based on, yet not reducible to, the experience of perceptions. This differs from the ontological claim of the phenomenalists: that an object is *only* and *simply* actual or possible perceptions. Further, the meaning-empiricist reading of Hume overlooks the distinction between common life and abstract thought that suffuses his work. Common life presupposes sociality and the importance of customs and traditions; the notion of experience that it relies on is much broader than meaning-empiricism allows. While abstract thought encourages confusion between experience and ideas, "this deficiency in our ideas is not, indeed, perceived in common life" (1.4.7.6). Meaning-empiricists overlook the importance of common life for Hume's thought. The mind's supposition of basic theism relies on a complex process of perception that includes social components.

Hume constricts the power of reason by using an approach similar to that described by Flew's phenomenalism and Dickers's meaning-empiricism. Yet Hume's moderate skepticism regarding the firm types of ontological commitment that phenomenalism demands, his sense that history and nature inform our mental contents, and his belief in cellular movement in the brain separate him from both the phenomenalist and meaning-empiricist interpretations. Hume's idea of power resides in our mind but it is also based on experience and nature. On his view, we can think of power as part mind-dependent and part mind-*in*dependent. It is potential, actual, and in some ways 'real.' The power of the mind cannot be reduced to *simply* a quality of the mind, but we can intelligibly discuss power in its basic theism as a feature of the mind (and have reasonable and moral grounds to do so).

## POWER IN NATURE AND THE NATURE OF POWER

To some, the *Treatise* suggests that the source of the mind's power comes from outside of the mind itself, and Hume accepted that there are secret powers and purposes in nature. I have tried to distinguish the idea of power, that is, power as an epistemological component, from its metaphysical status—that is, whether it is *real*. I emphasized that on the level of experience Hume observed the idea 'power' to be formed through natural and observable processes that infer, from repeated experiences of perceptions, that active energy is likely responsible for experience. The assumption of basic theism is that the mind naturally functions to assume power that orders and regularizes (an Author of Nature). On this way of thinking, power is an idea; it is mind-dependent. Now, I want to briefly shift my focus to the question of the *ontological* status of power: might Hume take there to be experience-independent power?

Hume's claim that "everything is conducted by springs and principles, which are not peculiar to man, or any one species of animal" (*T*, 2.2.12.1) suggests that secret powers and hidden purposes actually exist in the universe. He does not describe the content of these powers and purposes; he seems to accept that they operate in the background of experience and generally cannot be investigated empirically. He writes that "ultimate force and efficacy of nature is perfectly unknown to us, and that 'tis in vain we search for it in all the known qualities of matter" (1.3.14.8), and "the operations of nature are independent of our thought and reasoning" (1.3.14.27). The implication here is that power is real yet mysterious: we cannot penetrate its nature because it is ultimately inaccessible to our minds. As I read it, his claim "we can never distinctly conceive how any particular power can possibly reside in any particular object, we deceive ourselves in imagining we can form any such general idea" (1.3.14.12) means that we do not have an a priori idea of power. He does not deny, however, the mind's natural inference that something may exist beyond its perceptual reach. In fact, Hume appears to take it for granted that "in every part of nature there is contain'd a vast variety of springs and principles" (1.3.12.5). His empirical method, however, limits him from describing the nature of these "springs and principles." Thus, we can know little about the content of experience-independent power; a detailed description of it is beyond our purview.

*Interpretations: Skeptical Realism and Naturalism.* The question of whether power is real for Hume has become a controversial one within Hume scholarship. Two interpretive lenses have been generated from this feature of his thought, and each has elicited important responses. These interpretations are relevant for my argument about Hume's basic theism, so here I briefly describe the *skeptical realist* approach and the *naturalist* interpretation of Hume on the nature of power.

Skeptical realists confirm that Hume accepted experience-independent power as metaphysically real. They add, however, that Hume was skeptical of providing descriptive content to this power. Kenneth Richman represents his general position as follows: "A skeptical realist about some entity is realistic about the entity's existence, but agnostic about the nature or character of that thing because it is epistemically inaccessible to us in some non-trivial way."[38] John P. Wright, Galen Strawson, and Donald Livingston interpret Hume in this fashion. Though there are distinctions between their individual arguments, they generally agree that Hume accepts "there are real powers and forces in nature which are not directly accessible to our senses" and that Hume affirmed causal power "in some essentially non-Regularity theory way."[39]

Skeptical realists have reinvigorated controversies about the existence of mind-independent power in Hume.[40] Though he neither makes an explicit argument for the reality of these powers nor says much about them, on the skeptical-realist interpretation, Hume implicitly accepts and uncritically embraces extramental power as metaphysically real. But P. J. E. Kail offers an important rejoinder to this point. He claims that we had better not be "too agnostic" about the nature of the relevant item or entity, "otherwise we are left with an 'unknown something' which 'no skeptic will see fit to contend against.'"[41] One way to avoid falling prey to Kail's criticism is to contend (as Donald Livingston does in *Hume's Philosophy of Common Life*) that Hume relies on common life to supply at least some minimal content to what we take to be experience-independent power.

Projectivist accounts of experience-independent power provide a powerful counter to the skeptical realists here.[42] They contend that content for experience-independent power is derived from expectations of the mind based on a habit of our imagination. On the projectivist reading, belief in mind-independent power is no more than the expressive description of the productive faculty of the imagination and its "gilding and staining" of the world. Projectivist interpreters rightly affirm the limits of our minds and remind us of Hume's commitment to scaling back the inordinate powers we grant to reason. Skeptical realists agree with this. The distinction between the two is that projectivists view Hume as a realist about relations and properties; skeptical realists view Hume as a realist about powers in nature. While there are numerous textual details that one should take into account to effectively assess this debate, my argument for Hume's basic theism remains in the realm of his unique counterepistemology, which relied on common life.[43] It is unnecessary to take a stand on Hume's realism, because my concern is simply with *belief* in basic theism, not whether this belief points to anything metaphysically real. Hume's "intention never was to penetrate into the nature of bodies, or explain the secret causes of their operations" (*T*, 1.2.5.26); rather, it was only to locate and describe the principles that allow our minds to hold beliefs and make imaginative projections.

The aforementioned "rules" of nature invite us to unearth the naturalist interpretations of Hume.[44] While naturalist readings of Hume are diverse, generally speaking, they contend that what is most distinctive about his project is its assertion that we hold certain beliefs that we have no rational grounds for holding. We justify these beliefs, on the naturalist reading, and thereby try to stave off skepticism, simply by an appeal to nature. Naturalist interpreters emphasize Hume's statement that "Nature, by an absolute and uncontroulable necessity has determin'd us to judge as well as to breathe and feel" (*T*, 1.4.1.7) and accentuate his claims throughout the *Treatise* that lend credence to the reading that nature, not reason, is the ultimate guide for our behavior. We must exercise caution before concluding that Hume is a naturalist, however, for at least two reasons. First, his notion of human nature is fluid; it privileges history and includes custom. In other words, nature is not fully determinative for Hume (as most forms of naturalism declare). Second, Hume is not a scientific naturalist because he does not take nature to be self-explanatory. In other words, he avoids the traps of positivism, or the idea that reality is comprehensible and coextensive with nature. Hume's reflections both begin and end with practical human behavior in common life. To him, human behavior is guided by universal principles and derived from the powers of nature. We might describe him then as holding a type of naturalism by default. He does not believe that nature is self-explanatory, that it provides normative status, or that it is determinative. Principles of nature play an important role in motivating our minds and guiding our behavior, yet they do not completely determine it. Hume is not a conventional naturalist; however, reading him through the naturalist lens may help us to better comprehend belief in basic theism, which is crucial for a Humean true religion.

To take on the question of whether causal power is real in Hume is to consider power as "connexion." Accordingly, the issues that are revealed when viewed in this way are at least fourfold: that Hume's discussion of power is broader than simply causation; that the *Treatise* attends to the power of the mind, the power of the passions, and the power of political authority, among other things (each type of power may be linked to causal power, but they should not be reduced to causal power); and, finally, that his engagement with the issue of power includes at least two features: the idea of power (what is power?) and—our original question—the nature of power (is it real?). The larger claim of this chapter is that Hume's philosophy presupposes belief in basic theism, a mildly theistic rendering of something like ultimate cause or intelligent power that makes belief in an Author of

Nature irresistible, and that this basic belief is the source of both the vulgar theism of false religion and the genuine theism of true religion. I turn now to Hume's thoughts on belief to investigate how this mild theism might be intelligible on the grounds of Hume's philosophical schema.

## Natural Belief and Basic Theism

'Tis therefore demanded, *how it happens, that even after all we*
*retain a degree of belief, which is sufficient for our purpose, either*
*in philosophy or common life.*
—*T*, 1.4.1.9

It is difficult to positively establish the belief in basic theism, the mind's supposition of causal power, as an intelligible idea on the formal components of Hume's theory of mind. This is because his theory of mind is, in many ways, geared to show that the modern notion of an idea has become freighted with and burdened by the standards of philosophical thought. These standards, when considered under Hume's skeptical eye, are shown to be largely unintelligible. This is Hume's scathing skeptical critique of abstruse reason and false philosophy, and it is important and central to his thought. In some ways, it leaves him without a positive way to explain why we hold the ideas and beliefs that we do. The method he does find most useful, the empiricist method of inductive argument for mostly probable conclusions, by itself cannot justifiably "close the deal" for an intelligible idea of basic theism. Hume's philosophy of mind is simply too skeptical for us to casually smuggle in an intelligible notion of basic theism under its banner. At the same time, however, it refuses to allow for nihilism or despair in the face of the false standards of reason held by popular philosophers that have crept into common life. Thus Hume turns to nature and to our beliefs to support the broad, positive aims of his science. Beliefs have a much lower bar for intelligibility in Hume's work. Inextricably linked to our passions, they serve as sources of action and thereby play a crucial role in experience. Instead of responding to the rationalist standard by searching for justifiable grounds of our thoughts and actions, Hume gives an affective sense of nature and our beliefs that would satisfy his sense of reasonability. With this strategic move, perhaps he displays the fundamental investment of his thought project: to enhance human self-understanding and nourish social stability by demonstrating nature, not reason, to be the source of our most widely held and deeply moving beliefs.

*Hume's Views on Belief*

By his own admission, Hume's treatment of belief in the *Treatise* was, in some respects, incoherent (*T.*, app., 13).[45] I will not dwell on the specific tensions and contradictions in his description of belief, for others have thoughtfully exposed these critical details.[46] I focus on whether or not the basic belief in theism is intelligible on the terms of his early science. If it is, then we can assert that Hume's early philosophy, a science he believed to be "superior in utility to any other of human comprehension" (*T*, introd., 10), provides grounds for both the vulgar theism of false religion (which Hume explicitly argues for in the *NHR*) and genuine theism of a true religion (our speculative project). If the terms of Hume's thought do not allow us to justify the basic belief in theism, then we must drop the claims for this belief.

I take the following account of belief as Hume's general definition for what he means when he writes about belief.

> Belief consists not in the nature and order of our ideas, but in the *manner of their conception*, and in their *feeling to the mind*. I confess, that 'tis impossible to explain perfectly this *feeling* or *manner of conception*. We may make use of words that express something near it. But its true and proper name is *belief*, which is a term that every one sufficiently understands in common life. And in philosophy we can go no farther, than assert, that it is something *felt* by the mind, which distinguishes the ideas of the judgment from the fictions of the imagination. It gives them more force and influence; makes them appear of greater importance; infixes them in the mind; and renders them the governing principles of all our actions. (*E*, 5.2.3; italics added)

In the spirit of the mechanistic model on which he often relied but was also critical of, this account situates sense experience (impressions of reflection) as foundational for belief. For Hume, beliefs are neither a priori nor commanded by our will. Neither are they reducible to instinctive responses to what is given in experience, nor are they inspired by a supernatural spark. In significant part they are how our mental "machinery"—guided by rules and principles— responds to experience. They have a distinct "manner of conception" and are to be distinguished by the feelings of liveliness they exert on the mind. They are, also, the source of human action and behavior.[47] For Deleuze, "the virtual multiplicity of impressions and ideas is actualized, and is only actualized, by way of the beliefs that are inseparable from practical action."[48] Practical action, on the

Deleuzian view, actualizes the virtual multiplicity of preindividual singularities of belief.

What are the possible sources of the belief in basic theism? To answer this question we must consider its *formation*. Is belief in basic theism formed through custom; does it strike the mind with vivacity; does it impact our actions? Hume writes, "Now as we call everything Custom which proceeds from a past repetition, without any new reasoning or conclusion, we may establish it as a certain truth, that all belief, which follows upon any present impression, is derived solely from that origin" (*T*, 1.3.8.10). If custom is the source of beliefs, then force is its stamp, for belief "can only bestow on our ideas an additional force and vivacity" (1.3.7.5). Basic theism, on the schema Hume articulates, would start with a lively feeling and then be formed into a vivacious idea by a custom of the mind before becoming a belief. I offer a set of categories to clarify Hume's discussion and assist our inquiry into the question of whether basic theism is a belief in Hume's schema: *perceptual beliefs* and *projective beliefs*. The basic difference between these two categories of belief is the degree to which they are impacted by impressions. Perceptual beliefs are feelings that depend on recent memories or present impressions of sensation. Hume describes beliefs of this kind as "lively idea[s] related to or associated with a present impression" (1.3.7.5). Projective beliefs are also perceptions, but they have been more thoroughly mediated by the mind and therefore have less force. They emanate from impressions of reflection "related" (that is, redacted and collated) by the imagination. The common mistake here would be to take what I name "projective" beliefs as conclusions drawn from the understanding. Hume, however, is clear: properly calling something a belief has to do with "the manner of our conceiving" (1.3.7.4) or attending to the "force and vivacity" of the ideas. In other words, it is how the impression impacts the mind, the feeling, that is key for Hume. He writes that it is "impossible by words to describe this feeling, which everyone must be conscious of in his own breast."[49] While the impressions at the core of our projective beliefs do not enliven with the force of those behind perceptual beliefs, both forms of belief are action guiding.

Like all categories in Hume's schema, perceptual beliefs start with perceptions (for example, I went outside earlier and felt cold, now I *believe* that it is cold outside and will dress accordingly). The lively ideas derived from these vivacious impressions are crucial for these perceptual beliefs, for "an idea of an object is an essential part of the belief of it, but not the whole" (*T*, 1.3.7.1). Due to their heavy reliance on short-term memory and what seem to be recent impressions of sensation, we might provisionally describe perceptual beliefs as backward-looking and acknowledge them as stable sources of much of our practical behavior. These beliefs allow us to generate assumptions from past experience that assist in our organization of present and future ones. Their force prohibits them from being illusory or fictive: "'Tis evident, that whatever is present to the memory, striking upon the mind with a vivacity, which resembles an immediate impression, must become of considerable moment in all the operations of the mind, and must easily distinguish itself above the mere fictions of the imagination" (1.3.9.3). The belief in our experience-derived perception of causation—the capacity to remember observed repeating occasions where one event has successfully followed another— is determined by associative principles. The mind naturally infers cause from con- tiguity of events. So while it may seem to the human subject (or, more precisely, to the mind) that belief in causation is a valid idea derived from a lively impres- sion, Hume contends that there is no impression for causation. He shows that a customary inference of mind allows us to associate events that we feel are histori- cally contiguous and lead us to expect the future to resemble the past. We order our daily experience based on this fiction of mind. Because there is no impres- sion, belief in causation cannot be a perceptual belief.

Projective beliefs also begin as feelings. More specifically, however, they are beliefs that rely on impressions of reflection in the imagination more than mem- ory (for example, I have never opened this freezer before but I believe that when I open it, it will be cold). The imagination and impressions of reflection can, depending on the feeling of "force and vivacity" in the transaction between the mind and the impression, lead to what I call a projective belief. This type of "belief not only gives vigour to the imagination, but that a vigorous and strong imagina- tion is of all talents the most proper to procure belief and authority" (T, 1.3.10.8). The imagination and the principles that guide it are formative for our projective beliefs. The trouble is that the creative powers of the imagination can synthesize existing ideas and create new ones that are fictions (e.g., Centaur), theoretical concepts that we cannot directly experience (e.g., mind-independent objects), or beliefs that are meaningless for common life (e.g., the concept of substance).[50] Yet Hume neither indicts projective beliefs because they are speculative and may ori- ent us away from experience nor denies their potential impact on our behavior. His investment is, again, in assessing their process of formation. For him, the *content* of a belief is not of primary import because it does not authenticate the natural human disposition to a belief. Instead, by "belief" Hume simply means the historically evolving and custom-drenched "manners of conception" and "feel- ings to the mind" certain impressions tend to evoke.

Projective beliefs reveal the power of the imagination, a faculty driven by prin- ciples of human nature. We have established that causal power is not a perceptual belief because it cannot find an impression in sense experience. Our question now is if the imagination can create an impression of reflection, relate the ideas enliv- ened by this impression, and deliver a projective belief in causation. Or, maybe a better way to ask this question is the following: would Hume's philosophy allow us to label our habitual inferences from observable effects to unobservable causes "projective beliefs"? A growing body of scholars, including P. J. E. Kail, Simon Blackburn, Helen Beebee, and Angela Coventry, has provided some grounds for answering this question in the affirmative. These thinkers, building on the foundational work of Janet Broughton and Barry Stroud, read Hume as a projectivist about necessity in external objects per his claim that "the mind has a great propensity to spread itself on external objects, and to conjoin with them any internal impressions, which they occasion" (*T*, 1.3.14.24).[51] On their argument, the imagination projects its expressive language onto external objects, "gilding and staining" them "with the colours, borrowed from an internal sentiment" (*EPM*, app. 1.v.4). It linguistically co-opts sense experience in such a way that it collapses the multiplicity and singularity of its disparate, unconnected perceptions into necessarily connected and related ones. As mentioned earlier, the projectivist reading takes care to distinguish this weak claim for expressive speech about necessary connection in objects from the stronger, related one: that necessity and power reside in the objects. Further, projectivists acknowledge that belief in causal power and necessary connection (seminal for basic theism) relies on a habitual inference made by the mind after observation of contiguous and constantly conjoined events. That the source of our belief in necessary connection (as a feature that resides in objects) is an inference of the mind, not an impression derived from experience, means that we cannot legitimately classify it as a projective belief.

In many ways I am splitting hairs here in ways that Hume might not approve. My point is that our beliefs in causation, necessary connection, and external objects cannot be established as intelligible on the process of belief formation stipulated by Hume's philosophy. His investment, however, was neither to destroy these beliefs nor to demonstrate their veracity; it was simply to expose the process of their genesis and evolution. On his argument, our belief in the necessary connection of cause and effect was formed by a consistent habitual inference that was so strong that we "imagine" cause and effect "to be absolutely inseparable" (*T*, 1.3.9.10). This inference transcends what we are given in experience. Thus, on the standards of abstruse reason and philosophy, belief in cause and effect is, technically, unwarranted. Yet due to its crucial function in our practical lives, belief in cause and effect, as well as belief in basic theism, is an indispensable supposition of thought derived from sense impressions of reflection (passions) that inform all science, philosophy, and religion. Of course, human history would continue and human nature would persist without this belief. Yet reason and science would cease to exist in their present form if we did not presuppose certain laws of the universe and nature. Thus, we cannot confirm belief in basic theism as either a perceptual or projective belief for Hume. We may, however, embrace these "obvious and natural principles" as natural beliefs, that is, beliefs required for our minds to properly frame experience and make it coherent. The natural belief in basic theism or, from the perspective of our true religion, the acceptance of general providence, provides a religiophilosophical structure for reflective common life and backgrounds Hume's science of human nature. It is to a discussion of the natural beliefs that I now turn.

## Natural Beliefs

A 1905 article by Norman Kemp Smith assigned special status to a small set of beliefs that he argued were presupposed by Hume's work.[52] Kemp Smith dubbed these "natural beliefs," a term Hume never used. According to Kemp Smith, natural beliefs were distinct from other beliefs in Hume's schema because they were not derived from Hume's articulated views about ideas and beliefs. Hume's theory of belief stipulated that beliefs were derived from impressions, that they related through his associative principles, and that they were livelier and formed more powerfully than ideas. Kemp Smith's insight was that Hume endorsed certain beliefs that did not meet the standards explicated by his theory of mind. In other words, Humean naturalism allowed for us to hold beliefs from nondeductive inferences. The probable and likely sources of these beliefs were largely mysterious. The most we could say about them was that they were based on some combination of the innovative powers of nature, experience, and common life. Still, for Kemp Smith, these beliefs were of undeniable import: they were "indispensable" and "inevitable," and they enabled our proper functioning on the globe. On his writing, natural beliefs "provide the context—frame of reference, so to speak" for all our other beliefs; thus, they are validated pragmatically.[53]

Kemp Smith's argument for natural beliefs in Hume was an intervention in the field of Hume studies. Against both skeptical and positivist readings of Hume, he highlighted Hume's self-styled naturalism. Basing his naturalist interpretation on the claim that "reason is, and ought only to be, the slave of the passions, and can never pretend to any other office than to serve and obey them" (T, 2.3.3.4), Kemp Smith not only read Hume's veneration of the passions as both descriptive and normative but also took it as Hume's overall solution to the various problems of philosophy. On Kemp Smith's thinking, Hume believed that the passions were 'natural,' which was discernible by "the constancy and steadiness of [their] operations" (2.1.3.2). The passions "win out" over reason and should always do so, because nature is "providential"; it affords "human beings with mental mechanisms that allow them to cope successfully with the world."[54] This provides us with a viable and compelling account of Hume's naturalist approach to human nature on which we might build. It also gives us a category that makes basic theism intelligible on Hume's thought: natural belief.

Hume scholars generally agree that 'natural beliefs' are a class of beliefs we hold in spite of the fact that they cannot be demonstrated rationally or verified empirically by Hume's associative principles. There is little consensus, however, as to which beliefs in Hume should be classified as natural beliefs. Kemp Smith originally argued for three, but he later reduced these to two: belief in the continuous and independent existence of objects in the external world and belief in causal power. Other scholars add the belief in personal identity (originally included by Kemp Smith). A fourth idea posited as a natural belief is belief in an intelligent Designer of the universe. Stanley Tweyman, Beryl Logan, Miguel Badia-Cabrera, and R. J. Butler supported the belief in an intelligent Designer as a natural belief, while J. C. Gaskin, Terence Penelhum, Antony Flew, and Norman Kemp Smith held that belief in an intelligent Designer was not an "irresistible" belief and that it did not fit the criteria for natural belief.[55]

There is an important distinction between what I take to be Hume's basic theism and what Kemp Smith calls belief in an intelligent Designer. Hume's basic theism—the belief that order (and, therefore an Orderer) exists—is constituted by our natural sense of order and regularity and the causal function of the mind. This is the equivalent of what Kemp Smith calls causal power and describes as a natural belief. It is a presupposition of Hume's philosophy explained in the introduction to the *Natural History of Religion* as one of the "primary principles of genuine Theism and religion." As a natural belief, it is unmediated by the beliefs and principles of religion (false or true), for the "first religious principles must be secondary" (*NHR*, introd.); that is, they filter original instincts. Although our distinct interpretive lenses lead us to emphasize different aspects of the belief in basic theism, I agree with Kemp Smith that it is intelligible as a natural belief on Hume's philosophy. Further, we also agree that when Hume writes about belief in an intelligent, anthropomorphic Designer, he is referring to a belief of popular religion, not a natural belief (that is, not an invisible power). This distinction is important: it clarifies that what I dub "basic theism" is intelligible in Hume's philosophy as a natural belief.

Hume's experience inside of Evangelical Presbyterianism taught him to be highly critical of belief in a Designer. Thus he despised the deity of popular religion and natural theology. He embraced belief in a Designer only when it was used as a description of our basic belief in "causal power," "omnipotent mind," or, at times, "invisible, intelligent power." Hume detested false religion's belief in a *particular* providence, the faith that an all-perfect and sovereign deity was involved in the salvation and well-being of individuals for a larger redemptive world purpose. Yet his philosophical writing presupposed a basic theism based on our sense of regularity and purposive order. This basic theism was not a virtue, and it did not require religion. It was a basic belief that grounded our experience and oriented us in the universe. My claim is that to consider a Humean true religion, we should approach Hume through his basic theism, which under rare circumstances—if we read his project closely—evolves into a genuine theism, a belief in general providence. Hume writes, "The providence of the deity appears not immediately in any operation, but governs everything by those general and immutable laws, which have been established from the beginning of time. All events, in one sense, may be pronounced the action of the almighty: They all proceed from those powers, with which he has endowed his creatures."[56] But we must be careful here: the "God" of genuine theism is distinct from human beings (contra Hegel's *Geist*), has no particular concern with human happiness or morality (contra Leibniz), takes no interest in the redemption of the world (contra Edwards), and has no anthropomorphic characteristics and attributes (contra Clarke).

The debate about whether Hume's belief in a Designer is a natural belief is generally understood to hinge on how one constitutes a natural belief.[57] For my purposes, however, the interesting consequence of taking Hume's belief in a Designer as a natural belief is that it helps illumine Hume's two different senses about this topic. It is obvious that Hume was troubled by belief in the Designer of false religion. Kemp Smith, following Hume's argument against popular Christianity, asserted that Hume's belief in the Designer was not a natural belief (as it was not "irresistible"). On the other hand, the previous discussion demonstrates that Hume did accept a nonconventional theism: the basic belief in purposive order of the principles of human nature. R. J. Butler, working from this aspect of Hume's logic, claims that Hume did accept belief in a Designer. Kemp Smith and Butler are both correct: they simply seize two different inferences in Hume's discussion of a Designer and reason in opposite directions.

The debate about which beliefs in Hume are natural beliefs may be irresolvable. Still, the attempt to uncover that small set of elemental beliefs that lie outside of Hume's theory of mind is instructive. Perhaps the best we can do is to build on this conversation by condensing Kemp Smith's insights and supplementing them with the most sustainable ideas offered by Tweyman, Gaskin, and Butler. This approach yields three useful characteristics of a natural belief. First, beliefs that fall outside of Hume's formal theory of belief have *inscrutable* sources—they are not directly derived from impressions, ideas, or the creative power of the imagination. Second, these beliefs are *indispensable* for the ordering of experience—both science and rationality would cease to exist in any recognizable form without them. And third, these important beliefs are part of the *implicit* content or nonreflective wisdom that operates in custom. Thus construed, the basic theism noted by Hume's philosophy is a natural belief, but the genuine theism of true religion and the vulgar theism of false religion are *not*. The latter two beliefs are derived from complex ideas and mediated through symbolic and imaginative grasps for

and against sacrality. Though it is not a natural belief, genuine theism is instructive not only because it serves as the theistic worldview of our speculative true
religion but also because paying close attention to it can reveal Hume's basic theism and illuminate his thoughts on beliefs.

## True Religion and True Philosophy

Against many traditional interpretations of Hume, the work of Donald Livingston, particularly his second book *Philosophical Melancholy and Delirium*, is the
most instructive grappling we have with Hume's true philosophy and true religion.[58] With great scope and depth, Livingston eloquently argues that common
life and false philosophy work dialectically in Hume's thought. The resolution and
overcoming of this division is the rare, true philosophy. Livingston's philosophy of
common life confirms that some beliefs derived from inscrutable sources, for
example, natural beliefs, are worthy of embrace. His reading of Hume supports
my contention that basic theism (Livingston calls this "true theism") is the source
for both the vulgar theism of false philosophy and the speculative genuine theism
of true religion.

Keeping track of Livingston's argument for true philosophy and true religion
(he equates them) in Hume requires that we closely follow Hume's use of abstract
reason (the path to moderate skepticism) and attend to his notion "common life"
(that confirms our customs, prejudices, and natural propensities against this
skepticism). Hume explains the tension between the two modes as follows: "In
considering this subject we may observe a gradation of three opinions, that rise
above each other, according as the persons, who form them, acquire new degrees
of reason and knowledge. These opinions are that of the *vulgar*, that of a *false
philosophy*, and that of the *true*; where we shall find upon enquiry, that the true
philosophy approaches nearer to the sentiments of the vulgar, than to those of a
mistaken knowledge" (*T*, 1.4.3.9; italics added). Following this logic, the rare, true
philosophy reconciles the popular opinions of common life with the vulgar conclusions of false philosophy, but it reflects the general orientations of common life
that inhere in beliefs and ideas of false philosophy. Unlike false philosophers, true
philosophers are not alienated from the traditions of common life that produced
them. They explain, describe, and organize the conclusions of common life and
quietly challenge them. "The true philosopher," Livingston writes, "having worked
through the errors of false philosophy, recognizes the authority of the popular
system in his own thought."[59] Concerning the practice of religion, true philosophers may observe the religion of common life in practice and feel a sense of kin-
ship with the community of worshippers. It is likely, however, that they would feel
little connection to its theological content and sacred rituals. True philosophers

may even believe that he who practices true philosophy or true religion best does not know he is practicing it. A similar sentiment was expressed by Eric Gill: "he prays best who does not know that he is praying."[60] For true philosophers, ceremony has come to be an affirmation of common life that reveals its contamination by abstract thought; thus, Hume believes, our functions and practices must ultimately guide our philosophy. Extending Livingston one step further, we might say that he understands Hume's philosophy as a theory of what we *do*. False philosophy is a vulgar way of conceiving what we do. True philosophy is a reflective method of considering what we do. False religion is a popular way of conceiving our religious ways of doing that reveals the infestation of false philosophy— described earlier as modern religion that strove for philosophical legitimation. True religion is that rare way of conceiving our religious ways of being. It does not aim for legitimacy in the terms of abstract thought, nor does it opt for easy answers. Still, it can provide balance in the face of life's vicissitudes.

On Livingston's reading, Hume contends that we can be in the business of certifying or devalidating long-standing artifacts of our culture (e.g., reason and religion), or, more rarely, as true philosophers, we might bring attention to these practices, trace their origins, and formulate "critical rules, principles or ideals which seem to reflect the practice[s]."[61] True philosophy indicates the rarefied harmony of common life and philosophical self-reflection. It distinguishes between the surface of experience and that which precedes it. It "clears the way to make the surface itself the object of inquiry."[62] In this way, the true philosopher assumes a natural order while maintaining ignorance about its sources. We might understand this natural order as a parallel of basic theism.

We must remember that true philosophy is not obsessed with establishing the true as the certain as in some forms of rationalism and empiricism. It also rejects logical verification as in particular forms of positivism. Finally, it shows little interest in clarifying the epistemic status of our ideas or the justifiability of our beliefs. Again, it simply aims to explain the process of formation of our ideas and beliefs. This is how it sheds light on the surface of experience and, inadvertently, what lies below it. To do so, true philosophy must take into account the categories and prereflective convictions of common life, whose sources remain, it must ultimately admit, inscrutable. The epistemological humility of true philosophers position them to readily embrace our most useful and naturally occurring beliefs with both humility and confidence. On Hume's argument, the tacit wisdom of common life as well as the natural functioning of our minds generate our impulse to reflect on mind-independent power. This impulse may be distorted by too little reflection (false religion) or too much (false philosophy). True philosophy moderates this potential for distortion by remaining aware of the silent knowledge passed through the customs of common life and habits of mind. It accepts a basic theism, the belief that the world is a result of purposive activity, in spite of the fact that this belief flies in the face of the standards of evidence required by abstract thought. In this way, true philosophy and true religion both preserve the theistic impulse of common life in reflective form and protect the mind's process of habitual inference. But the true philosopher is aware that the belief in basic theism, though it helps us function by allowing us to order and organize experience, is caught up in a process ultimately guided by the passions. This means that belief in basic theism will, ultimately, manifest in some form of passionally driven religious activity. Hume confirms this in the *NHR* when he argues that the direct-passions hope and fear distort the belief in basic theism into a vulgar theism. Of course, true religion might include a way of deliberating that alters the belief in basic theism into a genuine theism, but the true philosopher is the only one who can correctly identify this process, reflect on the origins of our beliefs, and "methodize and correct" them. On the parameters of Livingston's argument, true theism—that we tend to think of the world as ordered by "springs and principles"—is a foundation for true philosophy. It affirms that the sources of what I have called "belief in basic theism" go beyond actual experience, and it acknowledges that prereflective belief in theism, spread through the customs of common life, cannot be justified on the standards of abstract reason. It seems that Livingston allows that the basic theism behind Hume's philosophical project can lead to genuine theism, a feature of true religion, a rare form of religion that contributes "to the amendment of men's lives, and their improvement in morality and social virtue" (*EPM*, 9.2.1).

On the argument of this chapter Hume's early philosophy holds a basic theism that irresistibly leads to belief in an Author of Nature. This basic theism sidesteps Hume's skepticism, is justified by his theory of ideas, confirmed by Kemp Smith's notion of natural beliefs, and made intelligible by Livingston's argument for true philosophy. This basic theism is typically distorted by the passions into its vulgar form, yet in its calmer moments it can evolve into genuine theism. How this happens is a function of how we moderate the passions. Thus, I turn to the question of the passions: what are they and how might we moderate them in a way that can fit into our Humean true religion?

# 3

## MODERATE HOPE

For my part, my only hope is, that I may contribute a little to
the advancement of knowledge, by giving in some particulars
a different turn to the speculations of philosophers, and pointing out to them more distinctly those subjects, where alone
they can expect assurance and conviction.
—*T*, 1.4.7.14

Hume's ideas about the passions were a seminal component of his early science
that shaped his entire thought project. In fact, his theory of ideas, thoughts on
belief, and his moral considerations all relied—to some degree and differently—
on the role of the passions. Book 1 of the *Treatise* argued that our most important
beliefs and ideas were drawn from customs of the mind (imaginative associations) and reflective traditions of common life both generated by secondary,
reflective impressions, or "passions" (2.1.1.1). Accordingly, the passions served as a
kind of oasis for Hume: they were the integral source of our natural ways of reasoning. Hume's classification of them in book 2 aimed to demonstrate how they
functioned on the theory of association he described in book 1. In service of this
end, it detailed the passions, the sources of both our beliefs and actions, and their
causes. The discussion of the passions in book 2 was also important to clear the
path for what some consider his complex subjectivist argument—that the standard of action rests primarily on the individual—concerning moral value and
judgment in book 3.

In the secondary scholarship, Hume's treatment of the passions has mostly
been subordinated to his work on moral motivation. This is unfortunate yet
understandable given the rationalist commitment to catalog the status of reason
and its relationship to the passions in Hume. To reduce Hume's passions to sources

of moral judgment and to probe how they motivate it, however, is to disfigure them to meet the rational standards of practical reason. Christine Korsgaard's extensive project on normativity, which repeatedly takes up Hume and the passions, mildly demonstrates this sort of disfigurement. Citing Hume's claim that "actions may be laudable or blameable; but they cannot be reasonable or unreasonable" (*T*, 3.1.1.10), Korsgaard shows the inability of Hume's account to classify an action as "irrational." For her, this leaves it open to the claim of absurdity ("'Tis not contrary to reason to prefer the destruction of the whole world to the scratching of my finger" [2.3.3.7]) and incapable of accounting for the normative content required to motivate judgment ("It seems evident, that reason, in a strict sense, as meaning the judgment of truth and falsehood, can never, of itself, be any motive to the will and can have no influence but so far as it touches some passion or affection"); to Korsgaard, practical reason is necessary for the act of judgment.[1]

Accordingly, she reads Hume as a subjectivist about the sources of our actions and as an antirealist regarding practical reason. Hume's explicitly stated intention, however, was to demonstrate *how* the "passions yield to our reason without any opposition" (*T*, 2.3.3.6), not to undermine practical reason. Korsgaard's interpretation then, while insightful, tempts us to overlook both the complicated psychological aspects of how passions associate in Hume's thought ("one passion will always be mixt and confounded with the other" [*DP*, 1.3.4]) and his sophisticated subjectivism that included nature, passions, reason, and common life. Further, reducing his theory of the passions to his moral thought obscures Hume's goal. He was not invested in either voicing support for 'internalism' (the view that moral motivation was built in to moral judgment) or 'externalism' (that moral judgments require independent motivation). Annette Baier reminds us that he merely wanted to reconcile our passions with our beliefs by highlighting some possible ways they might associate. Baier cites Hume's famous statement "Reason is, and ought only to be the slave of the passions, and can never pretend to any other office than to serve and obey them" (*T*, 2.3.3.4) not as Hume's censure against reason and its motivational capacity (Korsgaard's view) but as his way of confirming the psychological sources of our behavior, which always include customs of common life and habits of mind. In this way Baier maintains more of the imaginative power of Hume's treatment of the passions as she counters the constraints of the rationalist approach.[2]

Hume acknowledged that the desire to submerge his discussion of the passions in debates on moral motivation was driven by the passions, for we are led "astray, not only by the narrowness of [our] understandings, but by that also of [our] passions" (*EMPL*, 18.160). Hume's discussion of the passions then, both the section in his prodigious *Treatise* and its later, truncated articulation—the *Dissertation on the Passions*—was not undertaken specifically for moral concerns or against instrumental conceptions of reason. It was, more likely, an imaginative attempt to set up the broad causal background for our natural affections and sentiments. This generative effort to account for the inner history of our reflective, secondary impressions was related to his treatment of religion: against those who claimed that religious beliefs were divinely implanted, a necessity of the idea of heaven, or a constituent part of miracles, Hume argued that they were fully natural and derived from the direct-passion hopes and fears. My premise, that calm, moderate hopes and fears might constitute a feature of religion's proper office, follows from this. This chapter considers the role of moderate hope for my larger argument: that when combined with a genuine theism and a commitment to practical morality, calm or moderate hope can serve as an intelligible feature of a speculative true religion derived from Hume's thought.

The hope that Hume explicitly detailed in the *Treatise* was the direct-passion hope of false religion, not the moderate hope of the true. To locate this calm, moderate hope in Hume's thought it behooves us to decipher Hume's formal discussion of the passions along with his broader general references to hope. The work of John Bricke is instructive for how we might undertake this sort of enterprise. Bricke highlights an important tension between Hume's theoretical discussion of direct passions and his concrete deployment of more modest and subjective ones. He reasoned that Hume's direct-passion "desire" was "narrow" and "should not mislead" us from the more "inclusive," "theoretically important" concept of "desire" that was implicitly woven throughout his project. Bricke's argument about "desire" could be made for "hope" in Hume: the hope Hume defined as a direct passion was narrow and "should not mislead" us from the more moderate, stable hope that ran implicitly throughout his project. Bricke helps us realize that there may be a "hope" governing Hume's work that is external to his formal classificatory scheme of the passions. This point is powerfully supported by Joseph Godfrey's *A Philosophy of Human Hope*, a comprehensive survey and analysis of "deep grounded hope" that distinguishes "between two equally significant kinds of hope: hope that has an aim and is one's deepest hope, *ultimate hope*; and . . . hope without aim, a tone or disposition with which one faces the future—*fundamental hope*." Both Bricke and Godfrey implicitly acknowledge a form of hope that resides outside of the theoretical, ultimate, or direct-passion hopes in Hume.[3]

To trace the potential manifestations of what Bricke calls Hume's more "inclusive" passions and Godfrey names "hope without aim" is to redirect our attention from direct-passion hope to this more modest hope. To do so regarding religion is to begin by acknowledging that the *Natural History of Religion* (1757) confirms direct-passion hopes and fears as the sources of popular religion. On Hume's bifurcated view of religion we can fairly presume then, that a more *moderate* hope, if we could account for it in Hume's thought, would be the crucial source of a speculative true religion. Godfrey's framework sanctions this presumption. He showed that a deep consideration of hope reveals both of its types in the work of Kant, Marcel, and Bloch. Kant's well-documented *ultimate hope* in the "ethical commonwealth/kingdom of God" was reinforced by his *fundamental hope* that manifested as trust and informed his notion of a rational faith. This fundamental hope was also present in Kant's willingness to "obey and respect moral impera- tives without being able to grasp . . . outcomes" or "without having speculative hold on what grounds" the reasonableness of such imperatives.[4] Godfrey locates these two distinct types of hope in Kant's work. His unique interpretive lens uncovers both the tenor of Kant's social hope and the conviction with which he limited reason. Godfrey, however, did not extend his close reading of hope to thinkers that preceded Kant. Might Hume's project possess both an ultimate hope and a fundamental hope? If so, is fundamental hope available to support the pre- sumption that might inform religion's proper office? Is there a calm passion that we might name moderate hope in Hume? I answer in the affirmative to all these questions.

Godfrey maintains that fundamental hope orients us to the future but does not seek an object. He wrote, "The best preliminary characterization of fundamental hope is as an openness of spirit with respect to the future. . . . One faces up to the evidence. But openness also means a sense of the limits of evidence. . . . It knows the difference between 'This cause is lost,' and 'All is lost.'"[5] To rethink Hume's theory of the passions and his consideration of religion with this idea of hope is to thicken Hume's passions and deemphasize his critique of the hopes of popular religion. It is also to enlarge the way we characterize Hume's hopes. A Humean fundamental hope would be a hope that was not stirred by the attempt to over- come unhappiness and its opposite would not be fear. Its aims would be loose. Fundamental hope does not generate momentum solely from pursuit of objects, and it does not strive for dramatic transformation or spectacular improvement. Fundamental hope grounds us firmly in the present and stabilizes us for what may come (always impermanent and unpredictable). It would promote equipoise, a sense of well-being that we might consider "religious" in the broad sense of the term. This type of hope—a calm passion—could be a speculative feature of our Humean-inspired true religion.

One might wonder, however, if there is no aim and no goal, how can we dub this hope? Godfrey contends that we can call this fundamental hope because its "tonality . . . is thus distinguishable from optimism and presumption on the one hand and pessimism and despair on the other."[6] This present condition and future orientation of the mind is dubbed "hope" because hope is the extant category within common life that it most resembles. It is distinguishable from both "desire" and "wish," based on its closer relation to the probability that it might acquire its object. The likelihood that this disposition would reach its aim was high; that is why it was hope and not desire. Of course, this process of differentiating the energy of the disposition, its aim, and the probability of its acquisition was neither scientific nor fully predictable. It relied on the basic springs and principles of the universe and the particular moods of subjects as they responded to experiences. This type of complex subjectivity is constituted by personal feelings and attitudes as well as the feelings and attitudes of others; so both kinds of hope in Hume are personal and subjective yet linked to the collective conventions of common life.

To Hume, history proved that direct-passion hopes were the source of false religion. If religion ever appeared in its proper office, which it did very rarely, it is very likely that it would have been birthed by a calm and modest hope: a sense of confidence that what is needed is available and a disposition to trust that these resources will (somehow) be employed at the appropriate time. This calm passion, on Hume's account, is "a settled principle of action . . . the predominant inclination of the soul [that] produces no longer any sensible agitation" (*T*, 2.3.4.1). The two parts of this chapter (each with two sections) provide a framing of Hume's theory of passions that attends to the moderate hope that can fund the proper office of religion. In the first section of part 1, I briefly highlight the views of the passions held by some of Hume's predecessors and explore his theory of the passions as articulated in the *Treatise*. This overview is not exhaustive. It displays common trends in the Enlightenment discourse on the passions in general and hope in particular to lay the foundation for my argument that two kinds of hope persist in Hume's writings. The second, longer part of this chapter turns to Hume's religious writings. Its first section analyzes the *Natural History of Religion* and its second section treats his *Dialogues Concerning Natural Religion* to uncover how Hume's treatment of the passions—specifically regarding the two types of hope—applies to his discussion of both false and true religion. The thesis that guides my argument is that Hume's work allows for modest hope as a calm passion that can form the second constitutive feature of a Humean-inflected true religion. This mild hope vitiates the atheism and skepticism that so doggedly haunt Hume's legacy and clarifies a way to understand his theory of passions that is useful for the action-guiding project that we shall pursue in the next chapter.

## Enlightenment Passions and Hume's *Treatise*

I am not, however, without hopes, that the present system of
philosophy will acquire new force as it advances.
—*T*, 3.1.1.1

Hume's way of thinking about the passions did not originate in a vacuum; he derived it from the tradition of inquiry in which he was situated. Early modern reflections on the passions were based on the classical distinction between both the passive and active parts of the soul.[7] Enlightenment thinkers tended to work from assumptions about the passions grounded in this legacy, namely: (1) that the passions had an appetite for the good (not necessarily a moral good but a personal one); (2) that the passions produced action on their own (the motivation to act was internal to the passion, it did not require an external stimulus); and (3) that the passions needed to be regulated by reason. These assumptions led Hume and his contemporaries to prioritize the dynamic relationship between reason and the passions such that reason was the guide and motivator of the passions. Hume, however, took a skeptical approach to this relationship: he did not believe reason could or should authorize and control the passions. To him, the passions did not need to be tamed by reason, they simply required deeper and closer examination. To that end, he tried to discern the role of the passions for our actions and beliefs. I am interested in aspects of his thoughts on the passions that inform the imagination in ways that enhance our reflective experience in common life and result in equipoise and magnanimity, features we can link with our broad conceptualization of religion.

## Hume's Immediate Predecessors on the Passions

In the *Treatise* Hume seemed to playfully improvise on specific parts of definitions of the passions offered by three foundational thinkers that preceded him. First, against the voluntarists, Bacon had described the passions as the fully *natural and unavoidable* dispositions of persons excited by events in the mind/soul. Second, Spinoza had reasoned that the passions generally *specified ends*; that is, they were directed toward a future aim or object. Third, counter to the strict dualists and the Stoics, Descartes had held that the passions were always *interrelated* or 'mixed,' influenced by *both* mind and body, reason and sensation, other passions and ideas.[8] Of course, Hume disagreed with the granting of normative authority to reason over the passions, and he could not justify ascribing any theological content to the passions. Still, his work largely accepts the passions as natural, interrelated, and driven toward ends. In addition to the fundamental insights of Bacon, Spinoza, and Descartes, perhaps Locke's and Hutcheson's accounts of the passions may have even more significantly influenced Hume's consideration of them (even though Locke and Hutcheson embraced a Christian deity). Locke's intervention stressed that the passions arose from data received by our inner senses filtered through the mind, and Hutcheson's unique contribution was his emphasis on the social features of the passions. Hume disavowed their assertions that the passions were to be fully regulated by reflection (Hutcheson) or controlled by the mind (Locke). He also denied Locke's belief in rational principles that completely transcended the passions, and he disagreed with Hutcheson's claims that our other-directed passions were always benevolent. Still, the inner structure of Hume's passions partially reflected the Lockean inheritance, and their social features revealed Hutcheson's influence.

Hume's ideas regarding the passions were mostly derived from the thought of Locke, who had "sever[ed] the mind's connection to those organs of the body believed to be the source or conduit of the passions: the heart, the spleen, the liver, and even, paradoxically, the brain."[9] Locke connected the passions directly to feelings of pleasure and pain, which were determined rationally, not physically. His *Essay Concerning Human Understanding* (1690) stated, "Pleasure and pain, and that which causes them, good and evil, are the hinges on which our passions turn. And if we *reflect* on ourselves and *observe* how these under various considerations operate in us, what modifications or *tempers of mind*, what internal sensations they produce in us, we may thence form to ourselves the *ideas* of our passions [italics added]." While Hume limited Locke's notion of ideas and rejected the hedonism suggested by his view (if virtue was the equivalent of our greatest pleasure and highest happiness, then the passions were inherently self-indulgent), he borrowed the basic structure of Locke's passions as ideas that originated as sensations but became known to us post(minimal) cognition. Additionally for Locke, good increased pleasure, evil intensified pain, and our passions motivated us to pursue good and avoid evil: "For we love, desire, rejoice, and hope, only in respect of pleasure; we hate, fear, and grieve, only in respect of pain." Hope, in Locke's early writings, was a pleasure-driven passion—that is, a particular kind of idea— "which every one finds in himself, upon the thought of a probable future enjoyment of a thing" that aimed for a future, possible good.[10] Its opposite was fear. This naturally occurring hope was neither derived from nor dependent on any religious beliefs. It was generated by our rational desire to satisfy selfish pleasures, which were the equivalent of the good. Lockean passions affirmed our predilection to allow internal, guiding rational principles to manage sensations and self-interests. Hume accepted these positions.

Francis Hutcheson's intervention in discourse on the passions was the addition of a social dimension. Staying mostly within the parameters of the Lockean approach, Hutcheson linked our passions to the feelings of pleasure we received from the happiness of others. These "other-directed" sensations allowed him to avoid the latent hedonism of the Lockean view and provide a communal component.[11] Strongly influenced by Malebranche, Hutcheson's *Essay on the Nature and Conduct of the Passions and Affections* (1728) tweaked the Lockean self-interested pleasures by emphasizing "benevolent (or public) affections." He argued that "these can lead us, without any thought of self-interest, to pursue the happiness of others. Moreover, the satisfaction of these benevolent affections was a source of pleasure to the agent himself." Hutcheson filtered the selfishly-driven pleasures of Locke through the frame of our *social* relationships and thereby granted them more public usefulness and agreeability. For Hutcheson, it was our public sense of morality that proved more important than our private self-interest: what we did for others was ultimately more pleasing to us than what we did for ourselves. This affirmed a natural link between the passions and morality and provided the grounds for reading Hutcheson as a 'moral sense' theorist. He thought the passions should be regulated and argued that humans should allow "long-term affections" or "calm desires"—more controlled than the passions ("short-term affections")— to guide their lives.[12]

Hume was likely influenced by Hutcheson's theory of the passions in at least two crucial ways: first, he espoused the notion that the passions were driven by an inner disposition for the attainment of personal good, which was always social. Second, he accepted that the moderation of our passions was compelled by public sentiments and social modifications. Hume's passions—following his reading of Hutcheson—thus went beyond the internal dynamics of the human mind into the social realm: the passions were able to be modified by public affections and social sentiments. Hope, for Hutcheson, however, does *not* seem to be a public affection. He wrote, "Hope, if it be any way an affection, and not an Opinion, is 'a mixture of desire and joy, upon the probability of obtaining good, and avoiding evil.'"[13] Hume expands Hutcheson's more public affections to the way he conceived of the passion of hope.

Finally, an important influence on Hume is often overlooked: the moderate philosophical and personal hopes of his progenitors. Locke and Hutcheson held personal hopes that exemplified how the passions could be moderated. In one example, the hope that Hutcheson actually practiced and *enacted* in his texts—"I hope that I am contributing to promote the more moderate and charitable sentiments in religious matters in this country"—was a milder form of the hope on which he theorized.[14] This type of calm vision for progress or "posterity" (Carl Becker's thesis) was common to Enlightenment thinkers. The problem was that their overarching investment in reason left them largely unable to describe these personal hopes as *passions*. This comports with Bricke's analysis of Hume mentioned earlier, which suggested that in addition to the formal direct-passion hopes that were his theoretical focus, a more modest type of hope guided his broader vision for philosophy. Hume, of course, was skeptical of both reason and progressive concepts of history, yet he held a modest hope that his work might support the transition from violent, agitated passions to more modest, calm ones and thereby increase stability in politics, philosophy, and religion. He advocated a form of public learning through custom and the development of social conventions: for, "where experiments of this kind are judiciously collected and compared, we may *hope* to establish on them a science" (*T*, introd., 10; italics added). The quiet hope in Hume should not be discounted; as part of the trio of features I propose it is useful for religion's proper office.

## Hume's Theory of the Passions

For Hume, the passions informed our beliefs and were largely responsible for our actions. Hume's thought attempt, to locate the sources of human behavior, was framed by the dynamic bounds of both history and common life and guided by the hidden parameters of nature and the principles of the imagination. As in Locke, Hume's passions had much to do with our *ideas* ("hope and fear, which may properly be called impressions of reflexion, because derived from it . . . are copied by memory and imagination, and become ideas" [*T*, 1.1.2.1]), and they reflected "natural principles" (2.1.12.1). Hume's passions also, per Hutcheson, informed both our *internal sense* ("the beauty of our person, of itself, and by its very appearance, gives pleasure, as well as pride; and its deformity, pain as well as humility" [2.1.5.1]) and our *social sense* ("no quality of human nature is more remarkable, both in itself and in its consequences, than that propensity we have to sympathize with others, and to receive by communication their inclinations and sentiments, however different from, or even contrary to our own" [2.1.11.2]). And, as we shall see in the next chapter, passions influenced our *moral* judgment ("If a man have a lively sense of honour and virtue, with moderate passions, his conduct will always be conformable to the rules of morality" [*EMPL*, 8.169]); our *aesthetic sensibilities* ("'Tis not solely in poetry and music, we must follow our taste and sentiment, but likewise in philosophy" [*T*, 1.3.8.12]); and our *behavior* ("Nothing can be more real, or concern us more, than our own sentiments of pleasure and uneasiness; and if these be favourable to virtue, and unfavourable to vice, no more can be requisite to the regulation of our conduct and behavior" [3.1.1.25]).

Hume started from the idea that the passions were practical and conditioned secondary impressions experienced by complex and limited biohistorical creatures in particular contexts. These reflective sensations (of an individual) should not be thought of as *simply* reactions. It may be more useful to consider them as natural responses to experiences within the matrix of historical, natural, and social environments that were always informed by conventions, habits, and the imagination. Thus our passions neither bypassed the mind nor sidestepped common life. Hume believed that a deeper understanding of the causes and operations of the passions could help us transition to calmer ones. He formally discussed the mechanics of direct-passions hope and fear in book 2 of the *Treatise*. That he dealt with them secondarily (after ideas) should not decrease the importance of the modest hope that animated the tone and attitude of his broader corpus. This mild passion hope, the basis of the "strength of mind" of the true philosopher, sustained his vision, supplied the easygoing forward rhythm of his writing, and implied a sense of equipoise, or balance in the face of the unknown. Following Godfrey, we might consider this Hume's *fundamental hope* and contemplate its merit as a feature of religion's proper office.

## OF THE PASSIONS

Following Locke, Hume asserted that the passions were impressions of *reflection* and thus secondary. They were "antecedent to the ideas derived from them, but posterior to impressions of sensation from which they may be indirectly derived via an idea of pleasure or pain, this idea itself arising from an antecedent impression of pleasure or pain."[15] These reflective impressions were derived from and thus associated with other impressions, ideas, and passions, as "all resembling impressions are connected together, and no sooner one arises than the rest immediately follow" (*T*, 2.1.4.2). To Hume these sensations were processed by the mind, and they interacted as pairs on a continuum: for example, pride/humility, grief/joy, love/hatred, and hope/fear. When a particular continuum was excited, the relevant passions pushed and pulled against one another until one resonated more strongly than the other. Thus, a mechanical relationality was a feature of Hume's classification of the passions just as it was in his theory of mind.

One of the ways Hume displayed the Lockean legacy was with his division of the passions into the categories of "original" and "secondary."[16] Unlike Descartes and Malebranche, he jettisoned the account of bodily fluids as sources of our original passions, for "these depend upon natural and physical causes, [and] the examination of them wou'd lead me too far from my present subject" (*T*, 2.1.1.2). Again, following Locke's intervention, Hume maintained an investment in sensations processed by the mind: this explains why he named them "secondary" and "reflective." As with his distinction between the simple and complex impressions and ideas in book 1, Hume divided these secondary impressions even further, into two kinds, the calm and the violent. Violent passions, of which Hume only gave examples—"love and hatred, grief and joy, pride and humility"—were agitated sources of unstable behavior. Hume admitted that the division between calm and violent passions was "far from being exact" and "vulgar and specious," yet he banked on it to "proceed with the greater order" (2.1.1.3). Part of this order was the distinction between direct and indirect passions, for "when we take a survey of the passions, there occurs a division of them into *direct* and *indirect*. By direct passions I understand such as arise immediately from good or evil, from pain or pleasure. By indirect such as proceed from the same principles, but by the conjunction of other qualities" (2.1.1.4). Book 2 is mostly an account of the causes and mechanics of the indirect passions.

*The Indirect Passions.* The indirect passions, described as natural impulses insepa-rable from the soul, were Hume's original contribution. This makes sense given that their causes, which reflected his unique principles of association, were not evident in earlier discussions of the passions. The natural (though not original) cause of an indirect passion—say pride, for example—was distinct from its object, the self (*T*, 2.3.1.1–5). The indirect passion was always in "conjunction" (2.1.1.4), "succession," and "proportion" (2.1.2.3) with other perceptions, impulses, and ideas. If Hume's theory of ideas was a reflective consideration of our perception-based imaginative associations that highlighted human nature as well as the limi-tations of the mind (and abstruse philosophy), then his theory of the passions was a reflective emphasis on the structure of perceptive experience as it was channeled through the mind and manifested in our sentiment-based behaviors modified through participation in common life. Hume wrote, "The passions are often vary'd by very inconsiderable principles; and these do not always play with a perfect regularity, especially on the first trial. But as custom and practice have brought to light all these principles, and have settled the just value of everything; this must certainly contribute to the easy production of the passions and guide us, by means of general establish'd maxims, in the proportions we ought to observe in prefer-ring one object to another" (2.1.6.9).

Hume's "cautious observation" of the indirect passions, which he listed as "pride, humility, ambition, vanity, love, hatred, envy, pity, malice, generosity" (*T*, 2.1.1.4) obligated him—on the grounds of his science—to "pretend a description of them" or to shed light on both their genesis and their revelation. In service of this task, he established that the passions had an object and that the unique object of the indirect passions was the self.[17] Thus, for a passion to be classified as indi-rect, its cause had to be distinguishable from its object. For example, the cause of the indirect-passion pride could be, say, successfully closing a business deal, which "turns our view" (2.1.2.4) toward the self, an object distinct from the cause. The vast majority of book 2 canvassed the indirect passions of pride, humility, love, and hatred (which could be violent or calm), the objects of which were "something real, not something to be realized, and it makes no sense to talk of [them] as satisfied by the realization of [their] object."[18]

*The Direct Passions.* Direct passions were named "direct" because they directed us toward good and away from evil, both the aim and original stimulus of the pas-sion (*T*, 2.3.9.2).[19] The cause of a *direct* passion was its object, whereas, the cause of an *indirect* passion was distinct from its object. For example—and here I am paraphrasing and revising Hume's example from 2.3.9.25—if we have some sense that our child may be in danger we experience a mixture of direct-passions "desire and aversion, grief and joy, hope and fear along with volition" (2.3.9.2). The probability, and its particular kind ("uncertain, and to be determined by chance" or "certain, yet 'tis uncertain to our judgment" (2.3.9.20) [that is, we do not yet know about its certainty]), determine which of the direct passions will manifest with the most vivacity. Note the Newtonian mechanics at work again: the activation of a direct passion is mostly predictable and machinelike. The machinery, however, can be tweaked and the passions recalibrated. In other words, the strength of the seven direct passions Hume identifies are modifiable based on probability, proximity to their object, and the customs and conventions of common life. We learn how to modify them through a more acute understanding of how they originate and function, which we can pursue through the passion of hope, for "none of the direct affections seem to merit our particular attention, except hope and fear, which we shall here endeavour to account for" (2.3.9.9).

Similar to his philosophical predecessors, Hume described hope as a direct passion that arose "immediately from good and evil" (*T*, 2.1.1.4). By situating the direct-passion hope in a particular matrix of thoroughly natural causes (an "impression which [arose] from good and evil most naturally, and with the least preparation" [2.3.9.2]), Hume effectively disconnected hope from its status as a God-given virtue, a feature of Divine Revelation, or an act of Christian grace. This was a resilient move against the beliefs of popular and revealed religion. Hume was not simply being crafty by defining the passions as fully natural, historically conditioned, and culturally specific. He was indirectly undermining at least three ways that popular religion and false philosophy had traditionally deployed the concept of hope. First, hope had been confined to the purview of Christianity by those who had faith in the existence of heaven and the afterlife (e.g., Warburton). Second, hope had been relegated to the realm of religion by those who believed in miracles (e.g., Clarke). And third, hope was said to emanate naturally from bodily sensations (e.g., Descartes) yet somehow be controlled by an infinite God. Hume's conception of hope exposed Christian hopes for the afterlife, miracle-induced hopes of vulgar religion, and hopes tied to the flow of spirits through the brain (Descartes's "pineal gland") as illusory. Hope, on his view, was circumscribed by and activated within common experience, which was always social and historical. Hume exposed the Christian hope for heaven and miracles to be based on a human desire, *not* a divine mandate. This natural desire for the good was dictated by mysterious "springs and principles" and "general rules" of nature that guided the mind. Neither divinely implanted nor religiously encoded, direct-passion hopes were human-driven aims for probable, positive change in response to particular experiences. To Hume, all the passions, particularly hope, aided human functioning. They did not require remedy. The need to do so was indicated by how they informed our happiness, which was, in part, a social determination for "we can form no wish, which has not reference to society" (2.2.5.15).

Hume clarified his classification of the direct-passion hopes and fears with the reminder that these passions were always inspired by objects, events, and circumstances that provoked either the desire for or aversion toward their reoccurrence in the future. If achievement of the desired circumstances was *certain*, then the direct passions of "joy" or "grief" were activated (*T*, 2.3.9.9). That is, the possibility for hope or fear relies on *uncertainty*, the strong degree of probability that makes joy and grief less likely. For example, joy is the direct-passion sentiment someone feels when a highly pleasurable event recently occurred or is presently occurring. If the event had not yet transpired, but it was more than likely to do so (i.e., it was probable), the sentiment experienced is not joy but hope. The direct-passion hope originated with a pleasurable event or object, it required the event's or object's future uncertainty (probability), and it relied on desire for that event or object in the future.[20] Joy, however, was constituted simply by a pending (certain) pleasurable event (probability was not a factor). Direct-passion hope was rooted in a belief based on the future probability of good, a probability that was the result of one of two predicaments: when an "object is really in itself uncertain" or when "the object be already certain, yet 'tis uncertain to our judgment" (2.3.9.20).

## DELIBERATION AND THE DIRECT PASSIONS

Enlightenment theories of the passions generally aimed to remedy the seemingly irrepressible energies of the passions through practical reason. Hume, however, neither venerated reason nor was alarmed by the intensity of the passions. Instead of trying to reposition reason over the passions or attempting to revise the relationship between passions and actions, he highlighted the origin and function of the passions in the same way that he investigated the origin and function of our ideas. Hume's science of human nature was neither threatened by the passions nor invested in commandeering them for some higher purpose. His patient acceptance of these (sometimes) violent passions was itself an example of a "calm passion." Calm passions were not weak ones, for "generally speaking, the violent passions have a more powerful influence on the will; tho' 'tis often found, that the calm ones, when corroborated by reflection, and seconded by resolution, are able to controul them in their most furious movements" (*T*, 2.3.8.13). Violent passions generated jittery and uneasy feelings, while calm passions produced feelings of ease and "strength of mind" (2.3.3.16).[21] The proximity of a passion to its object distinguished it, for "a variation in this particular [was] able to change the calm and the violent passions into each other." Hume continued, "Both these kinds of passions pursue good, and avoid evil; and both of them are encreas'd or diminish'd by the increase or diminution of the good or evil. But herein lies the difference betwixt them: The same good, when near, will cause a *violent* passion, which, when remote, produces only a *calm* one" (2.3.4.1; italics added).

Generally, Hume believed that the calm passions led to proper coordination between human beings and more effective social conventions. These conventions inspired social stability and personal happiness. The violent passions made stability and happiness more difficult to realize because they discouraged successful coordination between persons. This was due to the fact that individual behavior was steadier when guided by calm passions, a balance that provoked our aesthetic sensibilities. Note Hume's description of the calm passions as "the *sense of beauty and deformity* in action, composition, and external objects" (*T*, 2.1.1.3; italics added).[22] The calm passions were crucial for developing "greatness of mind" or "magnanimity" (*EPM*, 7.4), the chief characteristic of the true philosopher (and a quality that Adam Smith admitted was one of Hume's most well-developed traits). In Hume's own words, "strength of mind, implies the prevalence of the calm passions above the violent" (*T*, 2.3.3.16).[23] Due to their steady and constant quality, Hume admitted that the calm passions were often mistaken for reason. Unlike reason, however, calm passions were sources of behavior. Humans did not have the volitional power to control their actions through an act of will. To Hume, it was only through active participation in reflective common life—with its artifices, customs, and conventions—that our violent passions might transition to calmer ones. "Custom," Hume wrote, "must certainly guide us, by means of general establish'd maxims, in the proportions we ought to observe in preferring one object to another" (2.1.6.9). I take this to mean that collective awareness of a passion and its affiliated object over a significant stretch of time could reveal the dynamic relations between an object and a passion to be dysfunctional or its passion to be too strong. In other words, custom would ultimately disclose the suitable level of energy (calm or violent) required for the appropriate object, and convention would finally divulge the most functional object of a properly calibrated passion. It seems that calm passions are strong (firm, but not violent) as a result of the shared feeling generated by sympathy of persons operating from a general point of view, and they are less agitated than the violent ones because custom had rendered their ends either more distant or less familiar.[24]

Hume applied the direct-passion hopes and fears from his philosophical work to his analysis of religion. In the *Natural History of Religion* he argued that vulgar or popular religion arose when contemplation of "unknown causes" of experience "became the object of our hope and fear" and kept our passions agitated and "in perpetual alarm" (3.1). Similarly, in his essay "Of Miracles," Hume described the popular religious believer, monk, and "itinerant or stationary teacher" as armed with a false narrative and a set of delusions that aimed at the "gross and vulgar passions" of his listeners (*E*, 10.2.5). In his essay "Of Superstition," he explicitly rooted "superstition and enthusiasm . . . two species of false religion" in the passions: "weakness, fear, melancholy, together with ignorance, are, therefore, the true sources of SUPERSTITION" and "hope, pride, presumption, a warm imagination, together with ignorance, are, therefore, the true sources of ENTHUSIASM" (note both indirect and direct passions in each). Hume characterized the incipient energies of enthusiasm as "furious and violent." He contended that they were founded on "strong spirits and a presumptuous boldness of character" that produced "the most cruel disorders in human society." Enthusiasm, for Hume, was similar to "thunder and tempest," which fizzled out quickly and "left the air more calm and serene than before" (*EMPL*, 10.77). Hume left no question: he believed false religion was endowed by direct passions, particularly the more agitated hopes and fears. It follows that true religion—in the rare circumstances it might appear—would be based on calm passions, for he writes that the "corruptions of true religion" can be diluted by the "calm sunshine of the mind" (*NHR*, 14.8). But how might this occur? By what mechanism could a violent passion become calm?

Scholars generally agree that in Hume's schema the violent passions, both direct and indirect, can be moderated, their ends shifted, and the actions they inspire altered. There is extensive discussion, however, about *how* this happens. Are transitions in the passions reflective of a change in the means we take to the objects and ends or simply a shift in the objects and ends themselves? Is the shift from a violent to a calm passion driven by practical reason or self-interest? Or might it be guided by authoritative norms or other natural tendencies and personal dispositions? The philosophical conversation around these issues has become quite intricate and somewhat convoluted, yet it is important to at least grasp its basic contours. I describe, briefly and in broad strokes, some interpretations of the mechanics of the passions to illuminate some contemporary philosophical approaches to how we might moderate the direct-passion hope.

In the set of lecture notes he disseminated to his students for more than twenty years (finally published in 2000 as *Lectures on the History of Moral Philosophy*), John Rawls patiently interrogated Hume's theory of the passions. He took Hume to hold practical reason to be a complex form of deliberation that could impact the passions in at least five ways: "Two [of these ways] consist[ed] of corrections to adjust the passions to true (or well-grounded) beliefs; three others [we]re specifying, scheduling, and weighting [of the passion]." On Rawls's account, violent passions were neither moderated by the normative authority of reason, nor regulated by valid judgments. Instead, they could be calmed by a thick deliberation that took into account practical reason and sociopolitical ends, as well as history, mood, temperament, and tradition. We learn this deliberation through practice (like playing an instrument, the more we do it, the easier it becomes) and the more successful deliberations we have, the stronger our calm passion for it becomes. Rawls wrote, "In persons of strength of mind, the calm passions have a central place in the total configuration of their passions and have taken control of the powers of rational thought."[25] The habit of deliberation, then, is an effective hindrance to the wily, broad range of the imagination. Deliberation enables calm passions.

Christine Korsgaard—trained under Rawls—pushed this point to its logical limit. She argued, "Hume sometimes seemed to think . . . that the authority of our reasons for action must be derived from the strength of our desires."[26] If I understand her correctly, Korsgaard accepts that Hume's passions were partially constituted by an instrumental reason whose authority (always a part of the passion and proportionally related to its strength) was the source of our actions. This meant that an action, on Hume's account, could never be "irrational" (though an action could be based on false beliefs). Thus Korsgaard pressed, "How can there be rational action, in any sense, if there is no irrational action?" For Korsgaard truly rational agents are motivated by the recognition that their mind had appropriately linked their beliefs and desires. Hume denied this type of rational necessity between beliefs, desires, and actions. Thus, to Korsgaard, Hume's thought suggested that "there is no such thing as practical reason at all." Her point was to raise the question about how, on Hume's argument, our actions could be guided by an instrumental principle, internalism requirement, practical reason, or deliberation. If they could not—and she has a hard time finding the resources in Hume that allow the requisite separation of a person's actions from their ends—then Hume's model of the passions is overdetermined by mechanical processes of association. "Desire, fear, indolence, and whim shape the Humean agent's ends, and, through them, her actions. When her passions change, her ends change, and when her ends change, so do her actions."[27] It follows that the transition from a violent passion to a calm one in Hume's thought is, for Korsgaard, largely unpredictable.

Against these rationalist interpretations, Annette Baier reads Hume as a psychological naturalist regarding the passions. Reminiscent of and largely dependent on Kemp Smith's reading of Hume's theory of ideas, Baier interprets Hume's contribution to the passions as a skeptical acknowledgment about the role of both practical reason and principle-dependent passions when it came to our beliefs and actions. Hume, she suggests, was making a psychological argument about association, that is, one that was interested not in regulating passions but in demonstrating how they were informed by complicated natural forces and shaped by customs and the imagination. For Baier, Hume's main interest was to reconcile these passions with our beliefs. He did so, she claimed, by walking us through the formation and progression of the psychological elements of subjective experience. Hume's patient description of these elements inspired Baier to observe that the violent passions had both proximity to their objects and a "frequent disharmony with other passions."[28] From this, we might reasonably presume that calm passions were not simply less agitated, distant from the object, and collective in their sympathy, but also somehow (temporarily) free of emotions. Baier acknowledged that though reason was subordinate to the passions when it came to our actions, morals still "excite[d] passions, and produce[d] or prevent[ed] actions" (*T*, 3.1.1.6). For Baier, and I concur with her position, the passions were calmed by a natural, psychological, and partially mysterious process.

MODERATE PASSIONS AND FUNDAMENTAL HOPE

A background hope patiently propels the *Treatise* and first *Enquiry* forward. This hope, however, is not amenable to Hume's description of hope as a direct passion that arises "from good and evil most naturally, and with the least preparation." Neither does it function as a direct passion in Hume's system (its cause is not its object). The hope built in to the attitude and background of the *Treatise* was less object-driven and more moderate than the direct-passion hopes Hume described. The objects of these special hopes were distant yet familiar, their energy firm and stable. Perhaps we can label these modest, open, and forward-looking hopes of the true philosopher as calm passions (for Hume) or fundamental hopes (for Godfrey).

*Hume's Fundamental Hope.* Godfrey's "fundamental hope" was an "objectless hope," "a hope without aim which is a tone or basic disposition with which one faces the future."[29] The moderate hope in Hume's writings corresponds with this. Though Hume was explicit about his philosophical hopes he made no argument for them, nor did he buttress his commitment to hope with facts or premises. This hope energy was revealed by the general temperament of his writing, displayed in his sense of civic progress and character development, and exposed as a logical outcome of the calm passions.[30] Hume's philosophical hope was neither a cheap optimism—that is, a mere expectation that the outcome will be in one's favor—nor a strong desire. It did not trouble itself with the far future or deeply invest in an object (as direct-passion hopes did). Thus, while it shares qualities with the calm passions, its objectless expectancy make it more akin to Godfrey's fundamental hope.

Is this moderate hope too general to be defined as hope or too commonplace to be worthy of serious mention? Does a disposition that silently accepts the future implicitly animate most philosophical writings? I take the latter question first: an implicit premise—if this moderate hope were simply one—should invite more rigorous analysis, not less. Second, we must take Hume at his word. This moderate hope in the *Treatise* is not only an "implicit premise" for Hume's argument but also an explicit basis for his claims. A close reading of the *Treatise* requires the careful reader to attend to two kinds of hope: direct-passion hope and fundamental hope (the latter closely resembles, but does not have the object attachment of a calm passion). When Hume wants to discuss direct-passion hopes, he uses the words "hope" and "fear" together. Yet when he displays the more moderate hope, it is detached from the term "fear." Examples of this include the following:

> I am not, however, without *hopes* that the present system of philosophy will acquire new force as it advances. (3.1.1.1)

> Where experiments of this kind are judiciously collected and compared, we may *hope* to establish on them a science, which will not be inferior in certainty, and will be much superior in utility to any other of human comprehension. (*T*, introd., 10)

> But were these hypotheses once remov'd, we might *hope* to establish a system or set of opinions, which if not true (for that, perhaps is too much to be hop'd for) might at least be satisfactory to the human mind, and might stand the test of the most critical examination. (1.4.7.14)

> I am sensible, that of all the paradoxes, which I have had or shall hereafter have occasion to advance in the course of this treatise, the present one is the most violent, and that 'tis merely by dint of solid proof and reasoning I can ever *hope* it will have admission, and overcome the inveterate prejudices of mankind. (1.3.14.23)

> The true state of the question is, whether every object, which begins to exist, must owe its existence to a cause; and this I assert neither to be intuitively nor demonstratively certain, and *hope* to have prov'd it sufficiently by the foregoing arguments. (1.3.3.8)

I take the articulation of moderate hope in these passages as an intentional representation of Hume's modest philosophical hope. Like a calm passion, it is "secure, unconflicting, regularly satisfied and demanding no sacrifice."[31] Critics might contend that these examples of hope speech actually service an aim, drive toward an object, and therefore qualify as direct passions, not simply calm ones. Admittedly, in many ways, Hume's moderate hopes do seem to correlate with a calm, direct passion. Reducing Hume's moderate hopes to a calm passion as described, however, conceals the degree to which moderate hope "may embrace ends, but its nature and power are largely independent of them."[32] It also obfuscates Hume's explicit description of the calm passions, which never includes hope. These hopes read more like Godfrey's fundamental hope than they do as a direct passion, even a calm one. They are not fixated on an aim, and they express an open disposition toward the future. Moderate hope is confident that the future will be what it will. This tempered, quiet hope fits with genuine theism and endures as a naturally derived equipoise in the face of life's vicissitudes. It may have a loose and largely unspecifiable expectation but it is not driven by this expectation, and, even more important, "it can live beyond its disappointment without a reduction in quality of life."[33]

Hume explicitly described direct-passion hopes *and* he mentioned a modest, fundamental hope in the *Treatise*. This was indicative of his overall approach, which tied his self-styled descriptive and critical emphasis with a mild constructivist and generative project. Hume was comfortable sharing his observations of human beings in common life, and he had no trouble giving mild, humble suggestions that might gently inspire the reader to self-actualization. His explicit situating of hope as a direct passion was important: it liberated hope from supernatural sources and showed popular religion to be a human enterprise. At the same time, his enacting a controlled and moderated hope provided a forward energy or purposiveness to his science. This moderate hope, when considered alongside genuine theism and practical morality, provides us with some possible content for the proper office of religion.

## Hope in Hume's Religious Writings

I was, I say, a man of mild disposition, of command of temper,
of an open, social, and cheerful humor, capable of attachment, but little susceptible of enmity, and of great moderation
in all my passions.
—*My Own Life*, para 22

Given the vast potential for harmful action, violence, and factionalism of superstition and enthusiasm, Hume recognized that direct-passion hopes required by traditional Christian dogma (false religion) were dangerous. Additionally, he abhorred the addictive hope that often became a toxin of its own, given its requirement for larger doses of itself to satisfy the terms of its illusion. From his earliest work Hume mildly hoped that we might create conditions that allowed us to moderate our passions. Our speculative true religion—a form of meliorism—is both spawned by and a facilitator of those conditions. In this part of the chapter,

I look closely at the relationship between the passions and religion in Hume's religious writings to support my argument that Hume's work inspires the idea that a moderate hope might serve as a constitutive feature of our Humean true religion.

The most productive period in Hume's career, 1749 to 1763, saw the publication of the six-volume *History of England* (published over a period of eight years, 1754–62); the *Enquiry Concerning the Principles of Morals* (1751, a reworking of book 3 of the *Treatise*); the *Political Discourses* (1752); the *Four Dissertations* (1757, of which the *Natural History of Religion* is part); and the four-volume *Essays and Treatises on Several Subjects* (1753–56). This was also the era where Hume wrote early drafts of the *Dialogues Concerning Natural Religion* (1779). While these works were marked by a slight but important shift in method and emphasis from the earlier *Treatise* (1739) and first *Enquiry* (1748), it is fair to say that they maintained Hume's two types of hope: hope he defined as a direct passion (the opposite of fear) and the fundamental hope that operated in the background of his work.

Until 1748, the year of the first printing of the *Philosophical Essays*, Hume deftly used empirical observation for his science of human nature.[34] His approach was mostly synchronic in this phase, as he described our beliefs and behaviors as naturally grounded in common life, the passions, the imagination. After 1748 Hume extended his philosophical framework along a broader trajectory. In this period, his aim was to assess the science of human nature diachronically, that is, to see how it played out across time and to test whether the theory explicated in his first two philosophical works could be used as the theoretical framework for his narrative historical project. To do this, Hume turned his concerns to the more expansive development of human society and the ideas endemic to it. This historical phase of Hume's writing is seminal for understanding his overall project, particularly its constructive elements.

In spite of this slight shift in emphasis, it is clear that much in Hume's thought remained consistent throughout both phases. His central interest in uncovering the sources of our beliefs and behaviors persisted, and his investment in affirming the limits of human reason continued. As these similarities indicate, the division of Hume's career into two phases might best be understood as a heuristic device that more poignantly draws our attention to his historical emphasis over his philosophical arguments.[35] Here I consider two compositions of the more historical phase of Hume's writings that explicitly focus on religion: the *Natural History of Religion* and the *Dialogues Concerning Natural Religion*. Given my larger intention to build on Hume's tacit suggestion for religion, I assess these works to examine the relationship between Hume's theory of the passions and his description of religion. I argue that his religious writings confirmed that direct-passion hopes were the source of popular religion and the moderate, fundamental hopes informed the proper office of religion.

The 1757 *NHR* is Hume's investigation of the "origin in human nature" of religion (*NHR*, introd.). It aimed to provide a historical account of the development of the religious ideal in human society. Beneath this aim, Hume applied his speculative framework from the *Treatise* to the history of human religiosity. Part social psychology, part philosophy of religion, and part history, the *NHR* gave a lucid account of Hume's dual uses of hope. The *NHR* was not simply an outright attack on the argument from design, as many interpreters suggest; rather, it was an attempt to locate direct-passion hopes as the source of popular religion. Additionally, the conception of history that informed Hume's narrative approach was cast in the mode of fundamental hope that pervaded Hume's thought. Finally, Hume implied a notion of true religion in the text of the *NHR*. I discuss these facets of the *NHR* and others in the first section that follows.

*Dialogues Concerning Natural Religion* (*DCNR*; published posthumously in 1779) is arguably the crowning achievement of Hume's career. Using the dialogue form, the work is best known for its critical discussion of the argument from design. My interest is in the type of hope the characters display and how this hope informs their ideas about religion. The literary form of the *DCNR* was crucial to its content, and we are mistaken if we frame our reading of this report of a conversation as if one single character represented Hume. In its form and substance—its discussion of piety, the a priori argument, the a posteriori argument, and finally its mentions of true religion—it presents a rich discussion of religion and an inspiring deployment of moderate hope in service of true religion. The concluding section details the *DCNR*.

## The Natural History of Religion

Hume's *Natural History of Religion* was first published along with three short essays as *Four Dissertations* on February 7, 1757. A narrative historical and scholarly treatment, the *NHR* was quite different from the other essays. To Ernest Campbell Mossner, the *NHR* was a study of the psychological basis of religion that arrived well ahead of its time. He wrote, "the problem presented [in it] is essentially modern, and to Hume should go the credit for being the first great modern to treat of it systematically."[36] Keith Yandell has argued that Hume's approach in this text was not only unique but also articulated more clearly here than in any of Hume's other works. To Yandell, this makes the *NHR* the "key to understanding Hume's philosophy of religion."[37] The text is now a classic: many take it to be Hume's seminal philosophical views distilled into a short volume on religion.

The standard reading of the *NHR*, repeated in countless overviews of Hume's work on religion, is fixated with establishing it as directly oppositional to the argument from design.[38] While there is a kernel of truth to this interpretation, it overemphasizes Hume's critical project and overlooks his explicit commitment to expose the origins of religion. Certainly the *NHR* contested central components of the argument from design, but the conventional reading exaggerates the degree and effect of this contestation. Still, it supplies three important insights: first, that Hume believed religion originated not in observation of nature, reflection on the cosmos, or unique revelation from the divine, but in human feeling. This renders our rational perception of design in nature—understood by deists as the source of religion—as fruitless for the grounds of religious belief. Second, it demonstrates that Hume thought polytheism preceded monotheism. This weakens the argument from design, for if history shows that the God of the theists (a single, powerful, and intelligent God) appeared *after* a set of polytheistic gods had been embraced by humans, then the argument from design (that reflection on nature proves just *one* intelligent, omnipotent God) is critically weakened. And, third, the standard reading suggests that Hume undermined the traditional argument from design on sociological and moral grounds. The logic for this position is Hume's contention in the *NHR* that monotheism was the basis of social discord. Traditional interpretations of the text conclude that the social ineffectiveness of religion fully undermines the argument from design by stipulating that if religion were natural, it would have a positive effect on society. Conventional assessments of the *NHR* misread religion to be the equivalent of monotheism and incorrectly conclude that Hume thought religion was always damaging to society.

Still, the conventional reading is correct in many of its points. When, however, it uses the sum of these points to conclude that the *NHR* was primarily concerned with attacking the argument from design, weakening rational appeals to natural religion, and confirming Hume's irreligion, it goes too far. The *NHR* did not argue against our disposition to assume "invisible, intelligent power." It did not deny the practical import of religious beliefs and rituals. It did not prove that Hume despised all forms of religion at all times. Over the past twenty years, a more nuanced contextualization of the *NHR* in Hume's overall thought has materialized. These secondary texts keep track of Hume's mitigated skepticism, his philosophy of the imagination, and his commitment to true philosophy and reflective common life. They generally confirm that the *NHR* established the direct passions as the source of popular religion, that it introduced a nonlinear conception of human history, and that it conjured (by default) the proper office of religion. This contextualization of the *NHR* in Hume's wider philosophy clarifies that direct-passion hopes and fears were the source of false religion. It also makes permissible our provisional claim that the proper office of religion might be constituted by a moderate hope.

## THE ESTABLISHMENT OF THE DIRECT PASSIONS

It is generally agreed that the aims, contents, and strategies of the *NHR* were largely circumscribed and defined by the *Treatise* and the first *Enquiry*. In fact, Hume gestured toward the *Treatise* in the first paragraph of the *NHR* when he wrote, "The first religious principles must be secondary; such as may easily be perverted by various accidents and causes, and whose operation too, in some cases, may, by an extraordinary concurrence of circumstances, be altogether prevented" (*NHR*, introd.). This sentence was a restatement of Hume's idea that the passions were secondary impressions of reflection, not instincts.

To reassure the reader that the source of vulgar or popular religion was not an instinct, Hume wrote, "It would appear, therefore, that this preconception springs not from an original instinct or primary impression of nature such as gives rise to self-love, affection between the sexes, love of progeny, gratitude, resentment; since every instinct of this kind has been found absolutely universal in all nations and ages, and has always a precise determinate object, which it inflexibly pursues. The first religious principles must be secondary" (*NHR*, introd.).

False religion depended on a secondary or reflective passion, what Hume had previously named a direct-passion hope and described as driving toward a probable, future object that it had naturally associated with the good. From its opening paragraph, then, the *NHR* was safely ensconced within the framework of Humean science, and popular religion was linked to the direct-passion continuum of hope and fear. When perceptions excited their particular continuum, the passions mechanically pushed and pulled against one another until one was pronounced with greater clarity and resonance than the other. This explains how "the first ideas of religion arose not from a contemplation of the works of nature, but from a concern with regard to the events of life, and from the incessant hopes and fears which actuate the human mind" (2.4). Hume put special emphasis on this argument in the *NHR*: "agitated by hopes and fears of this nature, these unknown causes, then, become the constant object of our hope and fear" (2.5) and "any of the human affections may lead us into the notion of invisible, intelligent power; hope as well as fear" (3.4). Later in the text, he returned to this point: "the unknown causes are still appealed to on every emergence; and in this general appearance or confused image, are the perpetual objects of human hopes and fears" (8.1).

Since violent passions were agitated and anxious, Hume slightly modified his description of the direct-passions hope and fear and sometimes replaced them with the descriptive phrase "anxious concern" for future happiness. He stated,

"No wonder, then, that mankind, being placed in such an absolute ignorance of causes, and being at the same time so anxious concerning their future fortune, should immediately acknowledge a dependence on invisible powers, possessed of sentiment and intelligence" (*NHR*, 3.2). Employing this phrase again, he claimed, "As the *causes*, which bestow happiness or misery, are, in general, very little known and very uncertain, our anxious concern endeavours to attain a determinate idea of them" (5.9). And to further drive the point home, he wrote, "But the same anxious concern for happiness, which begets the idea of these invisible, intelligent powers, allows not mankind to remain long in the first simple conception of them" (8.2).

The *NHR* firmly established direct-passions hope and fear as sources of popular religion and thereby showed that popular religion was not an instinct; our disposition for it originated in human nature and secondary impressions of reflection. By keeping religious belief in the realm of the natural and the human, Hume accomplished two tasks: he demonstrated that humans were not made in the image of God (they did not have a divine spark for religion), and he positioned religion fully within the secular history of humanity so that he could interrogate the complexity of religious belief. With religion fully analyzable as a social and psychological (as well as a symbolic and imaginative) activity of humans in time, place, and culture, Hume could trace its *natural* origins and development.

## HUME'S PHILOSOPHY OF HISTORY IN THE *NHR*

There are two primary starting points to Hume's philosophy of history as articulated in the *NHR*. First, as Edward Craig has argued in *The Mind of God and the Image of Man*, Hume shunned all Biblical conceptions of man as a creature made in God's image, and he rejected the theological idea of Adamic man as fallen from paradise. In other words, Hume did not embrace the idea that history was fundamentally the work of divinity. He understood himself to be a *natural historian*; therefore he focused on all visible, evident, and obvious motivations for human belief and activity. Like Voltaire and Montesquieu, he took the study of history to be a secular assessment of human and natural possibilities. Further, he did not assume, as did Turgot and Condorcet, that the current historical moment represented the highest phase of human development. Hume's approach to history was humble and moderate, prone to fits and starts, and unwilling to interpret certain historical moments as necessarily more valuable than others. In this regard, Hume provided a reasonably balanced sense of the past.

A sound and persuasive investigation of the origins of religion in human nature required both his well-developed sense of human nature and his balanced historical sensibility. The theory of the passions grounded his notion of human nature and the principles that guided it. To apply these theoretical insights regarding principles of human nature to the origins of religion, he needed a conception of history that could effectively illustrate how both human nature and religion manifested in and through time. The task was to be able to keep in view the constant and universal springs and principles that guided the human mind and, simultaneously, capture the sense of change that was part and parcel of the human journey through history. Hume described this type of dualism in relation to the faculty of the imagination: "To justify myself, I must distinguish in the imagination betwixt the principles which are permanent, irresistible, and universal; . . . and the principles, which are changeable, weak, and irregular" (*T*, 1.4.4.1).

In the *NHR* he displayed his historical conception through the dynamic movement between the "flux and reflux" of mono- and polytheism. Hume was not primarily interested in making a theological point, so he neither systematically defined religion nor formally explained monotheism or polytheism. His point was a historical one: that polytheism *preceded* monotheism in the development of religion. The evidence he cited to support this was that almost two thousand years ago "all mankind were polytheists" (1.2), and now most did not claim to be. That polytheism evolved into monotheism achieved two immediate victories for Hume: first, it destroyed the version of the argument from design that asserted observation of the "frame of nature" led us to "belief of *one* Supreme Being" (1.7; italics added) worthy of worship. Second, it portends the movement of Hume's philosophy of history, what he names "flux and reflux," a temperate back and forth that is patient yet does not long, that is circular without expectation. Its purposiveness is toward balance, consistency, and regularity. In other words, the drive of the religious idea in history from polytheism to monotheism is not a linear movement or progressive development in human society; it is perennially cyclical. "It is remarkable, that the principles of religion have a kind of flux and reflux in the human mind, and that men have a natural tendency to rise from idolatry to theism, and to sink again from theism into idolatry" (8.1). Hume, as Mossner concluded, "accepts neither the idea of decay nor the idea of progress, but believes in the possibility of both."[39] We might say that in its orientation to the future, Hume's philosophy of history reflected the disposition of moderate hope—it was gently open to the future as it unfolded, and it asserted no strong drive to an object. Probable, but mostly unlikely, Hume's moderate hope was fully conditioned and thoroughly historical.

HUME'S POSITIVE DESCRIPTION OF RELIGION

Though Hume did not use the term "true religion" explicitly in this text (he did mention genuine theism), the *NHR* implicitly suggested the proper office of religion. That is, Hume directly attended to vulgar religion, popular religion, and superstition while he implied their opposite, true religion.[40] The majority of humankind was vulgar and adhered to false religion. "The vulgar, that is, indeed, all mankind, a few excepted, being ignorant and uninstructed, never elevate their contemplation of the heavens, or penetrate by their disquisitions into the secret structure of vegetable or animal bodies; so far as to discover a supreme mind or original providence, which bestowed order on every part of nature" (8.1). The adherents of false religion are "ignorant of astronomy and the anatomy of plants and animals, and too little curious to observe the admirable adjustment of final causes; they remain still unacquainted with a first and supreme creator, and with that infinitely perfect spirit, who alone, by his almighty will, bestowed order on the whole frame of nature" (3.3).

These quotations confirm that Hume believed most of humankind, except a few, to be vulgar and to embrace popular religion. There were numerous instances in the *NHR* where he used the term "vulgar" to describe humankind in general and "vulgar religion" or "superstition" to describe popular religion. For example, "as an invisible spiritual intelligence is an object too refined for vulgar apprehension, men naturally affix it to some sensible representation" (5.9).[41] Additionally, he added, "it may safely be affirmed, that popular religions are really, in the conception of their more vulgar votaries, a species of daemonism" (13.6) and "*barbarity, caprice* . . . we may universally observe, form the ruling character of the deity in popular religions" (14.8). Hume contended throughout the text that the direct passions led the masses to embrace the beliefs of vulgar religion. These masses then attempted to recruit abstruse philosophy to sanction vulgar religion as rationally grounded and to legitimate its beliefs in common life. Hume was troubled by this. He was clear that even though we have a "universal propensity to believe in invisible, intelligent power" (not an "original instinct"), if we "consult this image, as it appears in the *popular religions* of the world . . . the deity [is] disfigured in our representations of him" and "degraded even below the character, which we should naturally, in common life, ascribe to a man of sense and virtue!" (15.5; italics added). Hume was troubled by the fact that the direct-passion hopes and fears drove us toward the beliefs and "depraved ideas" (14.8) of popular religion. The "[f]eeble apprehensions of men cannot be satisfied with conceiving their deity as a pure spirit and perfect intelligence; and yet their natural terrors keep them from imputing to him the least shadows of limitation and imperfection. They fluctuate between these opposite sentiments" (8.2).

Hume also showed that the moderation of our direct passions could lead to a more humble form of religion that quietly operated in the background of our lives and informed our character development. This is Hume's positive idea of religion, attainable only by a select few who elevated their reflections on the heavens and discovered a "supreme mind or original providence." But how does one do this, and what effect does this discovery have upon them? Hume regards this as an

exceptional occurrence, and while he does not explain how it occurs, he accepts it
as a benefit: "What a noble privilege it is of human reason to attain the knowledge
of the Supreme Being; and, from the visible works of nature, be enabled to infer so
sublime a principle as its supreme Creator?" (*NHR*, 15.6). And what are the effects
and consequences of the discovery of the "supreme mind" by those who have this
"noble privilege"? Again, Hume gives us little on this. Yet we may be able to glean
a bit about the contours of true religion from his description of what vulgar religion destroys. For example, he writes that a "manly, steady virtue" (14.8) is undermined by superstition. On my argument, such virtue must be preserved and even
enhanced by religion's proper office. Additionally, because vulgar religion produces in its adherents feelings of "protection and safety in this world, and eternal
happiness in the next," it is likely the case that the proper office of religion does not
do so. The proper office of religion inspires confidence to accept that the future will
be what it will be. Its (few) adherents, then, would possess the disposition of openness and the energy of acceptance.

A year prior to the publication of the *Four Dissertations*, Hume, in response to
criticism of his claims in the first volume of the *History* that the Roman Catholic
Church exhibited superstition and that the Protestant Reformers were "enthusi-
asts," explicitly mentioned "true and genuine piety" in the preface to the second
volume of his *History of England*. Later shortened and reduced to a footnote, the
original text read,

> It ought to be no matter of offence, that in this volume, as well as in the fore-
> going, the Mischiefs which arise from the abuses of Religion, are so often
> mentioned, while so little in comparison is said of the salutary Consequences
> which result from true and genuine Piety. The *proper Office of Religion* is to
> reform Men's Lives, to purify their Hearts, to enforce all moral Duties, and to
> secure Obedience to the Laws and civil Magistrate. While it pursues these
> useful purposes, its Operations, tho' infinitely valuable, are secret and silent;
> and seldom come under the Cognizance of History.[42]

The *NHR* leaves us with a powerful sense that a Humean-inspired true religion
would be of some practical social and political use; it also confirms that it would
be funded by a moderation of the passions.

## The *Dialogues Concerning Natural Religion*

The distinguishing feature that sets the *DCNR* apart from the rest of Hume's corpus is that it is written as a book-length conversation. We have neither a first-
person commentary that explains Hume's precise intentions nor details regarding

exactly why he employed the dialogue form in what he knew would be his final publication, but we can reasonably conjecture that Cicero's *De natura deorum* (45 B.C.E.) taught Hume that narrating an artful conversation regarding religion could expose the complexity of questions regarding the nature of the gods, sanction the advancement of contradictory positions on theological questions, and permit the author to disguise personal views. The *DCNR* then, as a unique type of dialogue, presents its readers with complex interpretive issues around rhetorical strategies, dramatic details, and formal devices.

Hume wanted to investigate wide-ranging questions about human nature that might shed light on our beliefs and behaviors. We might identify him as a seeker driven by the love of wisdom who shunned what we now take to be "the rationalistic ideal of close analysis, mathematical clarity and economy and system building" that marked abstruse philosophy.[43] Later in his writing career, after he had achieved literary fame and financial security, he eschewed the so-called objective ordering of arguments and impersonal systems of thought abstracted from common life. He proudly and intentionally turned to the dialogue form. Later, in fact, just eleven days before his death, Hume described the *Dialogues* in a letter to his close friend Adam Smith as follows: "On revising them (which I have not done these 15 years) I find that nothing can be more cautiously and more artfully written" (*LET*, 2.334.538).

Hume's previous work, as I have argued, challenged abstract reason and false philosophy largely through *content* of argument. The *DCNR*, however, challenged abstract reason and false philosophy on the level of both *form* and *content*. Hume asserted in the *Treatise* and poignantly in section 1 of the first *Enquiry* that comprehending the relationship between religion and reason demanded the proper execution of a different kind of philoliterary approach. His deftly crafted *DCNR* was not an anomalous experiment that Hume toyed with; it was designed with clarity of purpose. Its fastidiousness of construction preserved the dynamic character of a series of conversations to make a mark on reflective common life. Hume's use of dialogue form may be a suggestion that he believed it to be the best form to represent the hopes and fears of time-drenched and tradition-bound humans reflecting on something just beyond the reaches of their understanding. And his particular use of form enlightens, paradoxically, by partially obscuring the questions.

The *DCNR* is Pamphillus's reporting of a conversation between Philo, Cleanthes, and Demea to his buddy Hermippus. Although Hermippus has no lines of his own in the text, we know—based on a statement by Pamphillus—that he has previously heard a telling of these conversations by Pamphillus.[44] So the context of the work is set: the *DCNR* is a re-reporting of an earlier conversation overheard by Pamphillus. Part of the genius of Hume's choice here (following Cicero) is that it leaves open the possibility that Pamphillus's rendering of the conversation may be faulty; his memory, intentions, or subconscious desires might shape his story; and he may even attribute certain statements to the wrong person. Unlike intellectual exchanges of abstract reason and false philosophy, which are direct, rigorous, and confrontational, Hume's dialogue is painted "in the most amiable colours; borrowing all helps from poetry and eloquence, and treat[ing] the subject in an easy and obvious manner . . . as is best fitted to please the imagination, and engage the affections" (*E*, 1.1).

Pamphillus offers the best description of the usefulness of the dialogue form in the opening statement:

> There are some subjects, however, to which dialogue-writing is peculiarly adapted, and where it is still preferable to the direct and simple method of composition . . . Any question of philosophy, on the other hand, which is so obscure and uncertain that human reason can reach no fixed determination with regard to it—if it should be treated at all—seems to lead us naturally in to the style of dialogue and conversation. Reasonable men may be allowed to differ where no one can reasonably be positive: Opposite sentiments, even without any decision, afford an agreeable amusement; and if the subject be curious and interesting, the book carries us, in a manner, into company, and unites the two greatest and purest pleasures of human life: study and society. (*DCNR*, introd., 2, 4)

William Sessions, one of the few writers on the *DCNR* who remains particularly mindful of the dynamic aspect of this form, builds on Pamphillus's worldview. He states, "Arguments in a dialogue are not strings of propositions but series of points and shadings that take different meanings as they are made by and to different people."[45] It is precisely these philoliterary nuances that have made the *DCNR* a challenge for interpreters.

## THE CHALLENGE OF THE FORM OF THE *DCNR*

The attempt by some scholars to wholly ignore the form of the *DCNR* is perplexing. Through close reading and rigorous analysis of certain sentences, they point out inconsistencies of argument and flaws of logic as if the text were a straightforward rational reconstruction of logical positions in different voices. This move does violence to the broad compositional spirit of the *DCNR* and truncates its usefulness for common life. Michael Malherbe explains this as follows: "When philosophy becomes academic, it usually forgets that the search for truth requires a literary form, and that this form, rather than being something arbitrarily added, should be derived from the very nature of the enquiry."[46] Interpretations of the

*DCNR* that overlook its form lead to a logical dead end. Hume's voice is not identified in the text, yet these interpretations make claims about his position on reason and religion, and they attribute statements to him made by selected characters. This approach informs one of the most well-known and extensive debates about the *DCNR*, that is, which character speaks for Hume?[47]

There are conflicting interpretations about which character speaks for Hume; however, contemporary commentators generally argue that it is Philo, the most skeptical of the characters, who represents Hume.[48] Others claim that it is the host of the dialogues, Cleanthes.[49] Interestingly, the debates about who speaks for Hume could have encouraged scholars to attend to the form as part of Hume's argument. Yet they disregard the form at the expense of the *DCNR*'s delicate attention to "human life in various attitudes and situations" (*E*, 1.8). The preoccupation with locating Hume's singular voice renders many of the broader concerns of the text invisible. It fails to show that the *DCNR* "enters more into common life; moulds the heart and affects; and, by touching those principles which actuate men, reforms their conduct, and brings them nearer to that model of perfection which it describes" (1.3).[50]

Reading the *DCNR* as Hume's simple camouflaging of his own voice profoundly undermines its compositional uniqueness. In form and spirit, the author speaks through *all* the characters; if merely one character represented him, the others would be reduced to mere foils, simply a means for the Hume character to have adequate context to articulate his true perspective. And, if Hume had wanted to mask his thoughts behind one character, he probably would not have had such interweaving positions between interlocutors, and each character would have been more consistent in his views. In other words, there is an elusive quality to the text that we lose if we frame the text on the "Hume-as-Cleanthes" or "Hume-as-Philo" model. The *DCNR* (unlike the early Socratic dialogues but similar to the Ciceronian ones) is not structured to favor one voice at the expense of the others. There is relative equity in quantity of lines, a profound parity in content, and equality in complexity of argument for each of the three main characters.

Some have justified the position that one character speaks for Hume by arguing that a straightforward expression of his radical positions would have placed him in danger from the censors. There are at least two reasons why it does not follow that Hume used the *DCNR* to camouflage his positions from the censors. First, the most controversial claims of the *DCNR* are less offensive to orthodox religious views than many of the claims in Hume's earlier writings. Second, the *DCNR* was planned for posthumous publication; he had little reason to hide his perspective behind the voice of a character when he was dead, that is, well beyond the reach of censure.

Overall, the focus on "who speaks for Hume" that haunts interpretations of the text rests too easily on an assumption that Hume actually wanted to express one final, coherent position on the relation of religion to reason. Rather than drawing conclusions, however, Hume may be telling us more about *how* to discuss this relation, or perhaps revealing the inner dialogue of his own consciousness concerning false and true religion. He may also have had literary or comedic aspirations or simply wanted to encourage laughter in the face of the irresoluble. A reading of the DCNR that takes the complexities of its form seriously would attempt to gauge his interest in raising issues in creative and engaging ways that invited readers into their own dialogues about the relation of reason and religion in common life, rather than closing the book on the subject by ignoring the form or stipulating that Hume was one interlocutor or another.[51] Nonetheless, a puzzle remains: if no one character speaks for Hume, then how are we to extract the purposes and conclusions of the text?

### THE CLASH OF HOPES: WHAT DO THE DIALOGUES SAY?

The DCNR is a tapestry with multiple, twisting threads of contestations about the relations of reason and religion. In many ways, this dynamic set of dialogues is both the most effective and the least conclusive of all of Hume's writings. It is successful at inspiring "us with different sentiments, of praise or blame, admiration or ridicule" (E, 1.8) and mirroring some ways that we might reflectively and energetically engage common life. These dramatic dialogues meander through various moments with no clear resolution, yet the passion they ultimately seem to recommend is a moderate hope.

None of the three main characters is easily reducible to a single simple position on natural religion. Each voice is too nuanced to be confined to merely one easy approach. Yet even in this complexity and diversity, it is fair to say that each character loosely associates and is therefore identifiable with one particular feature of natural religion. Each character in the DCNR attempts to build a compelling argument for how religion relates to reason, and, more important for my argument here, each makes a claim about how to hope. Three conventional arguments for natural religion are rehearsed: the cosmological argument, the argument from piety, and the teleological argument. Most of the conversation, however, centers on the argument from design, which is the inference from our experience of nature that God exists and has a relationship with humans. Cleanthes and Philo both hold different forms of the argument from design, and they have distinct hopes. Cleanthes holds direct-passion hopes for an intelligible universe, while Philo possesses an open disposition and a moderate hope for the future. Demea—who venerates piety and the cosmological argument—is driven by direct-passion hopes, possibly violent ones, for God's inscrutability.

The positions of Cleanthes and Philo on the design, or a posteriori, argument verify that it has two distinct levels. On the first level—its traditional formulation—the argument from design stipulates that the experience of order in nature leads us to conclude that the Author of Nature is likely behind this order. On this level, simply due to the vastness of the order, the Orderer may generate a mild religious response, but we know nothing about this Orderer. Philo holds a position very close to this. The second level of the design argument presumes that we can posit attributes, characteristics, and wishes of the Author of Nature based on our observations and experience of nature. Cleanthes holds a position similar to this.

The *DCNR* also rehearses the cosmological, or a priori, argument for the existence of God. This is the idea that God is the necessary first cause of the universe. It is usually established in two steps. The first is that the existence of the world proves the presence of a necessary being that created it. The second step shows this necessary being is worthy of worship. Further, the text briefly takes on the practical issue of piety.[52] For Demea, piety is not driven by revelation or personal experience of the divine; it is a direct-passion–inspired desire for God as Mystery to ensure that human powers do not become sovereign. I begin with a discussion of Demea's piety, attend to the a priori and a posteriori arguments, and, finally, consider true religion.

*Piety*. Demea opens the *Dialogues* by expressing an unequivocal commitment to a form of popular piety. His piety is not driven by reason, but by habit, orthodoxy, and the direct-passions hope and fear. His most obvious statement in this regard is found in a claim he makes concerning the education of his children: "to season their minds with early piety is my chief care; and by continual precept and instruction, and I hope too, by example, I imprint deeply on their tender minds an habitual reverence for all the principles of religion" (*DCNR*, 1.2). Demea's popular form of piety venerates a conventional mode of submission. His "habitual reverence" is not derived from adherence to scripture, reason, or faith; it is inspired by the direct-passion fears and hopes that lead to veneration of the mystery of God and affirm the limits of the human mind. For Demea, the inscrutability of God keeps the human will from asserting itself beyond its boundaries:

> The question is not concerning the *being* but the *nature* of *God*. This I affirm, from the infirmities of human understanding, to be altogether incomprehensible and unknown to us. The essence of that supreme mind, his attributes, the manner of his existence, the very nature of his duration; these and every particular, which regards so divine a being are mysterious to men. Finite, weak, and blind creatures, we ought to humble ourselves in his august

presence, and, conscious of our frailties, adore in silence his infinite perfections which eye hath not seen, ear hath not heard, neither hath it entered
into the heart of man to conceive them. They are covered in a deep cloud
from human curiosity: It is profaneness to attempt penetrating through
these sacred obscurities; and, next to the impiety of denying his existence,
is the temerity of prying into his nature and essence, decrees and attributes.
(*DCNR*, 2.1)

The response to Demea is convoluted. In many ways, it replicates the normal
vicissitudes of a thoughtful conversation. Philo responds to Demea by challenging him, agreeing with parts of what he says (2.3 and 2.4) and at other times,
contradicting his position. Philo seems to recognize that Demea's piety is animated by direct-passion hopes and fears and that reason can do little in the face
of these passionate beliefs. Still, Philo is sensitive to Demea and offers no rational
argument against popular piety and the traditional view of inscrutability. Demea's
position remains in view and is never fully rebutted in his presence.

*The A Priori Argument.* Demea shifts his emphasis from submission and reverence to a more rigorous position in support of true piety.[53] The position he defends
is the cosmological, or a priori, argument for God.[54] He gives a succinct modern
formulation of it: "Whatever exists must have a cause or reason of its existence; it
being absolutely impossible for anything to produce itself, or be the cause of its
own existence" (*DCNR*, 9.3). Demea demonstrates that God is a perfectly necessary and worship-worthy Being based on causal logic. Still, his a priori argument
for God and his case for piety are similar: both are driven by intense, direct-
passion hopes and fears.

The *DCNR* does not belabor the a priori argument, but the discussion of it is
insightful. Cleanthes responds directly to Demea and contends, largely uncon-
vincingly, that Demea's argument is "ill grounded," which we might take to mean
that it is driven by direct-passion hopes and fears.[55] Cleanthes shows Demea's
claims to be both inchoate and absurd:

> There is an evident absurdity in pretending to demonstrate a matter of fact,
> or prove it by any arguments *a priori*. Nothing is demonstrable unless the
> contrary implies a contradiction. Nothing, that is distinctly conceivable
> implies a contradiction. Whatever we conceive as existent, we can also con-
> ceive as non-existent. There is no Being, therefore, whose existence implies
> a contradiction. Consequently there is no Being, whose non existence is
> demonstrable. I propose this argument as entirely decisive, and am willing
> to rest the whole controversy upon it. (9.5)[56]

With Demea's premises undermined, his conclusion—that God is a *necessary* fact—is weakened. Demea rejects Cleanthes's argument for two reasons: first, because it relies on an ineffective method (empiricism) and, second, because it can yield only probability, not the certainty that Demea needs. Demea's direct-passion hopes and fears drive him to expunge doubt, and though Cleanthes has a similar motivation, he appeals to experience to illuminate the rational structure of the universe. Both Cleanthes and Demea are driven by direct-passion hopes and fears; they simply employ different methods on the way to their conclusions about religion. This incongruity does not mean that the conversation is futile; in fact, Cleanthes's failure enables the conversation to flourish in its own enigmatic way. After critique and examination of the a priori argument, the reader can claim to have witnessed neither a perfectly articulated rebuttal nor a resounding affirmation of this position. The dialogues simply continue.

*The A Posteriori Argument.* The most significant part of the *DCNR* is dedicated to engaging the a posteriori argument: that the apparent design of the natural world suggests a Designer worthy of religious worship. This argument is first introduced by Cleanthes in part 2. It is criticized by Philo from parts 2 to 8. It is reanimated in part 10 through a consideration of the moral attributes of the Designer. Parts 11 and 12, integral to the argument here, demonstrate Philo's nifty and conclusive execution of a version of the design argument.

*Part 2.* Cleanthes presents a religiously based teleological perspective. To preserve the careful precision of Hume's work here, I cite the text at length:

> Look round the world: Contemplate the world and every part of it: You will find it to be nothing but one great machine, subdivided into an infinite number of lesser machines, which again admit of subdivisions, to a degree beyond what human senses and faculties can trace and explain. All these various machines, and even their most minute parts, are adjusted to each other with an accuracy which ravishes into admiration all men, who have ever contemplated them. The curious adapting of means to ends, through-out all nature, resembles exactly, though it much exceeds, the productions of human contrivance; of human design, thought, wisdom, and intelligence. Since therefore the effects resemble each other, we are led to infer, by all the rules of analogy, that the causes also resemble; and that the Author of Nature is somewhat similar to the mind of man; though possessed of much larger faculties, proportioned to the grandeur of the work which he has executed. By this argument *a posteriori*, and by this argument alone, do we

prove at once the existence of a Deity and, his similarity to human mind and intelligence. (*DCNR*, 2.5)

Two premises of Cleanthes's argument from design are noteworthy in this lengthy speech.[57] The first is his appeal to observable experience. Cleanthes's argument for God begins with a visual impression of nature: "look around the world." He then infers from this perception—and this is the second important premise—that one can analogize the world with the complex idea of a machine ("you will find it to be nothing but one great machine"). The claim that humans must be the effect of a first cause (Designer) just as human-made machines are the effect of a Designer is neither startling nor irrational. It is a seminal belief of popular religion and a standard argument of false philosophy.

*Part 2.7.* Unsurprisingly, Cleanthes's articulation of the argument from design is initially challenged by Philo on the grounds of its problematic use of analogy. Cleanthes's use of analogical reasoning is defective, according to Philo, because it compares objects *across* worlds. Philo might be willing to provisionally accept reasoning by analogy when both objects are within the realm of impression, but we have no impression of the creation of the world so we cannot analogize it to the human creation of machines. On Philo's logic Cleanthes has taken his analogy literally "out of this world":

> If we see a house, Cleanthes, we conclude, with the greatest certainty, that it had an architect or builder; because this is precisely that species of effect, which we have experienced to proceed from that species of cause. But surely you will not affirm, that the universe bears such a resemblance to a house that we can with the same certainty infer a similar cause, or that the analogy is here entire and perfect. The dissimilitude is so striking, that the utmost you can here pretend to is a guess, a conjecture, a presumption concerning a similar cause. (*DCNR*, 2.8)

Philo suggests that if one were to reason analogically from experience of the world, the more accurate inference would be that the world resembles an animal body or a vegetable: a growing unity, moving and actuated by "a like principle of life and motion." Philo says, "The world, therefore, I infer, is an animal; and the Deity is the Soul of the world, actuating it, and actuated by it" (*DCNR*, 6.3). For Philo, the world is better represented by analogy to systems that contain imma-nent energy than those that rely on a transcendent creator. The life forces and animating energies that Philo infers from experience suggest creation of the world might be better analogized to an "infinite spider who spun this whole complicated mass from his bowels, and annihilates afterwards the whole or any part of it, by absorbing it again, and resolving it into his own essence" (7.17). The design argument is useless if presented analogically beyond the limits of our actual experience.

Cleanthes attempts to clarify his position in the face of Philo's devastating criticisms. He suggests that analogy is successful only if the resemblance between objects is strong: "the liker the better" (*DCNR*, 5.4). For Cleanthes, if we suppose a greater similarity between God and humans, then we can effectively analogize them. If the mind of God operates like the mind of humans, then God is the architect of the world. This argument, however, opens Cleanthes up to another set of problems, and in part 5 Philo challenges him: how does God have any attributes that establish him worthy of worship if He resembles humans so closely? This question reasons that Cleanthes's use of analogy actually undermines the concept of God. It is a critical blow to Cleanthes's argument. Still, Philo allows that the a posteriori method is neither useless nor to be abandoned. "A man, who follows your hypothesis," he states, "is able, perhaps, to assert, or conjecture, that the universe, sometime, arose from something like design: But beyond that position he cannot ascertain one single circumstance, and is left afterwards to fix every point of his theology, by the utmost licence of fancy and hypothesis" (5.12). Philo affirms this basic theism but he never cosigns popular religion, vulgar theism, or false piety.

*Part 10.* The conversation in part 10 extends the arguments for natural religion and underscores the types of hope that mark the *DCNR*. In this most well-known section, the discussion revolves around the ubiquitous misery and dread in human life and the moral attributes of God. Demea passionately details a world full of pain, evil, and terror. Concomitantly, without much of an argument and in an almost nonreflective fashion, he asserts his own description of the source of religious beliefs: "that everyone feels religion in his own breast" (10.1). Demea explicitly admits that the passions move him to embrace religion.

Consistent with the aim of his earlier direct-passion hopes for the inscrutability of God, Demea hopes to expand this religious *feeling* in humans. To this end, he provides an explanation for religious belief that affirms popular forms of piety, in particular, Christian worship. His expression of direct-passion hopes through this form of vulgar piety has a profoundly practical emphasis, intending "to appease those terrors with which we are incessantly agitated." The end for which Demea hopes is the reduction of misery in human life, and his means to this end is to shift the focus of the mind to the afterlife. "Futurity is still the object of all our hopes and fears" (*DCNR*, 10.1), he says, "the present evil phenomena, therefore, are rectified . . . in some future period of human existence" (10.29).

Philo is the major interlocutor with Demea in part 10, as Cleanthes speaks only twice for a total of three brief paragraphs. Philo's line of argument has two important strategies. First, given the presence of evil, it seeks to render the capacity to infer God's moral attributes from the natural world impossible. The second strategy is to affirm the irresistibility of the design argument for establishing the existence of God. While it may seem surprising that Philo embraces the design argument after he has spent the majority of the conversation (parts 2–8) criticizing it, Philo's criticism has always aimed at the *grounds* and methods of Cleanthes's design argument, not at its *conclusions*. In other words, Philo was careful never to claim that inferring the existence of a Designer from the experience of order (basic theism) was unintelligible or unwarranted; rather, he questioned the grounds on which Cleanthes made his particular inferences and the degree of similarity in his analogical conclusions. Philo attacked Cleanthes's version of the design argument because it anthropomorphized God. Yet he affirmed a less anthropomorphic version of the design argument that leads to invisible, intelligent power.

Philo's main work in part 10 consists in his giving a full account of the misery, evil, and terror that are part and parcel of the human experience. Concurring with Demea, Philo embraces the human feelings of fear and failure and affirms that every animal is surrounded by enemies, even those created by the human mind (*DCNR*, 10.9). He further contends that "man is the greatest enemy of man" (10.12) and states that humans are terrified, "discontented, repining" creatures with an "anxious disposition" (10.16). He asks Cleanthes,

> Is it possible . . . that after all these reflections, and infinitely more, which might be suggested, you can still persevere in your anthropomorphism, and assert the moral attributes of the Deity, his justice, benevolence, mercy and rectitude, to be of the same nature with these virtues in human creatures? His power we allow infinite: Whatever he wills is executed: But neither man nor any other animal is happy; Therefore, he does not will their happiness. His wisdom is infinite; He is never mistaken in choosing the means to any end; But the course of nature tends not to human or animal felicity: Therefore, it is not established for that purpose. Through the whole compass of human knowledge, there are no inferences more certain and infallible than these. In what respect, then, do his benevolence and mercy resemble the benevolence and mercy of men? (10.24–26)

This famous—some might say climactic—moment of the *Dialogues* seems to compel Cleanthes. He can only reject Philo's description: "your misrepresentations [of evil] are exaggerated, your melancholy views mostly fictitious: your inferences contrary to fact and experience" (10.31). Yet Philo does not waver. He contends that no matter the facts, people *feel* pain to be a more profound and lasting experience than pleasure. This distinction, though rhetorically effective, ultimately turns out to be unimportant since Philo shows that neither position can be empirically quantified. It is the presence of evil, not the number of its occurrences, that makes it impossible simply to infer an infinite, wise, and benevolent God.

Philo's focus on terror, misery, and evil in the world set up his residual notion of hope in part 10. He does not explicitly use hope speech; his hope is silent in the background yet evident in his unwillingness to despair in light of ever-present evil. Though Philo does not detail his moderate hope, we can say that he participates in the life of hope because he maintains an open and accepting disposition toward the future. Philo is invested in expanding possibilities for meaning and extending the peace of a nondogmatic positive worldview in the face of impending catastrophe and approaching doom. His moderate hopes are not contingent on forces beyond his control; they are conditioned, rational, and grounded, unlike Demea's and Cleanthes's direct-passion hopes. Thus, Philo exhibits a more moderate or, following Godfrey, fundamental hope.

Philo's moderate hope is most evident in his description of terror and natural evil. He is adamant in his depiction of the severe evil endemic to the human condition because he wants others to affirm the reality of evil in life. His modest, philosophical hope manifests when he rejects the appeal to superstition in the face of suffering. Fundamental hope is the disposition to embrace the fullness of life, including misery, as a part of the human experience. Philo moderately hopes for humans to find a nonsuperstitious and nonenthusiastic way to live in the face of the misery. And his moderate hope, unlike the direct-passion hopes of Demea and Cleanthes, leaves humans vulnerable. It silently compels us to equipoise, the acceptance of all that life brings and the calm feeling of balance in our thoughts about the unknown.

*Parts 11–12.* In many ways, parts 11 and 12 extend the tone of Philo's expression of his moderate hope. He explicitly indicates that he wants humans to be more humble and affirm the fullness and the mystery of life in these sections. The first section of part 11 (11.1–11.6) is a continuation of part 10. In it, Cleanthes reaffirms his commitment to empirical theism as well as his hope for a rational, revealed religion, slightly revised based partially on Philo's criticisms. Cleanthes drops the commitment to an infinite Designer and proposes that perhaps God is "finitely perfect, though far exceeding mankind" (*DCNR*, 11.1). While this distinction is somewhat confusing (what exactly is a finitely perfect God?), it allows Cleanthes to confirm that evil is, possibly, a legitimate feature of the world (although he never actually says that it is a definite feature of life), at the same time that it allows him to retain the idea of God's perfection.

Cleanthes's "revised" Designer reads more like a desperate attempt to reassert his direct-passion hopes for an intelligible, happy, and predictable world than it does as a rational reply to Philo. He is unwilling to yield in his conviction that one can empirically infer an active and perfect God from nature. Cleanthes holds tight to the passionally informed belief that the world is fully comprehensible and that all questions are answerable. This worldview sustains him; he takes comfort in the vulgar theism and popular religion that it supports.

Philo's bare theism—he embraces design but can give no attributes to the Designer—and moderate hope that humans come to grips with the fact that the beliefs of popular religion are more dependent on our passions than on rationality are once again challenged by Cleanthes's relentless investment in the idea that the empirical method can provide knowledge of God's attributes. Philo has been trying to reveal the profound limitations of human reason all along. When it seemed that Philo had convinced him, Cleanthes immediately shifted the terms of his Designer. Philo, seemingly a veteran of this sort of inconsistency in conversation, patiently tries again:

> We know so little beyond common life, or even of common life, that, with regard to the economy of a universe, there is no conjecture, however wild, which may not be just; nor any one, however plausible, which may not be erroneous. All that belongs to human understanding, in this deep ignorance and obscurity, is to be skeptical or at least cautious; and not to admit of any hypothesis whatever; much less of any which is supported by no appearance of probability. (*DCNR*, 11.5)

He then gives "four circumstances of evil" to show Cleanthes that most pain and misery in the world are avoidable and unnecessary, preventable by humans or God (that is, a God with adequate power). While the specifics of his argument are not necessary here, its conclusions are useful. Philo argues that God's moral attributes cannot be inferred from experience and hence Cleanthes cannot prove even a "finitely perfect" being. He contends that the moral character of the world is probably guided by "neither goodness nor malice" (11.15) and that "the original source of all things is entirely indifferent to all these principles, and has no more regard to good above ill than to heat above cold, or to drought above moisture, or to light above heavy" (11.14). While asserting mystery and incomprehensibility at the core of the human experience, Philo is guided by a moderate hope. Demea, who viewed Philo as an ally based on their mutual commitment to the "incomprehensible nature of the divine Being" (11.18), at this point realizes that Philo does not share his reverence for the beliefs of popular religion; he becomes angry and exits the conversation. His dramatic departure frees Philo to become even more expressive about his form of hope in the lengthy, final part of the work.

On my reading, the conclusion of the *DCNR* accomplishes three things. First, it clarifies and solidifies Philo's commitment to a form of the argument from design. Second, it extends, without resolution, the clash of the direct-passion hopes of Cleanthes and the moderate hope of Philo based on their varying interpretations of experience. Third, it describes the category 'true religion.' I discuss the first two of these presently and treat true religion in a separate section later.

In what many scholars incorrectly regard as a reversal of positions, Philo proclaims early in part 12 that "no one has a deeper sense of religion impressed on his mind, or pays more profound adoration to the divine Being. A purpose, an intention, a design strikes everywhere the most careless, the most stupid thinker; and no man can be so hardened in absurd systems, as at all times to reject it" (*DCNR*, 12.2). This statement is neither ironic, nor a change of heart by Philo. Again, Philo *never* undermined the basic force of the design argument. He did, however, attack the attempt to establish attributes of the Designer by inference from nature, hence attenuating the traditional scope of the argument.

H. O. Mounce provides a unique perspective on this issue, arguing that Philo subscribes to a classical teleological position and that Cleanthes appeals to (what will become) a popular nineteenth-century version of the design argument. The classical position, according to Mounce, was articulated by Aristotle and Aquinas, who argued "that the order of the world has a source that transcends the world itself" and is unknowable. The popular formulation of this argument claims that "the order of the world must have a Designer analogous to the human."[58] The distinction between these two positions resides in the degree of similarity presumed or asserted between humans and God. Philo consistently denied the analogy between humans and God; hence he reflects the classical teleology.

Cleanthes's default positions throughout the *DCNR* were the following: that the world is a predictable place, that we are meant to be happy, and that God is moral, wise, and beneficent. His argument was derived from beliefs that he justified through simple appeal to sense experience (or the direct passions). Cleanthes's theism eases the fear of vulnerability in an unpredictable world. It is driven by the hope-fear continuum and displays a lack of preparedness to respond to the possibility of its falsehood. Perhaps Hume is trying to tell us that Cleanthes, and others like him, do not possess the psychic tools to grapple with a world that has a Designer whose attributes are impossible to discern (never mind a world without a Designer). Cleanthes's position shows him to be devoid of the psychic resources to survive in an unpredictable world. This may be why he lobbies so powerfully for his position: his fear has erected an illusory monument to a vulgar type of theism.

Philo ends his remarks reflecting on the hope-fear continuum. Echoing Hume's description of the direct passions in the *Treatise* and his explication of how direct passions are the source of religion in the *NHR*, Philo shows how hope and fear generate the popular impulse toward religion. He says, "It is true; both fear and hope enter into religion; because both these passions, at different times, agitate the human mind, and each of them forms a species of divinity, suitable to itself" (*DCNR*, 12.29). Given the power of these direct passions, Philo aims for their moderation through common life. His moderate hope, then, is for the de-escalation of factionalism and suffering caused by the intense direct passions that give rise to popular religion. Philo is magnanimous and open, full of equipoise in the vicissitudes of the dialogues. We might fairly presume that his exemplary participation here reflects his disposition for moderate or fundamental hope. It seems that this calm passion leaves him wide awake to what may come and largely in control of his responses to it.

TRUE RELIGION

The *DCNR* directly engages true religion. Each of its characters is armed with a distinct conception of true religion attached to a different type of hope. Viewing from the lens of true religion is important in the *DCNR*, then, not only in its own right but also because it helps to illuminate distinct types of hope at the foundation of each character's worldview. For example, Demea's conception of true religion seems to be religious piety, or the submission to the authority of religion and God based on revelation and tradition. This follows from the fact that his main hope is the direct-passion hope for salvation. Demea's direct-passion hope is a traditional Christian hope, an unconditioned hope, a hope that his own agency has very little to do with achieving. His strong sense of piety (a quasi-Calvinism, it seems) practically *assures* his salvation. Demea does not make himself vulnerable or leave himself open to the future; he completely relies on that which he *knows* will deliver.[59]

Though they differ in most areas, Cleanthes and Philo share a conception of true religion. A distinct sense of hope, however, underlies each. Cleanthes best articulates the conception of true religion when he says that "the proper office of religion is to regulate the hearts of men, humanize their conduct, infuse the spirit of temperance, order and obedience" (*DCNR*, 12.12). Philo confirms his commitment to true religion when he confesses "no one has a deeper sense of religion" (12.2) and claims that he has a "veneration of true religion" (12.9). While some scholars argue that Philo's sense of true religion has no religious value, fundamental acceptance of the future and openness to life, are, on my argument, spiritual dispositions and religious modes of being.[60]

An important disagreement between Philo and Cleanthes on true religion seems to inform their disparate styles of hoping. They disagree over the degree to which they believe true religion is popular religion. Cleanthes contends that popular religion, the popular beliefs and styles of worship, is the equivalent of true religion. Philo strongly counters this. While this distinction may seem trivial, it is not. The content of Cleanthes's true religion is at stake as is the very hope at its foundation. Cleanthes's sense of true religion emphasizes a very practical goal, "to regulate the hearts of men, humanize their conduct, infuse the spirit of temperence, order and obedience" (*DCNR*, 12.12). In other words, true religion is, according to Cleanthes, the means to the attainment of objects or practical ends. It is, therefore, based on a direct-passion hope because it is motivated by future, probable goods. Popular religion shares these same objective ends; thus, Cleanthes concludes that true religion *is* popular religion. Cleanthes's investment, however, is not necessarily in true religion itself but in what true religion serves: to regulate and humanize. His practical considerations lead him to argue that "religion, however corrupted, is still better than no religion at all" (12.10).

Cleanthes's direct-passion hopes, mirroring those of Demea, ultimately serve to protect him from vulnerability and the vicissitudes of life. Cleanthes has no doubt that, if accepted by all, the firm empirical argument from design guarantees the regulation of men's hearts and the humanization of their behavior; he therefore looks to the future with more assurance than faith, more confidence than hope. He stands against the parochial piety and theism of Demea and holds a notion of true religion that rejects the very revelation Demea wants. He reminds Philo to remain balanced in his approach to true religion in his final line of the dialogue: "take care: Push not matters too far: Allow not your zeal against false religion to undermine your veneration for the true" (*DCNR*, 12.24).

Philo generally embraces the substance of Cleanthes's true religion, but he disagrees with its form. For him, true religion is a very rare condition or an 'ideal type,' it is generally not religion "as found in the world" (*DCNR*, 12.22), and it is grasped by a very few individuals who can approach it only when they moderate their passions through common life. Cleanthes wants to use reason and nature to support an exacting vision and particular worldview that are justifiable on the standards of abstract reason. Philo's more moderate hope generates a different form of true religion. He says, "true religion, I allow, has no such pernicious consequences" (12:22). The moderate hope at its foundation is judicious yet offers no guarantees.

Prioritizing the form of the *DCNR* subdues our need to make strong claims about what the text concludes or what Hume's *definitive* position is. It does not, however, deplete our capacity to comprehend the fascinating way the text positions the passions in relation to religion. In fact, taking the form of the text under serious consideration more fully reveals that each character's position on religion and theism was informed by the different forms of hope he possessed. Paying attention to the varieties of hope in the *Dialogues* offers us a new vista on the text and a more complex understanding of the role of the passions in Hume's religious thought. On this reading, the *Dialogues* allow that a moderate hope might be integral to the proper office of religion, which helps us "regulate our hearts" and "humanize our conduct."

This chapter investigated the role of the passions for Hume's concept of true religion in light of his two types of hope. Godfrey's notion 'fundamental hope' was useful here in that it illuminated the latter of these hopes, an unexamined, moderate form of hope that serves as the positive thrust in the background of Hume's thought. Chapter 2 posited that the first leg of our speculative, Humean-influenced true religion might be a genuine theism. This chapter has tracked Hume's implicit, humble hopes and his project for the passions to establish the second (contingent) leg of moderate hope. I now turn to his moral project to locate the potential third element of religion's proper office: practical morality.

# PRACTICAL MORALITY

Nothing can be more real, or concern us more, than our own
sentiments of pleasure and uneasiness; and if these be favourable to virtue, and unfavourable to vice, no more can be requisite to the regulation of our conduct and behavior.
—*T*, 3.1.1.25

Hume explained his moral project as an examination of the "general foundation
of morals: whether they be derived from Reason, or from sentiment; whether we
attain the knowledge of them by a chain of argument and induction, or by an
immediate feeling and finer internal sense" (*EPM*, 1.3). Two of its goals regarding
religion were to demonstrate that popular religion undermined moral judgment
and to dismantle the belief that its deity possessed moral attributes.[1] There are
extensive implications to these two aims. For example, they weakened the belief
that man was made in the image of God (for neither man nor God was a moral
creature).[2] They also established that the deity of popular religion could not
unpredictably intervene in history (as the existence of moral evil confirmed) and
proved that popular religion had no positive consequences for practical morality
(as demonstrated by history).[3] On these terms I take Hume's moral project to have
been a success: it severely undermined the moral claims of popular religion and
undercut its excessive theism. His captivating opposition to conventional morality prefigured both Nietzsche's moral critique of Christianity and Mill's ethical
quest for happiness.

When we hold Hume's account of our social interactions and his Ciceronian
influence in mind, his scathing moral condemnation of popular religion takes on
a lighter hue. On the former, Hume partially agreed with Hobbes's insight that
human beings were motivated by self-interest. Against Hobbes, however, Hume

noted that we were likewise compelled by a natural dependence on the compassion of others. Hume's approach to morals reflected his belief that humans were driven by both self-interest and a natural benevolence toward others. In its general form this natural benevolence played a crucial role in our social interactions; thus a major Humean intervention in moral thought was the contention that social interaction consisted of organically occurring and repeated acts of strategic coordination between individuals in a quest to reinforce mutual interests. For example, Hume reasoned that individuals strategically coordinated the exchange of property due to their self-interested desire to protect their possessions and their natural benevolence to reassure others that their assets would be protected. This type of coordination aimed to "leave everyone in the peaceable enjoyment of what he may acquire by his fortune and industry" (*T*, 3.2.2.9). Humans uniquely recognized that their self-interests regarding property (and promises) were best served if they worked toward mutual advantage.

If the recognition of mutual interests drove the social component of moral judgment, it was the repetition of the successful coordination of these joint interests, say, in the exchange of property, that was a "remedy in the judgment and understanding, for what is irregular and incommodious in the affections" (*T*, 3.2.2.9). The repetition of successful coordination between human beings bolstered our sense of protection, reduced fears, and assisted in the sustenance of civic stability and social order. It also indicated probable success for future coordination and inspired its expectation. This expectation shaped "conventions" that formalized the means to social cohesiveness. On Hume's account, justice was an "artificial" virtue mediated by these conventions. On his depiction it is reasonable to analogize justice with religion.[4] Keeping in mind the public aspects of the formation of religion when it is in its proper office (calm passions, such as moderate hope, always have a *social* component), we might consider religion as a Humean social convention. This view repositions his criticism of religion. That is, instead of interpreting Hume as attacking the imaginative symbols and sacred practices formed in belief communities, we might read his critical comments on religion as a description of a social convention in decline. From this view, Hume's challenge to religion would be a potent expression of discontent at the failure of a social convention to effectively manage social concerns. As I have emphasized, Hume had major problems with the epistemological aspirations of modern religion and wanted to quell the direct-passion sources that drove popular religion. These issues would not have prohibited him from also thinking of religion as a social convention. In fact, the epistemological and affective realms are amenable to both his moral and historical framing of religion. Though his historical observations indicate that religion most often leads to factionalism, nowhere does Hume claim that religion, in each and every one of its forms, is *always* an obstacle to social stability and personal liberty. And if religion is a social convention, it follows that popular religion must be the convention for religion that delivers social instability and political volatility, and true religion one convention among many (including secular ones) that might enhance public life and augment civil stability.

Another element that casts Hume's moral criticism of popular religion in a new light is his Ciceronian influence. As I argued in chapter 1, Cicero's *religio* was a practical and strategic venture; it was invested in results. For Cicero, morality was a part of our nature that required cultivation. The convention *religio* was a tool that, if it were structured properly, could effectively cultivate virtue. That is, Cicero used *religio* to shift the conflicting desires of Roman social groups and curb their natural self-interests so that the republic could function better. At their best, the civic festivals and public rituals of Cicero's *religio* were collaborative and strategic efforts of individuals to order social space in ways that protected individual interests and affirmed social well-being. In other words, guided by the strong hand of Cicero's leadership, *religio* vitally served justice and political stability.

It seems highly likely that this functional conception *religio* influenced Hume's considerations of religion. Following Cicero, Hume wanted to articulate a moral system that would "help us to form a just notion of the *happiness* as well as of the *dignity* of virtue" (*T*, 3.3.6.6). He was clear that popular religion was malformed and too corrupted to assist in this venture. Had he been pressed directly on this issue, it is likely that Hume may have admitted that a strategically developed form of religion (with a mild theism and moderate passions) might serve as a useful convention for teaching the "social virtues" of happiness and justice. Of course, this conjecture should not diminish the importance of Hume's loathing of the vulgar systems of morality supported by popular religion. Neither should it encourage us to overlook that against popular religion and vulgar morality Hume advocated thoughtful and patient reflection, friendship, study, and leisure, *not* (any extant form of) religion for the development of virtuous character and the proper temperament. We must remember, however, even though Hume did not consistently state it, he was suspicious of the "*corruptions* of true religion" (*EPM*, 10.73; italics added), not true religion itself. It follows that Hume's moral vision did not foreclose the possibility that a socially derived religious artifice—a true religion—could have a positive impact for the development of character, the increase of personal happiness, and the stability of the social order. While his moral critique of popular religion was devastating, Hume was open to the idea of true religion, which would, given his interests in morality, be useful for the ethical formation of individuals in common life.

The importance of social interactions for Hume's moral thought and his Ciceronian influence open another possibility: that Hume's contribution to moral discourse may be rendered clearer and made more cogent when couched within the proper office of religion. Here Hume's choice not to give a detailed description of his category 'true religion' is beneficial: it remains available to marry with the most generative insights from his work on theism, the passions, and morality. Wedding Hume's "practical morality"—that is, how his moral worldview shapes his sense of human action—to a *convention* we might call "true religion" safeguards its social and political insights as well as its inspirational qualities. Further, it can provide us with the ability to give a richer account of Hume's distinctive response to the long shadow cast by Hobbes's moral thought. Of course, what I am naming Hume's "practical morality" does not *need* religion, but its core themes—including his psychological notion "sympathy" and his sense of how we might develop virtuous character—do not *require* secularity either. In fact, Hume's practical morality can be bolstered and sustained by either religious or secular "artifices." The proper religious artifice that might include Hume's practical morality is rare, and its appearance is at best intermittent, as humans will never escape their natural propensity to superstition and proclivity for easy answers.

One could take exception to the suggestion that Hume's practical morality comes into better view as a component of a speculative true religion. The worry that this view dilutes Hume's strong moral critique of religion or undermines his moral atheism bears consideration. It is akin to the position of those who believe that Hume's empiricist method allows *only* probable conclusions, a stance leveraged to support the argument that his moral project could be only *descriptive*.[5] This view is supported by a particular reading of Hume's well-known metaphor of anatomist and painter (book 3 of the *Treatise*).[6] Though it was "hideous" and "minute in view of things," the work of the metaphysician qua anatomist was prerequisite to the overarching vision of the moralist qua painter. To read Hume solely as an anatomist is to accept that his moral project was only descriptive and that he refused to make claims about what we *ought* to do.[7] Additionally, it is to hold that the painter provides only an aesthetic depiction of virtue, not a set of hints for ethical formation. *Descriptivists* interpret the anatomist-painter analogy as proof that Hume refused to express an ethical vision and that he was irreligious. They deride the suggestion that Hume's practical morality could be taken as a normative component of true religion.[8]

We might broadly and provisionally refer to those who highlight the constructive parts of Hume's ethical project as *normativists*.[9] Responding to the descriptivist's appropriation of the anatomist-painter metaphor, they regard Hume as a painter who provides aesthetically rendered descriptions of the moral scene in ways that convey how to best navigate it. *An Enquiry Concerning the Principles of Morals* depicts the quest for our moral sources, catalogs the virtues, and describes the poetic character of human life. Normativists rely on it to argue that Hume posited ethical norms and engaged in a type of virtue ethics. On their view, Hume noted traits most worthy of cultivation and made recommendations for how we might best develop virtuous character. His psychological approach, however, restricted his normativity. That is, Hume made suggestions about how we might better fulfill particular and evolving sociopolitical interests; he did not believe we were to satisfy some transhistorical, universally true, and morally "right" purposes. Following this subjectivist approach, the best we could do was to explain our feelings and describe how they might invoke moral judgments that would better serve our interests. Normativists and descriptivists generally agree that Hume's unique, naturalist reflections on morality were shaped by this kind of socioethical commitment. Virtuous behavior, for Hume, neither depended on the authority of a sovereign government or a supernatural entity nor relied on the teachings of popular religion. Virtue was instead grounded in our nature as human beings, linked to our changing historical conditions, and associated with our attempts to resolve social goals (which also served our self-interests).[10] Hume's basic theism (a form of naturalism) and his subjectivist normative project for morality supports the idea that a practical morality can serve as the third leg of religion's proper office.

In the final paragraph of the *Treatise* 3.1.1 Hume famously denied that one could derive a moral "ought" from a nonmoral "is." This well-known and fecund statement—often read as his retrenchment from and criticism of the prevailing view that a moral "logic" could make warranted claims about future virtuous behavior merely from observation of a present fact—is open to a variety of interpretations. For example, we might read it as a claim that moral judgments can never be taken as "fact" or that ethical "values" cannot be derived from evident "facts." Reflecting further on this latter reading invites some interesting questions. For instance, might Hume's point be a *historical* one, that what we take to be "facts" are already "values" in some sense or another? If what we consider to be moral "facts" always and already reflect social "values" and vice versa, then how would we formulate a moral project? A peek at Hume's larger argument about the social component of facts and values sheds some light on this issue.

Hume considered himself to be a scientist of morals and an analyst of the affections who believed the source of our morals lies in our *social* response to our fully subjective passions. This meant that he was both a (proto)sociologist and a (proto) psychologist. His emphasis on history as the intersection of the passional *and* the social confirms that his theory of moral judgment was inseparable from the social processes of the passions as observed in our actions. Concerning Hume, Deleuze explains that "one must be a moralist, sociologist, or historian, *before* being a psychologist, *in order to* be a psychologist."[11] There are two important points about this nexus of concerns as characterized by Deleuze and represented earlier. First, Hume believed, like Cicero and Hobbes, that social order was paramount for human well-being and that it was mediated by the conventions resulting from our strategic collaborations. Social interaction was shaped by constant coordination and continuous cooperation that reinforced both individual interests and collective welfare. These ever-shifting social conventions did not establish rules that were objectively or universally "right"; they provided us with particular modes of consideration mutually beneficial for a certain amount of time.[12] In this way the evolutionary path from self-interest to convention (through repeated coordination) did not suggest a move from fact to value. Instead of being rules by which we live, Humean conventions established expectations for how we might best consider certain social transactions. For example, Hume argued that we acquiesced to government rule due to convention (a convention is also responsible for existence of government). Similarly, convention was responsible for submission to the beliefs of popular religion. We must remember that conventions were historically derived and always fluid. Similar to the way our allegiance to government can change, the convention for popular religion could also shift. Hume confirmed this when he wrote that the religion of Scotland "is likely to keep possession, for a long time, of the minds of the people. And though it is much to be hoped, that the progress of reason will, by degrees, abate the acrimony of opposite religions all over Europe; yet the spirit of moderation has, as yet, made too slow advances to be entirely trusted" (*EMPL*, 15.510).

The links between the psychological, social, and political confirm a second crucial point: that Hume's moral project drove toward functionality over establishing a transcendent and objective notion of correctness. In other words, for Hume, human agents designated and explained an action as moral based on its result or how it functioned in common life and human community. This is not a reductive functionalism; rather, it is a product of Hume's practical naturalism. If a behavior was viewed as beneficial to individual happiness and the stability of the social order, then Hume was open to considering it virtuous and worthy of being maintained. This practical approach marked his considerations of religion: if a particular form of religion benefited our individual happiness and the stability of the social order, Hume generally took it to be virtuous and thought it should be maintained. The opposite was also true. If a form of religion did not benefit individual happiness and the stability of the social order, then it was not to be maintained. Since popular religion aided factionalism, abetted superstition, and thereby destabilized society, it was not only impractical but also dysfunctional. The proper office of religion was to "reform Men's Lives, to purify their Hearts, to inforce all moral Duties, & to secure Obedience to the Laws & civil Magistrate."[13] If a form of religion succeeded at these tasks, then it was a convention worth supporting and thereby might be labeled as "true." To lose sight of the practical aspects and functional aims of Hume's considerations of religion is to lose track of the distinctively Humean modulation between forms of religion that destabilized society and varieties of religion that did not.

Hume suggested that one of the ways we might shift away from the convention of popular religion was through moderation of certain passions ("the progress of reason will, by degrees, abate the acrimony of opposite religions all over Europe"). The previous chapter demonstrated that social deliberation was one way we might generate a change in the strength of the passions, alter our social coordination, and begin to spontaneously reform the convention for religion. I emphasized Hume's belief that popular religion offered little advantage to society; it either failed to find adequate ways to calm the passions or lost sight of the important social and political aspects of our moral judgment. Hume acknowledged that to some extent humans were moral subjects and that morality was a fact of our nature; his practical and functional investment was to keep track of how we might moderate the passions in service of excellence of character. To Hume, the vocation of true philosopher was constituted by a moral component. The aspiration for "greatness of mind" required the true philosopher to put forth both well-considered ideas regarding the sources of our moral norms and virtuous actions (human community and social conventions) and to provide insightful reflections on the intricate processes in our moral judgment (sympathy and approbation) to help moderate passions and improve the function of moral judgments. In this way, the true philosopher, reminiscent of Cicero, helps others develop beliefs that cultivate virtues of self-formation and serve mutual interests that stabilize social relationships.

Following his approach to the understanding, Hume's overall method regarding morality was significantly critical: he challenged "vulgar systems" (T, 3.1.1.26) of morality that misconstrued moral sources and misappropriated the causes of stable character development. These vulgar systems did not take history seriously enough to posit thick narratives that could effectively explain present moral conditions and posit future changes based on them. Hume attempted to rectify this with a moral view solidly informed by history that both exposed present social conditions and mildly projected a (gradual) means of transition to more stable ones. Of course, he recognized that human fears were inescapable and that there was neither remedy nor respite from the destructive capacities of human nature. There was merely flux and reflux—the temporary transition to social and psychic stability consistently and repeatedly up-ended by a regressive pull. Hume's abiding comfort and philosophical confirmation of this "two steps forward, two steps back" philosophy of history and his calm moral sanctioning in the face of ineluctable suffering that was "baked-in" to human experience reflected the mild disposition of one who kept religion in its proper office. He would support any convention, religious or otherwise, that confirmed these moderate aspirations and complied with social morality as they concomitantly crafted it.

The systems that Hume referred to as "vulgar" took on four varieties. The first vulgar system was the moral skepticism of Hobbes and Mandeville. Their moral schemas were thoroughly grounded in the psychological motivations of human agents as they worked from the premise that the human drive for pleasure was based in our uncontrollable self-interest. Morals were not divinely inspired, encoded in our nature, nor "real." To Hobbes and Mandeville, people must simply agree to submit to a sovereign authority to control the inevitable clash of individual self-interests. Samuel Clarke and William Wollaston came to the question of morals from an opposite set of commitments. Their vulgar system identified moral differences as real, necessary, and eternal elements in nature. Like mathematical truths, they believed moral ones were discernible through our faculty of reason. Hume took the work of Shaftesbury and Hutcheson as a third vulgar system that largely agreed with the "rationalists" Clarke and Wollaston on the idea that virtues were real. Against them, however, these "sentimentalists" argued that the source of our moral norms was in our nature as human beings, discoverable not by reason but by a moral "sense." Fourth, Warburton argued that humans required a divine source to obligate them to natural law (which was objective and independent from God); thus he posited an omnipotent God as central for our moral decisions.[14]

Though Hume understood all of these to be vulgar systems and his observational science rejected "every system of ethics, however subtle or ingenious, which is not founded on fact and observation" (*EPM*, 1.11), he is generally interpreted as a Hutchesonian sentimentalist regarding morality. There is both an aesthetic element to Hume's reappropriation of Hutcheson's moral thought (both believed that the good was the beautiful) and a socioethical aspect that he borrowed from Hutcheson's work (both believed that reason was not the source of moral action and that affections were public). Hume differed from Hutcheson, however, in an important way: first, he did not accept that our moral sense was simply our disposition for approbation. Hume asserted it was "absurd to imagine, that in every particular instance, these sentiments are produc'd by an *original* quality and *primary* constitution" (*T*, 3.1.2.6). That is, since our approval (and disapproval) was spread over a "multitude of precepts," the moral sentiment could not be produced by an "*original* quality" or "*primary* constitution" (like Hutcheson's sense of benevolence); there must then be "some more general principles"—or secondary ones—that animated our moral sense. Hume's observational science demonstrated that the psychological mechanism of "sympathy" was the secondary principle that funded our moral sentiment. Though secondary, it was fully natural: "when you pronounce any action or character to be vicious, you mean nothing, but that from the constitution of your nature you have a feeling or sentiment of blame from the contemplation of it" (3.1.1.25). As far as Hume was concerned, we could neither confidently ascribe objective sources to moral norms nor intelligibly argue that moral decisions had metaphysical significance.

We can provisionally order Hume's broad interest in the sources of our moral norms and how we gain access to these sources as his *metaethical* reflections. His insight, at this wider approach to morals, was that we could only "expect success" finding their sources "by following the experimental method, and deducing general maxims from a comparison of particular instances." Just as he was not convinced that there was a "moral arc" to history or the universe, Hume also carried extraordinary doubt regarding the capacity of our moral judgments to reflect any objective or independent moral standards. Thus, he approached the conclusions of moral realism (that moral norms were mind-independent), moral rationalism (that moral distinctions were derived from reason), moral theism (that moral judgments were determined by God), and moral sentimentalism (that our morals depended on an a priori moral sensibility) with a largely nondogmatic and mitigated skepticism. This mature skeptical vision that Hume brought to the questions we now refer to as "metaethical" was neither nihilism, nor moral atheism; it was, rather, an apt acknowledgment of the limits of our rational inheritance.[15] The capacity to understand the sources of moral judgment was not available to us, and he gave no indication that we would develop this capacity. Hume came at the question differently: he perceived that publicly observable behaviors inspired by virtuous motives had useful consequences. The causes of these motives, however, were *unobservable*. Hume proposed, following his theory of mind, that they were derived from "universal principles, from which all censure or approbation is ultimately derived" (*EPM*, 1.10). These universal principles were inaccessible to the human mind and could not "be accounted for" (*T*, 3.3.1.27). The best that we could do was to work from an observational method to describe our psychology of moral *approval*.

The rest of this chapter expands on the basic argument I have set out. The first part describes the background for the metaethical questions that Hume inherited and demonstrates his skeptical and naturalist responses to the Hobbesian legacy in morality to set up the contours for a *practical morality*. Though his moral framework constrained him from making particular types of moral claims, in part 2 I lay bare some of the elements of his limited normative approach. Hume's unique ideas such as the psychological mechanism "sympathy," his notion of the "common view," his discussion of promises, and his distinction between artificial and natural virtues are woven throughout as I use them to support my argument that a speculative, Humean-influenced notion of true religion is an artifice that enhanced social stability and happiness. Part 3 attends to the particular role of history for Hume's moral thought and a speculative true religion. Hume's *History of England* confirmed that the "man of morals" "gratefully acknowledges the bounty of his creator" (*EMPL*, 16.154). Further, his narration of certain historical figures revealed his quiet acknowledgment that true religion could play a role in the development of virtuous character. Annette Baier notes, regarding what is revealed in Hume's historical work, that "'true religion,' for Hume—what really ties and reties us to one another—is dedication to shared morality."[16] Overall, this chapter generally engages Hume as a pragmatic virtue ethicist: a thinker who values the Ciceronian approach to morality that emphasized the development of character traits against the modern focus on duty. Considering Hume in this way flags his thoughts on morality as central for discourse that helps "us to form a just notion of the happiness, as well as of the dignity of virtue" and leaves us with a notion of his "practical morality" (*T*, 3.3.6.6) that I propose as the moral core of our speculative project for religion, true religion.

## Hume's Metaethics

I found that the moral Philosophy transmitted to us by Antiquity, labor'd under the same Inconvenience that has been found in their natural Philosophy, of being entirely Hypothetical, & depending more upon Invention than Experience. Every one consulted his Fancy in erecting Schemes of Virtue & of Happiness, without regarding human Nature, upon which every moral Conclusion must depend. This therefore I resolved to make my principal Study, the Source from which I wou'd derive every Truth in Criticism as well as Morality.

—A Kind of History of My Life

Hume's idea of virtue on both the normative and practical levels was based on the notion that virtuous behavior was what humans found pleasing and what inspired their happiness. He claimed—loosely and without analytic precision—that a philosopher could generally make headway on the question of human virtue if he thoughtfully considered "whether or not he should desire to have this or that quality ascribed to him" (*EPM*, 1.10). His idea of virtuous character, however, did not stop at the level of the personal and the pleasurable. As I have been emphasizing, the *social* role and *public* affections were seminal for the development of virtuous character. Hume wrote, "justice is an essentially social and cooperative virtue."[17]

Hume's concerns about virtuous character and morality formed an integral component of his science of human nature, and the conclusions that he drew from them were connected to his thoughts on politics, economics, and religion. In this regard, Hume was indebted to Thomas Hobbes, who blazed the trail for the Scotsman in two other ways. First, Hobbes placed the sources of our moral norms and distinctions fully in the realm of the natural; Hume followed suit. Second, Hobbes prioritized human pleasure; Hume did also, but with a revision. He rejected Hobbesian egoism and asserted that humans were motivated by the pleasure of a nonegoist, socially directed attitude of approval from acting in mutually reinforcing ways. Hume did not completely concur with the Hobbesian premise that our drive for pleasure was fully reducible to the pursuit of our rational self-interest, and he did not accept that coercive state power secured social order. This left Hume standing between the rock of a Hobbesian moral skepticism and the very hard place of a Christian moral rationalism. The lacuna between these positions reveals the possibility that Hume's practical morality could be housed in religion's proper office.

## Hobbes's Legacy and the Moral Background to Hume

The ancient philosophers, though they often affirm, that virtue is nothing but conformity to reason, yet, in general, seem to consider morals as deriving their existence from taste and sentiment. On the other hand, our modern enquirers, though they also talk much of the beauty of virtue and the deformity of vice, yet have commonly endeavoured to account for these distinctions by metaphysical reasonings, and by deductions from the most abstract principles of the understanding.
—EPM, 1.4

The notion that our principal pleasure was to act in our rational self-interest was articulated most famously in Hobbes's 1651 *Leviathan* and again by Hume's close friend and student Adam Smith in his 1776 *Wealth of Nations*.[18] Thus the idea framed Hume's writing career. For Hobbes, morals did not exist. We discovered them in our obligation to submit to sovereign authority, which was mandated by our being motivated by the pleasure we received from pursuing our rational self-interest. For Smith, our moral commitment to competition was based on the belief that our primary human motive was rational self-interest, which would be transformed (and regulated) by free-market competition.

I have begun with the Hobbesian *psychological* claim that humans derive the most pleasure from pursuing their (rationally determined) self-interests and followed with the Hobbesian *moral* skepticism regarding the existence of morals, to illuminate the central role of pleasure and motivation in modern moral thought.

In many ways this is the Hobbesian legacy in morality, and it raises three fundamental issues crucial for the discussion of the moral features of our Humean true
religion. The first is the question of the sources of our moral norms, that is, moral
realism versus moral skepticism. Hobbes was a moral skeptic. The second is the
cause of our virtuous actions, or moral motivations versus moral obligations.
Hobbes contended that we were motivated by self-interests. Third, Hobbes's
method raised the question of how we access the virtues, the issue of moral sentiment versus moral reason. To Hobbes, moral behavior was determined by the
authority of sovereign power to which we submit to protect our self-interests. It is
likely that Hobbes's moral skepticism and his egoist conception of pleasure
inspired Hume, who had little interest in the idea that natural law guided our
moral behavior (i.e., Locke), had moved away from the belief in rational self-
control of the will (i.e., Descartes), had only slight patience for morals fully discernible through the faculty of reason (i.e., Clarke), and had disregarded the
moral claims of traditional theism (i.e., Warburton). If Hobbes was correct, Hume
would have to cosign the ideas that morals do not exist and our drive for pleasure
consistently threatened our communal existence.[19]

The two most powerful responses to Hobbes at the metaethical level, moral
rationalism (Clarke) and moral sentimentalism (Shaftesbury), argued that moral
norms were both real and accessible to the human mind. In this way, they shifted
the question from the motivation of our actions (Hobbes's view) to our obligation to honor reality. In his clever challenge to Hobbes, Samuel Clarke's *Discourse upon Natural Religion* (1706) privileged what he named moral knowledge
and argued that moral norms were both real and objective. Explicitly addressing
the "absurdity" of the Hobbesian scheme and the "falsity and weakness of Mr.
Hobbes's doctrine," Clarke asserted, based on the conception of a benevolent
God, that there were "necessary and eternal" distinctions between things in the
order of nature.[20] The very fact of these distinctions meant that it was already
determined that certain creatures should act in particular ways toward other
creatures. The "fitness" of an action was equivalent to its moral correctness, which
was real, objective, mind-independent, and a built-in component of nature. In
fact, the main feature of the mind, according to Clarke, was its capacity to penetrate the web of relationality and discern moral knowledge, the proper relations
between things. For Clarke, reason alone discovered existing moral truths and
allowed us to make proper moral judgments. These moral truths were the proper
relations of entities; thus they were immutable *and* discoverable, transcendent
*yet* accessible. He noted, "These things are so notoriously plain and self-evident,
that nothing but the extremest stupidity of Mind, corruption of Manners, or per-
verseness of Spirit can possibly make any Man entertain the least doubt concerning them."[21]

The unique status Clarke attributed to moral knowledge demonstrated his belief that our rational experience of reality was the actual experience of moral truth. Still, he allowed that humans were at liberty to choose to act in either a moral or immoral way. That is, reason could discern moral *obligation*, but it did not determine moral *conduct*. Clarke assumed that our conduct relied on a particular disposition of the will to be moved by the moral obligations discerned by reason.[22] To behave in concert with moral knowledge, that is, to engage in moral conduct, our will must be motivated in a particular way such that we act in accordance with reason and honor reality over illusion. If we reject the perception of moral truth, our will has not been impacted to moral behavior and we have simply disregarded reason and reality. Thus, reason has the power to influence action, and denying the truth of reason is absurd. For Clarke then, the certainty of moral truth was similar to the inevitability of mathematical truth, which is always self-evident, external to the mind, and eternally carved into the structure of nature (e.g., $2 + 2 = 4$). Both moral and mathematical truths are always fully discoverable by reason, the engine of moral conduct for Clarke.

In sum, Clarke's response to the Hobbesian premise was to establish an independent faculty that confirmed that moral norms were real, to assert that moral distinctions existed independent of our minds, and to affirm that reason affected our actions. Against Hobbes's fetishization of motivations that inspired the will to self-interest, Clarke emphasized the obligations that the knowledge of nature placed on us to act in accord with reason. He assumed that these obligations inspired our properly disposed will to act in a moral fashion. For after we discovered moral truths, we were obligated to act in accord with reason and perform in "fit" (or moral) ways. The idea of a moral universe reflected Clarke's rationalism and his interest in our obligation to Christian virtues. For him it was the power of real, necessary, and eternal knowledge (combined with abstract reason) that compelled the will of the human agent to act in service of moral truth. This rendered Clarke a realist concerning the source of our moral norms and a rationalist concerning our moral judgment (our faculty of reason has access to moral norms and shapes our moral judgments). To Clarke, the will was powered by reason.

Moral sentimentalism and moral rationalism are similarly structured. The sentimentalists simply replace the unique form of reason on which the rationalists depend with a special sense of the affections, and they swap out the notion that virtue emanates from a natural web of relationality with the idea that virtue is derived from human nature. We might even consider Shaftesbury—the representative of the sentimentalist approach—as part rationalist in the sense that "he allows no form of religious authority which cannot be made convincing to autonomous reason."[23] In this way the moral sense theorists actually had more in common with their rationalist predecessors than it seemed: both introduced an independent faculty that provided access to "real" moral knowledge and objective, ethical truth.

Shaftesbury moved against Hobbes's moral skepticism by demonstrating its logical instability and establishing his own moral realism based on human nature. His method was to simply extend Hobbes's skepticism to its logical limits. He stated that a full-blown skepticism did not diminish the clarity of our feelings: "Let us carry *Scepticism* ever so far, let us doubt, if we can, of every thing about us; we cannot doubt of what passes *within ourselves*. Our Passions and Affections are known to us. *They* are certain, whatever the *Objects* may be, on which they are employ'd." To Shaftesbury, our affections were indisputable: they could disclose the real, the certain, and the good, for it is "by Affection merely that a Creature is esteem'd good or ill, natural or unnatural."[24] For Shaftesbury (and Hutcheson), it was the affections, not reason, that inspired moral conduct and empowered the will.

In his "Inquiry" (a revision of part of the three-volume *Characteristicks of Men, Manners, Opinions, Times* [1711]) Shaftesbury argued that moral norms were built into human nature. It is when we accessed the real and entire nature of man through our affections that we would discover true moral knowledge and uncover the source of moral norms and distinctions. There were three kinds of affections for Shaftesbury: self-affections that led to private good, natural affections that led to public good, and unnatural affections that led nowhere. The self-affections were akin to Hobbes's self-interests. For Shaftesbury, however, they served only private interests—a small component of our human nature—and were too narrow to be virtuous.[25] To him, it was the natural affections that escorted us to the "Nature of Virtue," which consisted "in a certain just Disposition, or proportionable Affection of a rational Creature towards the moral Objects of Right and Wrong."[26] Though we label Shaftesbury a sentimentalist concerning morals because he esteemed the natural affections as the mode by which we gain access to moral norms, we might think of him as a moral realist about their sources: they are real and exist in human nature. Additionally, Shaftesbury thought that virtuous conduct was a result of the compelling obligations that were naturally generated when our sentiments discovered the good in our nature.

The point of departure for Hobbes's moral theory was the experience of pleasure and how it motivated the will to action. Shaftesbury and Clarke had a different starting point: they established an independent faculty that confirmed moral distinctions were real, moral knowledge was objective, and moral norms existed independently of the mind.[27] Thus, they avoided a direct confrontation with Hobbes on the motivating pleasure of self-interest. To be fair, it seems that Shaftesbury was more comfortable attending to the idea of pleasure and the passions than Clarke, but he did not link the pleasurable to the virtuous because pleasure was too selfish and irrational to serve morality. For Shaftesbury, pleasure was dangerous; it could lead us away from moral reality and into temptation.

Most interpretations of the sentimentalists and the rationalists emphasize the differences in these two methods and track what they understand to be of most importance in their strategies: whether our moral ideas are derived from reason or sentiment and how our conduct is powered by either reason or the affections. This contrast, however, obfuscates an important, shared element of their strategy. For the purpose of my argument regarding a constructive Humean true religion it is useful to assess the affinities between the rationalists and sentimentalists rather than emphasize their differences. What they share is a common stance in relation to Hobbes: the belief in an independent faculty that could discern the source of moral norms, establish them as real, and convey how they obligate us to ethical action.

## Hume's Moral Naturalism and Skepticism

That which renders morality an active principle and constitutes virtue our happiness and vice our misery . . . depends on
some internal sense or feeling, which nature has made universal in the whole species.
—*EPM*, 1.9

Hume reappropriated and reshaped some of the ideas of Clarke, Shaftesbury, and Hobbes.[28] His approach to the question of moral judgment seems to have at least four distinct aims: first, to demonstrate that we could not intelligibly trace our moral judgments back to rational, divine, or sovereign sources; second, to show that morality was partially derived from the social fabric of life; third, to establish a unique psychological mechanism called sympathy; and, finally, to establish grounds for his investment in virtuous character development. These aims are both philosophical and practical: they demonstrate his belief in improving common life, increasing social peace, and expanding toleration. Often unnoticed in analyses of Hume's moral thought is that virtuous character ultimately functions in what we might think of, broadly construed, as a religious fashion: it binds humans together and stabilizes the social order. I shall take up the normative side of Hume's thought in part 2, where I argue that his practical morality is a form of pragmatic virtue ethics. Here I want to discuss, in broader terms, his naturalist and skeptical response to metaethical discourse and briefly recap his concepts of sympathy and the common view.

The forethought to this section confirmed that Hume's argument cohered with components of the "moral sense" approach. There is substantive textual evidence for interpreting Hume as a sentimentalist regarding morality. For example, he claimed that "to have a sense of virtue, is nothing but to *feel* a satisfaction of a particular kind from the contemplation of a character. The very *feeling* constitutes our praise and admiration" (*T*, 3.1.2.3). This feeling inspired our actions; thus it seems that for Hume the sentiments were more responsible for our conduct than reason. Yet Hume's views can be distinguished from the sentimentalist view in at least two ways. First, Hume rejected the providential deity of both the rationalists and sentimentalists and showed little esteem for their reasoning that "our moral affections" were "analogous to God's and [that] our conscience" was "the voice of God within."[29] Second, Hume did not accept that moral knowledge—even if derived from a moral sense—was objectively true, and he was less sanguine than both Hutcheson and Shaftesbury regarding the altruistic motives of human beings.[30] In short, reading Hume comfortably within the sentimentalist trajectory inappropriately reduces and severely restricts his moral contributions.

Both the sentimentalists and rationalists established an autonomous faculty (either reason or sentiment) to demonstrate the motivational power of moral realism. Hume described an independent and post-egoist, social sentiment that provided natural motivation for moral agents. This sentiment, which Hume called "sympathy," was a psychological feature of our mind that animated our moral judgment. Sympathy, from Hume's use of the term in the *Treatise* (2.1.11), is having the same feeling as someone else while remaining in your own subject position. It is different from our contemporary notion of sympathy (to feel sorry for someone) and distinct from the current way we use the term "empathy" (to put yourself in someone else's shoes). It seems that for Hume, the motives (i.e., virtuous traits) of the moral agent were transferred by sympathy, the mechanism that allows the motive to gain public affection. The category "sympathy" distinguishes Hume's approach from both moral rationalists and moral sentimentalists. Additionally, the idea that the sources of our moral norms were social conventions (artifices) and the belief that the way we accessed the virtues was through our feelings of approbation allow us to reasonably conclude that Hume was neither a moral realist nor a moral skeptic. Hume believed morals were constructed by our natural propensities as processed through psychological mechanism and social artifice.

The point of departure for Hume's naturalism regarding morality was neither an autonomous subject nor a rational set of truths. Hume's approach to morality started with biohistorical agents fully situated in communities. It highlighted connectedness and stressed our sentiments, namely benevolence, as the first responders to experience. Moral judgment, as Hume considered it, was generally a public process that required deliberation and cooperation. It was partially kick-started by the sentimental motivation to social approval (and disapproval). It also relied on what Annette Baier described as "Cicero's 'undoubted maxim': that there must

be some natural motive to action before that action can be seen as morally obliga-
tory."[31] Hume admitted that the "natural motive" always combined with sentiments
that led to approbation or disapprobation was impacted by social conventions, one
of which was religion. He wrote that "religion . . . may be regarded as the great
spring of men's actions and determinations" (HE, 6.86). The sentiments excited by
moral judgment and "natural motive" functioned in a way that bound us to others
through our affections (the mechanism of sympathy is crucial here), brought us
a kind of social agreeability, and—these socially constructed and community-
moderated affections—influenced our will. Given this, and Hume's sense of true
religion, expressed in a letter that requested its recipient to object to religious
devotion, prayer, "and everything we commonly call religion, except the practice
of morality, and the assent of the understanding to the proposition that God
exists" (LET, 1.50.21), we can fairly presume that Hume articulated his moral project to comport with what he took to be religion's proper office. Ultimately, Hume's
moral contributions aimed to improve our conduct so we might better connect
and cooperate with one another. This was enhanced by natural coordination that
was both improvisational and strategic and by the formation of conventions that
encouraged more trust in the face of risk and betrayal. Claims like the following
confirm Hume's naturalist project for morality: "And indeed, when we consider
how aptly *natural* and *moral* evidence link together, and form only one chain of
argument, we shall make no scruple to allow that they are of the same nature, and
derived from the same principles" (E, 8.19).

One cannot deny that Hume's naturalism regarding morality had a skeptical
dimension. This allowed him to occupy a middle position between the moral realists' belief that moral judgments had independently existing truth-value and the
strong skeptical position that moral norms did not exist independently of the
mind. Moral value was, on the view of the realists, instantiated in the fabric of
the universe and merely *discovered* by human beings. For the skeptics, however,
transcendent, transhistorical moral value was nonexistent. To the moral realists,
moral facts were real and certain truths were *moral* ones; they reasoned that if our
minds worked properly, we could determine which action correlated with the
proper, preexisting moral principle. The Hobbesian moral skeptic, on the other
hand, asserted that we had to depend on authority to guide us to proper conduct.
Hume's skeptical naturalist approach started from the idea that abstract reason
could not locate the sources of our moral judgment. He claimed, against the
moral realists, that if an independent moral truth did exist, it was inaccessible to
the human mind. Against the strong skeptical position, he believed that our moral
imagination projected moral structure onto the world. Hume's investment in
excellence, greatness of mind, and virtuous character led him to argue that it was

our moral sensibilities that primarily informed our actions. He navigated between moral realism and moral skepticism by holding moral facts to be feelings about how we should behave that could evolve into conventions and endow our sense of moral virtue.

Hume also held a middle position between the moral obligationists (Shaftesbury) and the moral motivationists (Hobbes). Obligationists held that the simple awareness of the existence of morals compelled the moral agent to moral action. Motivationists argued that our volition contained a moral dimension that guided us to moral norms. Moral action is, on the view of the moral obligationists, dictated by the morals we discover. For the motivationists, moral action is the consequence of our motivation; what we are driven to do defines who we are morally (or not, per Hobbes). On the former view, we are obligated to do right. On the latter conception, what lies beneath our "right" actions determines what is right.

Hume rejected the obligationists' view that awareness of virtues *obligates* us to moral actions. He also resisted the motivationists' conception that moral motivations *lead* to virtuous action. His view was that virtuous motives obligated us to virtuous actions. How does a moral agent obtain virtuous motives for Hume? From virtuous actions. Perhaps this circularity can be explained as follows: by definition, all actions are public; that is, they are able to be observed by spectators. If an event has useful and agreeable consequences to the actor or the recipient, then the spectator experiences sympathy with the actor or recipient. This sympathy is—in Hume's early works—a morally neutral faculty of approval that transfers the affections between agent, recipient, and spectator. Another way to say this is that sympathy is the psychological device by which affections of the actor or recipient are actually experienced by the spectator. This complex psychological mechanism plays an important role in the process of confirming whether an act may be virtuous or not. Virtue, for Hume, is a motivating trait that generates approbation and informs the operation of the agent. The agent's virtuous actions motivate others to virtuous behavior. Highlighting Hume's unique notion of sympathy situates his moral theory between a theory of obligation and one of motivation.

Sympathy, on Hume's account, is inseparable from approbation, for *common approval* is required for a characteristic to be considered virtuous.[32] "The common point of view" is attained when he transcends his immediate historical experience and "departs from his private and particular situation, and must choose a point of view, common to him with others; he must move some universal principle of the human frame, and touch a string to which all mankind have an accord and symphony" (*EPM*, 9.1.6). This string is the human sentiments "which arise from humanity" and are "not only the same in all human creatures . . . but they also comprehend all human creatures" (*EPM*, 9.1.7). "And where that principle [sympathy] may take place and the quality approv'd of is really beneficial to society, a true philosopher will never require any other principle to account for the strongest approbation and esteem" (*T*, 3.3.1.10). Thus the language of the sentiments is broad, and our feeling of sympathy—at least in the *Treatise*—is the real propensity to feel what others feel.[33] To Hume, our sentiments are contagious.

Given that sympathy transfers emotions and sentiments between us and, by default, connects us with one another, we might say then that the function of "binding," traditionally associated with religion, is central to Hume's moral thought. If we approach Hume's concept of sympathy through the lens of true religion, it takes on a deeper religious hue and more of a binding resonance. Instead of simply transferring affections, it could be understood as a way of highlighting a special disposition between humans that propels us to expand our sense of self by taking on the affections of others. From the view of our speculative true religion, this transferring of the affections is not simply a superficial overlap of human passions or a neutral psychological mechanism; it is a soul-crafting experience of human solidarity and connectedness that provides psychic solidarity and stabilizes the social order.

In summary, moral sentimentalists accept that the most efficient pathway to moral norms and sources is through a special "moral sense," a part of our nature. Moral rationalists trust that it is the rational faculty that provides us with access to our moral sources and norms. Both camps work from the conclusion that morals are real, and then they explain the process by which we might approach these morals. Rationalists believe that moral questions can be worked out through the faculty of mind, while sentimentalists depend on a moral sense, something linked to a structure of moods. Hume, as I have explained, is not a moral realist (that is, he is *neither* a rationalist nor sentimentalist). For him, our moral lives are driven by social approval and pressed toward public utility. The psychological mechanism of sympathy is tantamount in this process. Socially speaking, we develop our moral sensibilities from conventions and artifices, not from an unmediated experience of nature. Ultimately, actions that generate approbation tend to forge social happiness and confirm that moral judgment is a collective process. On Hume's argument, humans do what is generally agreeable to and useful for one another. This creates the feeling of public happiness or "communitas" that—I might add—from the vista of our Humean-inflected true religion can be understood as a religious dimension of social experience.[34] For Hume, reason and the sentiments work together for public approbation that provides us, not with a clear path to some preexisting morals, but with a fully subjective convention to teach and guide virtuous development.

## Hume's Normative Project

Where would be the foundation of morals, if particular characters had no certain or determinate power to produce particular sentiments, and if these sentiments had no constant
operation on our actions?
—*E*, 8.1.18

On the normative level Hume relied on common life, the imagination, convention, and artifice to describe how we might best derive virtuous character traits.
Most basically, he contended that the traits we held to be virtuous were those we
wanted others to attribute to us. Annette Baier's extensive classification of these
traits confirms that Hume celebrated qualities of personality that were generally
pleasing and tended to make us happy.[35] As I have stated earlier, the natural sentiments for pleasure, happiness, and agreeability, in Hume's view, were shaped by
social artifices and conventions of common life. In this way the development of
virtuous character was deeply connected to the evolution of social artifices and
conventions for Hume. The significance of this is twofold: first, it affirms that
Hume's moral project was directed at outcomes and results; and, second, it suggests that if we consider religion as a convention, then the true religion would be
the form of religion that was the convention to help "humanize our conduct" and
develop our character.

The use of the concept "normative" in relation to Hume smuggles in baggage
that, in some ways, obfuscates his moral project. The term "normative" is con-
ventionally used in moral thought to designate something that has the authority
to guide our behavior to morally correct ends. Hume's mature skepticism dictated that we did not have reliable access to any transhistorical sources of morality. This meant that we could neither justifiably determine morally "correct" ends
nor intelligibly label a future action as objectively right. In short, we were both
ineffective in finding ends that were patently moral and inept at locating trust-
worthy escorts to them. Given this, Hume thought the best we could do was to
develop good character, for the correct behavior was that which functioned most
effectively for all involved. Another way to explain this is to say that right conduct was strategic for Hume; it served the mutual interests of the actors involved
and reflected their feelings of approval. In this way Hume's moral thought
rejected the conventional sense of normativity and left us impotent at making
*objective* moral claims. For example, on his account, nothing inherent in the act
of murder made it immoral. Murder was simply an occurrence of killing that was
morally wrong because we made it so. The laws that render it immoral are social

artifices evolved from our coordinated and repeated social disapproval of this particular mode of killing: "it is impossible for men so much as to murder each other without statutes, and maxims, and an idea of justice and honour" (*EPM*, 4.20). Hume's study of the artifice of justice disclosed that we were best served by treating the source of our moral norms and judgments as fundamentally grounded in our nature as human beings, not in divinity or a sovereign state. The normative aspect of his moral project then derived from his explanation of how this nature manifested in the mechanism "sympathy," expressed itself in approbation, and developed the artificial virtues. These dynamic, social features enhanced our character.[36]

## Hume's Virtue Ethics

A virtuous horse we can conceive; because from our own feeling, we can conceive virtue.
—*E*, 2.4

Hume is generally situated in the trajectory of the classical moralists who venerate *character* (who should I be?) over *duty* (what shall I do?) and employ a kind of virtue ethic. This way of approaching moral behavior stands against both the emphasis on duties (popularized by Kant) and the stress on consequences (first advanced by Bentham) that occupied the modern moral imagination. In philosophy, virtue ethics is often traced back to the work of Aristotle who held *eudaimonia*, a profound sense of well-being and happiness, to be the most important character trait and the ultimate virtue for which we should strive. In theology, virtue ethics is closely linked to the thought of Saint Thomas Aquinas, who provided a systematic description of the virtues that lead to our perfections.[37] Cicero was the classical figure concerned about the development of character traits that would sustain the social order. Hume followed neither Aristotle in the quest for *eudaimonia* nor Thomas in the pursuit of the perfections; instead, he argued, in more of a Ciceronian fashion, that "if any action be either virtuous or vicious, 'tis only as a sign of some quality or *character*. It must depend upon *durable principles of the mind*, which extend over the whole conduct, and enter into the *personal character*. Actions themselves, not proceeding from any *constant principle*, have not influence . . . and consequently are never considered in morality" (*T*, 3.3.1.4; italics added).

Hume contended that what was agreeable and useful for the development of virtuous character was based on the set of social and historical circumstances that constituted ethical formation in common life. In "A Dialogue" (crafted in Ciceronian style and tacked on to the appendix of the second *Enquiry*) he stressed how place, time, disposition, and situation ("fashion, vogue, custom and law") "were the chief foundation[s] of all moral determinations" (*EPM*, app. V, 26). One might read this dialogue as a study in comparative ethics. Hume, however, is neither a comparativist nor a moral relativist. He holds that basic and natural principles warrant the process of formation for our moral judgments. Importantly, these principles are not justified by rational criteria. Unlike Aristotle and Thomas, neither an overarching conception of happiness nor a drive for perfection provides the normative thrust for Hume's moral agent. It is the natural capacity of the mind for social approval that provides the foundations for Hume's virtue ethics. Note his definition of virtue: "it is the nature and, indeed, the definition of virtue, that it is *a quality of the mind agreeable to or approved of by every one who considers or contemplates it*" (8.1n).

This definition of virtue underscores two crucial facts. First, it validates his idea that actions or judgments are not intrinsically bad or good, but that we attach this value to them through a reflective act of the mind that reaches beyond reason and what is given in experience. Hume follows Hamlet's famous claim, "there is nothing either good or bad but thinking makes it so" and adds a social dimension to it. Second, it recognizes the "quality of mind" of a virtue by the *feeling* it produces. "An action, or sentiment, or character is virtuous or vicious; why? Because its view causes a pleasure or uneasiness of a particular kind" (*T*, 3.1.2.3). Hume describes this feeling as a social sentiment of approbation. "The approbation of moral qualities most certainly is not deriv'd from reason, or any comparison of ideas; but proceeds entirely from a moral taste, and from certain sentiments of pleasure or distrust, which arise upon the contemplation and view of particular qualities or characters" (3.3.1.15). Moral judgments create feelings of approval that are confirmed in social life and common experience (this is why some take him to be a sentimentalist).

This provisional definition of virtue—"*a quality of the mind agreeable to or approved of by every one who considers or contemplates it*" (*EPM*, 8.1n)—provides us with a basic sense of the notions of agreeability and common approval central to Hume's concept of virtue. Yet it does not fully capture the degree to which Hume believes the social usefulness of our actions is *decisive* for them to be considered virtuous or not. To note this emphasis, we might supplement this definition of virtue with a related one stated later in the moral *Enquiry*: "In all determinations of morality, this circumstance of *public utility* is ever principally in view; and wherever disputes arise, either in philosophy or common life, concerning the bounds of duty, the question cannot, by any means, be decided with greater certainty, than by ascertaining, in any side, the *true interests of mankind*" (2.2.12; italics added). I take this to mean that Hume believed virtuous character generally promoted the public interests of human society. Broadly, we might say that excellence was agreeable to the principles of human nature; it found approval from all who contemplated it.

To approach the question of virtue with an interest in feelings of public utility as they combined with approval or pleasure is often misunderstood as a simple appeal to set emotions as the guides of moral judgment. While I have spoken to Hume's position between the moral rationalists and moral sentimentalists, I have not addressed the broader issues conjured by those who regarded the strict reliance on personal feelings as the source of moral decisions. Analytic thinkers in ethics name this approach noncognitivism.[38] There is strong evidence for the interpretation of Hume as a noncognitivist regarding morality. As I have explained, however, one must take care before concluding that Hume fully reduces virtue to a matter of *feeling*, for this contradicts both his style as a philosopher (his moderate skepticism) and his idea of the passions (feelings are impressions of reflections and are thereby dependent on the mind). If Hume were simply a noncognitivist concerning morality, he would have little grounds on which to assert that certain moral actions were more correct than others, and it would therefore be difficult to resolve any moral conflict. Given his firm reliance on sympathy, the common point of view, and virtuous motives, as well as his refusal to posit a scientifically rigorous rule-based system of moral decision making, we might classify his work, for certain purposes, as a weak form of noncognitivism. Yet the most compelling strategy for situating Hume's practical morality as a part of our speculative true religion is, I think, to emphasize its naturalist elements over its noncognitivist ones, which a turn to some recent interpretations of Hume might loosely confirm.

## Interpretations of Hume's Approach

But 'tis not only the *natural* obligations of interest, which are distinct in promises and allegiance; but also the *moral* obligations of honour and conscience: Nor does the merit or demerit of the one depend in the least upon that of the other. And indeed, if we consider the close connexion there is betwixt the natural and moral obligations, we shall find this conclusion to be entirely unavoidable.

—*T*, 3.2.8.7

Rosalind Hursthouse's seminal text *On Virtue Ethics* provides us with one of the most detailed discussions of ethical naturalism.[39] Her micropresentation of the specifics of the naturalist project in moral theory, built on the foundations of the work of Philippa Foot and Elizabeth Anscombe and constructed largely in conversation with John McDowell, is unparalleled in its depth and detail.[40] Hurst-house reinvigorates the Aristotelian commitment to *eudaimonia* and marries it to a Humean moral naturalism that posits virtues as character traits that both ben-efit their possessor (enable them to flourish) and make their possessor a good human being qua human being. Hursthouse's virtue ethics, which are based on Hume's, posit four provisional ends for a virtue. Each is based on the particular characteristics of the species to which they are being applied (Hursthouse is care-ful about how virtue ethics must work across species). The ends she proposes are individual survival, continuance of species, freedom from pain and enjoyment, and good functioning of the social group.[41] She also importantly notes the crucial role of motivation and intention—again relying on Hume—for virtuous behavior.

Christine Swanton's *Virtue Ethics: A Pluralistic View* responds to some of the challenges that Hursthouse raises. She argues that the central problem of Hurst-house's view is that it is too teleological and therefore actually a misreading of Hume. For Hume, Swanton notes (and Hursthouse is equally aware of this), vir-tues do not solely serve ends. Swanton writes, "According to Hume, generally disutile traits can be understood as virtues if we approve of them having adopted a corrected (educated) sympathy. A generally disutile trait can be approved in virtue of its 'dazzling' qualities, or its ability to 'seize the heart' by 'its noble eleva-tion' or 'engaging tenderness.' And the reason that 'excessive bravery' and 'resolute inflexibility' are approved is that we take pleasure in 'splendour and greatness of appearance.'"[42]

Swanton also notes that the ends Hursthouse puts forward are all anthropo-centric, and she challenges them by offering a deeper pluralism that might priori-tize environmental ends over anthropocentric ones. Her revised "principle of virtue status" avoids anthropocentrism; it is a "disposition to respond in an excel-lent (or good enough) way (through the modes of respecting, appreciating, creat-ing, loving, promoting, and so on) to items in the fields of the virtue."[43] Hursthouse investigated the function of virtue ethics built on an Aristotelian ethical natural-ism that prioritized flourishing in light of Hume's emphasis on character traits of the possessor. Swanton employed a kind of Nietzschean naturalism that took self-love as its starting point yet expanded beyond mere human concerns in under-standing its task—as it reads Hume to do—as a theoretical one with generally, but not only, practical ends (to build community).

Michael Slote differs from both Hursthouse and Swanton: he argues for a Humean natural sentimentalism that begins with empathy (sympathy in Hume's usage). Slote writes, "Hume held that our capacity for approbation/approval and moral judgment depends on our 'propensity' or tendency to sympathize with oth-ers, but the sympathy at issue here is not the kind of sympathetic concern for others that we nowadays designate by using the term sympathy, but is rather for

Hume, a mechanism of psychological influence." Slote's agent-based (not agent-focused) approach explicitly aims to recover Hume's moral project by concentrating on the empathetic *motives* of the agent. Like Hursthouse and Swanton, Slote reads Hume as a naturalist regarding morality. Unlike Hursthouse and Swanton, Slote emphasizes the psychological dimensions of Hume's moral thought over his more historicist concerns. Slote maintains—and here I'm applying a formulation of Cornel West's—a "weak" form of moral relativism that holds universal standards and philosophical criteria to justify certain ethical choices and a "plurality of such procedures and standards between which there can be no adjudication."[44]

What is most fascinating about these three Humean-influenced virtue ethicists is how each creatively reads Hume with slightly different emphases. At the same time, what is troubling about these texts is that they remain wedded to a conception of morality that Hume, in many ways, largely abandoned. The implicit Kantian influence on Slote, Swanton, and Hursthouse has them reproducing categories of abstract reason and false philosophy that view ethics as a set of character traits that modulate between the objective and the relative, the subjective and the universal, the right and the less right. Stuck in this conventional muck about moral obligation, ethical principles, and sources, these thinkers entertain abstruse ideas about the proper grounds on which we might best calibrate our behavior, yet they understand their projects as largely Humean. But Hume showed little concern with pitching his moral project under the auspices of the conventional terms and approaches that had come to represent moral philosophy. He took himself to be freeing moral thought from its historical burdens and philosophical constrictions, and he wanted to reveal the agenda behind conventional approaches to morality and thereby show its deficiency for his practical morality. Concomitant to this effort, he navigated above the mire of these theoretical strategies and tried to contain his moral observations of human subjects in common life, strategically coordinating with one another for their mutual advantage, developing conventions, and building character. He kept track of human dynamism, community factionalism, and discontinuous traditions, as well as the human biases, needs, and desires that rendered the commitment to ahistorical, universal foundations as false. Simply put, he traced the personal and public use of our affections in ways that blurred the line between morality and prudence. Hursthouse, Swanton, and Slote want a clearer line. Their arguments for Hume as a nontraditional moralist have lots to offer, but only Hursthouse's reading leaves space for the sense of practical morality that we pursue.

Hursthouse helps us to recognize that a benefit of reading Hume as a naturalist regarding morals is that it leaves interpretive room for us to appreciate how the background "universal springs and principles" of our nature inform whether we generate subjective feelings of approbation or disapprobation regarding an action (useful or useless) that we have reflectively engaged in response to an event. The subjective pleasure we get from these feelings of approval reflects the moral value of the object or event. In this way, both the experience and the approbation are part subjective and part derived from outside of the realm of the mind. The feeling of approbation or disapprobation is therefore never fully private; it is saturated in experience, which is always multifaceted and thick, and it points toward a sense of reality that is inaccessible to our minds. Though our subjective experience is linked to the "moral" event, it ultimately reflects some aspect of what Hume takes to be a natural truth—that is, a truth beyond what has been given to us in experience. Reading Hume's moral naturalism in this way presents us with a nimble Hume that narrowly avoids the subjectivist trap of strong noncognitivism on one side and the speculative metaphysics of the moral realists on the other. It also reminds us that the understated power of Hume's approach to moral judgment lies in its humility. Hume is comfortable with the gray areas of moral uncertainty. He recognizes that no moral science could adequately comprehend the complexity and mystery of the nature of reality. Hume's moral thought was comfortable in uncertainties; his skeptical naturalism in morality means he is not provincial concerning the realm of virtue. Accordingly, Hume has two types of virtues: artificial and natural ones.

## Artificial and Natural Virtues

There are some virtues, that produce pleasure and approbation by means of an artifice or contrivance.
—*T*, 3.2.1.1

Two premises undergird Hume's discussion of the virtues. The first is the idea that the *motive* behind an action is key to whether or not the action is virtuous, for "no action can be virtuous, but so far as it proceeds from a virtuous motive" (*T*, 3.2.1.10). The second is that the motive to perform a good or virtuous action must reside "in human nature" (3.2.1.7). Hume divides this second premise into two parts: the natural propensity toward our "real or universal" virtuous motives (3.2.1.18), the "natural virtues"; and the natural propensity toward artifice, or the social invention of "obvious and absolutely necessary" virtuous teachings and laws, the "artificial virtues."[45]

The discussion of artificial and natural virtues in the *Treatise* (the only place he attends directly to these categories) is complicated and often misunderstood. If we approach this distinction with specific virtues in mind, however, it becomes less opaque. I shall focus on Hume's description of justice, an artificial virtue; and his notion of benevolence, a natural one.[46] The difference between these two virtues is that benevolence is a natural *inclination* of humans that arises primitively, while justice is a natural *invention* of humans trying to cooperate in social order. The natural inclination of benevolence is generally expressed privately or in a small group; it exhibits *partiality* and most often has direct benefit for another human subject. The natural invention of justice is expressed publicly; it exhibits *impartiality* and does not benefit any specific individual.

The distinction, then, between these two virtues is not derived from their basis in nature, reason, or the passions. Their difference is based on the relationship of the virtue to social conventions. For example, natural virtues (e.g., benevolence) are antecedent to the development of property-owning societies, while artificial virtues (e.g., justice) materialize after the organization of human society and the simultaneous development of private property and its concomitant dependence on contracts. It is interesting to note that at the historical moment when the transatlantic slave trade was at its apogee—with England at the forefront and Scotland amassing great wealth from chattel slavery (Glasgow was proudly a "slave merchant city")—Hume's notion of justice says *nothing* about the protection of the human body; its concern is solely the secure transfer of *property*.[47] In fact, Hume does not seriously address physical or bodily harm. He either (mistakenly) thinks benevolence will win the day, or he simply wants to ignore the issue of bodily harm altogether. Either way, for him the "subsistence of the species" curiously seems to have nothing to do with the human body.

To illustrate the distinction between the natural and the artificial virtues, Hume provides a "natural history" of the development of human society as it evolved from a collection of individuals with enlightened self-interest in close-knit friend and family structures to the complex arrangement of individuals both deeply dependent on and in competition with others outside of their social circle. He explained that artificial virtues naturally evolved from natural virtues as human beings organized into complex social groups (*T*, 3.2.1.1–3.2.12.9). When cooperation between social groups became complicated, particularly on the prickly details around transactions of property and contracts, the community naturally constructed moral edifices and social artifices to simplify the fine points and optimize collective functioning. These edifices and artifices, what Hume called "conventions," were foundational for the evolution of the virtue of justice.[48] For, on Hume's account, we are not automatically inclined—regarding property— to justice, promises, or honesty. These features evolve and reevolve out of our experience within a collective. "A man's property," Hume writes, "is some object related to him. This relation is not natural, but moral, and founded on justice." He continues, "'Tis very preposterous, therefore, to imagine that we can have any idea of property, without fully comprehending the nature of justice, and shewing its origin in the artifice and contrivance of men" (3.2.2.11). Justice, promises, and obligation are linguistic conventions to help us preserve social arrangements and protect what we own; they are symbols that point us toward something beyond ourselves.[49]

Hume's presentation of natural (benevolence) and artificial (justice) virtues reveals how abstract reason misleads us when it "assert[s] justice to be a natural virtue, and antecedent to human conventions" (T, 3.2.8.4). When we imagine justice and all it carries with it—promises, fidelity, honesty—as natural, we allow our imagination to delude us into an improper self-conception that leads us to misunderstand our motives. False philosophy mistakes justice for a natural quality, or simply as a rule imposed by government authority (Hobbes). This misleads us in two ways: first, it helps us ignore the *limited benevolence* of our true character; and, second, it makes it easier for us to overlook the power of our conventions that precede (and nourish) the presence of government. The proper perception of justice, promises, honesty, and fidelity—artificial virtues—is to consider them as a set of "civic commitments," for the "object of our civil duties be the enforcing of our natural" ones (3.2.8.5) allows the development of clarity of motive and propriety of intention. Natural virtues, like benevolence, inform the artificial virtues, like justice, which then become mistaken for natural ones.[50] Hume's effort here is both to keep the Hobbesian version of the state of nature at bay and to disrupt the assumptions that justice is natural, that property is universal, that promises are rationally sound agreements, and that public good and civil society are eternal and unchangeable entities.

The discussion of the natural and the artificial virtues serves to further accentuate the historical dimensions of the artificial virtues. To peek at their evolution and development is to get a sense of how they are parasitic on the social and political aspects of experience. This does not mean, however, that the artificial virtues are less important than natural ones. In fact, the opposite is true: the recognition that artifice and education assist in the regulation of our conduct is the first step toward this very regulation. Hume believes we suffer from the illusion that justice is a natural virtue and that we can rely on people to keep their promises, proceed with honesty, and employ "equitable conduct towards each other" (T, 3.2.2.8). His natural history of virtue—a story about the growth and development of human community and the virtues and values that it deems useful and agreeable—both demonstrates this and illuminates the importance and power of our social institutions. "Society is absolutely necessary for the well-being of men" (3.2.6.1) and the "moral beauty" (3.2.2.1) of its tale is the aesthetic evolution of the constraints that make us free and allow our happiness. As the complexity of our social relationships increases, the social conventions, public institutions, and community rules evolve to assist the common interest and channel our natural predilections, dispositions, and inclinations. For "it is only a general sense of common interest; which sense all the members of the society express to one another, and which induces them to regulate their conduct by certain rules" (3.2.2.10).

The world of social conventions is the web of relationality between mechanisms of edification, cultural training, persons in communities trying to cooperate, and the history of their success and failure. It is the sphere of the development of our social consciousness, moral ideas, religious beliefs, economic values, and political interests—the space our collective life engenders so that it might endure and we might better tolerate one another. Social conventions teach symbols-cum-beliefs that are systematized, codified, routinized, and ritualized. They take on a quasi-religious quality. Hume notes this in his depiction of the symbolic behavior of promising: "Since every new promise imposes a new obligation of morality on the person who promises, and since this new obligation arises from his will; 'tis one of the most mysterious and incomprehensible operations that can possibly be imagin'd, and may even be compar'd to *transubstantiation*, or *holy orders*, where a certain form of words, along with a certain intention, changes entirely the nature of an external object, and even of a human creature" (*T*, 3.2.5.14).

The artificial virtues are central to Hume's moral thought. After sorting out their sophisticated relationship to the natural virtues—which is handled largely in book 3 of the *Treatise*—the challenge that Hume leaves us with is how we might refine our awareness of the character and function of these artificial virtues to enhance the stability of the social order, increase our happiness, and improve our friendships. For my argument, this raises the question of the role of true religion in the development of virtuous character. Before turning directly to that question, however, I discuss an example of an artificial virtue, promises, and the importance of utility in Hume's moral thought.

## The Meaning of Promises

It is impossible for men so much as to murder each other without statutes, and maxims, and an idea of justice and honour. War has its laws as well as peace; and even that sportive kind of war, carried on among wrestlers, boxers, cudgel-players, gladiators, is regulated by fixed principles.
—*EPM*, 4.20

For Hume the "performance of promises, is not *natural*" (*T*, 3.2.5.1). He writes, "a promise is not intelligible naturally, nor antecedent to human conventions" because there is no "act of the mind" on which the words "*I promise*" depend (3.2.5.2). In other words, as Herman De Dijn argues, "words or signs like 'I promise' or like the shaking of one another's hand when striking a bargain, look like they possess magical power: the power of binding us to the future."[51] Hume accepts that the concept 'promise' is mysteriously linked to the concept 'obligation.' Since, on his argument, the association between these two concepts does not occur naturally to our minds, it must depend on our social formation. He interrogates how the idea of a promise functions to reveal the invisible glue that links the symbol 'promise' with the idea 'obligation.'

One of the more interesting results of Hume's contention that promise is an artificial virtue is his depiction of the act of promising as a symbolic behavior. A statement of promise has unique status in human communication because it creates a strong commitment to a future act. On the Deleuzian reading previously mentioned, we might think of promising as an act that represents something beyond itself. In this manner, Hume argues, it is similar to the symbolic rituals of popular religion, which point beyond themselves. I noted this on the previous page when I cited his explanation of the link between a promise and its obligation as "one of the most mysterious and incomprehensible operations that can possibly be imagin'd, and may even be compar'd to *transubstantiation*, or *holy orders*." This quotation confirms that the main difference between a symbolic phenomenon of popular religion (e.g., transubstantiation) and the symbolic phenomena of conventional social order (e.g., promises) is that the latter reflects the "interest of society" whereas the former does not. Promises are useful and agreeable; transubstantiation is a "monstrous doctrine" invented by priests with "no public interest in view" (*T*, 3.2.5.14).

For Hume, symbolic acts are not "natural." They have been constructed by the meaning-making machinery of cooperative living. The notion of property is a convention-derived symbol that represents or points toward something beyond it. The way it works is that we randomly create borders (that we justify by the use of practical reason) so that these fictional boundaries create the illusion of property, something stable, to be possessed, protected, and transferred. Hume writes, "Property . . . when taken for something real, without reference to morality, or the sentiments of the mind, is a quality perfectly insensible, and even inconceivable; nor can we form any distinct notion, either of its stability or translation." He goes on to describe the transference of property and all its associated contracts, titles, and legal tomfoolery as intricate inventions, a "*symbolical* delivery" of a "kind of superstitious practice in civil laws, and in the laws of nature, resembling the *Roman catholic* superstitions in religion" (*T*, 3.2.4.2).[52]

Hume's account of the links between social convention and (the artificial virtue of) justice illuminates the crucial role of the meaning-making structures we create. "Common interest" induces us to "regulate our behavior by certain rules." This "sense of interest has become common to all our fellows, and gives us a confidence of the future regularity of their conduct: And 'tis only on the expectation of this, that our moderation and abstinence are founded" (*T*, 3.2.2.10). Popular religion reflects this common interest. It does not occur naturally, but it is an artifice dependent on human imagination, education, and fictive beliefs. That is, popular religion relies on organizational capacities, technical skills, and creative propensities of human beings in communities. Yet popular religion does not inspire the stability of justice, for "the greatest crimes have been found, in many instances, compatible with a superstitious piety and devotion" (*NHR*, 14.7). Here, Hume equates superstition with popular religion and is critical of both.

On Hume's moral-historical narrative, which Jacqueline Taylor has thoughtfully described as a "cultural transformation of instinct," popular religion has inspired some extreme behaviors that are not "useful or agreeable to ourselves or others."[53] These "monkish virtues," including "celibacy, fasting, penance, mortification, self-denial, humility, silence, solitude," have been propagated by the "delusive glosses of superstition and false religion." They serve "no manner of purpose; neither advance a man's fortune in the world, nor render him a more valuable member of society; neither qualify him for the entertainment of company nor increase his power of self-enjoyment." On Taylor's argument, when instincts are transformed through vulgar or popular religion, they often "stupify the understanding and harden the heart, obscure the fancy and sour the temper" (*EPM*, 9.1.3).

As explained earlier, direct-passions hope and fear actuate the human mind toward false theism and the "first ideas of religion" (*NHR*, 2.4). Glimpsing these "obscure traces of divinity" (2.5) in such a fear- or hope-based way leads to and is inspired by the development of popular, false religion, which co-opts the first ideas of religion with selfish institutional motives of clerics who have constructed systems of indoctrination for their own power and control. Still, Hume holds out the very narrow possibility that in the "flux and reflux" of history a very few rare individuals might engage religion in its true form to develop the social affections such that they elevate themselves to the highest level of character. It seems those few individuals might, with some luck, enhance their dispositions to become a hero of the social passions, what he names a "generous warrior" (*HE*, 2.16).

Hume scholar Timothy Costelloe concurs with my overall point here: that Hume's description of the artificial virtues parallels the development of popular religion. The way this happens is that as the cooperative social order evolves, the artificial virtue of religion develops. Costelloe emphasizes that Hume reserves a space for the rare true religion as an essential part of "every civilized community" (*HE*, 3.135). He argues that Hume was against the false religion, superstition, and enthusiasm that distort the development of virtuous character in common life. But Costelloe acknowledges that Hume was never completely against the idea of religion itself: he severely challenged religion derived from the direct-passions hope and fear, which did a disservice to the very peace and serenity our social conventions were constructed to deliver.[54] In this way the vulgar, popular form of religion betrayed the very artifices that produced it.[55]

## Beauty of Virtue and Excellence of Character

The social virtues must, therefore, be allowed to have a natural beauty and amiableness, which, at first, antecedent to all precept or education, recommends them to the esteem of uninstructed mankind, and engages their affections.
—*EPM*, 5.1.4

For our constructive project based on Hume, I have argued that we should regard genuine theism and moderate hope as elements of Hume's true religion. Genuine theism is the humble philosophical theism derived from the basic theism in Hume's theory of understanding; moderate hope is the mild feeling-content that is a result of his project on the passions, namely a calm passion. Hume's moral thought invites us to put forward a third element of true religion: a practical morality.

While morality was clearly important to Hume, he neither fully reduced it to nor completely severed it from religion. As dictated by the discursive conventions of his day, Hume's moral and religious thought were inextricably linked. The type of impact he aimed to have on discourse about religion was neither to articulate the details of a positive contribution in thought nor recommend a particular way to be religious. It was to expose the weak foundations of the arguments of his peers while quietly holding a conception of religion's proper office. Autonomous reason, nature, and revelation were not able to support the claims about religion and morality that Enlightenment thinkers wanted. Pointing this out, in a persuasive and engaging way, was one of the aims of his critical project. In service of this critical work he also demonstrated that morals were not derived simply from an autonomous standard of reason and that goodness did not reside in the essence of any act.

It seems that at the core of Hume's moral considerations were the notions that virtuous character traits were deeply grounded in nature but relied on artifice and depended on our feelings and that our reflections on our feelings were shaped by history and could reveal "the beauty of virtue" (*EPM*, 1.4). Aesthetically speaking, virtue was harmony between injustice and justice and the balance between beauty and deformity. The feeling of virtue fosters the recognition of—yet cannot defeat—the tragic irony of nature itself. Still, our sense of the beautiful as the agreeable provides some grounds on which we might stake our socioethical claims. Hume writes,

Our sense of *beauty* depends very much on this principle; and where any object has a tendency to produce pleasure in its possessor, it is always regarded as beautiful; as every object, that has a tendency to produce pain, is disagreeable and deform'd. . . . Here the object, which is denominated beautiful, pleases only by its tendency to produce a certain effect. That effect is the pleasure or advantage of some other person. Now the pleasure of a stranger, for whom we have no friendship, pleases us only by sympathy. To this principle, therefore, is owing the *beauty*, which we find in every thing that is useful. How considerable a part this is of *beauty* will easily appear upon reflexion. Wherever an object has a tendency to produce pleasure in the possessor, or in other words, is the proper *cause* of pleasure, it is sure to please the spectator, by a delicate sympathy with the possessor. Most of the works of art are esteem'd beautiful, in proportion to their fitness for the use of man, and even many of the productions of nature derive their *beauty* from that source. Handsome and beautiful, on most occasions, is not an absolute but a relative quality, and pleases us by nothing but its tendency to produce an end that is agreeable. (*T*, 3.3.1.8, italics mine)

Hume's brief mention of true religion suggested a clear and strong moral position: to humanize conduct. This moral claim was at the core of his depiction of religion's proper office, for the best way to be religious was in a way that developed virtuous character. Popular religion, due to its lack of moderating passions, did not develop excellence of character and compel aesthetic harmony. It was only when religion remained in its proper office that it motivated public benevolence: "ennobling sentiment[s] of the mind" (*EMPL*, 16.152) that aroused a character of "natural beauty and amiableness" (*EPM*, 5.1.4). For Hume, this is a social virtue— a kind of practical morality—that I posit as a feature of our speculative true religion. Hume's historical project speaks directly to this issue, so it is to this area of his work that I turn.

## Hume's Historical Project

History, the great mistress of wisdom, furnishes examples of all kinds; and every prudential, as well as moral precept, may be authorized by those events, which her enlarged mirror is able to present to us.

—*HE*, 5.545

Most studies of book 3 of the *Treatise* ("Of Morals") and Hume's moral *Enquiry* highlight their critical components. They often overlook how the sagacity of Hume's observational science in this early work manifests in his later works, particularly the historical and narrative writings, as well as his various dialogues. To my knowledge, only Annette Baier and Don Siebert have thoroughly investigated the links between Hume's historical efforts and his moral ones.[56] In significant part, Hume presents his most vital arguments in three ways: with his "observational" science, as in the *Treatise* and both *Enquiries*; in the form of dialogue as in the *DCNR* and book 11 of the first *Enquiry*; or through historical narrative as in the *NHR* or the six-volume *History of England*. His Ciceronian-style adoption of multiple literary forms is intentional and well considered; not only do these showcase his creative abilities as a writer, but also they allow him to elucidate new angles in content and provide a slightly different emphasis on certain points.

Hume's vast historical work was, in many ways, a study in the art of virtue and moral assessment as described in the *Treatise* and the moral *Enquiry*. I agree with Donald Siebert's contention that "of all Hume's works, it can be argued that the *History of England* is his only attempt at practical moral instruction."[57] The *History* and, similarly, his "Essays on Happiness" offer a particular sort of moral teaching through the depiction of virtuous or nonvirtuous characters in real time. These writings give us a sense of how what I posit as two components of true religion (genuine theism and moderate hope) invite public benevolence and practical morality.

## Historical Narrative and Hume's Moral Thought

There is also an advantage in that experience which is acquired
by history, above what is learned by the practice of the world,
that it brings us acquainted with human affairs, without
diminishing in the least from the most delicate sentiments of
virtue.
—*EMPL*, 6.567

Hume's observational science in books 1 and 2 of the *Treatise* established that autonomous reason is simply unequipped to justify our beliefs, which are verifiable through common life, the imagination, and the passions. Book 3, described in the preceding section, detailed the sources of our moral judgment and examined the development of virtuous character. It is Hume's later work, however, particularly his *History of England*, that is, to my mind, more illustrative of his direct approach to morals. In this text he showed how, in practical terms, one might prioritize the complex questions of character (what type of person should I be?) over the question of behavior (what deed should I do?). The *History* provides examples of how social experience both undermined and supported his idea of practical morality. In other words, we can glean direct insight into how religion functions regarding our moral judgment by assessing history. Borrowing a useful framework from Roberto Unger, three features of Hume's moral theory are made clearer by the *History of England* and the four essays on happiness: (1) that we are "soaked in particularity"; (2) that "the institutions of society and the conventions of culture" shape our character; and (3) that "society and thought can be organized" in a way that invites and is inspired by the proper office of religion.[58] The *History* provided a first-person, active perspective on the effects of common life and the imagination, history, and social institutions in our ethical lives, and it revealed the conceptually unavoidable yet necessarily penetrable veil between moral agent and the moral spectator. These writings, therefore, substantially augment the complex matrix of "delicate sentiments" with which we engage as we develop virtuous character; thus, they speak to our interest in practical morality.

My turn to the more historical and literary parts of Hume's corpus in service of my argument about the role of his work on morals for the category 'true religion' is an attempt to demonstrate how Hume's historical writings allow direct access to common life and its moral quandaries, show the influences of popular religion on public benevolence, and challenge us to reconcile the moral distinctions made by false philosophy and abstract reason that create deeper factionalism. For the purposes of understanding Hume's moral thought, the *History* is irresistible. It demonstrates that the modern subject is steeped in nature and custom yet invested in reason; that virtues are shaped by history yet strive to push us beyond it; and that we are dependent on our individual moral sensibilities and reliant on social life as well as guided by "universal springs and principles" of our nature and open to the possibility that the virtues we construct together might have derivative value but no intrinsic value. Further, unlike his presentation of the understanding and the passions in books 1 and 2, a proper consideration of moral judgment requires more than the self-assessment of the moral agent; it requires *spectators* to evaluate and approve the actions and sympathize with the sentiments of the (moral) actor. In other words, it shows that character development is a dance within social formation. Hume seemed to believe that morality was best understood when it was framed historically or narratively, for these forms of discourse best expose the dynamic between agent and spectators on which our sense of excellence of character rests.

My emphasis on Hume's historical work and its interrelatedness with his moral thought dovetails with his inference that history and narrative literature are the most useful contexts to display the relationality of moral agent and moral evaluators. Historians attend to moral subjects inside of ethical reality: "I think it a remark worthy the attention of the speculative, that the historians have been, almost without exception, the true friends of virtue, and have always represented it in its proper colours, however they may have erred in their judgments of particular persons" (*EMPL*, 6.567). As the *Natural History of Religion* served to ground Hume's philosophy of the passions, his *History of England* (six volumes appearing between 1754 and 1762) granted a distinctive glance into the way he appropriated, and therefore the way we might appropriate, moral language to describe the dynamic character of moral actors.

Patient engagement with Hume's historical texts can provide a clearer vista on the two-sided ethical task of happiness that expands true religion. By "two-sided" I designate that both moral agents and moral spectators are co-conspirators concerning virtue: the moral *agent* humanizes his conduct when his actions generate sympathy such that we approve it and thereby confirms that his virtuous traits show him to be "a person capable of contributing to the happiness or enjoyment of his fellow creatures" (*T*, 3.3.5.5). The moral *spectator* (Hume, the historian) is separated from both the action of the moral agent and the approval of the moral community through time and place. This separation allows him to exact moral judgment on *both* the moral agent and the social context that has granted approbation. This is why the historical and narrative work gives Hume such power: it provides him with a bird's-eye position on the vastness of moral life and complexity of virtuous character. He writes, "When a philosopher contemplates characters and manners in his closet, the general abstract view of the objects leaves the mind so cold and unmoved, that the sentiments of nature have no room to play, and he scarce feels the difference between vice and virtue. History keeps in a just medium betwixt these extremes, and places the objects in their true point of view" (*EMPL*, 2.568). The moral philosopher is a spectator in regard to the possessor of virtue, but the historian is an evaluator of both the possessor of the virtue and its social context.

Donald Livingston contends that "the task of the true philosopher is to moderate forms of experience and, through a poetic act of the imagination, to unite what reflection must consider to be contraries into one amiable character."[59] This statement can be read as a way to support Hume's turn to *narrative* discourse as a means of revealing the moral elements of his true philosophy. Narrative history or storytelling is the site where contradictory and complex characters become objects of reflection. Another way to put this is to say that if Hume believed, as Kant did, that humans were fully rational agents and that moral duty was rationally justifiable, then he would pursue abstract reason and false philosophy to designate the moral ecology justifiable by imperious reason. But Hume's investment in the development of character along with his extensive historical efforts allow us to conclude that he is committed to historical narrative for *moral* purposes. Gerald Bruns's discussion of Alasdair MacIntyre's historical project on morality, *After Virtue*, reflects this sensibility: "That a morality of character and virtue is essentially a morality of storytelling, since only stories can show what it is to be a human being, have a character and pursue the good of that character. Narrative, one might say, is foundational for moral philosophy."[60]

## History, Virtue, and Religion

In every religion, except the true, [the diligence of the clergy] is
highly pernicious, and it has even a natural tendency to pervert the true, by infusing into it a strong mixture of superstition, folly, and delusion.
—*HE*, 3.135

Hume's fascinating *History of England* inspires a wide range of questions. My interest, however, is to bear witness to Hume as moral spectator to get a clear sense of how he employed his own moral theory.[61] Perhaps a useful way to extract the moral content of Hume's thought from his *History of England* is to discuss specific examples from the text. I shall briefly rehearse just three: Hume's character descriptions of Thomas Wolsey, almoner to King Henry VIII; George Villiers, First Duke of Buckingham; and Charles I, king of England. The questions that I confront are related to those I raised earlier: How does moral approbation and the process of moral judgment actually work in historical narrative? What are the virtuous characteristics or motivating passions that Hume notes (and, peripherally, is he guilty of presentism or assessing the past on its own terms)? Finally, how might Hume, a spectator with such historical distance, generate sympathy both with the moral actor and his reading audience at the same time? The answers to these questions can shed light on the moral dimensions of religion's proper office.

Hume describes the historic ascendance of Thomas Wolsey from butcher's son to confidant of King Henry VIII as a testament to Wolsey's insatiable ambition for power. It makes sense that Wolsey, the Anglican cleric who was elevated to cardinal, would raise Hume's anticlerical hackles and be the poster child for all that was wrong with popular religion. Surprisingly, Hume does not describe Wolsey in harsh terms; in fact, his depiction of Wolsey is generally moderate, and his actual moral judgment on Wolsey is interestingly balanced. Note the narrative tone:

> By this rapid advancement and uncontrouled authority, the character and genius of Wolsey had full opportunity to display itself. Insatiable in his acquisitions, but still more magnificent in his expence: Of extensive capacity, but

still more unbounded enterprize: Ambitious of power, but still more desirous of glory: Insinuating, engaging, persuasive; and, by turns, lofty, elevated,
commanding: Haughty to his equals, but affable to his dependants; oppres-
sive to the people, but liberal to his friends; more generous than grateful; less
moved by injuries than by contempt; he was framed to take the ascendant in
every intercourse with others, but exerted this superiority of *nature* with such
ostentation as exposed him to envy, and made every one willing to recall the
original inferiority or rather meanness of his *fortune*. (*HE*, 3.100)

There are two noteworthy elements in this description. The first is that Hume
does not ascribe explicitly virtuous traits to Wolsey. He is critical of Wolsey
("exerted this superiority of *nature* with such ostentation," "less moved by injuries
than by contempt"), but he writes of him in a mildly sympathetic and a morally
unprejudiced fashion such that his critique is mostly balanced. Hume also presents Wolsey as an affable family man, a generous social being, and a liberal friend.
Given this, Hume seems to embrace the complexity of Wolsey's moral character
in a way that most of Wolsey's contemporaries did not. Most simply, on Hume's
account, Thomas Wolsey's peers thought he was selfish. Hume describes them as
harboring envy toward Wolsey and relishing the fact of his less-than-fortunate
early life. This establishes that the moral judgment of the time on Wolsey was
harsh: he was disliked and thought to lack virtue due to the lack of agreeableness
and usefulness of his actions.

    On Hume's historical and moral imagination, Wolsey—though motivated by
the advancement of his own self-interests and personal pleasures—was not con-
demnable for his status as cleric, his selfishness, or his ambition for power. Wolsey's motivations did not generate pleasurable sentiments from others and were
therefore not considered virtuous, but Hume did not expose Wolsey to a thor-
oughgoing critique. Some may find this to be something of a small point, but it
is worthy for my argument in this way: though Hume was critical of popular
religion and extremely anticlerical in his *History of England*, he did not lose
track of the humanity of the individuals that operated inside of the institutional
structure of popular religion. I point this out not because it directly furthers my
argument for practical morality as a third constitutive feature of true religion,
but because it does not correlate with the conventional interpretations of Hume.
Against those, it shows that Hume's criticism of those involved in institutional
religion was actually moderated by the humanity of these individuals filtered
through the complexity of their circumstances. The literally thousands of discussions of religious individuals in the *History* demonstrate little of the critical
venom that one would expect from reading the secondary sources on his religious thought.

A second noteworthy element in the passage on Wolsey is that Hume generates sympathy from the reader for Wolsey by presenting him in a morally balanced way. The reader perceives Hume's lack of bias, particularly regarding a
cleric, as useful and agreeable, and therefore it brings the reader pleasure. Hume,
as author, has become moral agent and the reader is the moral spectator. In
Hume's moral economy the moral act is the actual presentation of Wolsey in a
balanced way. This generates sentiments of pleasure and approbation from the
reader that are transferred between readers and the author through the faculty of
sympathy. The result is that Hume's motivating passions are understood as virtuous and his act of writing is considered good. Thus the narrative choices of the
*History* are deliberate moral enactments. Again, Hume's presentation of Wolsey
stands in diametric opposition to more critical assessments of Wolsey by other
historians. His refusal to place moral judgment on Wolsey reflects his own virtuous character, and at the same time it suggests the affective power of his historical
approach.[62]

Hume's depiction of the First Duke of Buckingham, George Villiers, is similarly notable for its evocation of sentiment. Villiers rose through the ranks of the
court of King James I and became his confidant and personal favorite. He
remained there during the first two years of the reign of King Charles I (1625–27).
In 1623 he accompanied Charles (then Prince of Wales) to Madrid to negotiate a
marriage for the teenage Maria Ana, Infanta of Spain. Buckingham, according to
Hume's narrative, not only secretly persuaded the prince, in an attempt to get
back into his good graces, into believing that he would be better off pursuing his
own bride instead of being assigned one, but also concocted the whole idea that
the Infanta Maria would be desperate to marry the prince if he were to simply
visit her and express his interest to free her from Madrid. Hume attended to this
story (and Buckingham) at some length and, unlike his narrative of Wolsey, he
presented this courtier as a man in need of character development:

> Ever since the fall of Somerset, Buckingham had governed, with an uncon-
> trouled sway, both the court and nation; and could James's eyes have been
> opened, he had now full opportunity of observing how unfit his favourite
> was for the high station, to which he was raised. Some accomplishments of
> a courtier he possessed: Of every talent of a minister he was utterly desti-
> tute. Headlong in his passions, and incapable equally of prudence and of
> dissimulation: Sincere from violence rather than candour; expensive from
> profusion more than generosity: A warm friend, a furious enemy; but with-
> out any choice of discernment in either: With these qualities he had early
> and quickly mounted to the highest rank; and partook at once of the inso-
> lence which attends a fortune newly acquired, and the impetuosity which

belongs to persons born in high stations, and unacquainted with opposition. (*HE*, 5.102)

Again, it is noteworthy that Hume tried to present a balanced moral portrait of Buckingham's character, but Buckingham's life left him little with which to work. It seems to be the extreme passions and violent qualities of Buckingham's experience—that he could not control—that made him compelling to observers yet "destitute" of the qualities required for his job and impetuous in carrying them out. The best Hume can claim is that Buckingham was a "warm friend," which he qualified by adding that even in friendship he lacked "discernment." What we might glean from Hume's retelling of the Buckingham incident—in addition to Buckingham's agitated passions that worked against excellence of character—is a sense of Hume's moral grace; Buckingham was a liar and committed many deceitful acts, yet Hume refused to unfairly diminish his character or speak only in a negative tone about him. Hume, in the role of "intelligent spectator," presented Buckingham as impetuous, selfish, and somewhat mean, but he refused to be a moral judge, for it is the reporter of history that has moral responsibility.[63] Instructively, Hume does not use history to make judgments about an individual's moral character; those judgments can be made only by others in the same historical moment and social context. The flux and reflux of history, the shift in the emphasis of our social conventions, and the general human dynamism that ushers in different moral sensibilities and changes in temperament cannot be applied in a transhistorical way. Hume simply tries his best to retell stories and represent characters in a descriptively accurate yet morally neutral way to appeal to readers. The popularity of his *History of England* suggests his approach was successful.

What might Hume's lengthy and patient historical narrative—a moral act in itself—have to say about the proper office of religion? Perhaps Hume's historical work can stand in for his theoretical work on the passions and his written reflections on morality, for both explicitly confirm that with some historical distance the passions of the moral spectator become more calm. Since the *spectator*, when in the act of historical narration, becomes in some senses the moral *agent*, moral behavior persists in the act of narrating. Moral judgment that reflects magnanimity and excellence of character manifests when the calm passions set the tone of the historical report such that past occurrences are described evenly and without bias. This is similar to the position Hume takes in his important essay "Of Miracles" (*E*, 10), a critique of miracle testimony or, from another angle, an assertion of Hume's moral project.[64]

Mostly directed against Samuel Clarke's Boyle lectures of 1705, Hume's argument against miracle testimony proceeded directly from the theory of knowledge and concept of probability delineated in the *Treatise* and rehearsed in section 6 of the first *Enquiry*. It also reflected Hume's argument for calm passions and moral deliberation. In it, Hume asserted that humans naturally formed habits that lead them to hold future expectations for patterns of events that they observed in the past. Testimony for miracles was—by his definition—pronouncement of an event that violated a law of nature (that is, it was dissimilar to patterns of events we have observed in the past). The question was, therefore, under what conditions might we accept testimony for such an event? Or when does this sort of testimony have the highest probability of authenticity? How does Hume's morally informed project for historical reporting play out in the face of miraculous occurrences? Can we speak of miracles with a detached, calm passion and well-developed character that Hume's moral project invites?

The well-known section 10 is divided into two parts. The first part begins with a reaffirmation of Hume's observation that "experience be our only guide in reasoning concerning matters of fact," then it quickly asserts that experience is fallible and "apt to lead us into errors" (*E*, 10.1.3). The point here is that the observational science can give us only probable conclusions: we can develop beliefs and expectations for the future based on past experiences, but these future events may not occur. The reason is that "all effects follow not with like certainty from their supposed causes" (10.1.3). Because of this, "the wise man, therefore, proportions his belief to the evidence" (10.1.4) and tends to believe that which has a higher probability of occurrence. Additionally, since the most reliable evidence from experience comes in the form of a proof (in section 9 he has already defined proofs as "such arguments from experience as leave no room for doubt or opposition" [6.1n]), beliefs grounded on the "infallible experience" of a proof are more confident than those that are simply probable (10.1.4).

The distinction between proof and probability highlights the utter contingency of probability, such that when applied to miracle testimony, the argument practically writes itself. First, Hume shows that narrative testimony—like the recording and analysis of events and persons in his *History of England*—is both common and important for humans and that "as the evidence, derived from witnesses and human testimony, is founded on past experience, so it varies with the experience, and is regarded either as a *proof* or a *probability*" (*E*, 10.1.6). Thus, there are times when the testimony, witnesses, events, and the historian are more believable than others, that is, less subject to doubt. When multiple witness accounts do not contradict one another, when the character of the reporter is known to be strong, when the delivery of the testimony is without hesitation, and when what the testimony "endeavour[s] to establish" (10.1.8) is a fact easily conformable to our past experience, we are more likely to accept the testimony. Further, I would add, when reporters seem to be motivated by calm passions and not violent ones and when historians understand themselves as both moral spectator and moral agent, their work is more balanced and reasonable. On both cases, our assurance regarding the veracity of testimony increases the probability of its authenticity, and we tend to accept it more readily.

Hume's definition of a miracle as a "violation of the laws of nature" (*E*, 10.1.12) makes it analytically the case that miracle testimony is inauthentic.[65] But we must be careful to note that the framework of his approach and argument allow him to contend only against miracle *testimony*, particularly in light of the earlier distinction he has made between proof and probability. In fact, he has made it a proof that testimony for a miracle is unintelligible: "Thus, the plain consequence is (and it is a general maxim worthy of our attention), 'That no testimony is sufficient to establish a miracle, unless the testimony be of such a kind, that its falsehood would be more miraculous, than the fact, which it endeavours to establish; and even in that case there is a mutual destruction of arguments, and the superior only gives us an assurance suitable to that degree of force, which remains, after deducting the inferior'" (10.1.13). Hume simply uses the occasion of miracle testimony to assert the proof against it, and this neatly ends part 1 of the essay.[66]

The second half, "Of Miracles," takes up four objections to the credibility of miracle testimony. These are supplementary to his central argument (based on probability) against miracle testimony in part 1. Hume's first point against the credibility of miracle testimony takes it to be an obvious fact of history that witnesses who give testimony for miracles are usually very few and not of a reputable character: "there is not to be found, in all history, any miracle attested by a sufficient number of men, of such unquestioned good sense, education, and learning as to secure us against all delusion in themselves" (*E*, 10.2.2). Second, he undermines the credibility of miracle testimony by demonstrating that the acceptance of miracles does not adhere to the usual pattern of human conduct that his observational science has revealed. Since, based on observation, the acceptance of miracle testimony goes directly against probable reasoning and our normative pattern of conduct, it must be that some other psychological forces enable our acceptance of this testimony. For Hume, the reliance on these other forces indicates that the acceptance of miracle testimony is an abandonment of our normal principles of experience at a time when we should rely on them most. A third reason Hume discounts miracle testimony is because it derives from "ignorant and barbarous nations" (10.2.7). When we find belief in miracles among a culture of civilized peoples, it is due to the fact that it has been passed down from their ignorant and barbarous ancestors; thus, it is not credible. The fourth reason he deploys against the verisimilitude of testimony for miracles begins with his assertion that there are always competing miracle claims in different religious systems; thus, testimony for one set of miracles automatically cancels out the others. Hume asserts that miracle claims are the source of all religion; thus, if one accepts one religion (one set of miracles), one is implicitly denying the legitimacy of another set of miracles that support the belief system of another religion. In this way, miracle claims are always being destroyed, so the "credit of the testimony . . . destroys itself" (10.2.11).

In summary, scholars have read section 10 as an argument against the occurrence of miracles past and future. To claim that Hume was against the possibility of miracles is, however, to overlook how his moderate skepticism does not permit these kinds of conclusions, how his empiricism constrains his discussion largely to the realm of observable experience, and his nondogmatism keeps him focused on probability over possibility. Hume believed that there was no way to get at the true or essential nature of objects; thus he could make no firm metaphysical or strong ontological claims for or against the possibility of miracles in the past or in the future.[67] All he could confidently discuss was that which is manifest, that is, human experience, and he allowed this experience to shape his insights into the human mind. Stephen Buckle describes this section as "an account not of what is or is not possible—logically or physically—but of the proper functioning of mechanisms of belief formation in an instinctive being."[68] What Hume gives us in section 10 is simply a reiteration of his core observations in the *Treatise* as they relate to miracle testimony. His notions of experience, probability, causal reasoning, and the uniformity of nature as applied to miracles show only that miracle testimony is "not sufficient to establish a miracle unless the testimony be of such a kind that its falsehood would be more miraculous than the fact which it endeavors to establish" (*E*, 10.1.13).[69] And his thoughts on moral judgment and historical narrative are implicated in this section.

Finally, to turn back to Hume's historical writings, the most deliberate focus on sentiments and possibly the most intriguing implications for the idea of virtue in the *History* is Hume's account of the execution of Charles I. Hume provides extensive details regarding the life of Charles in volume 5, but as he describes his sentencing and execution, Hume pushes the boundaries of his own commitments as a historical writer and begins to write less as a recorder or a historian and more as a "man of feeling."[70] He sets up this sentimental history with a description of Charles's demeanor: "The king's behaviour, during this last scene of his life, does honour to his memory. . . . He never forgot his part, either as a prince or as a man. Firm and intrepid . . . mild and equable. . . . His soul, without effort or affectation, seemed only to remain in the situation familiar to it, and to look down with contempt on all the efforts of human malice and iniquity" (*HE*, 5.539). Hume goes on to describe how soldiers "spit in his face, as he was conducted along the passage to the court. To excite a sentiment of piety was the only effect, which this inhuman insult was able to produce upon him" (5.537). Charles I possessed virtuous motives, but Hume spends little time on the virtues here. It is the affections of the people that are seminal for his description. The focus on public sentiments allows Hume to transcend the divide of time and place that, if mishandled by the historian, are a fault line unable to be overcome by the passions.[71] The following are just a few examples of Hume's sense of the moral spectators' (the people's) response to this historic event:

> The people, though under the rod of lawless, unlimited power, could not forbear, with the most ardent prayers, pouring forth their wishes for his preservation; and, in his present distress, they avowed *him*, by their generous tears, for their monarch, whom, in their misguided fury, they had before so violently rejected. (5.537–538)

> The people remained in that silence and astonishment, which all great passions, when they have not an opportunity of exerting themselves, naturally produce in the human mind. (5.538)

> It is impossible to describe the grief, indignation, and astonishment, which took place, not only among the spectators, who were overwhelmed with a flood of sorrow, but throughout the whole nation, as soon as the report of this fatal execution was conveyed to them. (5.541)[72]

The affections of the people have been transformed in light of the events of the life of Charles I. These historical depictions mirror Hume's earlier theoretical descriptions of how the psychological mechanism of sympathy and its source of benevolence work. His description of the "progress of sentiments" exercises our sympathy because it connects us with the affectional component of our humanity, and therefore it potentially strengthens our virtues. Hume's narrative choices here both demonstrated historical sympathy and attempted to create it between people through a focus on similar sentiments across history. This form of a narrative artifice brings social conventions from the past into the purview of the present. It tests the capacity of the reader or spectator to embrace or reject these sentiments and thus offers a challenge to the enlivening of the reader's sympathy.

There are remaining dynamics in the narrative of Charles I worthy of observation that I will not delve into here, for example, the capacity of people to overthrow their sovereign, the role of justice when authority is corrupt, and the bodily virtues of the king. For my purpose, to show how Hume's historical work exemplifies his moral theory, it may be best to simply highlight his final depictions of Charles I: "The character of this prince, as that of most men, if not of all men, was mixed; but his virtues predominated extremely above his vices, or, more properly speaking, his imperfections" (*HE*, 5.542). This assessment of Charles I in the "most favourable light" positioned him as free from "pride," "weakness," "rashness," "austerity," and "avarice" and made it seem that "all these virtues, in him, maintained their proper bounds, and merited unreserved praise." Hume also acknowledged that "his good qualities were attended with some latent frailty. . . . His beneficent disposition was clouded by a manner not very gracious; his virtue was tinctured with superstition; his good sense was disfigured by a deference to persons of a capacity inferior to his own; and his moderate temper exempted him not from hasty and precipitate resolutions." Hume concludes that Charles I "deserves the epithet of a good, rather than of a great man" (5.542).

One way to understand Hume's sympathy and balance here is to acknowledge that Hume was committed to reading Charles I in his own context. He admitted that historians "have rashly questioned the good faith of this prince," but he is determined to simply describe and not evaluate the actions and decisions of Charles I. For "if we consider the extreme difficulties, to which he was so frequently reduced . . . we shall avow, that probity and honour ought justly to be numbered among his most shining qualities . . . and though some violations of the petition of right may perhaps be imputed to him; these are more to be ascribed to the necessity of his situation . . . than to any failure in the integrity of his principles" (*HE*, 5.543). The emphasis on describing Charles I in his own context is a means of writing from the detached, moderate passions that reflect excellence of character and is exemplary of the applied moral project in Hume's historical writing. Assuredly, there are other potentially rich ways to link Hume's historical writing to his moral writing (e.g., the execution of Charles could be taken as a lesson on the powers of public affections), yet these brief, few examples suggest that Hume's historical writings were informed by his moral thought. Interestingly, his conclusion of the events around Charles I sound a somewhat futile note for the popular (especially religion); he writes, "but, it must be confessed, that these events furnish us with another instruction, no less natural, and no less useful, concerning the madness of the people, the furies of fanaticism, and the danger of mercenary armies" (5.545–46).

These examples from Hume's *History of England* speak directly to the questions presented at the beginning of this section. First, they demonstrate that historical work is, in many ways to Hume, moral work, part of which meant that one must assess the past in its own terms, not in those of the present. Second, they allow us to consider that moral approbation can happen in two ways: on one level, approbation is between the author (Hume), the moral actor as historian (spectator), and the reader as spectator to the author's act; and between the historical actor and the historical spectators, affective members present at the time and place of the act. Third, these briefly presented historical examples are amenable to the notion that we bestow the idea of virtue on those who have virtuous motives.

Finally, Hume's historical work shows that the faculty of sympathy can work across history and society, though it does not fully transcend either.

Hume's moral thought fascinatingly presents ideas of sympathy, social happiness, and the regulation of our conduct—notions usually encoded with "religious sensibilities"—in nonreligious terms. He believed that popular religion was full of superstition and had a craving for the miraculous, elements that actually worked against the development of morality. Our speculative project for religion, if it is to reflect Hume's thoughts on moral judgment, should be driven by and lend support to a kind of practical morality that informs the most functional of our social conventions and binds us together as sentient beings. Further, it should elevate our awareness of the present, enable social happiness, and inspire the development of excellence of character. Yet, with no symbolic rituals, no deity with attributes, and no sacred text, what makes our Humean true religion religious? It is to this final issue that I now turn.

# A HUMEAN TRUE RELIGION

The Proper Office of Religion, is to reform Men's Lives, to purify their Hearts, to inforce all moral Duties, & to secure Obedience to the Laws & civil Magistrate. While it pursues these useful Purposes, its Operations, tho' infinitely valuable, are secret & silent; and seldom come under the Cognizance of History. . . . The Idea of an Infinite Mind, the author of the Universe seems . . . to require a Worship absolutely pure, simple, unadorned; without Rites, Institutions, Ceremonies; even without Temples, Priests, or verbal Prayer & Supplication.
—Draft of Preface, *HE*, 5.2

It could be argued that public discourse on religion is somewhat thin and, in some ways, haunted by a nihilistic tone. This may be the result of critical work on religion, whose most significant studies allow a glimpse of both the resplendent beauty and the ghastly horror of human beings. This discourse—at its best— speaks compellingly and compassionately about how we might attend to the peculiar mixture of beauty and horror in the variety of all-too-human imaginative attempts to reach beyond ourselves. Since mastery in the study of religion demands an eye for history, it both reveals the perennial violence of unregulated human passions and confirms that analysis unregulated by moral insight lacks social utility. History, on Hume's reading, further discloses that the mind is circumscribed by nature, social forces, political contexts, and conventions of common life and that it has a predilection for illusions and fantasies even as it names itself rational in the modern West. Overwhelmed by the peaks and valleys of the history of religion and paralyzed by attacks on the discourse of religion by both modern science and evangelical fervor, a creeping nihilism turns many a brave thinker away from a *visionary* approach to religion. Instead, among other things, public and academic discourse on religion obsesses on debates regarding the sweeping metaphysical claims of theology or turns to the safe harbors of ethnographic assessment of eras bygone. While much of this work is useful and enlightening, a visionary philosophy of religion guided by an explicit grasp of history and human psychology that takes into account social and political contexts and is guided by a gentle moral vision that attends to theism and the passions with care situates us to transition the sets of social conventions we name, most generally, religion. The very possibility of shifting these conventions can motivate us to play a role in balancing our passions and impacting religious practice and doctrine. *Toward a Humean True Religion* wrestles with Hume's work in an attempt to establish it as a viable possibility for this sort of effort.

I have argued that Hume's thoughts on religion, instead of being reduced simply to a paralyzing criticism, celebratory atheism, or a dogmatic skepticism (and thereby rendered useless for a constructive project), can be a generative resource for scholars. In particular, for philosophers of religion who want to take history, morality, and political culture seriously and are interested in working out a substantive, nonconventional notion of religion based on Enlightenment resources, I have tried to show that Hume's religious thought might be a resource. In significant part, the reading I have provided of Hume's unconventional theism, his sense of the psychological as well as social sources of religion, and his postulations regarding how we might modify passions as well as social conventions, prioritized the *functional* aspects of his thoughts about religion. I have argued that this view is amenable to the Ciceronian influence on his thought, that it resonates with his philosophical commitments, and that it fits—at the same time that it challenges—the religious discourse of his day. It also comports with his historical work that faced the inescapable messiness of human nature, its beauty as well as its horror, and demonstrated how religion might (and largely might not) inculcate stability. My hope was that these factors, when taken cumulatively, established that we get only half of the picture when we deem Hume simply a critic, skeptic, or nihilist. Hume's work avoided the nihilism that has become a persistent part of the public conversation regarding religion (especially treatments of Hume's philosophy of religion!). He seems to have realized that there was neither remedy for the destructive costs of religion nor respite from its benefits. There was only flux and reflux in history, the temporary transition to stability always followed by a regressive pull. The best religion could do was to remain in its proper office. As a social convention, it could help "reform Men's lives, to purify their hearts, to inforce all moral duties, and to secure obedience to the laws and civil magistrate."[1] The benefit of considering the constructive side of Hume's approach to religion as the cumulative result of his positive projects on the understanding, the passions, and moral judgment is that it provides us with a model of how to take history seriously but not give up on a moral vision; gives us an example of how to preserve a sense of nondogmatic skepticism regarding purposiveness yet assert a basic theism and some (weak) moral norms; and shows us how to acknowledge the complexity of human motivations yet remain committed to effective social functioning of human agents in common life. It also teaches us how to moderate our hopes.

## A Generative Resource for Public Dialogue on Religion

The overarching aim of this book has been to establish Hume as a generative resource for religious thought. Part of what I mean by a "generative resource" is made clear with a few examples. My interpretation of Hume's work can be an asset in the recent dustup surrounding Thomas Nagel's *Mind and Cosmos*, a debate that has garnered much attention in both public and academic spheres. Nagel, arguing strongly against the neo-Darwinians, claims that modern science is predicated on a materialist, naturalist view that reduces all matter, the mind (consciousness and cognition), and value to physical properties obedient to the laws of physics (biology is explained by chemistry, which ultimately relies on physics). For Nagel, this crude reductionism has become the prevailing view of Western science and culture. He claims it is offensive to common sense and should be abandoned by science because it does not provide an adequate account of the universe and abandoning it would "have no effect on most scientific research." Nagel's alternative, to which he is barely committed, is a form of natural teleology, which he describes as a "teleology without intention" that includes physical laws as well as other laws of nature. This form of teleology, Nagel admits, is "far too unimaginative," and he remains open to a "much more radical departure from the familiar forms of naturalistic explanation" than he can conceive at this point.[2]

In some ways, the "radical departure" Nagel mentions may have been articulated more than 250 years ago in Hume's basic theism. This form of theism is shorn of the supernaturalism Nagel detests and can serve as a cornerstone in his "teleology without intention." In some ways, Hume's notion of stability could be a unique *telos*, or end, that Nagel acknowledges. It has the natural directionality (not the intention) of the nonvulgar. He seemed to think that—as far as our minds could tell—reflection, common life, politics, and religion, when not corrupted by abstraction or the passions, naturally moved toward stability. The Humean disposition of the mind—which I dub "basic theism"—demonstrated for Deleuze our reliance on something beyond the given in experience; thus, it was a form of theology that did not allow for supernatural intervention in history or a deity with human attributes, only the consistent reach of our mind going beyond experience in search of a cause or purpose. This basic theism, a radical departure from Nagel's conventional sense of theology, can be marshaled as a supplement for Nagel's idea of natural teleology. Since Hume thought that we intuited that "a purpose, an intention, a design, is evident in everything" (*NHR*, 15.1) as a natural belief of common life, a Humean already accepts something like Nagel's natural teleology as basic. This is an example of how Hume's work could be of constructive use in contemporary work in the philosophy of religion.[3]

Further, Nagel gives a metaphysical argument in his attempt to rival modern science. A Humean approach that remained mostly within the empirical realm teaches that the challenge to Darwinian-inspired scientific naturalism does not *require* a metaphysical argument. For example, one could claim, inspired by what our quest for the proper office of religion has uncovered, that Darwinian reasoning reflects the natural tendency of our minds to draw conclusions about unobservable causes based on observable effects. Hume's methodological considerations, namely his inductive method based on experience that could assert only probable conclusions, could be deployed as a first order retort to Darwin had his work not preceded Darwin's. Nagel's choice of a metaphysical approach to support his argument for a naturalist teleology was a practical and political one. He recognized that modern science—especially the Darwinian version of evolution—operated under the illusion of metaphysical truth and the guise of universal certainty. While Nagel admitted, against this, that the truth may well be beyond our cognitive reach, he opted to respond to science in its terms in search of a "systematic understanding of how we and other living things fit into the world." Nagel's chosen method, then, is actually just a slightly modified version of the quest for truth of modern science. Had Nagel annexed the Humean approach, however, his work could have remained largely in the realm of history, nature, and epistemology and challenged the premises of scientific discourse by reminding it of its own limiting biases and political intentions. What I am saying here is that the most incisive challenge to scientific naturalism of the Darwinian sort is not a direct one, as Nagel offers; it is one that indirectly takes *scientism* out at the knees, that is, that destroys the idea that science is the bastion of truth. This is closer to the mode of Hume's argument, which challenged the conclusions of philosophy by exposing their weak foundations and emphasizing the importance of common sense. Nagel's critique of scientific naturalism would do well to approximate Hume's argument against popular religion and abstract philosophy as sources of transhistorical and transcultural knowledge. This Humean approach would allow Nagel to remain neutral on the question of the existence of God (he claims atheism) yet still be able to effectively argue for a mild natural teleology in terms of the tendency of the human mind to understand "the universe as basically prone to generate life."[4]

In another example, our speculative Humean true religion could be a useful resource in the debate between militant atheists and evangelical believers in God. Richard Dawkins, Daniel Dennett, and Christopher Hitchens (just to name a few) have built a public following around the idea that religion is built on false claims, that there is no evidence for the idea of God, and that faith naturally breeds extremism. It is likely that Hume would have agreed with these claims (with some modifications). It is just as likely that he would have been deeply disturbed by the claims of figures like Alvin Plantinga, Stanley Hauerwas, and Richard Swinburne, who assert analytic arguments for God, scientific defenses of religion, and socio-ethical logic for Christian faith. A Humean true religion, as I have constituted it, allows the militant atheists to be correct about vulgar theism and popular religion but displays their intolerance for religion in general and their complete dismissal of both a useful social convention like religion and its genuine theism to be short-sighted. On the other side, the evangelical believers make a sound defense of religion on the grounds of abstruse thought and epistemological truth, yet their reliance on methods of science and claims of faith reveal little about human estrangement and the existential conditions of humans grasping for ways to cope in light of the traditions that have been bequeathed to them in common life. Both sides miss the richness of the enterprise of religion for fear of its dangers.

Hume's middle way out of the tension in the debate between the atheists and evangelicals has the flavor of American pragmatism in the mode of William James and John Dewey. Our speculative, Humean true religion demonstrates—as prag-matism confirms—that epistemological and metaphysical truth claims are not the issues when it comes to religion. Hume's commitment, like the investment of early pragmatists who took religion seriously, is in the justifiability of the idea of God and the effects of religion in common life. Accordingly, in this framing the ques-tion is about how religion functions, not about its truth-value. When Dawkins claims that religion is toxic and, oppositely, Hauerwas asserts its value, both the Humean and the pragmatist beg for further contextualization and more specific-ity. For them, religion is not a rational exercise or cognitive effort that transcends history or allows transcultural assent to a higher power, it is a category we fre-quently use to describe a set of symbols, beliefs, hopes, and practices that always take place in a particular community at a particular moment for particular pur-poses, which might remain unclear. In fact, on the Humean view, one cannot justifiably make the claim that religion is toxic or valuable; that way of speaking about religion denies the very specific psychological and social (practical) aspects of religious activity from which we must begin our encounter with religion.

There are other ways that our Humean true religion can be a resource for con-temporary debates in religious studies. My task has been to break new ground in the study of Hume's philosophy of religion and thereby provide some foundations for a Humean approach to religion. If I have done a satisfactory job, I will have made Hume's work slightly more accessible for thinkers in religious studies.

By way of a conclusion, my hope is that the reader is convinced that when viewed together, the genuine theism engendered by our feelings of basic theism; the equanimity brought by collective, calm hopes and fears; and the development of virtuous character inspired by practical morality can help us revise our understanding of Hume's positive contribution to religion; impact how we might reformulate the category 'religion'; and, more important, invigorate a philosophy of religion regulated by moral vision and historical awareness. What may remain more of an open question, though I have attended to it a few times in the body of the argument, is why I consider the positive result of Hume's considerations of religion to have *religious* value instead of simply moral or philosophical value. As I have instructed, the religious value of Hume's project is not conventional. I attribute religious value to his basic theism, moderate hope, and practical morality for three reasons. First, they enhance stability of self and social order, the effect of which is to bind us more closely to one another, nature, and that which is greater than experience. Second, Hume's historical sensibilities led him to appreciate the fact that religious belief was a significant feature of practically every Western society; therefore, he knew that his science, if it were to be effective, had to make an intervention in *religious* discourse and—even if only slightly— in the religious beliefs of common life (popular religion). From what we can gather, his mild hope was that superstition, enthusiasm, and popular religion could be moderated by calm reflection and social deliberation. We can reasonably conclude from this that his work had *religious* interests, that it was positively valuable for discourse in *religion*, and that it had *religious* value: it posited another (rare) way we might be religious. Third, and closely linked to the previous point, Hume reasoned that the passions informed our beliefs *prior* to their being taken up by philosophical reflection. In other words, the passions led toward beliefs and actions that immediately manifested in common life (e.g., basic theism) and then were likely seized by social forces to form beliefs of popular religion (e.g., vulgar theism). They would later become available to philosophical reflection, which could lead to true philosophy and true religion (e.g., genuine theism). Thus it was the prudence and deliberation born of the passion for reflection that could excite the transition from the beliefs of vulgar religion to the beliefs of the true. In this way, as I have argued, a Humean true religion is just a moderate form of what Hume called vulgar or popular religion. Important here, however, is the reiteration that the religious actually *precedes* the philosophical, and as Hume's discussion of the passions confirms, he aimed for practical impact at the more primary (yet not original) level of the religious. This is why we can say Hume's work had value for religion.

Further, Hume explicitly (though infrequently) used the words "true religion." He did not describe the most functional form of religion that he could imagine as a virtuous atheism, philosophical theism, radical fideism, natural belief, or secular moralism. Neither did he use the descriptors deism, atheism, moralism, or skepticism to frame his suggestion for religion. Hume's choice partially reflected the tenor of the discourse of his day, which was circumscribed by the idea 'true religion.' Secondary literature is littered with descriptions that try to grasp at Hume's project for religion by using terms that he never employed: moral atheism, moral naturalism, mitigated skepticism, skeptical realism, attenuated deism, and projectivist realism. These important contributions clarify Hume's work and allow us to interrogate how contemporary categories might relate to his project. My argument pursued Hume's discussion of religion based on his own categories 'false religion' and 'true religion.' It took these terms at face value and put some meat on the bones of his sparingly used idea 'true religion' in hopes to illustrate ways in which this term might be made applicable for the generative work that he hoped his science would inspire.

It seems to me that, ultimately, the question of whether or not a Humean-inspired true religion has religious value should hinge two things: Hume's understanding of religion and our own cultural politics regarding the idea 'religious value.' Most scholars import their conventional ideas about religion onto Hume's work right out of the gate; they argue, like Gaskin, that "true religion has none of the distinctive features of actual religions."[5] In some ways this is true, but it is overdetermined by the idea that actual religions are a set of orthodox Biblical views and conventional worship practices. Gaskin's claim, and others like it, diminishes the religious significance of Hume's true religion before it so much as ventures an attempt at seeking Hume's sense of religion. Of course, Hume's venom against popular religion is, in part, a critique of conventional views of religion. But his bifurcated approach makes it clear that this is only a portion of the story he wants to tell. Hume acknowledged conventional features as content for vulgar religion but he refused to *reduce* religion to these features. Hume grasped the fundamental dynamism, sociohistorical forces, and political investment in the idea 'religion'—that it was always in the process of being redefined and that those definitions reflected social and political interests—and he may have contributed his underdeveloped notion of true religion as a way to invite us to reevaluate the very way we applied the descriptor "religious." This may be why he stated, "It is remarkable, that the principles of religion have a kind of flux and reflux in the human mind" (*NHR*, 8.1). It also may explain why he called for "a public establishment of religion in every civilized community" and stated that "in every religion, except the true, [the diligence of the clergy] is highly pernicious and it has even a natural tendency to pervert the true, by infusing into it a strong mixture of superstition, folly, and delusion" (*HE*, 3.135–36). Though scholarship on Hume has not acknowledged this point, it is my (moderate) hope that this book will have at least a slight impact on the conversation.[6]

Hume's positive suggestion for religion can be supplied with intelligible and provisional content such as a mild philosophical theism, moderate hope, and practical morality. This gives Hume's work value for religion as well as value for philosophical discourse on religion. It also reinvites Hume as a lover of wisdom (not Hume the skeptic, naturalist, or atheist) into dialogue in religious studies as a *constructive* interlocutor. It allows us to use his rich and fertile thought not only to support our vituperations against religion but also to fuel visionary work in the philosophy of religion and public discourse on religion. If our conventional notions of (false) religion are informed by the direct-passions (hopes and fears), then they evade the calm moderation and elide the factionalism that true religion resolves. Accordingly, a Humean-inspired true religion expands our very sense of the religious in three ways that this book has described: it affirms our belief in basic theism, calms our passions, and assists in the development of character and practical morality. Its impact on our lives is quiet yet crucial—it stabilizes our philosophical foundations, enhances reflective common life, and allows us to approach the world with equipoise. In short, it takes us beyond ourselves, not necessarily to a supernatural deity, but possibly to more generous conduct with others, to lighter expectations for the future, and to a more cautious commitment to our abstract reason. These are not simply *moral* issues. I shall assess the ways in which the conventional definitions of religion block the effectiveness of Hume's true religion by framing the remainder of this chapter around Jonathan Z. Smith's statement (which reflects Hume's schema): "Most frequently, the religious is identified with rationality, morality, or feeling."[7]

## Conventional Theism Versus Hume's Philosophical Theism

Conventional claims for religion are often derived from a strong notion of deity that inspires devotion. It is arguably the case that a strong theism—connected to worship—is the most easily identifiable trait we attach to the idea of religion. In fact, one could argue that we have normalized the connection between a strong, worshipful deity and religion to such a degree that even when confronted by unconventional theistic ideologies (say, a polytheism full of evil deities), if the holders of this belief worship those gods (even in a nontraditional way, say, through the drinking of urine), we would tend to identify this twisted theism and the sadistic reverence it inspires as having value and significance as *religion*. On this view, religion is largely reduced to its function of reverent worship.

Hume, in many ways, recognized that the logic of religion as worship was at best misguided and at worst dangerous. He aimed to mitigate against it by framing the idea of religion in terms that he thought might serve against the type of factionalism and violence that could potentially be supported by the logic of religion as worship. Still, as I stated earlier, scholars generally do not recognize or assign religious value to his idea of true religion. When they do grasp the basic theism in Hume's project (which is not very often), interpreters of Hume generally identify it as thin, underdeveloped, and useless for religion. J. C. A. Gaskin writes, "Assent to the existence of god in the sense allowed by Hume is valueless for any theistic religion. It carries no duties, invites no action, allows no inferences and involves no devotion." Gaskin here affirms Hume's intention and rightly notes that Hume's theism is meek and that it does not inspire commitment. Yet when he describes Hume's "plain, philosophical assent to the existence of a god as indicated by the vestiges of the design argument, a god whose sole attribute is intelligence which may bear some remote analogy to the intelligence of man, as 'attenuated deism,'" he goes too far in at least two ways.[8] First, Hume specifically denied that he was a deist on methodological grounds: deists grounded their claims on a rational argument from design. Since Hume asserted the *passions* were the source of our beliefs and actions, he did not support the rational argument from design and could not be identified as a deist. Second, Hume's Author of Nature—the mind's projection at the level of metaphysics—likely had intelligence *and* power, not simply intelligence as Gaskin argued. Gaskin was correct, however, that Hume's notion of invisible, intelligent power did not invoke religious devotion, allow for revelation, or leave space for a personal God. Gaskin diminishes the extent, however, to which Hume's basic theism "makes a difference in how we think and act in the world," and he failed to even entertain the religious significance of Hume's true religion.[9] Thus, Gaskin's position is ultimately dogmatic concerning religious significance and value. It assumes if there "can be no duty to love god," then there is no religious value. Stated positively, his position equates to the following: *if* there is adoration of god, *then* we have religion.[10] Gaskin's dismissal of the religious significance of Hume's more moderate notion 'true religion' and his failure to take note of Hume's revision of religious value itself is fueled by his conflation of religion with the robust theism that inspires devotion. This approach largely ignores theory in the study of religion that preserves room to attend to nontheistic traditions (Buddhists, Quakers), pantheism (Spinoza, Taoism), and panentheism (Hartshorne, Hinduism). Finally, it collapses the matrix of complexity that the broad use of the term "religion" might capture into a fairly crass and simple adoration of deity. On this standard for religion, Hume's theism is irreligious.

Donald Livingston posits that we might provisionally understand religion as a brand of theism that simply has an effect in one's life. Livingston—attending to the broadly functionalist interpretation of religion—demonstrates that Hume's ultimate theism impacts our lives because it functions as an "antidote" to false philosophy and allows us to avoid the "philosophical error" of abstract reason.[11] In short, on Livingston's argument, Hume's philosophical theism cures us from imperious reason and better orients us to reflexive common life and true philosophy, spaces that allow us to acknowledge the role of the passions, the imagination, habit, history, and culture in our understanding. Hume's philosophical theism impacts our daily life for the better; thus it has religious value.

## Absolute Dependence and Hume's Moderate Passions

One strategy that philosophers of religion have taken is to assign the term "religion" to a particular constellation of feelings, beliefs, or actions. These feelings are either generated by a depth experience or are its source. Either way, on this view religion is defined by the substance or content of our feelings, for example, feelings of "absolute dependence" and "immediacy" (Schleiermacher), the "numinous" (Otto), "luminous presence" (Thurman), and "hierophany" (Eliade). This approach emphasizes the experience of extraordinary feelings of wonderment and offers that these feelings may best be categorized with the adjective "sacred." Religion is neither what this feeling produces nor how this feeling functions regarding the wider social order; it is the substance of the feeling itself.

The enterprise of assigning religious value to specific feelings is a risky one fraught with challenges. Hume seemed to be aware of this, and though he argued that our beliefs and behaviors were ultimately derived from the passions, he was very clear and direct about the particular feelings, sentiments, and passions that played a role in religion. Vulgar religion, as I have detailed, was derived from direct-passions hope and fear, "which arise from good and evil most naturally" (T, 2.3.9.2). It follows that true religion relied on calm hopes and fears. Hume was sure to avoid the pitfall made by many of his interpreters: he did not reduce the feelings that inspired true religion to religious feelings. That is, Hume's discussion of the passions was quite modest. It asserted that with distance from its object and collective support our hopes could be tempered and moderated. This calm hope could be considered religious because of how it functioned, not because it contained any intrinsic religious value. For Hume, passions are neither religious or not; they may lead to *beliefs* that later are characterized as belonging to either vulgar or true religion.

Chapter 3 argues that a few scholars identify Hume's discussion of the direct-passions fear and hope as the source of vulgar or popular religion. They do not, however, accentuate the more moderate hope that "regulates the hearts of men" and, in my interpretation, constitutes a Humean true religion. Miguel Badia-Cabrera is an exception to this; he explicitly connects religious value to the realm of intense feeling and depth experience and discusses Hume's direct-passions hope and fear in light of Schleiermacher's feelings of immediacy and "absolute dependence." Confirming that Hume's idea of the passions does not quite meet Schleiermacher's more broad, romantic notion of sentiment or feeling, he writes, "Hume's language here seems to suggest that he was aware of the fact that a 'feeling of dependence' is at the basis of religion. [However, it] would be preposterous for us to try to derive, out of Hume's few remarks, Friedrich Schleiermacher's metaphysical interpretation of religion." Still Hume becomes, for Badia-Cabrera, a kind of proto-Schleiermacher. On his reading, Hume accepts that religion or religious experience is associated with an intense feeling. Badia-Cabrera is correct when he states, "Hume could say that such hopes and fears, or such a natural feeling of dependence connected with the origin of religious representations are the result of the operation of the world upon us." But he goes too far when he suggests that Hume holds the seed of an idea of a "peculiarly religious" "modality of being" or "dimension of human sensibility."[12] For Hume religious belief was arrived at only *after* the passions, which were themselves "secondary" or dependent on reflection, training, or common life. The moderate feeling at the core of a speculative true religion is thus incompatible with Schleiermacher's more ethereal, immediate, and sometimes erotic "revelation of the Infinite in the finite."[13] Even though he rightfully uses Schleiermacher as a point of comparison, Badia-Cabrera, like most philosophers of religion, loses track of the calm feelings that motivate Hume's quiet recommendation for religion.

Though it does not lead to worship or veneration, the moderate hope of true religion impacts the lives of those who live from it: it creates distance between the object and the passion and thereby generates calm passions. In this way, it regulates the heart. Another way to put this is that the effect of calm hope is that it teaches us to control our perceptions. One of the most powerful ways we can use our minds, on Hume's argument, is to allow our reflective impression of moderation to be filtered through common life. This produces a two-fold result: first, it helps generate belief in balance and therefore incites action that contributes to personal and social stability. When our volition springs from moderate passions the impact on the level of the understanding is profound: we are reminded of the importance of common life and the moral sentiments. Second, on the level of the passions, moderate hope affects our daily life by reducing the range of our passional responses. If the parameters of the passions are decreased, then equanimity is more likely to prevail and our daily lives may possibly become simpler and cleaner. The impassioned superstitions and enthusiasms that steal so much of our time and energy become less of a preoccupation for us. Annette Baier reminds us that Hume's calm passions (not "emotionless reason") "motivate us without any discernible turbulence in the soul or in the body, just as reasoning can go on in 'calmness and tranquility.'"[14] Might we assign some religious value and significance to these quiet and calm motivations?

## Religious Value and Hume's Practical Morality

Religious value is often apportioned to worldviews that articulate a strong moral code. This is, in part, because of the legacy of the Cartesian notion—inherited from Aquinas and Scotus and revised in the service of a strong commitment to modern rationalism—that morality comes from God. Hume, as I described in the previous chapter, did not chime with this position. For him, the source of our moral judgment was not some objective will of a Designer; rather, it was the social conventions of common life that, based on our feelings of sympathy, instructed us in virtuous character traits and habits of excellence. Still, Hume's work allowed that our socially derived morality could be attached to a particularly nuanced concept of religion. His humble vision for religion's proper office was likely constituted by this sort of morality, which he imbued with both religious value and secular sensibilities. The religious value stems from his historical awareness of the pervasiveness of religious ways of being due to the human propensity to religious belief. The secular sensibilities are derived from his commitment to sympathy and practical morality. It is these concerns and dispositions (not laws and principles) that inform our "determinations of morality" that are always dependent on the "circumstance of public utility" (EPM, 2.2.12), which should motivate our actions and may be best understood as the moral feature of Hume's true religion.

Those who believe that moral commitments automatically have religious significance tend to assert at least one of the following positions: that morality has historically been linked to religion; that our moral reflection is conceptually inseparable from religious reflection; or that moral law is dependent on the commands of God. Hume did not support any of these positions: his close study of history demonstrated that popular religion often supported factionalism and religious warfare. He also contended that benevolence and the "softer affections" (EPM, 2.1.1) that should inform our moral reflection might be enhanced by a further separation from popular religion. Finally, Hume did not affirm the notion of supernaturalism incorporated into divine command theory. His urgent disavowal of our capacity to posit moral attributes for God led many to believe in his time (William Warburton), and some in ours (Paul Russell), that Hume was an atheist who articulated a philosophy of irreligion that forged an autonomous moral life to which religion was superfluous. But as I have shown, Hume's considerations of religion had an explicitly moral thrust: "to regulate the heart of men, [and] humanize their conduct" (*DCNR*, 12.12). He did not hold a "virtuous atheism" because he realized our powerful human propensity for both religion and morality.

Paul Russell gives an extensive and nuanced discussion of the relationship between morality and religion in the *Treatise*. He situates Hume in the context of the competing interests of his day, that is, between the skeptical moral theory of Hobbes and the moral naturalism of Hutcheson. Russell investigates how Hume's moral theory is amenable to both the "religious philosopher" and the "speculative atheist" to conclude that Hume's moral thought cannot be easily pigeonholed, for "the truth of the matter is that Hume *blends together* the 'optimistic' elements found in Shaftesbury and Hutcheson along with the 'pessimistic' elements he found in Hobbes's work. His moral system is, therefore, both *mixed* and *complex*."[15] Russell's discussion stands counter to the conventional reading of Hume on morality and religion, and I agree with large parts of it. Because it attends to only one of Hume's writings (the *Treatise*), however, it cannot grasp the full historical and social importance of Hume's discussion—across his corpus—of religion in common life. Hume's later works, particularly his explicit grappling with religion in the *DCNR* and *NHR*, demonstrate that he was convinced of the power of religion in history and common life, both its beauty and its terror. He thought the best strategy, in face of the dilemma religion created, was to focus on the dilemma that created it: the quest for harmony. Accordingly, Hume argued that instead of abandoning religion altogether we should develop a moderate religious consciousness.

On Humean standards for virtuous characteristics, atheism was neither useful nor agreeable. Neither was superstition. What was useful and agreeable was a moderate approach to religion that both affirmed and moderated the passions. True religion was Hume's description for this positive and constructive vision. It was a convention that could develop virtuous traits and therefore should be, he claimed, an important part of "every civilized community" (*HE*, 3.135–36). Hume's generative project disclosed that our moral propensities, if fostered, might grow into a humble religious worldview, which he dubbed true religion. He clearly wanted a true *religion*, not a deeper secularism or a more virtuous atheism. Sympathy—a kind of affective solidarity with others—the common point of view on which our moral sentiment relies, and the fundamental interrelatedness that our morality takes for granted, are better understood when we approach them as components of a moderate religious worldview, not simply a moral one.

## Mindfulness and True Religion

The beauty of Hume's corpus is that it leaves open to its readers a vast array of possible interpretations, some more useful and accurate than others at different historical moments. On the one hand, this quality invites a variety of interesting, thoughtful, and sometimes contentious interpretations; on the other hand, it encourages hackneyed, self-interested interpretation and enables misguided readings of religion in Hume's overall project.

To some, my discussion of the notion 'true religion' in Hume may suggest that I believe he held beliefs in a peculiar mode of worship that he obscured in his writings. Or it may provoke readers to wonder if my interpretive agenda is simply to impose my own religious desires onto Hume and privilege religion in his thought. But neither of these is accurate; Hume did not have a set of secret religious beliefs or intentions, and neither do I. And I do not want to privilege religion but simply enhance our understanding of it. The aim here was to increase the chances that Hume's thought could have a positive impact on the discourse on religion. Thus my goals, like those of true religion, are modest. I have made the political and philosophical choice to assert that we gain from viewing Hume's positive projects in reason, the passions, and morality cumulatively as a Humean true religion. If my argument is correct, then scholars in religious studies might find Hume's work to offer something generative for the philosophy of religion. This does not mean that Hume's true religion is a panacea for the problems of philosophy, religion, or society, for he does not suggest that true religion become more prominent, take on an institutional form, or challenge vulgar religion. It must remain mostly quiet and manifest only inside of the individual soul through outward behaviors of excellence. We might think of it materializing when we ease our commitment to the conclusions of our causal thinking, regulate our moral conduct, and moderate our passions. Still, it is unseen. Mostly, we are reminded of it after its effects have registered, and it is then we quietly aspire to it again.

The whole of a Humean-inflected true religion is greater than the sum of its parts. Genuine theism, moderate passions, and practical morality, when approached as a collective set of terms under the rubric "true religion," become more than ideas, passions, and sentiments—they form a quality of mindfulness that orients us in relation to complete presence or the totality of experience. This might be described as sacred experience. Of course for Hume, unmitigated and unmoderated language of the sacred was too dangerous; it invited factionalism, superstition, enthusiasm, and belief in miracles. The *sensibility* this language points toward at its best, however, was valuable to Hume, and he did not want to lose it. He may concur with those who associate with the variety of forms of Westernized Buddhism: that true religion is mindful presentness without the baggage of conventional religion. It invites us to a deep appreciation of the unexplainable order and Orderer, embraces the incomprehensibility of our feelings, and keeps us in harmony with the collective sympathy of all persons and therefore fully present in the moment. This sensibility is rare and difficult to sustain as it seems we are never fully able to escape our nature, history, tradition, and culture. We can, however, as

Hume's description of true religion reminds us, "humanize our conduct" to temporarily appeal to what Lincoln called "the better angels of our nature" and strive for equipoise in common life. It is to this poetical, postreligious religion where these reflections on the work of David Hume have brought us, and it is here that our task must, for the time being, end.

# NOTES

## Introduction

1. Ernest Campbell Mossner, *The Life of David Hume* (Oxford: Clarendon Press, 2001), 306.

2. Christopher Williams's brilliant discussion of Humeanism is instructive for this entire introduction. See his *A Cultivated Reason: An Essay on Hume and Humeanism* (University Park: Pennsylvania State University Press, 1999).

3. An example of this is Hume's famous "Letter to a Physician" (1734), in which the young Hume describes his mental health with a comparison to the mystic: "I have notic'd in the Writings of the French Mystics, & in those of our Fanatics here, that when they give a History of the Situation of their souls, they mention a Coldness and Desertion of the Spirit, which frequently returns; and some of them, at the beginning, have been tormented with it many years. As this kind of Devotion depends entirely on the Force of Passion, & consequently of the Animal Spirits, I have often thought that their case and mine were pretty parallel" (*LET*, 1.17.3). While this is not an endorsement for religion, it certainly does not completely dismiss it. The best discussion of this letter is by John P. Wright, "Dr. George Cheyne, Chevalier Ramsay, and Hume's 'Letter to a Physician,'" *Hume Studies* 29, no. 1 (2003): 125–41.

4. For example, writing about the "genius and spirit" of the "Roman catholic superstition," Hume states, "the popular religion consisted more of exterior practices and observances, than of any principles, which either took possession of the heart, or influenced the conduct" (*HE*, 1, foreword).

5. Charles Taylor, *Sources of the Self: The Making of Modern Identity* (Cambridge: Harvard University Press, 1989), 344; Isabel Rivers, *Reason, Grace, and Sentiment: A Study of the Language of Religion and Ethics in England, 1660–1780*, vol. 1 (Cambridge: Cambridge University Press, 1991), 7–8; Donald W. Livingston relies on the work of Michael Polanyi for this point. Polanyi, *The Tacit Dimension* (London: Smith, 1983); and *Personal Knowledge: Toward a Postcritical Philosophy* (Chicago: University of Chicago Press, 1974).

6. Hume, quoted in Ernest Campbell Mossner, *The Life of David Hume* (Oxford: Clarendon Press, 2001), 306–7.

7. John Immerwahr intervenes in our understanding of Hume's use of the idea 'true religion.' See his "Hume's Aesthetic Theism" in *Hume Studies* 22, no. 2 (1996): 325–37.

8. Hume writes, "Some nations have been discovered, who entertained no sentiments of Religion, if travelers and historians may be credited; and no two nations, and scarce any two men, have ever agreed precisely in the same sentiments." (I read "Religion" here as monotheism, or what he calls genuine theism.) The wider, more general category 'religion' exists in some form in all human societies: "It is a matter of fact incontestable, that about 1700 years ago all mankind were polytheists" (*NHR*, introd.).

9. Hume specifically addresses the charges of atheism in his 1745 *Letter from a Gentleman to his Friend in Edinburgh*, ed. Ernest Campbell Mossner and John V. Price (Edinburgh: Edinburgh

University Press, 1967), 21. He confirms his anti-atheism here when he writes, "wherever I see order, I infer from experience that *there*, there hath been design and contrivance. And the same principle which leads me into this inference, when I contemplate a building, regular and beautiful in its whole frame and structure; the same principle obliges me to infer an infinitely perfect architect, from the infinite art and contrivance which is displayed in the whole fabric of the universe" (25–26).

10. Peter Gay, *The Enlightenment: The Rise of Modern Paganism* (New York: Norton, 1977); Carl L. Becker, *The Heavenly City of the Eighteenth-Century Philosophers* (New Haven: Yale University Press, 1967).

11. See Terence Penelhum, *Themes in Hume: The Self, the Will, Religion* (Oxford: Clarendon Press, 2003), 177–260; and Keith E. Yandell, *Hume's "Inexplicable Mystery": His Views on Religion* (Philadelphia: Temple University Press, 1990). While Penelhum's views on this question evolved over the course of his thinking on Hume, he concluded that Hume's project ultimately helped Hume "keep his atheism in the closet." See Penelhum, "Hume on Religion: Cultural Influences," in *A Companion to Hume*, ed. Elizabeth Radcliffe (Malden: Blackwell, 2008), 336. Yandell's fascinating tour de force through Hume's religious writings suggests that Hume is wrong about some things and right about others, yet his epistemology "provides no way for Hume to justify his own theory of religious belief and experience" (340–41).

12. Penelhum, *Hume (Philosophers in Perspective)* (London: Macmillan, 1975) 163.

13. Paul Russell, *The Riddle of Hume's "Treatise": Skepticism, Naturalism, and Irreligion* (Oxford: Oxford University Press, 2008); Thomas Holden, *Spectres of False Divinity: Hume's Moral Atheism* (Oxford: Oxford University Press, 2010). Annette C. Baier claims that Russell "persuasively argues that irreligion is the main agenda of Hume's *Treatise*." *Death and Character: Further Reflections on Hume* (Cambridge: Harvard University Press, 2008), 280. I think Russell and Baier would be more precise to argue that in the *Treatise* Hume is against *popular* religion. In fact, Baier admits on the same page that Hume treats religion in a nuanced fashion and that she is unclear how to classify his ultimate position on religion.

14. Donald Livingston, *Philosophical Melancholy and Delirium: Hume's Pathology of Philosophy* (Chicago: University of Chicago Press, 1998), 148; Joseph J. Godfrey, *A Philosophy of Human Hope* (Dordrecht: Nijhoff, 1987), 55; and Annette C. Baier, *A Progress of Sentiments: Reflections on Hume's "Treatise"* (Cambridge: Harvard University Press, 1991), 279.

15. Penelhum mentions true religion very briefly. See Penelhum, *Hume*, and Yandell, *Hume's "Inexplicable Mystery"*; both acknowledge a veiled theism in Hume but they write very little about it.

16. J. C. A. Gaskin contends that Hume makes "the most formidable attack on the rationality of religious belief ever mounted by a philosopher" in his introduction to *Principal Writings on Religion Including "Dialogues Concerning Natural Religion" and "The Natural History of Religion,"* Oxford World's Classics (Oxford: Oxford University Press, 1993). Flew writes, "The 'true religion,' to which Hume professed his devotion, was persuasively defined to exclude all actual religious belief and practice." David Hume, *Writings on Religion*, ed. Antony Flew (La Salle, Ill.: Open Court Press, 1992), vii. Gaskin is unable to see how Hume's project for religion has any practical value and he is wrong to foreclose the possibility that a basic theism is necessarily irreligious. With this logic nontheistic religion could not exist.

17. This is separate from the claim that all arguments that overlook true religion do not assist our understanding Hume on religion. For example, Edward Craig's argument that Hume works against the idea that man was made in the image of God confirms Hume's way of undermining the idea of God normally associated with religious belief. Craig is correct in this argument, but he stops too soon. He fails to show how Hume's naturalism might function religiously. Similarly, Justin Broackes's reading of Hume's inconsistent modes of belief in the *Treatise* and first *Enquiry* point toward Hume's attack on traditional religious belief. This is instructive and, I think, mostly correct. But Broackes's argument also pulls up early. He does not discuss the potential religious

significance of natural beliefs in Hume. See Edward Craig, *The Mind of God and the Image of Man* (Oxford: Oxford University Press, 2006); and Justin Broackes, "Hume, Belief, and Personal Identity," in *Reading Hume on Human Understanding*, ed. Peter Millican (Oxford: Oxford University Press, 2002), 187–202.

18. See Baier, *Progress of Sentiments*; Baier, *The Cautious Jealous Virtue: Hume on Justice* (Cambridge: Harvard University Press, 2010); Baier, *Death and Character: Further Reflections on Hume* (Cambridge: Harvard University Press, 2008); Baier, "Promises, Promises, Promises," in *Postures of the Mind: Essays on Mind and Morals*, ed. Annette C. Baier (Minneapolis: University of Minnesota Press, 1985), 174–206; Donald W. Livingston, *Hume's Philosophy of Common Life* (Chicago: University of Chicago Press, 1984); and Livingston, *Philosophical Melancholy and Delirium*.

19. Jennifer Herdt supports the idea that Hume's "epistemological concerns are derivative of his broader social concerns." See *Religion and Faction in Hume's Moral Philosophy* (Cambridge: Cambridge University Press, 1997).

20. Hume's notion of utility is simply a quality of an act. Bentham's maximization of utility through the evaluation of acts based on consequences was different from Hume's idea that utility is what makes something virtuous.

21. In fact, the statement by Sir James at the beginning of this introduction is a quick study in how Hume's complexity was received (as well as the complexity of his reception). It is probably the case that Hume's celebrity in France among the general public may have been buoyed by the recently signed Treaty of Paris of 1763, which ended the conflict between the French and English and unleashed an unspoken Anglophilia among the French elite. In this new social milieu, his Scottish heritage elevated him: the French could celebrate him without risk of being stigmatized as direct supporters of Great Britain. Additionally, his historical writings fit perfectly with the interests of the French reading public, who were groomed to appreciate historical work, most notably due to the recently published thirty-six-volume masterpiece *Historie naturelle* (1749) by Georges-Louis Leclerc Buffon. Finally, Hume's social skills and his large size endeared him to the French, "their original admiration for his intellect was consequently augmented by affection for his person." Mossner, *Life of David Hume*, 447. In terms of philosophy, while there is no record of any direct conflict between Hume and the philosophes while he was in France, the choice by writers such as Maupertuis, Diderot, D'Holbach, and Helvetius not to embrace Hume's philosophical project publicly demonstrates that they did not take Hume to be an ally. A major difference between the philosophes and Hume was their distinct methods of criticism of religion. They were much more dogmatic in their critique of religion than Hume because they generally understood religion to be a scheme of domination. Hume had distaste for any flat-footed dogmatism that held religion to be bad in all times and all places.

Hume's critique of religion—intensely aimed at the superstition and enthusiasm he so closely associated with the Calvinism and Evangelical Presbyterianism of his day—rested on both his historical analysis, which showed that popular religion often had deleterious social and moral effects, and his philosophy of the passions, which argued that reason had little to do with religious belief. His investment in considering religion through the lens of history, custom, human nature, common life, the passions, and morality prevented him from concluding, as the philosophes did, that religion was, at all times, bad.

22. See Joel Weisenhemer, *Eighteenth-Century Hermeneutics: Philosophy of Interpretation from Locke to Burke* (New Haven: Yale University Press, 1993).

23. The "action" that this belief inspires is equanimity (a "nonaction" to some). Richard Rorty articulates something like this moderate form of hope when he describes the hope of John Dewey. He calls Dewey's hope a "criterionless hope" or "that ability to believe that the future will be unspecifiably different from, and unspecifiably freer than, the past." *Philosophy and Social Hope* (New York: Penguin, 1999), 120.

*Chapter 1*

1. When paired with the term "religion," Hume used "false," "popular," and "vulgar" interchangeably and for cross-purposes.

2. Isabel Rivers, *Reason, Grace, and Sentiment: A Study of the Language of Religion and Ethics in England, 1660–1780* (Cambridge: Cambridge University Press, 1991), 1:7–8.

3. Moving toward a Humean true religion requires closely attending to the suggestive claims for religion in statements such as "the corruption of the best things gives rise to the worst" and "solid belief and persuasion . . . governs us in the affairs of common life" (*NHR*, 12.14). Hume used this line at least three times regarding religion: 10.1 and 11.1; see also *EMPL*, 10.73.

4. Joseph Ellin writes, "there is no evidence that for Hume there is any form of religion which can be identified as 'true religion.'" See "Streminger: Religion a Threat to Morality," *Hume Studies* 15, no. 2 (1989): 296. J. C. A. Gaskin claims Hume "cannot conceal his critical analysis of actual religion behind a commendation of something as unreligiously abstract as the 'true religion' which he describes and which he admits." *Hume's Philosophy of Religion* (New York: Macmillan, 1978), 149. Erik J. Wielenberg writes that "Humean 'true religion' has almost no implications for how we ought to act in everyday life." *God and the Reach of Reason: C. S. Lewis, David Hume, and Bertrand Russell* (Cambridge: Cambridge University Press, 2008), 188. The work of Donald Livingston, Timothy Costelloe, Van Harvey, Gerhard Streminger, William Sessions, Nicholas Capaldi, Annette C. Baier, Ryan Patrick Hanley, Don Garrett, William Lemmons, and Timothy Yoder challenges this reading. See Nicholas Capaldi, "The Dogmatic Slumber of Hume Scholarship," *Hume Studies* 18, no. 2 (1992): 117–35; Capaldi, "Hume's Philosophy of Religion: God Without Ethics," *International Journal for Philosophy of Religion* 1, no. 4 (1970): 233–40; Annette C. Baier, *A Progress of Sentiments: Reflections on Hume's "Treatise"* (Cambridge: Harvard University Press, 1991); Ryan Patrick Hanley, "Hume's Critique and Defense of Religion," in *Enlightenment and Secularism: Essays on the Mobilization of Reason*, ed. C. Nadon (Lanham: Lexington Books, 2013), 89–101; Don Garrett, "What's True About Hume's 'True Religion'?" *Journal of Scottish Philosophy* 10, no. 2 (2012): 199–220; Willem Lemmens, "Beyond the Calm Sunshine of the Mind: Hume on Religion and Morality," *Aufklarung und Kritik* 27 (2011): 214–50; and Timothy Yoder, *Hume on God: Irony, Deism, and Genuine Theism* (London: Continuum, 2011). There are different degrees, however, to which these thinkers attribute religious value to Hume's true religion. Donald W. Livingston, "Hume's Conception of 'True Religion,'" in *Hume's Philosophy of Religion: The Sixth James Montgomery Hester Seminar*, ed. Antony Flew (Winston-Salem: Wake Forest University Press, 1986), 33–73. Livingston, *Hume's Philosophy of Common Life* (Chicago: University of Chicago Press, 1984); and Livingston, *Philosophical Melancholy and Delirium: Hume's Pathology of Philosophy* (Chicago: University of Chicago Press, 1998) are the most useful and elegant discussions of true religion in Hume. Livingston argues that the religious value of true religion is that it takes us away from the barbarism of reason. Timothy M. Costelloe, in "'In Every Civilized Community': Hume on Belief and the Demise of Religion," *International Journal for Philosophy of Religion* 55 (2004): 171–85, also reads true religion as an important means of binding people in the social order. Van Harvey—the source for the expression "useless rump"—believes that Hume's true religion has a spiritual quality akin to Buddhism. He argues this in "Philo's 'True Religion,'" in *Religion and Hume's Legacy*, ed. D. Z. Phillips and T. Tessin (London: Macmillan, 1999), 68–80. Gerhard Streminger attributes moral and religious value to Hume's notion of true religion. See his "Religion a Threat to Morality: An Attempt to Throw Some New Light on Hume's Philosophy of Religion," *Hume Studies* 15, no. 2 (1989): 277–93. William Sessions claims to assess true religion in his *Reading Hume's "Dialogues": A Veneration of True Religion* (Bloomington: Indiana University Press, 2002), but he focuses solely on the *DCNR*.

5. In his essay "Of National Characters" (1748), Hume wrote, "all mankind have a strong propensity to religion at certain times and in certain dispositions." The three-thousand-word footnote from which this claim is extracted is an extensive criticism of clerics (*EMPL*, 21.199).

6. See also the draft of a paragraph in the preface that Hume removed from volume 2 of his *History of England*, as cited by Ernest Campbell Mossner, *The Life of David Hume* (Oxford: Clarendon Press, 2001), 306–7. "The proper Office of Religion is to reform Men's Lives, to purify their Hearts, to inforce all moral Duties, & to secure Obedience to the Laws & civil Magistrate. While it pursues these useful Purposes, its Operations, tho' infinitely valuable, are secret & silent; and seldom come under the Cognizance of History." These lines were removed, subsequently placed in a footnote in the 1757 first edition of volume 6 and then removed again in 1770. A revision of these lines is given by Cleanthes in *DCNR*, 12.12.

7. Timothy Fitzgerald's work *Discourse on Civility and Barbarity: A Critical History of Religion and Related Categories* (New York: Oxford University Press, 2010) reminds us that the term "religion" is undefinable without its oppositional binary (nonreligion or secular); thus the use of the term is fraught with both academic as well as ideological commitments. On his argument, discourse on "religion" is an enterprise that strategically constructs rhetorical boundaries and thereby severs the fundamental unity that the symbol 'religion' claims to promote. Hume took religion to be a distinct category that originated in human nature and experience. For Fitzgerald, Hume's co-signing of the binaries religious/secular and natural/supernatural reflects an ideological commitment and has material consequences. The account that follows both illuminates Fitzgerald's important insight and invites us to think beyond it.

8. The following works specifically discuss the influence of Cicero's *De natura deorum* on Hume's *Dialogues Concerning Natural Religion*: J. C. A. Gaskin, in the introduction to *Principal Writings on Religion Including "Dialogues Concerning Natural Religion" and "The Natural History of Religion,"* Oxford World's Classics (Oxford: Oxford University Press, 1993), xx–xxiii; Peter Fosl, "Doubt and Divinity: Cicero's Influence on Hume's Religious Skepticism," *Hume Studies* 20, no. 1 (1994): 103–20; John Vladimir Price, "Sceptics in Cicero and Hume," *Journal of the History of Ideas* 25, no. 1 (1964): 97–106; and Christine Battersby, "The *Dialogues* as Original Imitation: Cicero and the Nature of Hume's Skepticism," in *McGill Hume Studies*, ed. David Fate Norton, Nicholas Capaldi, Wade L. Robinson (San Diego: Austin Hill Press, 1979), 239–53. I supplement the consensus of these essays, that Cicero's skepticism in *De natura deorum* influenced Hume's writing in the *Dialogues*, and attempt to give a broader reading of both Hume and Cicero.

9. Works that have addressed the broader links between Cicero and Hume are Adam Potkay, *The Passion for Happiness: Samuel Johnson and David Hume* (Ithaca: Cornell University Press, 2000); and Peter Jones, *Hume's Sentiments: Their Ciceronian and French Context* (Edinburgh: Edinburgh University Press, 1982). Hume mentions Cicero throughout his corpus (Peter Jones says that he names Cicero more than fifty times. Two general and introductory examples: in a letter to Francis Hutcheson, Hume wrote that "Upon the whole, I desire to take my catalogue of Virtues from Cicero's *Offices*, not from the *Whole Duty of Man*. I had, indeed, the former Book in my Eye in all my Reasoning's" (*LET*, 1.34.13). In Hume's autobiographical work, *My Own Life*, he writes, "My studious Disposition, my Sobriety, and my Industry gave my Family a Notion that the Law was a proper Profession for me: But I found an unsurmountable Aversion to every thing but the pursuits of Philosophy and general Learning; and while they fancyed I was pouring over Voet and Vinnius, Cicero and Virgil were the Authors which I was secretly devouring" (*EMPL*, introd., xxxiii).

10. Eli Edward Burriss, "Cicero and the Religion of His Day," *Classical Journal* 21, no. 7 (1926): 526.

11. Cicero's notion *religio* contained ambiguities and contradictions and, as some scholars note, became more skeptical after *De legibus* (51 B.C.E.) (New York: Loeb Classical Library, 1928). For a useful, basic discussion of this fluid category, see Wilfred Cantwell Smith, *The Meaning and End of Religion: A New Approach to the Religious Traditions of Mankind* (New York: Macmillan, 1991); and Benson Saler, "*Religio* and the Definition of Religion," *Cultural Anthropology* 2, no. 3 (1987): 395–99. Useful discussions of Cicero and *religio* are Arnaldo Momigliano, "The Theological Efforts of the Roman Upper Classes in the First Century BC," *Classical Philology* 79,

no. 3 (1984): 199–211; Mary Beard, "Cicero and Divination: The Formation of a Latin Discourse," *Journal of Roman Studies* 76, no. 3 (1986): 33–46; and Robert J. Goar, "The Purpose of *De divinitione*," *Transactions and Proceedings of the American Philological Association* 99 (1968): 241–48.

12. The speech, "De domo sua" (57 B.C.E.), is Cicero's public attempt to compel the Senate to rebuild his house on Palatine Hill after it had been taken and consecrated as a temple by Clodius during Cicero's exile. It commenced with an affirmation of the link between *religio* and *res publica*.

> Many things, O priests, have been devised and established with divine wisdom by our ancestors; but no action of theirs was ever more wise than their determination that the same men should superintend both what relates to the religious worship due to the immortal gods, and also what concerns the highest interests of the state, so that they might preserve the republic as the most honorable and eminent of the citizens, by governing it well, and as priests by wisely interpreting the requirements of religion.

Marcus Tullius Cicero, *The Orations of Marcus Tullius Cicero*, trans. C. D. Yonge (London: Bell and Sons, 1891), 1. Cicero concludes his argument by stating that it would be fatal for the ceremonies, rituals, and priests of popular religion if an incorrect verdict in this matter was rendered. This speech eloquently adumbrates his understanding of the bond between religion and the state, a theme also emphasized in the poem "*De consulatu suo*," which confirmed that good judgment and virtuous decisions reflected infinite wisdom of the gods. Cicero, *De divinatione* (New York: Loeb Classical Library, 1923), bk. 1.11.17, p. 244. Cicero ridicules parts of the poem as he presents it. Key here is that the poem, which survived only because Cicero referenced it in the later *De divinatione* (44 B.C.E.), was generally agreed to be his attempt to aestheticize his autobiography and indicate divine support for his political actions. This boldness was extended, less abstractly, in a letter to his friend Atticus (July 61 B.C.E.) that attributed success of the Republic to his own personal understanding of "divine providence." Cicero, *Cicero's Letters to Atticus*, ed. David R. Shackleton Bailey (Cambridge: Cambridge University Press, 1965), 1:155. The letter continues on this point:

> Thirty of the most irresponsible rascals in Rome pocket their bribes and play ducks and drakes with religion and morality, in which Talna and Plautus and Spongi and the other riff-raff find that an offence was not committed when every man and beast too knows it was. And yet, to offer you some comfort on public affairs, rascality does not exult so merrily in victory as bad men had expected after the infliction of so grave an injury upon the body politic. They quite supposed that with the collapse of religion and good morals, of the integrity of the courts and the authority of the Senate openly triumphant villainy and vice would wreak vengeance on the best in our society for the pain branded by the severity of my consulship upon the worst.

Finally, he revisited the same theme directly but from the negative position in *De officiis*, where he argued that the quest for authority and power often led to a depraved imagination and an inconsiderate leader. Cicero, *De officiis*, trans. Walter Miller (Cambridge: Harvard University Press, 1913), 136.

13. Cicero leveled an extensive critique in the second book of *De divinatione* (44 B.C.E.), where, in the voice of Marcus, he deployed a trenchant skepticism that undermined the very possibility of divination and its concomitant religious practices, positions that Quintus—the other interlocutor in this dialogue—supported in book 1. In effect, he masterfully accomplished a profound critique as well as a deep affirmation of religion in the same text. Of course, Cicero's actual viewpoint was not reducible to either position. Mary Beard explains, "The second book is balanced by the first: the arguments against divination must be seen alongside the arguments in favour of the practice. Both positions are laid out, and no conclusion, supporting one side or the other, is offered." See "Cicero and Divination," 34. Cicero ends the dialogue:

"It is characteristic of the Academy to put forward no conclusions of its own, but to approve those which seem to approach nearest to the truth, to compare arguments; to draw forth all that may be said in behalf of any opinion; and without asserting any authority of its own, to leave the judgment of the inquirer wholly free. That same method, inherited from Socrates, I shall, if agreeable to you, my dear Quintus, follow as often as possible in our future discussions."

"Nothing could please me better," Quintus replied. (*De divinatione* 2.72.150)

14. An example of this in the first part of book 2 of Cicero's *De legibus* (51 B.C.E.) is when the greatness of the republic is described as a consequence of certain ancestral religions of Rome. *De legibus* depicts the laws concerning worship, festivals, and religious ceremonies of the model state and thereby gives support for a specific type of sacred worship. The text portrays the proper religion as that exemplified by Numa Pompilius, the second king of Rome, and thereby denies the value of other types of religious expression.

15. An effort from late in his career, the dialectical discussion *De divinatione* (44 B.C.E.), is an interesting source for attending to Cicero's thoughts on theism. Arguably, both interlocutors in the dialogue accept two provisional conclusions: that religion confirms a general order in nature and that it is the set of communal rituals directed to the gods that produce greater social harmony. Cicero, seemingly against his own earlier poem (recontextualized in this work in the voice of Quintus), acknowledges this in the voice of Marcus: "Furthermore, the celestial order and the beauty of the universe compel me to confess that there is some excellent and eternal Being, who deserves the respect and homage of men. Wherefore just as it is a duty to extend the influence of true religion, which is closely associated with the knowledge of nature, so it is a duty to weed out every root of superstition" (2.72.148–9). The Latin here for religious practice is *religio*. Of course, we should not reduce Marcus's view here to Cicero's overall position.

16. The historical essay of Robert H. Hurlbutt III, "David Hume and Scientific Theism," *Journal of the History of Ideas* 17, no. 4 (1956): 495–96, details the links in both style and content between Cicero and Hume.

17. Marcus Tullius Cicero, *De haruspicum responsis oratio*, trans. N. H. Watts (Cambridge: Harvard University Press, 1923), 341.

18. In "Sceptics in Cicero and Hume," Price describes this mild or empirical theism in the character Balbus in *De natura deorum* and Cleanthes in the *DCNR*. Regarding Cicero's personal religious beliefs, Hume wrote, interestingly in the *NHR*:

> If ever there was a nation or a time in which the public religion lost all authority over mankind, we might expect, that infidelity in Rome, during the Ciceronian age would openly have erected its throne, and that Cicero himself, in every speech and action, would have been its most declared abettor. But it appears, that, whatever skeptical liberties that great man might take, in his writings or in philosophical conversation; he yet avoided, in the common conduct of life, the imputation of deism and profaneness. Even in his own family, and to his wife Terentia, whom he highly trusted, he was willing to appear a devout religionist; and there remains a letter, addressed to her, in which he seriously desires her to offer sacrifice to Apollo and Æsculapius, in gratitude for the recovery of his health. [Note the close association Hume makes between deism and profaneness.] (12.12)

He notes, a few paragraphs later, that Cicero, "who affected, in his own family, to appear a devout religionist, makes no scruple, in a public court of judicature, of treating the doctrine of a future state as a ridiculous fable, to which nobody could give any attention." Hume seems to distinguish between Cicero's personal experience of religion and his public understanding of its function.

Hume recognized Cicero's sense of *religio* and distinguished these aspects of his thought from the idea of personal providence.

19.  Hume stated in a letter to Hutcheson that he took his "Catalogue of Virtues" from Cicero's *De officiis* and claimed that he kept this work of Cicero's consistently in "his eye" (*LET*, 1.32.13).

20.  Marcus Tullius Cicero, *De inventione*, in *The Orations of Marcus Tullius Cicero*, vol. 4, trans. Charles D. Yonge (London: Bell, 1988), 42.

21.  Marcus Tullius Cicero, *De finibus bonorum et malorum; or, On Moral Ends*, ed. Julia Annas (Cambridge: Cambridge University Press, 2004), 94.

22.  Ibid., 3.

23.  For an informative discussion of "The Stoic," see John Immerwahr, "Hume's Essays on Happiness," *Hume Studies* 15, no. 2 (1989): 307–24.

24.  Tertullian, *The Apology of Tertullian*, trans. and annotated by William Reeve (London: Newberry House, 1889); *Meditations of the Emperor Marcus Aurelius Antoninus*, trans. J. Collier (London: Scott, 1887), 24:80.

25.  Celsus's *Aletheia logos; or, On True Doctrine*, of 177 C.E. There is debate about whether the title should be translated *True Doctrine*, *True Discourse*, or *True Word*. See Tomas Hagg, "Hierocles the Lover of Truth and Eusebius the Sophist," in *Parthenope: Studies in Ancient Greek Fiction*, ed. Lars Boje Morensen and Tormod Eide (Denmark: Museum Tusculanum Press, 2004), 407. Nevertheless, the text has been handed down to us in detailed reconstruction only from extensive quotations by Origen of Alexandria, an early Christian apologist. He presented the positions of Celsus, then eloquently argued against them in *Contra Celsum*, ed. Henry Chadwick (Cambridge: Cambridge University Press, 1953). From these citations, we are able to glean that Celsus promoted the practical disposition for religion derived from the ancestral traditions as a response to what he believed was an insincere religious movement on the margins of Roman culture (Christianity). Porphyry's *Against the Christians* (around 300 C.E.) is an extant collection of fragments only because of extensive discussion of it by those who opposed it. Michael B. Simmons articulates the problems of analyzing Porphyry in a review of Robert Berchman's *Porphyry Against the Christians* when he writes, "Trolling in the deep and often murky waters of Porphyrian studies can be risky and dangerous simply because many of the works of the disciple of Plotinus are either lost or, as in the case of his anti-Christian literature, in deplorable, fragmentary condition. To compound the latter problem one must keep in mind also that all the fragments both of Porphyry's *Contra Christianos* (C.C.) and *Philosophia ex oraculis* (which contains some anti-Christian oracles) derive from the works of his greatest enemies, the Christians. Scholars are still not in agreement as to how many of Harnack's fragments of the C.C., originally published in his *Porphyrius Gegen die Christen, 15 Bücher, Zeugnisse, und Referate* (Berlin, 1916), are genuinely Porphyrian or whether they mainly come from the *Apocriticus* of the fifth-century Macarius Magnes." See *Journal of Early Christian Studies* 16, no. 2 (2008): 263–65.

26.  Jeremy Schott makes a compelling argument for the idea that early Christians and Greek thinkers who engaged in religious discourse both claimed their systems of religious belief were universal and therefore true. "Porphyry on Christians and Others: 'Barbarian Wisdom,' Identity Politics, and Anti-Christian Polemics on the Eve of the Great Persecution," *Journal of Early Christian Studies* 13, no. 3 (2005): 277–314.

27.  See Ramsey MacMullen, *Paganism in the Roman Empire* (New Haven: Yale University Press, 1981); and Michael Frede, "Celsus' Attack on the Christians," in *Philosophia Togota II: Plato and Aristotle at Rome*, ed. Jonathan Barnes and Miriam Griffin (New York: Oxford University Press, 1997), 218–39.

28.  "Neither Celsus nor Porphyry could have any fault to find with these arguments in point of form: all positive religions have a mythical element; the 'true religion' lies behind the religions." Adolf Harnack, *History of Dogma*, trans. Neil Buchanan (Boston: Little, Brown, 1907), 2:340, 125.

29. Important differences appear in the work of Celsus and Porphyry. After Christianity became the religion of the Roman Empire, the site of true religion slightly shifted. Constantine, ever the savvy politician, convinced Christians that he embraced the belief that Christianity was a separate and higher mode of discourse—a revealed truth—by converting to Christianity in 312 C.E. and legalizing it in 313 C.E. Largely a genius at manipulating the public, he claimed to subordinate his imperial agenda in service to God, and what was considered his strong faith was understood as the key to Rome amassing more political power, economic success, and material prosperity to spread the Christian gospel.

30. On the natural law of Grotius, see T. J. Hochstrass, *Natural Law Theories in the Early Enlightenment* (Cambridge: Cambridge University Press, 2004). On the natural religion and humanism of Herbert, see Peter Byrne, *Natural Religion and the Nature of Religion* (New York: Routledge, 1989), 22–36.

31. Generally understood as the basis for modern natural law, this explicitly political work confirms the importance of religion. In it, Grotius describes four fundamental religious "truths" that lead to "true religion, which is the same at all periods of time." *The Rights of War and Peace*, abridged and translated by William Whewell (Cambridge: Cambridge University Press, 1853), 245.

32. For a detailed history of this work, see Jan-Paul Heering, *Hugo Grotius as an Apologist for the Christian Religion: A Study of His Work "De veritate religionis christianae"* (Leiden: Koninklijke Brill, 2004).

33. Hugo Grotius, *The Truth of the Christian Religion in Six Books*, trans. John D. Clarke (Oxford: Baxter Press, 1818), 4, 157, 72.

34. Edward, Lord Herbert of Cherbury, *De veritate*, trans. Meyrick H. Carre (Bristol: Arrowsmith, 1937), 75. His later writings, namely the religious text *Religio laici* (1645) and the historical work *De religione gentilium* (1663), asserted that a constellation of true beliefs formed true religion. These true beliefs were certain: the result of the proper application of the principles of universal reason, which emanated from an interior disposition of the person marked by God.

35. Cherbury, *De veritate*, 77.

36. The "five common notions" that constituted the universal true religion in *De veritate* are (1) there is a supreme God; (2) God should be worshipped; (3) "the connection of Virtue with Piety, defined in this work as the right conformation of the faculties, is and always has been held to be, the most important part of religious practice"; (4) repentance is useful; and (5) there is reward or punishment after this life (296). Herbert continues, a few pages later, "The only Catholic and Uniform Church is the Doctrine of Common Notions which comprehends all places and all men. This church alone reveals Divine Universal Providence, or the wisdom of nature. This church alone explains why god is appealed to as the common father. And it is only through this Church that salvation is possible" (Cherbury, *De veritate*, 303).

37. Grotius, *Rights of War and Peace*, 452; Edward, Lord Herbert of Cherbury, *Pagan Religion: A Translation of "De religione gentilium,"* ed. John Anthony Butler (Ottawa: Dovehouse, 1996), 17.

38. Grotius, *Truth of the Christian Religion*, 12. He also wrote, "we must observe that 'true religion,' which is the same at all periods of time, rests upon four evident and universally acknowledged truths" (Grotius, *Rights of War and Peace*, 245) and declares that "we must establish the fundamental principles of religion by means of universal wisdome" (Cherbury, *De veritate*, 290).

39. Peter Harrison argues that "the deists of the eighteenth century opted for exclusive but explicit belief in natural religion rather than the universal and implicit belief which Herbert proposed." *"Religion" and the Religions in the English Enlightenment* (Cambridge: Cambridge University Press, 1990), 87.

40. My selection of Tindal and Morgan is not a claim that they are the most important representatives of this era or the most prominent deists. This would require debate about the specific parameters and distinguishing features of deism. Using Tindal and Morgan as my figures

here—like Grotius, Herbert, Celsus, and Porphyry—is strategic. I chose them because they used the dialogue form, articulated the constructive part of their projects as true religion, and emphasized the ethical aspects of true religion. In short, they helped establish the historical foundations that support my constructive argument for a Humean true religion.

41. Matthew Tindal, *Christianity as Old as Creation; or, The Gospel: A Republication of the Religion of Nature* (London, 1730), 22.

42. Ibid., 21, 3–5, 50.

43. Thomas Morgan, *The Moral Philosopher in a Dialogue Between Philalethes, a Christian Deist, and Theophanes, a Christian Jew* (London: 1737), 230–31; italics added. Compare this to Isaac Newton: "so then the first religion was the most rational of all others till the nations corrupted it. For there is no way (without revelation) to come to knowledge of a Deity but by the frame of nature." Richard S. Westfall, "Isaac Newton's *Theologiae gentilis origines philosophicae*," in *The Secular Mind: Essays Presented to Franklin L. Baumer*, ed. W. Warren Wagar (New York: Holmes and Meier, 1982), 25.

44. One of the reasons for the intense focus on natural religion is due to this statement by Morgan. There are "two species of religion. The first is the Religion of Nature, which consisting in the eternal, immutable rules and principles of moral Truth, Righteousness or Reason, has been always the same, and must for ever be alike apprehended, by the understandings of all Mankind, as soon as it comes to be fairly proposed and considered. But besides this, there is another sort or species of Religion, which has been commonly call'd positive, instituted, or revealed Religion, as distinguished from the former. And to avoid circumlocution, I shall call this the political religion, or the Religion of the hierarchy in which I do not design to distinguish between one sort of clergy and another, because, in this case, they are scarce distinguishable." *Moral Philosopher*, 94.

45. Morgan writes, "And therefore the acts of charity, bounty and munificence, when men part with their property, ease, or pleasure, for the good of others, to promote the happiness of society, and especially to maintain the honour of God, or the credit and interest of virtue and 'true religion' in the world; these are the most acceptable and valuable sacrifices of all, as they are the most natural and direct means of pleasing God" (ibid., 211).

46. Ibid., 200.

47. J. B. Schneewind, "Hume and the Religious Significance of Moral Rationalism," *Hume Studies* 26, no. 2 (2000): 212.

48. Hume's biographer Ernest Campbell Mossner confirms that Hume was responding to the deists, particularly Tindal, when he describes the energy of 1730s London as "a ferment of philosophical-religious controversy" and a "period of easy publication." He writes, "into this atmosphere of controversy, Hume would inevitably have been plunged," and "his philosophy, Hume was confident, would put an end to all such controversies as that between the Deists and the Christians by proving that both sides were wrong, that rationalistic proof of matters of fact is as invalid as authoritarian proof, that the scope of analogy is strictly delimited. The publication of the *Treatise*, he felt certain, would cause a tremendous stir in the intellectual world." *Life of David Hume*, 112–13.

49. Ibid., 306–7.

50. Annette C. Baier says Hume believed "religion is supposed to tie and retie us together." *Death and Character: Further Reflections on Hume* (Cambridge: Harvard University Press, 2008), 91.

## Chapter 2

1. By "basic belief" I mean "a belief such that it is rational to hold it in the *basic* way, that is, not on the basis of argument or evidence from other things I believe." Alvin Plantinga, *Where the Conflict Really Lies: Science, Religion, and Naturalism* (Oxford: Oxford University Press, 2010), 341.

2. John Rawls describes Hume's belief in an "Author of Nature." He asserts, and I agree with him, that this was not the God of Christianity (that is the object of prayer or worship). He argues, and here I disagree, that Hume had no use at all for religion. I accept that Hume had no use for popular or false religion, but Hume did have an idea of religion's proper office. *Lectures on the History of Moral Philosophy* (Cambridge: Harvard University Press, 2000), 12.

3. Paul Russell, *The Riddle of Hume's "Treatise": Skepticism, Naturalism, and Irreligion* (Oxford: Oxford University Press, 2008), 94, 132. Russell's premise is both correct and helpful: the *Treatise* had much to say about religion. I qualify the central premise of his book, that the *Treatise* contained "systematic irreligious intentions," by noting that Hume argues against conventional religion and theism but leaves room for a nonconventional theism and true religion.

4. Peter Millican has a wonderful paragraph that describes Hume's "antagonism" toward religion. He writes that Hume "thought of religion, at least in its 'popular' forms, as a thoroughly evil and pernicious influence, which is born out of superstitious fears (*NHR* II, III, and VI; "Of Superstition and Enthusiasm"), corrupts morality in a variety of ways (*NHR* XIV; 'Of Superstition and Enthusiasm'; "Of Suicide"), and in particular recommends spurious 'monkish virtues' (*M* 270, *NHR* X), promotes intolerance (*NHR* IX), and encourages the vices of hypocrisy ("Of National Characters" 204n), self-deception (*NHR* XIII), and simple-minded credulity (*E* 117–18, *NHR* XI–XII)." "The Context, Aims, and Structure of Hume's First *Enquiry*," in *Reading Hume on Human Understanding: Essays on the First Enquiry*, ed. Millican (Oxford: Clarendon Press, 2002), 38.

5. In the final section of this chapter I discuss what has become known as the "New Hume" debate between traditional interpretations of Hume as skeptic about causal powers and objects and interpretations that take him to be a skeptical-realist about causal powers and objects. Millican, ed., *Reading Hume on Human Understanding*, 38.

6. Ernest Campbell Mossner, *The Life of David Hume* (Oxford: Clarendon Press, 2001), 597.

7. Explaining the relationship between the two texts in a 1745 letter to Gilbert Elliot of Minto, Hume wrote, "The philosophical Principles are the same in both: but I was carry'd away by the Heat of Youth & Invention to publish too precipitately. . . . I have repented my Haste a hundred, & a hundred times" (*LET*, 1.158.73). The *Enquiry* begins with the following disclaimer: "Henceforth, the author desires, that the following Pieces may alone be regarded as containing his philosophical sentiments and principles" (*E*, advertisement).

8. The easiest question to answer is my investment in the *Treatise*. Rehabilitating positive contributions from Hume's philosophy for contemporary religious studies requires that we attend to his religious writings as well as their philosophical foundations, which are in the *Treatise*. Of course, the commitment to studying Hume's philosophy, however, does not require that we rely on the *Treatise* more than the first *Enquiry*. I agree with Strawson, Millican, and Buckle, who argue that the first *Enquiry* is more important for studying Hume's philosophy and that Hume's mature philosophical vision is best presented in it. The context of the composition of the *Treatise* and raw energy of the work make it a more interesting read for me. It also visits our ideas about religion and deity in ways that are more revealing than the first *Enquiry*. Simply put, the *Treatise* contains Hume's original philosophical insights and discoveries. Its creative energy and inventive flair captivate me as a reader in ways that the more polished first *Enquiry* does not. I do try to restrict my attention to issues in the *Treatise* that are compatible with those that persist in the rewrite.

9. Gilles Deleuze, *Empiricism and Subjectivity: An Essay on Hume's Theory of Human Nature*, trans. Constantin V. Boundas (New York: Columbia University Press, 1991), 77.

10. Ibid., 22.

11. This is a citation from the preface that Hume removed from volume 2 of his *History of England*. Mossner, *Life of David Hume*, 306–7.

12. John Immerwahr, "Hume's Aesthetic Theism," *Hume Studies* 22, no. 2 (1996): 325–37; Millican, *Reading Hume*, 37.

13. Russell takes this position in *The Riddle of Hume's "Treatise."* See also Timothy Mitchell, *Hume's Anti-theistic Views: A Critical Appraisal* (Lanham: University Press of America, 1986).

14. On this view antitheism (or atheism) is indistinguishable from nontheism, so Hume may be cast as an atheist or a nontheist. It is well known that Hume explicitly denied he was an atheist.

15. Fideism was the view of two early German interpreters of Hume, J. G. Hamaan and F. H. Jacobi. For a contemporary consideration of this view, see Donald Klinefelter, "Scepticism and Fideism in Hume's Philosophy of Religion," *Journal of the American Academy of Religion* 40, no. 2 (1977): 222.

16. Deleuze, *Empiricism and Subjectivity*, 24.

17. Keith E. Yandell, *Hume's "Inexplicable Mystery": His Views on Religion* (Philadelphia: Temple University Press, 1990), 75; J. C. A. Gaskin, *Hume's Philosophy of Religion* (New York: Macmillan, 1978).

18. The source of Hume's Pyrrhonism is unclear. While he most likely should have derived his understanding of it from Sextus Empiricus in *Outlines of Pyrrhonism*, he does not confirm this. (The second *Enquiry* refers directly to Sextus.) He may have read of the life of Pyrrho from Cicero, yet there is a difference between Pyrrhonic skepticism as a school of thought and the life of Pyrrho himself. Of the four extant sources that we have for information about Pyrrho (Aristocles, Sextus Empiricus, Diogenes, and Cicero [Diogenes's treatment relies on Antigonus of Carystius]), Cicero tends to read Pyrrho as a moralist more than a skeptic, while Sextus presents Pyrrhonism as a suspension of belief aiming for tranquility. While I have noted the importance of Cicero for Hume, other possible sources are Montaigne's *Apologie pour Raimond Sebond* and Pierre Bayles's *Dictionnaire historique et critique*. Richard Popkin—against my position—argues that Hume is actually more of a Pyrrhonian than he believes himself to be. See "David Hume: His Pyrrhonism and His Critique of Pyrrhonism," in *Hume*, ed. Vere C. Chappell (New York: Doubleday, 1966), 53–98. For a good description of Hume's context, see Thomas Olshewsky, "Classical Roots of Hume's Scepticism," *Journal of the History of Ideas* 52 (1991): 269–87.

19. Rene Descartes, "Meditations on First Philosophy," in *Descartes: Selected Philosophical Writings*, trans. John Cottingham, Robert Stoothoff, and Dugald Murdoch (Cambridge: Cambridge University Press, 1988), 108.

20. David Hume, "Immortality of the Soul," in *David Hume: Writings on Religion*, ed. Antony Flew (La Salle, Ill.: Open Court Press, 1992), 30.

21. Nicholas Capaldi, "The Dogmatic Slumber of Hume Scholarship," *Hume Studies* 18, no. 2 (1992): 128. There is a significant amount of quality scholarship on Hume's skepticism. I take the work of David Fate Norton, *David Hume: Common-Sense Moralist, Sceptical Metaphysician* (Princeton: Princeton University Press, 1982), 262–69; Peter Jones, *Hume's Sentiments: Their Ciceronian and French Context* (Edinburgh: University of Edinburgh Press, 1982), 161–79; Barry Stroud, *Hume* (London: Routledge and Kegan Paul, 1995); John P. Wright, "Hume's Academic Scepticism: A Reappraisal of His Philosophy of Human Understanding," *Canadian Journal of Philosophy* 16 (1986): 407–35; and Nicholas Capaldi, *David Hume: The Newtonian Philosopher* (Boston: Twayne, 1975) as instructive. These writers generally emphasize that Hume's position cannot be reduced to a skeptical one.

22. Donald C. Ainslie, "Hume's Scepticism and Ancient Scepticism," in *Hellenistic and Early Modern Philosophy*, ed. Jon Miller and Brad Inwood (Cambridge: Cambridge University Press, 2003); and Robert Fogelin, *Hume's Scepticism in the "Treatise of Human Nature"* (London: Routledge, 1985) read the *Enquiry* as concluding with a calm mitigated skepticism and the *Treatise* as more Pyrrhonian. Yves Michaud, "How to Become a Moderate Sceptic: Hume's Way Out of Pyrrhonism," *Hume Studies* 11, no. 1 (1985): 33–46, contends that the skepticism in the first *Enquiry* is more mild than that found in the *Treatise* due to the fact that Hume embodies the skeptical position in the *Treatise* and merely reports on it from afar in the *Enquiry*. My position borrows more from Miriam McCormick, "A Change in Manner: Hume's Skepticism in the *Trea-*

*tise* and the First *Enquiry,*" *Canadian Journal of Philosophy* 29 (1999): 413–31. She stresses the continuity between both texts. An insightful overview of these issues is provided by Peter Millican, "Critical Survey of the Literature," in Millican, *Reading Hume,* 421–23 and 461–72. The *Treatise* states, "Whoever has taken the pains to refute the cavils of this *total* skepticism, has really disputed without an antagonist. . . . Neither I, nor any other person was ever sincerely and constantly of that opinion" (*T,* 1.4.1.7). The *Enquiry* states, "For here is the chief and most confounding objection to *excessive* skepticism, that no durable good can ever result from it; while it remains in its full force and vigour" (*E,* 12.2.7). In this regard Pyrrhonism is a relatively easy target, and Hume joins the historical chorus of critics that proclaim nature and common life force us to make judgments; therefore, a total suspension of judgment is simply not possible. "The great subverter of Pyrrhonism or the excessive principles of skepticism is action, and employment, and the occupations of common life" (12.2.5).

23. Thoughtful work that would take issue with my position that Hume is not a Pyrrhonist includes James Fieser, "Hume's Pyrrhonism: A Developmental Interpretation," *Hume Studies* 15, no. 1 (1989): 93–119; Fogelin, *Hume's Scepticism;* Terence Penelhum, *David Hume: An Introduction to His Philosophical System* (West Lafayette: Purdue University Press, 1992); and the impressively detailed argument by Graciela De Pierris, "Hume's Pyrrhonian Scepticism and the Belief in Causal Laws," *Journal of the History of Philosophy* 39, no. 3 (2001): 351–83.

24. There are many interpretive treatments of this theory. Some read it imagistically and contend that Hume identifies ideas with images, so thinking and imagining are the same. For more on this argument, see Don Garrett, *Cognition and Commitment in Hume's Philosophy* (Oxford: Oxford University Press, 1997). Some read it as a form of meaning-empiricism; see Georges Dicker, *Hume's Epistemology and Metaphysics: An Introduction* (London: Routledge, 1998). Others suggest that the theory of ideas is best understood as a theory of consciousness— see Wayne Waxman, *Hume's Theory of Consciousness* (Cambridge: Cambridge University Press, 1994)—or as a theory of language; see Antony Flew, *Hume's Philosophy of Belief: A Study of His First "Inquiry"* (1961; repr., Bristol: Thoemmes Press, 1997). Each position is viable.

25. Deleuze, *Empiricism and Subjectivity,* 24. The next sentence reads, "But the subject can go beyond the given because *first of all* it is, *inside the mind,* the effect of principles transcending and affecting the mind."

26. Ibid., 77.

27. John Locke, *An Essay Concerning Human Understanding,* ed. Peter H. Nidditch (Oxford: Clarendon Press, 1979). Locke and Hume had different conceptions of impressions. In book 2.1.23 Locke viewed impressions as more physiological than Hume. There are two classes of impressions: those of sensation and those of reflection. The latter one comes to us through introspection. In the *Enquiry* Hume calls impressions of reflection an "inward sentiment" (*E,* 2.4).

28. H. O. Mounce, *Hume's Naturalism* (London: Routledge, 1999), 24.

29. Jeffrey A. Bell, *Deleuze's Hume: Philosophy, Culture, and the Scottish Enlightenment* (Edinburgh: Edinburgh University Press, 2009), 153.

30. The idea that nature is ordered, uniform, and regular is not basic theism. Basic theism requires belief in an Orderer.

31. Veronique M. Foti effectively charts the evolution of Descartes's views on the imagination. "The Cartesian Imagination," *Philosophy and Phenomenological Research* 46, no. 4 (1986): 631–42.

32. Later Hume writes, "Amongst the effects of this union or association of ideas, there are none more remarkable, than those complex ideas, which are the common subjects of our thoughts and reasoning and generally arise from some principle of union among our simple ideas" (*T,* 1.1.4.7).

33. Timothy M. Costelloe gives the most in-depth and detailed discussion of the imagination and the fictions it produces. The three powers he locates and their fictions are as follows: "From the imagistic power come generic fictions, which are ideas copied from simple and complex

impressions that give rise to true belief (in the case of memory) and perfect belief (in the case of the imagination); from the conceptual power arise real fictions and mere fictions, both traceable to impressions, but distinguished by the fact that the former inspire real beliefs while the latter only belief-like states; and from the productive power come necessary fictions, objects of real belief but not traceable to any impressions whatsoever." "Hume's Phenomenology of the Imagination," *Journal of Scottish Philosophy* 5, no. 1 (2007): 31–32. Costelloe's assessment of the imagination builds on that of Jan Wilbanks, *Hume's Theory of the Imagination* (The Hague: Nijhoff, 1968); and Gerhard Streminger, "Hume's Theory of the Imagination," *Hume Studies* 6, no. 2 (1998): 91–118. Saul Traiger's classic essay is foundational for Hume on the fictions; see his accessible discussion "Impressions, Ideas, and Fictions," *Hume Studies* 13, no. 2 (1987): 381–99.

34. While Hume is concerned with the intelligibility of ideas, he does not privilege their epistemic status. On his science, ideas are made true neither by their analytic value through logical clarity of argument nor by their correspondence with sense experience. The insight of the *Treatise* is that complex ideas compose the mind and that they are intelligible when formed by the natural associative processes of the imagination. The best that his science of human nature can do is to describe the formation and evolution of ideas that experience leads us to have. Whether an idea is true or not is a different issue: the more an idea comports with the principles of association, the more intelligible it is, for "to explain the ultimate causes of our mental actions is impossible" (1.1.7.11). Hume's depiction of the operations of the mind is, in some important ways, an attempt to present a dynamic philosophy conversant with evolving Enlightenment standards of scientific verifiability. Simultaneously, Hume delimits the power of the mind and elevates, without romanticizing, principles of the imagination as well as ideas that we reflectively affirm in common life: "all knowledge resolves itself into probability, and becomes at last of the same nature with that evidence, which we employ in common life" (1.4.1.4).

35. Theodore W. Adorno and Max Horkheimer, *Dialectic of Enlightenment*, trans. John Cumming (New York: Continuum, 1972), 1.

36. Locke, *Essay Concerning Human Understanding*, 32 and bk. 3, "On Words."

37. Dickers, *Hume's Epistemology and Metaphysics*, 5.

38. Kenneth A. Richman, introd. to *The New Hume Debate*, ed. Rupert Read and Kenneth Richman (London: Routledge, 2000), 1.

39. John P. Wright, *The Sceptical Realism of David Hume* (Minneapolis: University of Minnesota Press, 1983), 129. Galen Strawson, *The Secret Connexion: Causation, Realism, and David Hume* (Oxford: Clarendon Press, 1989), vii; Donald Livingston, *Hume's Philosophy of Common Life* (Chicago: University of Chicago Press, 1984), 153.

40. See Read and Richman, eds., *New Hume Debate*.

41. P. J. E. Kail, "Is Hume a Causal Realist?," *British Journal for the History of Philosophy* 11, no. 3 (2003): 515. Kail notes in response to Ken Winkler's foundational essay that Hume's "most accurate explication of the idea of power is given" on page 76 of the first *Enquiry* (518n22). It is there that Hume writes, "No conclusions can be more agreeable to skepticism than such as make discoveries concerning the weakness and narrow limits of human reason and capacity." Kail rightfully acknowledges the power-weakness dialectic in Hume but overemphasizes the importance of this particular statement. The context of this claim regards our idea that two objects "become proofs of each other's existence" by an inference of our mind formed by connecting them through associating repeated experiences of causes with observation of their effects. Hume says that this conclusion "in our thought" (the connection) is "somewhat extraordinary" but "founded on sufficient evidence." He goes on, "nor will its evidence be weakened" by suspicion or skepticism. Thus, the power of skepticism or suspicion cannot shake or weaken our holding the inference of our thought that leads to the conclusion that holds the two objects have "become proofs of each other's existence" (*E*, 7.2.23).

42. Simon Blackburn, "Hume and Thick Connexions," in Read and Richman, eds., *New Hume Debate*, 100–112.

43. Some scholars believe that Millican has ended this debate once and for all. Peter Millican, "Hume, Causal Realism, and Causal Science," *Mind* 118, no. 471 (2009): 647–712.

44. As mentioned earlier, there is significant overlap between the interpretation of Hume as a Common Sense thinker and that of Hume as a naturalist. The "Common Sense" school of thought ultimately resolves into the naturalist position. Mounce, *Hume's Naturalism*; Norton, *David Hume*; and Norman Kemp Smith, *The Philosophy of David Hume: A Critical Study of Its Origins and Central Doctrines* (London: Macmillan, 1960) are important for both interpretations. The discussion of naturalism in Hume is extended in M. Jaime Ferreira, *Scepticism and Reasonable Doubt* (Oxford: Clarendon Press, 1986); Daniel Kaufman, "Between Reason and Common Sense: On the Very Idea of Necessary (Though Unwarranted) Belief," *Philosophical Investigations* 28, no. 2 (2005): 134–58; and Stroud, *Hume*.

45. This section covers the discussion of belief in the *Treatise* in 1.3.7.8; app. 1–13; David Hume, *Abstract of a Book Lately Published Entitled "A Treatise of Human Nature" Wherein the Chief Argument of That Book Is Farther Illustrated and Explained*, in *Reading Hume on Human Understanding: Essays on the First Enquiry*, ed. Peter Millican (Oxford: Clarendon Press, 2002), paras. 17–23.

46. Some of the best critical work on Hume's theory of belief in the *Treatise* and first *Enquiry* are Henry E. Allison, *Custom and Reason in Hume: A Kantian Reading of the First Book of the "Treatise"* (Oxford: Clarendon Press, 2008); J. C. A. Gaskin, "God, Hume, and Natural Belief," *Philosophy* 49, no. H189 (1974): 281–94; Justin Broackes, "Hume, Belief, and Personal Identity," in Millican, ed., *Reading Hume*, 187–202; and Martin Bell, "Belief and Instinct in the First *Enquiry*," in Millican, ed., *Reading Hume*, 175–210; and Michael Hodges and John Lachs, "Hume on Belief," *Review of Metaphysics* 30 (1976): 3–18. Broackes warns us that Hume has no coherent theory of belief, just a set of views about it.

47. Broackes's "Hume, Belief, and Personal Identity" presents the most thorough consideration of the various tensions, inconsistencies, and developments in Hume's treatment of belief in both the *Treatise* and the first *Enquiry*. He makes a compelling argument that there can be no "feeling" of belief because Hume's theory of mind will not permit a feeling that is completely separable from the idea that caused it. Further, he convincingly shows that the "manner of conception" view of belief does not cohere with Hume's theory of personal identity. I find Broackes's close reading of Hume on belief to be very informative and well argued. Ultimately, however, our interests and intentions are different. My broad interests in redeploying Hume for religious studies keep my focus on Hume's larger critique of abstract reason and situate his theory of ideas as both critical and constructive, not totalizing (that is, to me Hume allows for much more than just impressions and ideas). Further, I take Hume to be both a participant-subject and observer-reporter of his science, so he is giving a firsthand statement of the "manner of conceiving" of a belief. Thus, though Broackes might disagree, when discussing Hume's theory of belief on the way to a larger argument, we may cautiously proceed with "manner of conceiving" and "feeling to the mind" as the central components of belief in Hume.

48. J. Bell, *Deleuze's Hume*, 29.

49. Hume, *Abstract of a Book*, 22.

50. Theoretical beliefs can certainly be meaningful. Hume's discussion of the *vis inertiae* (*E*, 7.1.23n) and relative ideas (*T*, 1.2.6.8) are important exceptions to this general point.

51. Janet Broughton, "Hume's Ideas About Necessary Connection," *Hume Studies* 13, no. 2 (1987): 217–44; Stroud, *Hume*, 68–90. Broughton discusses what she calls the "epistemological" view of Hume's treatment of necessary connection and causal power, that we can mean what we say when we talk about necessary connection, but we cannot justify it in Hume's categorical schema.

52. Norman Kemp Smith, "The Naturalism of Hume," *Mind* 14 (1905): 147–73.

53. Kemp Smith, *Philosophy of David Hume*, 124.

54. Don Garrett, introd. to Kemp Smith, *Philosophy of David Hume*, xxxiv.

55. Stanley Tweyman, *Scepticism and Belief in Hume's "Dialogues Concerning Natural Religion"* (Boston: Nijhoff, 1986); Beryl Logan, *A Religion Without Talking: Religious Belief and Natural Belief in Hume's Philosophy of Religion* (New York: Lang, 1993); Miguel Badia-Cabrera, *Hume's Reflection on Religion* (Dordrecht: Kluwer Academic Publishers, 2001); Ronald J. Butler, "Natural Belief and the Enigma of Hume," *Archiv für Geschicte der Philosophie* 42, no. 1 (1960): 73–100, all argue that belief in an intelligent Designer is a natural belief in Hume. Gaskin, *Hume's Philosophy of Religion*; Terence Penelhum, "Hume on Religion: Cultural Influences," in *A Companion to Hume*, ed. Elizabeth Radcliffe (Malden: Blackwell, 2008), 323–37; Antony Flew, *Hume's Philosophy of Belief: A Study of His "First Inquiry"* (Bristol: Thoemmes Press, 1997), 214–42; Kemp Smith, "The Naturalism of Hume."

56. David Hume, *Of Suicide*, in *Dialogues Concerning Natural Religion and the Posthumous Essays: Of the Immortality of the Soul and of Suicide*, ed. Richard H. Popkin (Indianapolis: Hackett, 1983), p. 99.

57. Gaskin offers four qualities that determine a natural belief: universally held, nonrational (but not irrational or unreasonable), naive common sense, and a precondition for action. See Gaskin, *Hume's Philosophy of Religion*, 132–33. Stanley Tweyman holds six requirements for a natural belief. He contends that a natural belief cannot be fully analyzed in terms of Hume's account of perceptions or impressions and ideas; a natural belief goes beyond data of experience, and we are thus only aware of its effects; we are not aware of exactly how we come to hold natural beliefs; what we believe naturally may not be at all; a natural belief is unavoidable and therefore universal; and holding a natural belief is such an important affair that we cannot trust this to our "uncertain reasonings and speculations" (Tweyman, *Scepticism and Belief*, 10–17). Norman Kemp Smith lists five features of a natural belief. For him, natural beliefs are not justifiable by reason; they are inevitable and beyond skeptical doubts; they are indispensable for common life; they are more certain than the mechanisms by which they operate; and they are beliefs in general. Ronald J. Butler notes features similar to those presented by Tweyman (he does not really put forward a direct list of the features like Tweyman or Gaskin or in the 1905 essay of Kemp Smith). Butler, "Natural Belief." (Kemp Smith uses the terms "inevitable" and "indispensable" to describe natural beliefs. "Naturalism of Hume," 152. Gaskin uses "unavoidable" and "universally held." *Hume's Philosophy of Religion*, 133. Tweyman claims "a natural belief is unavoidable and therefore universal." *Scepticism and Belief*, 15.)

58. Donald W. Livingston, *Hume's Philosophy of Common Life* (Chicago: University of Chicago Press, 1984); and Livingston, *Philosophical Melancholy and Delirium: Hume's Pathology of Philosophy* (Chicago: University of Chicago Press, 1998). Important discussions of common life and true philosophy are Fred Wilson, review of *Hume's "Philosophy of Common Life,"* by Donald Livingston, *Philosophy of Social Science* 18 (1988): 139; Marina Frasca-Spada, review of *Philosophical Melancholy and Delirium*, by Donald Livingston, *Mind*, n.s., 110, no. 439 (2001): 783–89; David Fate Norton, "Hume's 'Philosophy of Common Life,'" *Journal of History of Philosophy* 25, no. 2 (1983): 300–302; and P. J. E. Kail, "Reason, Custom, and the True Philosophy," *British Journal for the History of Philosophy* 9, no. 2 (2001): 361–66.

59. Livingston, *Hume's Philosophy of Common Life*, 22.

60. Eric Gill, *Art-Nonsense and Other Essays* (London: Cassell, 1929), 198.

61. Livingston, *Hume's Philosophy of Common Life*, 56.

62. Livingston, *Philosophical Melancholy and Delirium*, 68.

*Chapter 3*

1. David Hume, "Dissertation on the Passions," in *Four Dissertations and Essays on Suicide and the Immortality of the Soul* (South Bend: St. Augustine's Press, 1995), 99.

2. Christine Korsgaard, "Skepticism About Practical Reason," *Journal of Philosophy* 83 (1986): 5–25; see also Korsgaard, *The Sources of Normativity* (Cambridge: Cambridge University

Press, 1996); and Annette C. Baier, *A Progress of Sentiments: Reflections on Hume's "Treatise"* (Cambridge: Harvard University Press, 1991), 61, 130.

3. John Bricke, *Mind and Morality: An Examination of Hume's Moral Psychology* (Oxford: Clarendon Press, 1996), 36–37; Joseph J. Godfrey, *A Philosophy of Human Hope* (Dordrecht: Nijhoff, 1987). Godfrey's text is a seminal reference point for those who take hope seriously as a philosophical topic. For other rich discussions of hope, see Jayne Waterworth, *A Philosophical Analysis of Hope* (New York: Palgrave Macmillan, 2004); Patrick Shade, *Habits of Hope: A Pragmatic Theory* (Nashville: Vanderbilt University Press, 2001); Curtis Peters, *Kant's Philosophy of Hope* (New York: Lang, 1993).

4. Godfrey, *Philosophy of Human Hope*, 101.

5. Ibid., 64.

6. Ibid.

7. This Aristotelian division is based on his fundamental distinction between form and matter as articulated in the *Metaphysics*. See Jonathan Barnes, ed., *The Complete Works of Aristotle* (Princeton: Princeton University Press, 1984), 2:1050a4–15. Susan James makes it clear that the early modern theories of the passions were deeply indebted to but trying to move beyond Aristotle's crucial distinction between form (active) and matter (passive) as well as Aquinas's Christianization of this basic Aristotelian distinction. See *Passion and Action: The Emotions in Seventeenth-Century Philosophy* (Oxford: Clarendon Press, 1997), 1–156. Martha Nussbaum challenges my position on the usefulness of the passions. *Upheavals of Thought* (Cambridge: Cambridge University Press, 2003).

8. Descartes believed that the passions were habitual responses to stimuli that functioned mechanistically and inspired actions. Built in his concept of the passions was the idea of motion, because the passions always moved toward or away from their object. The Cartesian emphasis on how passions informed our imagination influenced Hume. He remained, however, averse to Descartes's idea that the pineal gland was the site of competition between reason and the passions (the gland linked mind and body and processed spirits through the nerves and blood). Overall, Hume was influenced by Descartes's confident acceptance of the passions as directors of human action and his seemingly weaker investment (than Locke or Hutcheson) in the need for them to be regulated by reason. Still, Cartesian passions, unlike Humean ones, contained moral import and were to be managed effectively. There are also similarities between the Cartesian and Humean concepts of hope. For Descartes, hope was derived from desire, one of the six "primitive passions" (i.e., wonder, love, hatred, desire, joy, and sadness). It was aroused when a "desire for the acquisition of a good or the avoidance of an evil" was accompanied by the probability that this could be accomplished." Rene Descartes, "The Passions of the Soul," in *The Philosophical Writings of Descartes*, trans. John Cottingham, Robert Stoothoff, Dugald Murdoch, 2 vols. (Cambridge: Cambridge University Press, 1984–85), vol. 1, pt. 2, art. 58. He wrote, "Hope is a disposition of the soul to be convinced that what it desires will come about. It is caused by a particular movement of the spirits, consisting of the movement of joy mixed with that of desire." For Descartes, hope did not arrive alone. It occurred together with anxiety, "another disposition of the soul, which convinces it that its desire will not be fulfilled" and required desire (something external to it) to motivate action. "These two passions," he wrote of hope and anxiety, "although opposed, may nevertheless occur together, namely when we think of reasons for regarding the fulfillment of the desire as easy, and at the same time we think of other reasons which make it seem difficult" (arts. 165, 389).

9. Nancy Armstrong and Leonard Tennenhouse, "A Mind for Passion: Locke and Hutcheson on Desire" in *Politics and the Passions, 1500–1850*, ed. Victoria Kahn, Neil Saccamano, and Daniela Coli (Princeton: Princeton University Press, 2006), 142.

10. John Locke, *An Essay Concerning Human Understanding*, ed. Peter H. Nidditch (Oxford: Clarendon Press, 1979), 230, 231, 138.2.20.8.

11. Sharon R. Krause has provided in-depth analysis on the political use-value of the passions in Hume. She is the leading voice from political science on the important overlaps between

Hume's thought and contemporary politics, the political dimensions of Hume's moral theory (particularly his sentimentalism), and the potential for impartiality within his moral psychology and the possibilities it offers for a deliberative project for justice. For Krause, Hume fits securely behind Shaftesbury and Hutcheson in the sentimentalist trajectory. I emphasize Hume as more critical of the sentimentalists regarding their notion of the divine, their general optimism, and their reliance on a "moral sense" to confirm that an act is good (my reading of Hume is that an act is good only if it has pleasurable effects). Our differences in emphasis are more a function of our larger concerns—her project for deliberative democracy and mine for true religion—than a disagreement in content. See her *Civil Passions: Moral Sentiment and Democratic Deliberation* (Princeton: Princeton University Press, 2008); "Hume and the (False) Luster of Justice," *Political Theory* 32, no. 5 (2004): 628–55; and "Passion, Power, and Impartiality in Hume," in *Bringing the Passions Back: The Emotions in Political Philosophy*, ed. Rebecca Kingston (Vancouver: University of British Columbia Press, 2007), 126–49.

12. Andrew Ward, introd. to *Essay on the Nature and Conduct of the Passions and Affections*, by Francis Hutcheson (Manchester: Clinamen, 1999), viii. Page x states,

> Hutcheson stresses that we should make our particular (short-term) affections yield appropriately to our more general (long-term) affections. Equally, we should ensure, as far as possible, that none of our affections ever becomes passionate. For, when this occurs, we may be so ruled by the given affection that we both prevent ourselves from effective reasoning concerning the attainment of its goal and hinder within us the operation of other equally or more important affections. Control of our various affections is achieved by stopping ourselves from holding confused opinions, or what he calls wrong "associations of ideas," concerning their objects. Once this control is fully attained, we shall be guided in our conduct by calm deliberative desires, and the proper ranking between these desires— with the benevolent, of course taking precedence—will fall into place.

13. Hutcheson, *An Essay on the Nature and Conduct of the Passions and Affections*, 41.

14. This line is Hutcheson's reply to a minister after describing that only one out of his seven children had survived. William Robert Scott, *Francis Hutcheson: His Life, Teaching, and Position in the History of Philosophy* (Cambridge: Cambridge University Press, 1900), 134.

15. John Rawls, *Lectures on the History of Moral Thought* (Cambridge: Harvard University Press, 2000), 25.

16. This division conjured the previous distinction between impressions of sensation and impressions of reflection from book 1: "This division of the impressions is the same with that which I formerly made use of when I distinguish'd them into impressions of sensation and reflexion." He continued,

> Original impressions or impressions of sensation are such as without any antecedent perception arise in the soul, from the constitution of the body, from the animal spirits, or from the application of objects to the external organs. Secondary, or reflective impressions are such as proceed from some of these original ones, either immediately or by the interposition of its idea. Of the first kind are all the impressions of the senses, and all the bodily pains and pleasures: Of the second are the passions, and other emotions resembling them. (*T*, 2.1.1.1)

17. This insight undermined the argument against the existence of the self in book 1 of the *Treatise*. In book 2 he took the existence of the self for granted as a vital idea on which the indirect passions depended. He wrote, "'tis evident, that pride and humility, tho' directly contrary, have yet the same OBJECT. This object is self" (*T*, 2.1.2.2). Thus, the indirect passions reflexively pointed us toward the idea of a (historical and socially situated) self.

18. Páll S. Árdal, *Passion and Value in Hume's "Treatise"* (Edinburgh: Edinburgh University Press, 1966), 19.

19. There are also original (primary) passions, a set of direct passions that arise from instinct but cannot be explained by general principles. They produce pain and pleasure and do not proceed from it. Benevolence is this sort of passion (see, *T*, 2.3.3.8).

20. In his later "Dissertation on the Passions," Hume writes, "in the production and conduct of the passions, there is certain regular mechanism, which is susceptible of as accurate a disquisition as the laws of motion, optics, hydrostatics, or any part of natural philosophy" (166). The direct-passion hope is a homeostatic passion; that is, it disappears when the hope is fulfilled or the object of the hope attained.

21. John Immerwahr contends that we might read Hume using the "calm/violent distinction for two related purposes." On the one hand, Immerwahr writes, "sometimes he uses calmness and violence to signify the kind of passion that is being experienced" and on the other, he uses "calm" and "violent" to "refer to the way passions are experienced." See "Hume on Tranquillizing the Passions," *Hume Studies* 28, no. 2 (1992): 295.

22. Timothy M. Costelloe's work on Hume's aesthetics has crucially informed my position on this aspect of Hume's work. See *Aesthetics and Morals in the Philosophy of David Hume* (New York: Routledge, 2007). Neil Saccamano's work also informs my argument here. See his "Parting with Prejudice: Hume, Identity, and Aesthetic Universality" in Kahn, Saccamano, and Coli, eds., *Politics and the Passions*, 175–95; and his "Aesthetically Non-dwelling: Sympathy, Property, and the House of Beauty in Hume's *Treatise*," *Journal of Scottish Philosophy* 9, no. 1 (2011): 37–58.

23. An important discussion of this appears later:

All men, it is allowed, are equally desirous of happiness; but few are successful in the pursuit: One considerable cause is the want of *strength of mind*, which might enable them to resist the temptation of present ease or pleasure, and carry them forward in the search of more distant profit and enjoyment. Our affections, on a general prospect of their objects, form certain rules of conduct, and certain measures of preference of one above another: and these decisions, though really the result of our *calm passions* and propensities, (for what else can pronounce any object eligible or the contrary?) are yet said, by a natural abuse of terms, to be the determinations of pure reason and reflection. But when some of these objects approach nearer to us, or acquire the advantages of favourable lights and positions, which catch the heart or imagination; our general resolutions are frequently confounded, a small enjoyment preferred, and lasting shame and sorrow entailed upon us. And however poets may employ their wit and eloquence, in celebrating present pleasure, and rejecting all distant views to fame, health, or fortune; it is obvious, that this practice is the source of all dissoluteness and disorder, repentance and misery. A man of a strong and determined temper adheres tenaciously to his general resolutions, and is neither seduced by the allurements of pleasure, nor terrified by the menaces of pain; but keeps still in view those distant pursuits, by which he, at once, ensures his happiness and his honour. (*EPM*, 6.1.15)

24. There is some debate as to how a violent passion might transition to a calm one. One possible explanation might be taken from the work of John Rawls, who argued that a form of practical or rational deliberation could "transform the system of the passions." *Lectures*, 40. Bernard Williams claimed that the stimulus to moderate a passion was internal to the subjective, psychological disposition itself; "Internal and External Reasons," *Moral Luck* (Cambridge: Cambridge University Press, 1986). I think it better to describe the passions in Hume as relying on both internal and external stimuli, personal and collective energies, to be calmed.

25. Rawls, *Lectures*, 33–34.

26. Korsgaard, *Sources of Normativity*, 33.

27. Christine Korsgaard, *The Constitution of Agency: Essays on Practical Reason and Moral Psychology* (Oxford: Oxford University Press, 2008), 40, 34, 46.

28. Baier, *Progress of Sentiments*, 168. This discussion has a number of sources: Elijah Millgram, "Was Hume a Humean?," *Hume Studies* 21, no. 1 (1995): 75–93; Jean Hampton, "Does Hume Have an Instrumental Conception of Practical Reason?," *Hume Studies* 21, no. 1 (1995): 57–74; and Hampton, *The Authority of Reason* (Cambridge: Cambridge University Press, 1998); Korsgaard, "Skepticism About Practical Reason"; see also Korsgaard, *Sources of Normativity*; David Phillips, "Hume on Practical Reason: Normativity and Psychology in Treatise 2.3.3," *Hume Studies* 31, no. 2 (2005): 299–316; and Sharon R. Krause, *Civil Passions: Moral Sentiment and Democratic Deliberation* (Princeton: Princeton University Press, 2008).

29. Godfrey, *Philosophy of Human Hope*, 3.

30. James T. King makes an interesting overture to there being different types of hope in Hume. "Despair and Hope in Hume's Introduction to the *Treatise of Human Nature*," *Hume Studies* 20, no. 1 (1994): 59–71. Because he focuses solely on the introduction to the *Treatise*, he cannot compare the type of hope he finds there with the direct-passion hope. Yet King is a sensitive reader who is more than adequately tuned to Hume's indirect-passion hope. He writes, "As I see it, this Introduction evinces a quite real tension between the hope for a new system of the sciences and the despair of achieving knowledge satisfactory to the mind" (61). Also he says that Hume has "uplifting hope" (62), "hope of a New Era" (60), and "hope anchored in the experimental method" (69).

31. Baier, *Progress of Sentiments*, 167.

32. Shade, *Habits of Hope*, 135.

33. Godfrey, *Philosophy of Human Hope*, 38.

34. In 1758 Hume changed the name *Philosophical Essays Concerning Human Understanding* to *Enquiry Concerning Human Understanding*. Also, he publicly acknowledged his authorship of the collection in its printing of April 1748. See Ernest Campbell Mossner, *The Life of David Hume* (Oxford: Clarendon Press, 2001), 223.

35. One feature of Hume's thought that supports the distinction between the two phases is his handling of religion. Hume is much more explicit about religion in all of his writings after 1748; he leaves behind the indirect method of his earlier discussions of religion.

36. Mossner, *Life of David Hume*, 333. Mossner's reading of the *NHR* is foundational among Hume interpreters. He writes,

> The thesis of the *Natural History of Religion* is the paramount one in all of Hume's philosophical productions, the essential a-rationality of human nature, here applied specifically to religion, which is treated as a natural product of the human mind. Sentiment, emotions, affections precede reason and philosophy in human nature and always remain dominant. The monotheistic deity of Christianity is, therefore, an advanced concept far beyond the primitive or popular mind in early or in late ages. The popular mind is ruled by hopes and fears, and out of these hopes and fears creates a religion of multifarious outside controlling forces; in short, polytheism. Polytheism thus antedates monotheism and even after the general acceptance of philosophy still survives in the popular mentality.

37. Keith E. Yandell, *Hume's "Inexplicable Mystery": His Views on Religion* (Philadelphia: Temple University Press, 1990), 3.

38. The standard reading of the *NHR* is grounded in William Warburton's "Remarks on Mr. David Hume's *Essay on the Natural History of Religion*," 1777, in *Hume on Natural Religion*, ed. Stanley Tweyman (Bristol: Thoemmes Press, 1996), 237–48. Mossner's *Life of David Hume* is also a foundational standard reading. Some recent popular standard readings of the *NHR* are given by David O'Connor, *Hume on Religion* (New York: Routledge, 2001); D. C. G. MacNabb, "David Hume," in *Encyclopedia of Philosophy*, ed. Paul Edwards, vol. 4 (New York: Macmillan, 1967);

and others. Some writers who discuss Hume on religion totally ignore the *NHR* and focus only on the *DCNR*; see H. O. Mounce, *Hume's Naturalism* (London: Routledge, 1999), 99–130; James McCosh, *The Scottish Philosophy* (Bristol: Thoemmes Press, 1990), 113–60; and John J. Jenkins, *Understanding Hume* (Edinburgh: Edinburgh University Press, 1992), 181–204.

39. Ernest Campbell Mossner, "An Apology for David Hume, Historian," *PMLA* 56, no. 3 (1941): 664.

40. J. C. A. Gaskin supports this idea: "The point is that, for Hume, religion as it has commonly been found in the world, the vulgar religion whose causes and effects are considered in the *N.H.R.* and whose working in human history and society is so baleful, is superstition. Thus, in the *N.H.R.* 'Popular religion' and 'superstition' are treated as interchangeable terms." *Hume's Philosophy of Religion* (London: Macmillan, 1978), 148.

41. Ibid. Hume argues that both monotheism and polytheism are forms of vulgar or popular belief that create "impious conceptions of the divine nature" (176). "Polytheism or idolatrous worship, being founded entirely in vulgar traditions, is liable to this great inconvenience, that any practice or opinion, however barbarous or corrupted, may be authorized by it" (160). Note also the very strong implication that since there are "impious" then there are quite possibly "pious" conceptions in Hume's formulation.

42. The episode and the "manuscript of the suppressed preface" are in Ernest Campbell Mossner, *Life of David Hume*, 306–7.

43. James Collins, *The Emergence of Philosophy of Religion* (New Haven: Yale University Press, 1967), 15.

44. William Sessions provides important insights concerning the underdiscussed Pamphillus, including the following: (1) His agency is involved in the recital of the conversation; (2) He is writing this to Hermippus (i.e., the best way to report a lively conversation is through dialogue form) and therefore is the writer of the *Dialogues*; (3) His recital is based on and complicated by the nexus of his own lens, interests, relationships, beliefs and concerns; (4) He has the important role of auditor of the dialogues, while Hume is the author. To my knowledge, Sessions is also the only writer that attends to the notion of plural dialogues in the text. *Reading Hume's "Dialogues": A Veneration for True Religion* (Bloomington: Indiana University Press, 2002), 15–17.

45. Sessions, *Reading Hume's "Dialogues,"* 8.

46. Michel Malherbe, "Hume and the Art of Dialogue," in *Hume and Hume's Connexions*, ed. M. A. Stewart and John P. Wright (University Park: Pennsylvania State University Press, 1995), 201. This article gives a superb discussion of both the modern history of the writing of philosophical dialogue and the value of the *DCNR* as literary art.

47. James Noxon provides a wonderful example of this flawed way of assessing the text: "The *Dialogues*, however, have not proven to be the key to the riddle of David Hume. On the contrary, they have themselves posed a riddle: who speaks for Hume? Unless this question can be answered, Hume's last philosophical testament provides us with no clue to his own religious convictions." "Hume's Agnosticism," in *Hume: A Collection of Critical Essays*, ed. Vere C. Chappell (New York: Doubleday, 1966), 363.

48. Most Hume scholars strongly support Philo as the representative of Hume, including A. J. Ayer, Peter Gay, Norman Kemp Smith, and Ernest Campbell Mossner.

49. Referring to a "sample" or portion of an early draft of the manuscript, Hume wrote that Cleanthes was "the hero of the Dialogue" in a letter to Gilbert Elliot of Minto in 1751. David Hume, *Writings on Religion*, ed. Antony Flew (LaSalle, Ill.: Open Court Press, 1992), 21. Early interpreters took the position that Cleanthes was the voice of Hume in the *DCNR*. B. M. Laing concurs with this position in his "Hume's *Dialogues Concerning Natural Religion*," *Philosophy* 12 (1937): 175–90.

50. Henry D. Aiken argues that Hume is both Philo and Cleanthes; see the introduction to his *Hume's "Dialogues Concerning Natural Religion"* (New York: Hafner, 1948), xiii. John Bricke, "On the Interpretation of Hume's *Dialogues*," *Religious Studies* 11, no. 1 (1975): 1–18; Beryl Logan,

*A Religion Without Talking: Religious Belief and Natural Belief in Hume's Philosophy of Religion* (New York: Lang, 1993); and Sessions, *Reading Hume's "Dialogues,"* all agree that the question of who speaks for Hume is an impoverished way into the *DCNR*.

51. Sessions makes a very important point regarding the lack of sensitivity of those interpreters who claim to know Hume's beliefs as articulated through the *DCNR*: "It is always possible that, even when we have understood this text's intentions, we will still be unable to determine what Hume's own views were, for perhaps the work does not express those views or does not express them clearly and unambiguously or was not intended to express the author's views but rather to provoke readers into examining their own views." *Reading Hume's "Dialogues,"* 6.

52. One may wonder, if Hume is investigating the "rational" foundations of religion, how a category like piety, which is not based on rational grounds, fits. My response is that the piety described by Demea is not based on rational argument, necessity, or analogy but on—as far as Demea is concerned—the rational decision to accept God as mysterious. Demea's claim that God's existence is self-evident and that God's attributes are inscrutable is a very well thought-out and conscious attempt to limit the power of humans to center themselves instead of God. Thus, it is rational choice.

53. I cite Demea's use of these two different arguments to once again affirm the problems with the common approach to the text. Searching for "who represents Hume" does not allow one to make a full appreciation of the multiplicity of each character's view. Part of the artfulness of the text is that it allows the presentation of these sometimes disparate views to come from the mouth of one character.

54. The particular type of modern cosmological argument that Hume uses is in the form originally presented by Samuel Clarke in his series of Robert Boyle lectures of 1704. See *A Demonstration of the Being and Attributes of God and Other Writings*, ed. Ezio Vailati (Cambridge: Cambridge University Press, 1998). James Dye writes that Demea does not arrive at the Deity by tracing the chain of causes from present existence to a temporally first cause. Instead of terminating the causal series, he adopts the standpoint of one who believes in an infinite causal succession and argues that "there must be a reason for the existence of the whole series." "A Word on Behalf of Demea," *Hume Studies* 15, no. 1 (1989): 266.

55. Most contemporary scholars are in agreement that Demea's argument is not successfully refuted by Cleanthes or by Philo. See Sessions, *Reading Hume's "Dialogues,"* 139–46; D. C. Stove, "Part IX of Hume's *Dialogues,"* *Philosophical Quarterly* 28 (1978): 300–309; James Franklin, "More on Part IX of Hume's *Dialogues,"* *Philosophical Quarterly* 30 (1980): 69–71; and M. A. Stewart, "Hume and the 'Metaphysical Argument a Priori,'" in *Philosophy, Its History and Historiography*, ed. Alan J. Holland (Dordrecht: Reidel, 1985), 243–65. However, Ernest Campbell Mossner argues that Cleanthes and Philo have successfully refuted the a priori argument. "Hume and the Legacy of the Dialogues," in *David Hume: Bicentenary Papers*, ed. George P. Morice (Austin: University of Texas Press, 1977), 18.

56. The best in-depth treatment of Cleanthes's response to Demea in part 9 is found in Edward J. Khamara, "Hume Versus Clarke on the Cosmological Argument," *Philosophical Quarterly* 42 (1992): 48–53.

57. Robert H. Hurlbutt III contends that Cleanthes's argument borrows heavily from the argument presented in the work of Newtonian theists George Cheyne and Colin Maclaurin. *Hume, Newton, and the Design Argument* (Lincoln: University of Nebraska Press, 1965). D. Hansen Soles argues that the greatest support for the existence of intelligent cause in the universe is found not in the argument but in the nature of Cleanthes's language. "Hume, Language, and God," *Philosophical Topics* 12, no. 3 (1981): 109–19.

58. Mounce, *Hume's Naturalism*, 105.

59. Patrick Shade writes critically about this type of hope that lacks faith: "Hope does need to sustain us, but insisting that it be able to do so in every possible situation is to drain it of actual

connections with actual states of affairs. A hope whose realization can only or primarily be affected though an unconditioned supernatural agency leaves us with nothing to do but await its arrival." *Habits of Hope*, 7.

60. A discussion of true religion in Hume occurs in D. Z. Phillips and Timothy Tessin, eds., *Religion and Hume's Legacy* (London: Macmillan, 1999), 47–108.

*Chapter 4*

1. "The greatest crimes have been found . . . compatible with a superstitious piety and devotion" (*NHR*, 14.7).

2. Edward Craig, *The Mind of God and the Image of Man* (Oxford: Oxford University Press, 2006); Kenneth Merrill and Donald Wester, "Hume on the Relation of Religion to Morality," *Journal of Religion* 60, no. 3 (1980): 272–84.

3. For divine interventions in history, see Thomas Holden, *Spectres of False Divinity: Hume's Moral Atheism* (Oxford: Oxford University Press, 2010).

4. Paul Russell, *The Riddle of Hume's "Treatise": Skepticism, Naturalism, and Irreligion* (Oxford: Oxford University Press, 2008), 290.

5. The most important descriptivist readings are Stephen Darwall, *The British Moralists and the Internal "Ought," 1640–1740* (Cambridge: Cambridge University Press, 1995); Stephen Darwall, "Hume and the Invention of Utilitarianism," in *Hume and Hume's Connexions*, ed. M. A. Stewart and John P. Wright (University Park: Pennsylvania State University Press, 1995), 58–82; and John L. Mackie, *Hume's Moral Theory* (London: Routledge, 1980).

6. The best discussion of this metaphor is in John Immerwahr, "The Anatomist and the Painter: The Continuity of Hume's *Treatise* and *Essays*," *Hume Studies* 17, no. 1 (1991): 1–14.

7. Hume implied in a 1739 letter to Hutcheson and in the *Treatise* 1.4.6.23 that he took himself to be an anatomist.

8. See Ken Binmore, *Natural Justice* (Oxford: Oxford University Press, 2005). An important review of that book is Dieter Birnbacher, "Binmore's Humeanism," *Analyse und Kritik* 28 (2006): 66–70. Additionally, see Robert Shaver, "Hume's Moral Theory?," in *History of Philosophy Quarterly* 12, no. 3 (1995): 317–31.

9. Annette C. Baier and Donald W. Livingston read Hume as having a normative project, as does Rachel Cohon, *Hume's Morality: Feeling and Fabrication* (Oxford: Oxford University Press, 2008).

10. Jennifer Herdt, *Religion and Faction in Hume's Moral Philosophy* (Cambridge: Cambridge University Press, 1997), 80–81. Herdt gives a very patient, sensitive, and persuasive treatment of Hume's notion of sympathy. Her attempt to resituate the development of our "sympathetic understanding" as key in light of our political and social concerns comports with my emphasis on Hume's investment in the intentions of the moral agent, social utility, and the development of character through the cultivation of the artificial virtues. Also, I generally agree with her idea that sympathy displaces providence as that which accounts for moral approval or disapproval. Where Herdt and I slightly disagree is with her treatment of religion. She wants to show that Hume does two things: (1) he demonstrates that morality does not rely on religious foundations, and (2) he details how religion distorts moral judgment. I want to show that we can get a new (and usable) vista on Hume's moral thought if we comprehend it as a provisional component of true religion. Hume realized the power of our disposition toward religion to be such that he had to reformulate religion, not reject it.

11. Gilles Deleuze, *Empiricism and Subjectivity: An Essay on Hume's Theory of Human Nature*, trans. Constantin V. Boundas (New York: Columbia University Press, 1991), 22.

12. Hume writes, "But as human society is in perpetual flux, one man every hour going out of the world, another coming into it, it is necessary, in order to preserve stability in government, that the new brood should conform themselves to the established constitution, and nearly

follow the path which their fathers, treading in the footsteps of theirs, had marked out to them" (*EMPL*, 12.476).

13. This is a citation from the preface that Hume removed from volume 2 of his *History of England*. Ernest Campbell Mossner, *The Life of David Hume* (Oxford: Clarendon Press, 2001), 306–7.

14. All these positions are much more complicated than this oversimplified and introductory sketch illuminates. I shall clarify the moral sense theory and rationalist positions later. For the best background information and Hume's general approach to it, see Mackie, *Hume's Moral Theory*; J. B. Schneewind, *The Invention of Autonomy* (Cambridge: Cambridge University Press, 1998); Herdt, *Religion and Factionalism*; David D. Raphael, ed., *British Moralists, 1650–1800* (Indianapolis: Hackett, 1991); and Darwall, *British Moralists*. Finally, for a thorough and interesting overview of the issues as they precede Hume, see Terence Irwin, *The Development of Ethics from Suarez to Rousseau: A Historical and Critical Study* (Oxford: Oxford University Press, 2008).

15. John L. Mackie provides the most thorough argument for the difference in the normative and the metaethical arguments. See his *Ethics: Inventing Right and Wrong* (New York: Penguin Books, 1977). James Fieser discusses Mackie's argument in "Is Hume a Moral Skeptic?," in *Philosophy and Phenomenological Research* 50, no. 1 (1989): 89–105.

16. Annette C. Baier, *The Cautious Jealous Virtue: Hume on Justice* (Cambridge: Harvard University Press, 2010), 8. She also makes this claim in *Death and Character: Further Reflections on Hume* (Cambridge: Harvard University Press, 2008), 91. Baier's position supports my argument: "Hume, of course, speaks of 'false religion' as the enemy of his humane and human version of morals, not of religion as such, and always disclaimed being an atheist." *Cautious Jealous Virtue*, 236.

17. Hume, quoted in Baier, *Cautious Jealous Virtue*, ix.

18. Thomas Hobbes, *Leviathan*, ed. Richard Tuck (Cambridge: Cambridge University Press, 1971). Adam Smith, recognized as the father of modern economics, had, in fact, held a chair in moral philosophy at the University of Glasgow, and his first published work was the deeply Humean-inspired *Theory of Moral Sentiments* in 1759. He follows Hume in privileging sympathy in his moral thought. His notion of sympathy, however, does not provide the observer with the experience of pleasure or pain of the moral actor; it simply allows one to experience the indirect passions of the moral actor (pride, humility, love, and hatred). Smith, *The Theory of Moral Sentiments*, ed. David D. Raphael and Alec L. Macfie (Oxford: Clarendon Press, 1976), 12–23.

19. Three studies of Hobbes are integral to my understanding of him: David Gauthier, *The Logic of Leviathan: The Moral and Political Theory of Thomas Hobbes* (Oxford: Oxford University Press, 1969); Howard Warrander, *The Political Philosophy of Hobbes: His Theory of Obligation* (Oxford: Oxford University Press, 1957); and Gregory S. Kavka, *Hobbesian Moral and Political Philosophy* (Princeton: Princeton University Press, 1986).

20. Samuel Clarke notes,

> And now, from what has been said upon this Head, 'tis easy to see the Falsity and Weakness of Mr. Hobbes's Doctrines; That there is no such thing as Just and Unjust, Right and Wrong originally in the Nature of Things; That Men in their natural State, antecedent to all Compacts, are not obliged to universal Benevolence, nor to any moral Duty whatsoever, but are in a state of War, and have every one a Right to do whatever he has Power to do; And that, in Civil Societies, it depends wholly upon positive Laws or the will of Governours, to define what shall be Just or Unjust. The contrary to all which, having been already fully demonstrated, there is no need of being large, in further disproving and confuting particularly these Assertions themselves. I shall therefore only mention a few Observations, from which some of the greatest and most obvious Absurdities of the chief Principles, upon which Mr. Hobbes builds his whole Doctrine in this Matter, may most easily appear.

Samuel Clarke, "Discourse upon Natural Religion," in *British Moralists, Being Selections from Writers Principally of the Eighteenth Century*, ed. Lewis A. Selby-Bigge (Oxford: Clarendon Press, 1897), 2:37 [512].

21. Ibid., 2:6 [484]. Clarke continues, "For a Man endued with Reason, to deny the Truth of these Things, is the very same thing, as if a Man that has the use of his Sight, should at the same time that he beholds the Sun, deny that there is any such thing as Light in the World; or as if a Man that understands Geometry or Arithmetick, should deny the most obvious and known Proportions of Lines or Numbers, and perversely contend that the Whole is not equal to all its parts, or that a Square is not double to a triangle of equal base and height."

22. There is extensive conversation in Hume studies about the difference morals make in conduct. The most noted text in this regard is Sophie Botros, *Hume, Reason, and Morality: A Legacy of Contradiction* (London: Routledge, 2006). Botros provides a careful assessment of Hume's argument in book 3.1 of the *Treatise*. Because she does not discuss the first *Enquiry*, her work cannot be considered to represent Hume's moral thought in a more "full" way.

23. Charles Taylor, *Sources of the Self: The Making of Modern Identity* (Cambridge: Harvard University Press, 1989), 254.

24. Ibid., 64, 5. And our "Sense of Right and Wrong" was "as natural to us as *natural Affection* itself, and being a first Principle in our Constitution and Make; there is no speculative Opinion, Persuasion or Belief, which is capable *immediately* or *directly* to exclude or destroy it" (23). In other words, moral distinctions are real for Shaftesbury, and the independent faculty that gives access to them is natural, rational, and passional. This is the "moral sense" (24).

25. Directly against the Hobbesian premise, Shaftesbury writes,

> YOU have heard it (my Friend!) as a common Saying, that *Interest governs the World*. But, I believe, whoever looks narrowly into the Affairs of it, will find, that *Passion, Humour, Caprice, Zeal, Faction*, and a thousand other Springs, which are counter to *Self-Interest*, have as considerable a part in the Movements of this Machine. There are more Wheels and *Counter-Poises* in this Engine than are easily imagin'd. 'Tis of too complex a kind, to fall under one simple View, or be explain'd thus briefly in a word or two.

Anthony Ashley Cooper, Earl of Shaftesbury, *Characteristicks of Men, Manners, Opinions, Times*, ed. Douglas den Uyl (Indianapolis: Liberty Fund, 2001), 1:115–16.

26. Anthony Ashley Cooper, Earl of Shaftesbury, "Inquiry Concerning Virtue or Merit," in Selby-Bigge, *British Moralists*, 1:21.

27. See Christine Korsgaard, *The Sources of Normativity* (Cambridge: Cambridge University Press, 1996).

28. Though his work did reflect some Hobbesian elements—particularly concerning justice—his "views cannot be neatly assimilated to those of Hobbes or his moral sense critics (Shaftesbury and Hutcheson). Hume's moral theory is a complex blend of elements from Hobbes, Shaftesbury, and others, with a view to defending a more nuanced account of the principles of (genuine) virtuous atheism." Russell, *Riddle of Hume's "Treatise."* I disagree with Russell's conclusion about Hume's "virtuous atheism" and think he would be more precise if he described it as virtuous atheism regarding popular religion.

29. Selby-Bigge, introd. to *British Moralists*, 1:8.

30. The best secondary sources on the Hume-Hutcheson connection are James Moore, "Hume and Hutcheson," in *Hume and Hume's Connexions*, ed. M. A. Stewart and John P. Wright (University Park: Pennsylvania State University Press, 1995), 23–56; and Ian S. Ross, "Hutcheson on Hume's *Treatise*: An Unnoticed Letter," *Journal of the History of Philosophy* 4 (1966): 69–72.

31. Baier, *Death and Character*, 69.

32. Herdt, *Religion and Faction*, provides a thorough discussion of sympathy.

33. Describing sympathy, Hume writes, "Thus it appears, *that* sympathy is a very powerful principle in human nature, *that* it has a great influence on our taste of beauty, and *that* it produces our sentiment of morals in all the artificial virtues. From thence we may presume, that it also gives rise to many of the other virtues; and that qualities acquire our approbation, because of their tendency to the good of mankind" (*T*, 3.3.1.10).

34. Victor Turner, *The Ritual Process* (Piscataway: Rutgers University Press, 1969), 131–212. When viewed through the lens of true religion, this notion of communitas is saturated with a spirit of provisional unity and momentary togetherness.

35. Annette C. Baier, *A Progress of Sentiments: Reflections on Hume's "Treatise"* (Cambridge: Harvard University Press, 1991), 198–219.

36. Another problem with applying the term "normative" to Hume's moral thought is that some might take it to imply the existence of ahistorical rules and standards by which we might allow our behavior to be guided. This is not Hume's approach. While we would generally be correct to assert that the foundational norms of his moral thought are the sentiments of approval and usefulness, if we tarry too long with this premise we flatten our capacity to capture the different modes and levels of moral activity (moral sentiments, artificial virtues, natural virtues, extensive sympathy, limited sympathy, contiguity); miss the extent to which Hume was not reducible to a normative thinker concerning morals; and lose the dynamism between moral agent and moral spectator that is evident in his narrative work. Holding a fixed or conventional notion of normativity does not allow us to approach Hume's moral thought with requisite fluidity and openness. Hume's work is action guiding and norm generating but it does not rely on autonomous reason as the source for our moral ends, and it keeps close track of history.

37. Eric Gregory teaches an important issue related to Thomistic ethics as virtue ethics: when understood through the idea of Christian love, the Augustinian tradition can, in many ways, be read as an important early articulation of a weak form of virtue ethics. Gregory masterfully rejects the strong version of virtue ethics yet is not subsumed by "deontological or consequentialist accounts of act-specification." *Politics and the Order of Love: An Augustinian Ethic of Democratic Citizenship* (Chicago: University of Chicago Press, 2008), 70.

38. One of the best discussions of Hume's subjectivism is Philippa Foot, *Natural Goodness* (Oxford: Oxford University Press, 2001). Foot challenges the readings of A. J. Ayer, R. M. Hare, Alan Gibbard, Simon Blackburn, and John Mackie on the grounds that they are based on a mistake. She argues that they reduced the meaning of moral evaluation to simply the attitude, intentions, and state of mind of the speaker or moral evaluator. They often attributed this approach to Hume. Another very compelling and interesting reading of Hume's subjectivism is David Wiggins, "A Sensible Subjectivism," in *Foundations of Ethics: An Anthology*, ed. Russ Shafer-Landau and Terence Cuneo (Oxford: Blackwell Press, 2007), 145–56. Wiggins rejects the strong subjectivism often attributed to Hume.

39. Rosalind Hursthouse, *On Virtue Ethics* (Oxford: Oxford University Press, 1999), has become the essential text for those in the field of virtue ethics.

40. Christopher Miles Cooper argues quite vociferously that Hursthouse is not properly representative of Anscombe (who was his teacher) due to the invisibility of the concept of justice in her argument and her translation of *phronesis* to moral wisdom over practical wisdom. "Modern Virtue Ethics," in *Values and Virtues: Aristotelianism in Contemporary Ethics*, ed. Timothy Chappell (Oxford: Oxford University Press, 2006), 20–52.

41. Hursthouse, *On Virtue Ethics*, 210; see also 167. She attends to two important issues (peripheral to my argument but worthy of mention). First, when we consider whether or not a virtue, say, temperance, is a virtue by nature (or naturally), we can only come to this question with our own conception of temperance. Thus, if ethical naturalism is correct, we are always imposing our moral conceptions or ideas about virtue onto nature, not vice versa. Second, she discusses the issue of how a naturalist ethics may not be able to speak to the different ways that virtues work in different circumstances of human ethical life.

42. Christine Swanton, *Virtue Ethics: A Pluralistic View* (Oxford: Oxford University Press, 2003), 90–95, 93. It is not clear to me why the "'dazzling' qualities," "noble elevation," and so on are not useful ends to Swanton.

43. Ibid., 93.

44. Cornel West, *The Ethical Dimensions of Marxist Thought* (New York: Monthly Review Press, 1991), 8.

45. There is disagreement about Hume's use and definition of these terms. See David Fate Norton, "The Foundations of Morality in Hume's *Treatise*," in *The Cambridge Companion to Hume*, ed. David Fate Norton and Jacqueline Taylor, 2nd ed. (Cambridge: Cambridge University Press, 2009), 270–310; and Cohon, *Hume's Morality*, 161–231.

46. Numerous natural virtues exist, but they generally fall under two rubrics: benevolence and greatness of mind. Artificial virtues in Hume are justice, honesty regarding property, fidelity to promises and obligations, allegiance, chastity, and good manners.

47. For a brief contemporary presentation of this history, see Stephen Mullen, *It Wisnae Us! The Truth About Glasgow and Slavery* (Edinburgh: Royal Incorporation of Architects in Scotland, 2009).

48. Herman De Dijn describes this evolution: "It is the same as with language; people didn't sit down and invent language for the sake of better communication, it simply evolved; but once it is there, its advantages are clear to everyone." See his thoughtful essay, "Promise and Ritual: Profane and Sacred Symbols in Hume's Philosophy of Religion," *Journal of Scottish Philosophy* 1, no. 1 (2003): 62.

49. Some note that regarding the development of a kind of social grammar Hume is proto-Wittgensteinian. See William H. Brenner, "Morality and Religion: Towards Meeting Hume's Challenge," in *Religion and Hume's Legacy*, ed. D. Z. Phillips and Timothy Tessin (London: Macmillan, 1999), 27–31.

50. Hume writes, "'Tis the voluntary convention and artifice of men, which makes the first interest take place; and therefore those laws of justice are so far to be consider'd as artificial. After that interest is once establish'd and acknowledge'd, the sense of morality in the observance of these rules follows naturally, and of itself; tho' 'tis certain, that it is also augmented by a new artifice, and that the public instructions of politicians, and the private education of parents, contribute to giving us a sense of honour and duty in the strict regulation of our actions with regard to the properties of others" (*T*, 3.2.6.11).

51. De Dijn, "Promise and Ritual." Thoughtful work on this issue is done by Annette C. Baier. Her chapter "Promises, Promises, Promises," in *Postures of the Mind: Essays on Mind and Morals*, ed. Annette C. Baier (Minneapolis: University of Minnesota Press, 1985), 174–206; and her *Progress of Sentiments*, 244–64, are crucial starting points. Cohon, *Hume's Morality*, 190–214, puts forward a sensitive, detailed, and compelling presentation of the myriad philosophical dimensions of Hume's discussion of promises. Yet in spite of her positive reading of Hume, she allows for his moral contributions to have occurred only in his explicitly moral writings (she overlooks his history and the essays on happiness). See also David Gauthier, "Artificial Virtues and the Sensible Knave," *Hume Studies* 18, no. 2 (1992): 401–27; and Bernard Wand, "Hume's Account of Obligation," *Philosophical Quarterly* 6, no. 23 (1956): 155–68, who both provide unique angles on the artificial virtues. Gauthier illustrates inconsistencies between the *Treatise* version and the *EPM* version of artificial virtues and undermines Hume's argument about the role of the moral grounds of our social conventions.

52. Hume develops this link between artificial virtues and superstition in the *EPM*:

> It may appear to a careless view, or rather a too abstracted reflection, that there enters a like superstition into all the sentiments of justice; and that, if a man expose its object, or what we call property, to the same scrutiny of sense and science, he will not, by the most accurate enquiry, find any foundation for the difference made by moral sentiment. I may

lawfully nourish myself from this tree; but the fruit of another of the same species, ten paces off, it is criminal for me to touch. Had I worn this apparel an hour ago, I had merited the severest punishment; but a man, by pronouncing a few magical syllables, has now rendered it fit for my use and service. Were this house placed in the neighboring territory, it had been immoral for me to dwell in it; but being built on this side the river, it is subject to a different municipal law, and by its becoming mine I incur no blame or censure. The same species of reasoning it may be thought, which so successfully exposes superstition, is also applicable to justice; nor is it possible, in the one case more than in the other, to point out, in the object, that precise quality or circumstance, which is the foundation of the sentiment.

But there is this material difference between *superstition* and *justice*, that the former is frivolous, useless, and burdensome; the latter is absolutely requisite to the well-being of mankind and existence of society. When we abstract from this circumstance (for it is too apparent ever to be overlooked) it must be confessed, that all regards to right and property, seem entirely without foundation, as much as the grossest and most vulgar superstition. Were the interests of society nowise concerned, it is as unintelligible why another's articulating certain sounds implying consent, should change the nature of my actions with regard to a particular object, as why the reciting of a liturgy by a priest, in a certain habit and posture, should dedicate a heap of brick and timber, and render it, thenceforth and forever, sacred. (3.2.16)

53. Jacqueline Taylor, "Justice and the Foundations of Social Morality in Hume's *Treatise*," *Hume Studies* 24, no. 1 (1998): 6–7.

54. Norman Kemp Smith describes Hume's moral naturalism in book 3 of the *Treatise* as deeply indebted to the work of Hutcheson. *The Philosophy of David Hume: A Critical Study of Its Origins and Central Doctrines* (London: Macmillan, 1960). Jennifer Herdt's *Religion and Faction in Hume's Moral Philosophy* (Cambridge: Cambridge University Press, 1997) gives a detailed description of the relationship between Hume and Hutcheson on morals and the passions that thoughtfully challenges Kemp Smith's argument.

55. Timothy M. Costelloe, "'In Every Civilized Community': Hume on Belief and the Demise of Religion," *International Journal for Philosophy of Religion* 55 (2004): 171–85.

56. Baier, *Cautious Jealous Virtue*, especially the introduction "What the Historian Taught the Moralist," 1–18, is crucial for this section, as is her *Death and Character*, 3–111. Donald Siebert, *The Moral Animus of David Hume* (Newark: University of Delaware Press, 1990) is vital for my argument here as well. Herdt also speaks to the importance of Hume's historical work for his moral argument, *Religion and Faction*.

57. Siebert, *Moral Animus of David Hume*, 40.

58. Roberto Unger, *The Self Awakened: Pragmatism Unbound* (Cambridge: Harvard University Press, 2007), 55–56.

59. Donald W. Livingston, *Philosophical Melancholy and Delirium* (Chicago: University of Chicago Press, 1998), 142.

60. Gerald L. Bruns, *Tragic Thoughts at the End of Philosophy* (Evanston: Northwestern University Press, 1999), 73.

61. Just some of the questions it inspires are, What philosophy of history does its author employ? Is it written in the style of the ancient or modern philosophy? What was its intended audience? What was Hume's purpose in writing it?

62. See Spencer K. Wertz, "Moral Judgments in History: Hume's Position," *Hume Studies* 22, no. 2 (1996): 350.

63. David Wooten, "David Hume, 'the Historian,'" in *The Cambridge Companion to Hume*, ed. David Fate Norton (Cambridge: Cambridge University Press, 1993), 284.

64. Beckwith and Yandell argue that Hume is after miracles in this section and not miracle testimony. My argument is that Hume's system prevents him from arguing against that which is unobservable. Thus, he attacks the veracity of testimony for miracles, not miracles themselves.

65. This controversial definition is articulated in Robert J. Fogelin, *A Defense of Hume on Miracles* (Princeton: Princeton University Press, 2003); and John Earman, *Hume's Abject Failure: The Argument Against Miracles* (Oxford: Oxford University Press, 2000). Hume actually provides two definitions of miracles in this essay. In *E*, 10.1.12, he writes in a footnote that "A miracle may be accurately defined [as] *a transgression of a law of nature by a particular volition of the Deity, or by the interposition of some invisible agent.*" The key distinction between this and his earlier definition of a miracle as "a violation of the laws of nature" is that the second definition gives more specificity to what constitutes a miracle and thereby shows that only a "Deity" or "invisible agent" is able to be ultimately responsible for a miracle. This confirms he has religion in mind.

66. Note: we have a proof, *not* a demonstration here. A demonstration concerns only the intrinsic relation between ideas (*E*, 4.2.5) and "the denial of their conclusion involves a contradiction." Don Garrett, *Cognition and Commitment in Hume's Philosophy* (Oxford: Oxford University Press, 1997), 143.

67. J. C. A. Gaskin concurs with this when he describes this section in the following way: "What Hume does not do in this argument, what he does not need to do, and what it may not be possible to do, is to show that miracles could never happen and that the evidence for a miracle could never be credible to a rational man." *Hume's Philosophy of Religion* (London: Macmillan, 1978), 120.

68. Stephen Buckle, *Hume's Enlightenment Tract: The Unity and Purpose of "An Enquiry Concerning Human Understanding"* (Oxford: Clarendon Press, 2001), 259.

69. Hume closes section 10 with what have now become some of his most famous and misinterpreted statements. He writes, "Our most holy religion is founded on *Faith*, not on reason; and it is a sure method of exposing it to put it to such a trial as it is, by no means, fitted to endure" (*E*, 10.2.27). Hume scholars most often describe this claim and the strong religious statements that immediately follow it as part of Hume's "prudential irony," his own safe way of negotiating the powerful forces of his day that could potentially prosecute and jail him for articulating antireligious sentiments. ("Prudential irony" is Gaskin's terminology; see his "Hume on Religion," in *The Cambridge Companion to Hume* [Cambridge: Cambridge University Press, 1993], 321.)

I suggest that this reading is deficient for two main reasons. First, Hume is mostly describing what he *observes* about humans and religion. His observation that most humans operate from the basis of faith concerning their religious beliefs is neither ironic nor inconsistent with his argument against miracle testimony. His statement, that for most humans "religion is founded on Faith, not on reason," on its own, is not particularly controversial.

Second, Hume's fideist language is neither ironic nor inconsistent if it is read as merely one possible explication for how his moderate skepticism and nondogmatism might inform something like the rare, true religion over and against the popular, vulgar religion. While Hume himself is not invested in faith as a foundation of knowledge against reason, as *fides* implies, his fundamental or moderated hope relies on a belief in nature and, therefore, a trust or faith in its broad sense. These fideist claims at the end of section 10 are neither ironic nor inconsistent; they can best be read as an invitation to the mild, true religion supported by Hume's constructive project. The best discussion of this issue is Delbert J. Hanson, *Fideism and Hume's Philosophy: Knowledge, Religion, and Metaphysics* (New York: Lang, 1993). While I think Hanson overreads Hume's fideism, I think his text is a very important counterweight to those who ignore fideism in Hume. Hanson does a particularly good job of providing evidence that shows Hume was more of a religionist than he is usually considered to be (the story of Hume's response to his mother's death on page 69–71 is particularly compelling).

70. J. C. Hilson, "Hume: The Historian as Man of Feeling," in *Augustan Worlds*, ed. J. C. Hilson, M. M. B. Jones, and J. R. Watson (Bristol: Leicester University Press, 1978), 205–22.

71. Hume's description of the execution of Charles I is powerful, and I cite it here at length:

> The street before Whitehall was the place destined for the execution: For it was intended, by choosing that very place, in sight of his own palace, to display more evidently the triumph of popular justice over royal majesty. When the king came upon the scaffold, he found it so surrounded with soldiers, that he could not expect to be heard by any of the people: He addressed, therefore, his discourse to the few persons who were about him; particularly colonel Tomlinson, to whose care he had lately been committed, and upon whom, as upon many others, his amiable deportment had wrought an entire conversion. He justified his own innocence in the late fatal wars, and observed, that he had not taken arms, till after the parliament had inlisted forces; nor had he any other object in his warlike operations, than to preserve that authority entire, which his predecessors had transmitted to him. He threw not, however, the blame upon the parliament; but was more inclined to think, that ill instruments had interposed, and raised in them fears and jealousies with regard to his intentions. Though innocent towards his people, he acknowledged the equity of his execution in the eyes of his Maker; and observed, that, an unjust sentence, which he had suffered to take effect, was now punished by an unjust sentence upon himself. He forgave all his enemies, even the chief instruments of his death; but exhorted them and the whole nation to return to the ways of peace, by paying obedience to their lawful sovereign, his son and successor. When he was preparing himself for the block, bishop Juxon called to him: "There is, Sir, but one stage more, which, though turbulent and troublesome, is yet a very short one. Consider, it will soon carry you a great way; it will carry you from earth to heaven; and there you shall find, to your great joy, the prize, to which you hasten, a crown of glory." "I go," replied the king, "from a corruptible to an incorruptible crown; where no disturbance can have place." At one blow was his head severed from his body. A man in a vizor performed the office of executioner: Another, in a like disguise, held up to the spectators, the head, streaming with blood, and cried aloud, *This is the head of a traitor!* (*HE*, 5.540)

72. This citation continues,

> Never monarch, in the full triumph of success and victory, was more dear to his people, than his misfortunes and magnanimity, his patience and piety, had rendered this unhappy prince. In proportion to their former delusions, which had animated them against him, was the violence of their return to duty and affection. . . . On weaker minds, the effect of these complicated passions was prodigious. Women are said to have cast forth the untimely fruit of their womb: Others fell into convulsions, or sunk into such a melancholy as attended them to their grave: Nay some, unmindful of themselves, as though they could not, or would not survive their beloved prince, it is reported, suddenly fell down dead. The very pulpits were bedewed with unsuborned tears; those pulpits, which had formerly thundered out the most violent imprecations and anathemas against him (*HE*, 5.541).

*Chapter 5*

1. Again, this is the description of true religion (which he later excised) in the preface to volume 2 of Hume's *History of England*. See Ernest Campbell Mossner, *The Life of David Hume* (Oxford: Clarendon Press, 2001), 306–7.

2. Thomas Nagel, *Mind and Cosmos: Why the Materialist Neo-Darwinian Conception of Nature Is Almost Certainly False* (Oxford: Oxford University Press, 2012), 4, 93, 127.

3. The problem here remains that Hume wanted to address human problems, while Nagel attended to problems of philosophy and science. Hume generally removed problems from the privileged realm of philosophical discourse and grounded them in a discussion about self-understanding that has relevance to ordinary people in common life.

4. Nagel, *Mind and Cosmos*, 127. Nagel noted Hume's subjectivist approach to moral value, yet he neglected to comment on Hume's investment in common sense and his (largely) epistemological approach.

5. J. C. A. Gaskin, *Hume's Philosophy of Religion* (London: Macmillan, 1978), 190.

6. Gerhard Streminger, "A Reply to Ellin," *Hume Studies* 15, no. 2 (1989): 303, is an exception here. He writes, "With some reservations, 'true religion' may be characterized in the following way: It consists in the private worship for the Creator, without superstitious beliefs, but in the spirits of tolerance and open-mindedness."

7. Jonathan Z. Smith, "Religion, Religions, Religious," in *Critical Terms for Religious Studies*, ed. Mark C. Taylor (Chicago: University of Chicago Press, 1998), 274.

8. Gaskin, *Hume's Philosophy of Religion*, 222, 223.

9. Donald W. Livingston, "Hume on the Divine and Philosophic Barbarism," in *Philosophy and Culture: Essays in Honor of Donald Phillip Verene*, ed. Glenn A. Magee (Charlottesville: Philosophy Documentation Center, 2002), 37.

10. Gaskin, *Hume's Philosophy of Religion*, 223.

11. Livingston, "Hume on the Divine," 36–53.

12. Miguel Badia-Cabrera, *Hume's Reflection on Religion* (Dordrecht: Kluwer Academic, 2001), 89, 90.

13. Friedrich D. E. Schleiermacher, *On Religion: Speeches to Its Cultured Despisers*, trans. Richard Crouter, 2nd ed. (Cambridge: Cambridge University Press, 1996), 79.

14. Annette C. Baier, *A Progress of Sentiments: Reflections on Hume's "Treatise"* (Cambridge: Harvard University Press, 1991), 167.

15. Paul Russell, *The Riddle of Hume's "Treatise": Skepticism, Naturalism, and Irreligion* (Oxford: Oxford University Press, 2008), 259.

# BIBLIOGRAPHY

*David Hume: Primary Sources*

Hume, David. *Abstract of a Book Lately Published Entitled "A Treatise of Human Nature"
Wherein the Chief Argument of That Book Is Farther Illustrated and Explained.* 1740.
In Millican, ed., *Reading Hume on Human Understanding,* 399–411.
———. *David Hume: Writings on Religion.* Edited by Antony Flew. La Salle, Ill.: Open
Court Press, 1992.
———. *Dialogues Concerning Natural Religion.* In *Principal Writings on Religion,* 29–130.
———. *Dialogues Concerning Natural Religion and the Posthumous Essays: Of the Immor-
tality of the Soul and of Suicide.* Edited by Richard H. Popkin. Indianapolis: Hackett,
1983.
———. "Dissertation on the Passions." In *Four Dissertations and Essays,* 99.
———. *An Enquiry Concerning Human Understanding.* 1748. In Selby-Bigge and Nidditch,
eds., *Enquiries Concerning Human Understanding,* 1–165.
———. *An Enquiry Concerning the Principles of Morals.* 1751. In Selby-Bigge and Nidditch,
eds., *Enquiries Concerning Human Understanding,* 168–323.
———. *Essays: Moral, Political, and Literary.* Edited by Eugene F. Miller. Indianapolis:
Liberty Classics, 1985.
———. *Four Dissertations and Essays on Suicide and the Immortality of the Soul.* Key Texts
in the History of Ideas. South Bend: St. Augustine's Press, 1995.
———. *The History of England: From the Invasion of Julius Caesar to the Revolution in 1688.*
6 vols. Indianapolis: Liberty Fund, 1983.
———. *A Kind of History of My Life.* In Norton, ed., *Cambridge Companion to Hume,*
345–50.
———. *A Letter from a Gentleman to His Friend in Edinburgh.* 1745. Edited by Ernest Camp-
bell Mossner and John V. Price. Edinburgh: Edinburgh University Press, 1967.
———. *The Letters of David Hume.* Edited by J. Y. T. Greig. 2 vols. Oxford: Clarendon
Press, 1932.
———. *My Own Life.* In Norton, ed., *Cambridge Companion to Hume,* 351–56.
———. *Natural History of Religion.* In *Principal Writings on Religion.*
———. *New Letters of David Hume.* Edited by Raymond Klibansky and Ernest C. Mossner.
Oxford: Clarendon Press, 1969.
———. *Of Suicide.* In *Dialogues Concerning Natural Religion and the Posthumous Essays,* 99.
———. *The Philosophical Works.* Edited by Thomas Hill Green and Thomas Hodge Grose.
Vol. 4. London: Scientia Verlag Aalen, 1964.
———. *Principal Writings on Religion Including "Dialogues Concerning Natural Religion"
and "The Natural History of Religion."* Edited, with an introduction and notes, by
J. C. A. Gaskin. Oxford World's Classics. Oxford: Oxford University Press, 1993.

————. *A Treatise of Human Nature.* Edited, with an analytical index, by Lewis A. Selby-Bigge. 15th ed. Oxford: Clarendon Press, 1978.

*Secondary Sources*

Adorno, Theodore W., and Max Horkheimer. *Dialectic of Enlightenment.* Translated by John Cumming. New York: Continuum, 1972.

Aiken, Henry D. Introduction to Hume's *"Dialogues Concerning Natural Religion,"* edited by Henry D. Aiken, vii–xvii. New York: Hafner, 1948.

Ainslie, Donald C. "Hume's Scepticism and Ancient Scepticism." In *Hellenistic and Early Modern Philosophy,* edited by Jon Miller and Brad Inwood. Cambridge: Cambridge University Press, 2003.

Allison, Henry E. *Custom and Reason in Hume: A Kantian Reading of the First Book of the "Treatise."* Oxford: Clarendon Press, 2008.

Andre, Shane. "Was Hume an Atheist?" *Hume Studies* 19, no. 1 (1993): 141–66.

Árdal, Páll S. *Passion and Value in Hume's "Treatise."* Edinburgh: Edinburgh University Press, 1966.

Armstrong, Nancy, and Leonard Tennenhouse. "A Mind for Passion: Locke and Hutcheson on Desire." In Kahn, Saccamano, and Coli, eds., *Politics and the Passions,* 131–50.

Arp, Robert. "Hume's Mitigated Skepticism and the Design Argument." *American Catholic Philosophical Quarterly* 72 (1998): 539–58.

Asad, Talal. *Genealogies of Religion: Discipline and Reasons of Power in Christianity and Islam.* Baltimore: Johns Hopkins University Press, 1993.

Bacon, Francis. *The Advancement of Learning.* Edited by Stephen Jay Gould. New York: Modern Library of America, 2001.

————. *The Major Works.* Edited, with an introduction, by Brian Vickers. Oxford World's Classics. Oxford: Oxford University Press, 2002.

————. *The Philosophical Works of Francis Bacon.* Edited, with an introduction, by John M. Robertson. New York: Dutton, 1905.

————. *The Works of Francis Bacon.* Edited by James Spedding. London: Longman, Green, 1859.

Badia-Cabrera, Miguel. *Hume's Reflection on Religion.* Dordrecht: Kluwer Academic Publishers, 2001.

Baier, Annette C. *The Cautious Jealous Virtue: Hume on Justice.* Cambridge: Harvard University Press, 2010.

————. *Death and Character: Further Reflections on Hume.* Cambridge: Harvard University Press, 2008.

————. *A Progress of Sentiments: Reflections on Hume's "Treatise."* Cambridge: Harvard University Press, 1991.

————. "Promises, Promises, Promises." In *Postures of the Mind: Essays on Mind and Morals,* edited by Annette C. Baier, 174–206. Minneapolis: University of Minnesota Press, 1985.

Barnes, Jonathan, ed. *The Complete Works of Aristotle.* Princeton: Princeton University Press, 1984.

Basu, Dilip. "Who Is the Real Hume in the *Dialogues*?" *Indian Philosophical Quarterly* 6 (1978): 21–28.

Battersby, Christine. "The *Dialogues* as Original Imitation: Cicero and the Nature of Hume's Skepticism." In Norton, Capaldi, and Robinson, eds., *McGill Hume Studies,* 239–53.

Beard, Mary. "Cicero and Divination: The Formation of a Latin Discourse." *Journal of Roman Studies* 76, no. 3 (1986): 33–46.

Beck, Lewis White. *Essays on Kant and Hume*. New Haven: Yale University Press, 1978.

Becker, Carl L. *The Heavenly City of the Eighteenth-Century Philosophers*. New Haven: Yale University Press, 1967.

Beckwith, Francis. *David Hume's Argument Against Miracles: A Critical Analysis*. Lanham: University Press of America, 1989.

Beiser, Frederick C. *The Fate of Reason: German Philosophy from Kant to Fichte*. Cambridge: Harvard University Press, 1987.

———. *The Sovereignty of Reason: The Defense of Rationality in the Early English Enlightenment*. Princeton: Princeton University Press, 1996.

Bell, Jeffrey A. *Deleuze's Hume: Philosophy, Culture, and the Scottish Enlightenment*. Edinburgh: Edinburgh University Press, 2009.

Bell, Martin. "Belief and Instinct in the First *Enquiry*." In Millican, ed., *Reading Hume*, 175–210.

Benjamin, Andrew. *Present Hope: Philosophy, Architecture, Judaism*. New York: Routledge, 1997.

Berchman, Robert. *Porphyry Against the Christians*. Boston: Brill, 2005.

Berman, David. "David Hume and the Suppression of Atheism." *Journal of the History of Philosophy* 21 (1983): 375–87.

Berry, Christopher J. *Hume, Hegel, and Human Nature*. London: Nijhoff, 1982.

Betty, L. Stafford. "The Buddhist-Humean Parallels: Postmortem." *Philosophy East and West* 21, no. 3 (1971): 237–53.

Blackburn, Simon. "Hume and Thick Connexions." In Read and Richman, eds., *New Hume Debate*, 100–112.

Blair, Hugh. *Sermons*. London: Smith, 1828.

Binmore, Ken. *Natural Justice*. Oxford: Oxford University Press, 2005.

Birnbacher, Dieter. "Binmore's Humeanism." *Analyse und Kritik* 28 (2006): 66–70.

Bloch, Ernst. *The Principle of Hope*. Oxford: Blackwell, 1986.

Botros, Sophie. *Hume, Reason, and Morality: A Legacy of Contradiction*. London: Routledge, 2006.

Brenner, William H. "Morality and Religion: Towards Meeting Hume's Challenge." In Phillips and Tessin, eds., *Religion and Hume's Legacy*, 27–41.

Bricke, John. *Hume's Philosophy of Mind*. Princeton: Princeton University Press, 1980.

———. *Mind and Morality: An Examination of Hume's Moral Psychology*. Oxford: Clarendon Press, 1996.

———. "On the Interpretation of Hume's *Dialogues*." *Religious Studies* 11, no. 1 (1975): 1–18.

Briggs, John C. *Francis Bacon and the Rhetoric of Nature*. Cambridge: Harvard University Press, 1989.

Broackes, Justin. "Hume, Belief, and Personal Identity." In Millican, ed., *Reading Hume*, 187–202.

Broadie, Alexander, ed. *The Cambridge Companion to the Scottish Enlightenment*. Cambridge: Cambridge University Press, 2003.

———. *The Scottish Enlightenment: An Anthology*. Edinburgh: Canongate Books, 1997.

Broughton, Janet. "Hume's Ideas about Necessary Connection." *Hume Studies* 13, no. 2 (1987): 217–44.

Brown, Colin. *Miracles and the Critical Mind*. Grand Rapids: Eerdmans, 1984.

Bruns, Gerald L. *Tragic Thoughts at the End of Philosophy*. Evanston: Northwestern University Press, 1999.

Buckle, Stephen. *Hume's Enlightenment Tract: The Unity and Purpose of "An Enquiry Concerning Human Understanding."* Oxford: Clarendon Press, 2001.

Burriss, Eli Edward. "Cicero and the Religion of His Day." *Classical Journal* 21, no. 7 (1926): 524–32.

Butler, Ronald J. "Natural Belief and the Enigma of Hume." *Archiv für Geschicte der Philosophie* 42, no. 1 (1960): 73–100.

Byrne, Peter. *Natural Religion and the Nature of Religion*. New York: Routledge, 1989.

Calvin, John. *Institute of the Christian Religion*. Edited by John T. McNeill. Vol. 2. Philadelphia: Westminster Press, 1960.

Capaldi, Nicholas. *David Hume: The Newtonian Philosopher*. Boston: Twayne, 1975.

———. "The Dogmatic Slumber of Hume Scholarship." *Hume Studies* 18, no. 2 (1992): 117–35.

———. "Hume's Philosophy of Religion: God Without Ethics." *International Journal for Philosophy of Religion* 1, no. 4 (1970): 233–40.

Capps, Walter H. "Mapping the Hope Movement." In *The Future of Hope*, edited by Walter H. Capps, 1–49. Philadelphia: Fortress Press, 1971.

Cassirer, Ernst. *The Philosophy of the Enlightenment*. Princeton: Princeton University Press, 1951.

Celsus. *On the True Doctrine: A Discourse Against the Christians*. Translated by R. Joseph Hoffman. New York: Oxford University Press, 1987.

Chappell, Vere C., ed. *Hume: A Collection of Critical Essays*. New York: Anchor Books, 1966.

Cherbury, Edward, Lord Herbert of. *De veritate*. Translated, with an introduction, by Meyrick H. Carre. Bristol: Arrowsmith, 1937.

———. *Pagan Religion: A Translation of "De religione gentilium."* Edited by John Anthony Butler. Ottawa: Dovehouse, 1996.

Christensen, Jerome. *Practicing Enlightenment: Hume and the Formation of a Literary Career*. Madison: University of Wisconsin Press, 1987.

Church, Ralph W. *Hume's Theory of the Understanding*. London: Allen, 1935.

Cicero, Marcus Tullius. *Cicero's Letters to Atticus*. Edited by David R. Shackleton Bailey. Vol. 1. Cambridge: Cambridge University Press, 1965.

———. *De divinatione*. New York: Loeb Classical Library, 1923.

———. *De finibus bonorum et malorum; or, On Moral Ends*. Edited by Julia Annas. Cambridge: Cambridge University Press, 2004.

———. *De haruspicum responsis oratio*. Translated by N. H. Watts. Cambridge: Harvard University Press, 1923.

———. *De inventione*. In *The Orations of Marcus Tullius Cicero*, vol. 4, translated by Charles D. Yonge. London: Bell, 1988.

———. *De legibus*. New York: Loeb Classical Library, 1928.

———. *De officiis*. Translated by Walter Miller. Cambridge: Harvard University Press, 1913.

———. *Orationes: Recognovit brevique adnotatione critica instruxit Albertus Curtis Clark*. 1891. With Albert Clark and William Peterson. Translated by Charles D. Yonge. Scriptorum Classicorum Bibliotheca Oxoniensis. Oxford: Typographeo Clarendoniano, 1909.

———. *The Orations of Marcus Tullius Cicero*. Translated by C. D. Yonge. London: Bell and Sons, 1891.

Clarke, Samuel. *A Demonstration of the Being and Attributes of God and Other Writings*. Edited by Ezio Vailati. Cambridge: Cambridge University Press, 1998.

———. "Discourse upon Natural Religion." 1706. In Selby-Bigge, ed., *British Moralists*, 2:482–525.

Cohen, L. Jonathan. "Some Historical Remarks on the Baconian Conception of Probability." *Journal of the History of Ideas* 41, no. 2 (1980): 219–31.

Cohon, Rachel. *Hume's Morality: Feeling and Fabrication*. Oxford: Oxford University Press, 2008.

Coleman, Dorothy. "Hume's Dialectic." *Hume Studies* 10, no. 2 (1984): 139–55.

Collingwood, Robin G. *The Idea of History*. New York: Oxford University Press, 1977.

Collins, James. *The Emergence of Philosophy of Religion*. New Haven: Yale University Press, 1967.

Collins, John. "Belief, Desire, and Revision." *Mind* 97, no. 387 (1988): 333–42.

Cooper, Christopher Miles. "Modern Virtue Ethics." In *Values and Virtues: Aristotelianism in Contemporary Ethics*, edited by Timothy Chappell, 20–52. Oxford: Oxford University Press, 2006.

Costelloe, Timothy M. *Aesthetics and Morals in the Philosophy of David Hume*. New York: Routledge, 2007.

———. "Hume's Phenomenology of the Imagination." *Journal of Scottish Philosophy* 5, no. 1 (2007): 31–45.

———. "'In Every Civilized Community': Hume on Belief and the Demise of Religion." *International Journal for Philosophy of Religion* 55 (2004): 171–85.

Craig, Edward. *The Mind of God and the Image of Man*. Oxford: Oxford University Press, 2006.

Damrosch, Leo. *Fictions of Reality in the Age of Hume and Johnson*. Madison: University of Wisconsin Press, 1989.

Darwall, Stephen. *The British Moralists and the Internal "Ought," 1640–1740*. Cambridge: Cambridge University Press, 1995.

———. "Hume and the Invention of Utilitarianism." In Stewart and Wright, eds., *Hume and Hume's Connexions*, 58–82.

Davie, George. *A Passion for Ideas: Essays on the Scottish Enlightenment*. Vol. 2. Edinburgh: Polygon, 1994.

Day, J. P. "Hope." *American Philosophical Quarterly* 6, no. 2 (1969): 89–102.

———. "Hope: A Philosophical Inquiry." *Acta Philosophica Fennica* 51 (1991): 11–51.

De Dijn, Herman. "Promise and Ritual: Profane and Sacred Symbols in Hume's Philosophy of Religion." *Journal of Scottish Philosophy* 1, no. 1 (2003): 57–67.

Deleuze, Gilles. *Empiricism and Subjectivity: An Essay on Hume's Theory of Human Nature*. Translated, with an introduction, by Constantin V. Boundas. New York: Columbia University Press, 1991.

De Pierris, Graciela. "Hume's Pyrrhonian Scepticism and the Belief in Causal Laws." *Journal of the History of Philosophy* 39, no. 3 (2001): 351–83.

Descartes, Rene. *Descartes: Selected Philosophical Writings*. Translated by John Cottingham, Robert Stoothoff, and Dugald Murdoch. Cambridge: Cambridge University Press, 1988.

———. *Discourse on Method and Meditations*. Translated, with an introduction, by Laurence J. Lafleur. New York: Liberal Arts Press, 1960.

———. "Meditations on First Philosophy." In Descartes, *Descartes*, 73–122.

———. "The Passions of the Soul." In Descartes, *Descartes*, 218–38.

Dicker, Georges. *Hume's Epistemology and Metaphysics: An Introduction*. London: Routledge, 1998.

Dole, Andrew. *Schleiermacher on Religion and the Natural Order*. Oxford: Oxford University Press, 2010.

Dye, James. "A Word on Behalf of Demea." *Hume Studies* 15, no. 1 (1989): 258–79.

Earman, John. *Hume's Abject Failure: The Argument Against Miracles*. Oxford: Oxford University Press, 2000.

Ellin, Joseph. "Streminger: Religion a Threat to Morality." *Hume Studies* 15, no. 2 (1989): 295–300.

Faulkner, Robert K. *Francis Bacon and the Project of Progress*. London: Rowman and Littlefield, 1993.

Ferreira, M. Jaime. "Hume's Naturalism: Proof and Practice." *Philosophical Quarterly* 35, no. 138 (1985): 45–57.

———. *Scepticism and Reasonable Doubt*. Oxford: Clarendon Press, 1986.

Fieser, James. "The Eighteenth-Century British Reviews of Hume's Writings." *Journal of the History of Ideas* 57, no. 4 (1996): 645–57.

———. "Hume's Pyrrhonism: A Developmental Interpretation." *Hume Studies* 15, no. 1 (1989): 93–119.

———. "Is Hume a Moral Skeptic?" *Philosophy and Phenomenological Research* 50, no. 1 (1989): 89–105.

Fitzgerald, Ross, ed. *The Sources of Hope*. Australia: Pergamon Press, 1979.

Fitzgerald, Timothy. *Discourse on Civility and Barbarity: A Critical History of Religion and Related Categories*. New York: Oxford University Press, 2010.

Flage, Daniel E. *David Hume's Theory of Mind*. London: Routledge, 1990.

Flew, Antony. *David Hume: Philosopher of Moral Science*. Oxford: Basil Blackwell, 1986.

———. *Hume's Philosophy of Belief: A Study of His First "Inquiry."* 1961. Reprint, Bristol: Thoemmes Press, 1997.

Fodor, Jerry A. *Hume Variations*. Oxford: Clarendon Press, 2003.

Fogelin, Robert J. *A Defense of Hume on Miracles*. Princeton: Princeton University Press, 2003.

———. *Hume's Skepticism in the "Treatise of Human Nature."* London: Routledge, 1985.

Foot, Philippa. *Natural Goodness*. Oxford: Oxford University Press, 2001.

Forbes, Duncan. *Hume's Philosophical Politics*. Cambridge: Cambridge University Press, 1975.

Fosl, Peter. "Doubt and Divinity: Cicero's Influence on Hume's Religious Skepticism." *Hume Studies* 20, no. 1 (1994): 103–20.

Foti, Veronique M. "The Cartesian Imagination." *Philosophy and Phenomenological Research* 46, no. 4 (1986): 631–42.

Frankenberry, Nancy, ed. *Radical Interpretation in Religion*. Cambridge: Cambridge University Press, 2002.

Franklin, James. "More on Part IX of Hume's *Dialogues*." *Philosophical Quarterly* 30 (1980): 69–71.

Frasca-Spada, Marina. Review of *Philosophical Melancholy and Delirium*, by Donald Livingston. *Mind*, n.s., 110, no. 439 (2001): 783–89.

———. *Space and Self in Hume's "Treatise."* Cambridge: Cambridge University Press, 1998.

Frede, Michael. "Celsus' Attack on the Christians." In *Philosophia Togota II: Plato and Aristotle at Rome*, edited by Jonathan Barnes and Miriam Griffin. New York: Oxford University Press, 1997.

Garrett, Don. *Cognition and Commitment in Hume's Philosophy*. Oxford: Oxford University Press, 1997.

———. Introduction to *Philosophy of David Hume* by Norman Kemp Smith. New York: Palgrave Macmillan, 2005.

———."What's True about Hume's 'True Religion'?" *Journal of Scottish Philosophy* 10 (2012): 199–220.

Gaskin, J. C. A. "God, Hume, and Natural Belief." *Philosophy* 49, no. 189 (1974): 281–94.

———. "Hume on Religion." In Norton, ed., *Cambridge Companion to Hume*, 480–514.

———. *Hume's Philosophy of Religion*. London: Macmillan, 1978.

Gauthier, David. "Artificial Virtues and the Sensible Knave." *Hume Studies* 18, no. 2 (1992): 401–27.

———. *The Logic of Leviathan: The Moral and Political Theory of Thomas Hobbes*. Oxford: Oxford University Press, 1969.

Gay, Peter. *The Enlightenment: An Interpretation*. Vol. 2, *The Science of Freedom*. New York: Knopf, 1969.

———. *The Enlightenment: The Rise of Modern Paganism*. New York: Norton, 1995.

Giles, James. "The No-Self Theory: Hume, Buddhism, and Personal Identity." *Philosophy East and West* 43, no. 2 (1993): 177–93.

Gill, Eric. *Art-Nonsense and Other Essays*. London: Cassell, 1929.

Goar, Robert J. "The Purpose of *De divinitione*." *Transactions and Proceedings of the American Philological Association* 99 (1968): 241–48.

Godfrey, Joseph J. *A Philosophy of Human Hope*. Dordrecht: Nijhoff, 1987.

Gregory, Eric. *Politics and the Order of Love: An Augustinian Ethic of Democratic Citizenship*. Chicago: University of Chicago Press, 2008.

Grotius, Hugo. *The Rights of War and Peace*. Abridged and translated by William Whewell. Cambridge: Cambridge University Press, 1853.

———. *The Truth of the Christian Religion in Six Books*. Translated by John D. Clarke. Oxford: Baxter Press, 1818.

Hacking, Ian. *The Emergence of Probability*. New York: Cambridge University Press, 1975.

Hagg, Tomas. "Hierocles the Lover of Truth and Eusebius the Sophist." In *Parthenope: Studies in Ancient Greek Fiction*, edited by Lars Boje Morensen and Tormod Eide, 405–16. Denmark: Museum Tusculanum Press, 2004.

Hampton, Jean. *The Authority of Reason*. Cambridge: Cambridge University Press, 1998.

———. "Does Hume Have an Instrumental Conception of Practical Reason?" *Hume Studies* 21, no. 1 (1995): 57–74.

Hanley, Ryan Patrick. "Hume's Critique and Defense of Religion." In *Enlightenment and Secularism: Essays on the Mobilization of Reason*, edited by C. Nadon, 89–101. Lanham: Lexington Books, 2013.

Hanson, Delbert J. *Fideism and Hume's Philosophy: Knowledge, Religion, and Metaphysics*. New York: Lang, 1993.

Harnack, Adolf. *History of Dogma*. Vol. 2. Translated by Neil Buchanan. Boston: Little, Brown. 1907.

Harrison, Peter. *"Religion" and the Religions in the English Enlightenment*. Cambridge: Cambridge University Press, 1990.

Harvey, Van. "Philo's 'True Religion.'" In Phillips and Tessin, eds., *Religion and Hume's Legacy*, 68–80.

Hecht, Jennifer Michael. *Doubt: A History*. New York: Harper Collins, 2003.

Heering, Jan-Paul. *Hugo Grotius as an Apologist for the Christian Religion: A Study of His Work "De veritate religionis christianae."* Leiden: Koninklijke Brill, 2004.

Herdt, Jennifer. *Religion and Faction in Hume's Moral Philosophy*. Cambridge: Cambridge University Press, 1997.

Hilson, J. C. "Hume: The Historian as Man of Feeling." In *Augustan Worlds*, edited by J. C. Hilson, M. M. B. Jones, and J. R. Watson, 205–22. Bristol: Leicester University Press, 1978.

Hobbes, Thomas. *Leviathan*. Edited by Richard Tuck. Cambridge: Cambridge University Press, 1971.

Hochstrass, T. J. *Natural Law Theories in the Early Enlightenment*. Cambridge: Cambridge University Press, 2004.

Hodges, Michael, and John Lachs. "Hume on Belief." *Review of Metaphysics* 30 (1976): 3–18.

Holden, Thomas. *Spectres of False Divinity: Hume's Moral Atheism*. Oxford: Oxford University Press, 2010.

Holland, Alan J. *Philosophy, Its History and Historiography*. Dordrecht: Kluwer Academic, 1985.

Howson, Colin. *Hume's Problem: Induction and the Justification of Belief*. Oxford: Clarendon Press, 2000.

Hurlbutt, Robert H., III. "David Hume and Scientific Theism." *Journal of the History of Ideas* 17, no. 4 (1956): 495–96.

———. *Hume, Newton, and the Design Argument*. Lincoln: University of Nebraska Press, 1965.

Hursthouse, Rosalind. *On Virtue Ethics*. Oxford: Oxford University Press, 1999.

Hutcheson, Francis. *Collected Works*. Hildesheim: Olds, 1969.

———. *An Essay on the Nature and Conduct of the Passions and Affections*. 1728. Manchester: Clinamen, 1999.

———. *On Human Nature*. Edited by Thomas Mautner. Cambridge: Cambridge University Press, 1993.

———. *An Inquiry into the Original of Our Ideas of Beauty and Virtue*. Hildesheim: Olds, 1971.

Immerwahr, John. "The Anatomist and the Painter: The Continuity of Hume's *Treatise* and *Essays*." *Hume Studies* 17, no. 1 (1991): 1–14.

———. "Hume on Tranquillizing the Passions." *Hume Studies* 28, no. 2 (1992): 295–310.

———. "Hume's Aesthetic Theism." *Hume Studies* 22, no. 2 (1996): 325–37.

———. "Hume's Essays on Happiness." *Hume Studies* 15, no. 2 (1989): 307–24.

Innes, David C. "Bacon's New Atlantis: The Christian Hope and Modern Hope." *Interpretation* 22 (1994): 3–36.

Irwin, Terence. *The Development of Ethics from Suarez to Rousseau: A Historical and Critical Study*. Oxford: Oxford University Press, 2008.

Jacobsen, Anne Jaap, ed. *Feminist Interpretations of David Hume*. University Park: Pennsylvania State University Press, 2000.

Jacobson, Nolan. "The Possibility of Oriental Influence in Hume's Philosophy." *Philosophy East and West* 19 (1969): 17–37.

James, Susan. *Passion and Action: The Emotions in Seventeenth-Century Philosophy*. Oxford: Clarendon Press, 1997.

Jenkins, John J. *Understanding Hume*. Edinburgh: Edinburgh University Press, 1992.

Johnson, Oliver A. *The Mind of David Hume: A Companion to Book I of "A Treatise of Human Nature."* Chicago: University of Illinois Press, 1995.

Jones, Peter. *Hume's Sentiments: Their Ciceronian and French Context*. Edinburgh: University of Edinburgh Press, 1982.

Kahn, Victoria, Neil Saccamano, and Daniela Coli, eds. *Politics and the Passions, 1500–1850*. Princeton: Princeton University Press, 2006.

Kail, P. J. E. "Is Hume a Causal Realist?" *British Journal for the History of Philosophy* 11, no. 3 (2003): 509–20.

———. "Reason, Custom, and the True Philosophy." *British Journal for the History of Philosophy* 9, no. 2 (2001): 361–66.

Kant, Immanuel. *Critique of Pure Reason*. Translated by Norman Kemp Smith. New York: St. Martin's Press, 1965.

Kaufman, Daniel. "Between Reason and Common Sense: On the Very Idea of Necessary (Though Unwarranted) Belief." *Philosophical Investigations* 28, no. 2 (2005): 134–58.

Kavka, Gregory S. *Hobbesian Moral and Political Philosophy*. Princeton: Princeton University Press, 1986.

Kemp, John. *Ethical Naturalism: Hobbes and Hume*. London: Macmillan, 1970.

Kemp Smith, Norman. "The Naturalism of Hume." *Mind* 14 (1905): 147–73.

———. *The Philosophy of David Hume: A Critical Study of Its Origins and Central Doctrines*. London: Macmillan, 1960.

Kenny, Anthony. *Action, Emotion, and Will*. London: Routledge and Kegan Paul, 1963.

Khamara, Edward J. "Hume Versus Clarke on the Cosmological Argument." *Philosophical Quarterly* 42 (1992): 48–53.

King, James T. "Despair and Hope in Hume's Introduction to the *Treatise of Human Nature*." *Hume Studies* 20, no. 1 (1994): 59–71.

Klinefelter, Donald. "Scepticism and Fideism in Hume's Philosophy of Religion." *Journal of the American Academy of Religion* 40, no. 2 (1977): 222–38.

Korsgaard, Christine. *The Constitution of Agency: Essays on Practical Reason and Moral Psychology*. Oxford: Oxford University Press, 2008.

———. "Skepticism about Practical Reason." *Journal of Philosophy* 83 (1986): 5–25.

———. *The Sources of Normativity*. Cambridge: Cambridge University Press, 1996.

Kraay, Klaas J. "Philo's Argument for Divine Amorality." *Hume Studies* 29, no. 2 (2003): 283–304.

Krause, Sharon R. *Civil Passions: Moral Sentiment and Democratic Deliberation*. Princeton: Princeton University Press, 2008.

———. "Hume and the (False) Luster of Justice." *Political Theory* 32, no. 5 (2004): 628–55.

———. "Passion, Power, and Impartiality in Hume." In *Bringing the Passions Back: The Emotions in Political Philosophy*, edited by Rebecca Kingston and Leonard Ferry, 126–49. Vancouver: UBC Press, 2007.

Laing, B. M. "Hume's *Dialogues Concerning Natural Religion*." *Philosophy* 12 (1937): 175–90.

Laird, John. *Hume's Philosophy of Human Nature*. New York: Archon Books, 1967.

Le Doeuff, Michele. "Hope in Science." In *Francis Bacon's Legacy of Texts*, edited by William A. Sessions, 9–24. New York: AMS Press, 1990.

Lemmens, Willem. "Beyond the Calm Sunshine of the Mind: Hume on Religion and Morality." *Aufklarung und Kritik* 27 (2011): 214–50.

Lewis, David. "Desire as Belief." *Mind* 97, no. 387 (1988): 323–32.

Livingston, Donald W. "Hume on the Divine and Philosophic Barbarism." In *Philosophy and Culture: Essays in Honor of Donald Phillip Verene*, edited by Glenn A. Magee, 37–55. Charlottesville: Philosophy Documentation Center, 2002.

———. "Hume's Conception of 'True Religion.'" In *Hume's Philosophy of Religion: The Sixth James Montgomery Hester Seminar*, edited by Antony Flew, 33–73. Winston-Salem: Wake Forest University Press, 1986.

———. *Hume's Philosophy of Common Life*. Chicago: University of Chicago Press, 1984.

———. *Philosophical Melancholy and Delirium: Hume's Pathology of Philosophy*. Chicago: University of Chicago Press, 1998.

Locke, John. *An Essay Concerning Human Understanding*. Edited, with a foreword, by Peter H. Nidditch. Oxford: Clarendon Press, 1979.

———. *The Reasonableness of Christianity with a Discourse on Miracles and Part of a Third Letter Concerning Toleration*. Edited, abridged, and introduced by Ian T. Ramsey. Stanford: Stanford University Press, 1958.

Loeb, Louis. *Stability and Justification in Hume's "Treatise."* Oxford: Oxford University Press, 2002.

Logan, Beryl. *A Religion Without Talking: Religious Belief and Natural Belief in Hume's Philosophy of Religion*. New York: Lang, 1993.

———. "Why Hume Wasn't an Atheist: A Reply to Andre." *Hume Studies* 22, no. 1 (1996): 193–202.

MacIntosh, John J., and Hugo A. Meynell. *Faith, Scepticism, and Identity*. Calgary: University of Calgary Press, 1994.

MacIntyre, Alasdair. *Whose Justice? Which Rationality?* Notre Dame: University of Notre Dame Press, 1988.

Mackie, John L. *Ethics: Inventing Right and Wrong*. New York: Penguin Books, 1977.

———. *Hume's Moral Theory*. London: Routledge, 1980.

MacMullen, Ramsey. *Paganism in the Roman Empire*. New Haven: Yale University Press, 1981.

MacNabb, Donald G. C. "David Hume." In *Encyclopedia of Philosophy*, edited by Paul Edwards, vol. 4. New York: Macmillan, 1967.

———. *David Hume: His Theory of Knowledge and Morality*. Hamden: Archon Books, 1966.

Macquarrie, John. *Christian Hope*. New York: Seabury, 1978.

Malherbe, Michel. "Hume and the Art of Dialogue." In Stewart and Wright, eds., *Hume and Hume's Connexions*, 199–215.

Marcel, Gabriel. *Creative Fidelity*. New York: Farrar, Strauss, and Giroux, 1964.

———. "Desire and Hope." In *Readings in Existential Phenomenology*, edited by Nathaniel Lawrence and Daniel O'Connor, 277–85. Englewood Cliffs: Prentice Hall, 1967.

———. *Homo Viator: Introduction to a Metaphysic of Hope*. New York: Harper and Row, 1962.

McCormick, Miriam. "A Change in Manner: Hume's Skepticism in the *Treatise* and the First *Enquiry*." *Canadian Journal of Philosophy* 29 (1999): 413–31.

———. "Hume on Natural Belief and Original Principles." *Hume Studies* 19, no. 1 (1993): 103–16.

McCosh, James. *The Scottish Philosophy*. Bristol: Thoemmes Press, 1990.

Merrill, Kenneth, and Robert W. Shahan. *David Hume: Many-Sided Genius*. Norman: University of Oklahoma Press, 1976.

Merrill, Kenneth, and Donald Wester. "Hume on the Relation of Religion to Morality." *Journal of Religion* 60, no. 3 (1980): 272–84.

Meyer, Michel. *Philosophy and the Passions: Toward a History of Human Nature*. Translated by Robert Barsky. University Park: Pennsylvania State University Press, 2000.

Michaud, Yves. "How to Become a Moderate Sceptic: Hume's Way Out of Pyrrhonism." *Hume Studies* 11, no. 1 (1985): 33–46.

Millgram, Elijah. "Was Hume a Humean?" *Hume Studies* 21, no. 1 (1995): 75–93.

Millican, Peter. "The Context, Aims, and Structure of Hume's First *Enquiry*." In *Reading Hume on Human Understanding: Essays on the First Enquiry*. Oxford: Clarendon Press, 2002.

———. "Critical Survey of the Literature." In Millican, ed., *Reading Hume*, 421–23.

———. "Hume, Causal Realism, and Causal Science." *Mind* 118, no. 471 (2009): 647–712.

———, ed. *Reading Hume on Human Understanding: Essays on the First Enquiry*. Oxford: Oxford University Press, 2002.

Mitchell, Timothy. *Hume's Anti-theistic Views: A Critical Appraisal*. Lanham: University Press of America, 1986.

Momigliano, Arnaldo. "The Theological Efforts of the Roman Upper Classes in the First Century BC." *Classical Philology* 79, no. 3 (1984): 199–211.

Moore, James. "Hume and Hutcheson." In Stewart and Wright, eds., *Hume and Hume's Connexions*, 23–56.

Morgan, Thomas. *The Moral Philosopher in a Dialogue Between Philalethes, a Christian Deist, and Theophanes, a Christian Jew*. London, 1737.

Morice, George P., ed. *David Hume: Bicentenary Papers*. Austin: University of Texas Press, 1977.

Mossner, Ernest Campbell. "An Apology for David Hume, Historian." *PMLA* 56, no. 3 (1941): 657–90.

———. "Hume and the Legacy of the *Dialogues*." In Morice, ed., *David Hume*, 1–22.

———. *The Life of David Hume*. Oxford: Clarendon Press, 2001.

Mounce, H. O. *Hume's Naturalism*. London: Routledge, 1999.

Mullen, Stephen. *It Wisnae Us! The Truth about Glasgow and Slavery*. Edinburgh: Royal Incorporation of Architects in Scotland, 2009.

Muyskens, James L. *The Sufficiency of Hope*. Philadelphia: Temple University Press, 1979.

Nagel, Thomas. *Mind and Cosmos: Why the Materialist Neo-Darwinian Conception of Nature Is Almost Certainly False*. Oxford: Oxford University Press, 2012.

———. *The Possibility of Altruism*. Oxford: Clarendon Press, 1970.

Neu, Jerome. *Emotion, Thought, and Therapy*. Berkeley: University of California Press, 1977.

Noonan, Harold W. *Hume on Knowledge*. London: Routledge, 1999.

Norton, David Fate, ed. *The Cambridge Companion to Hume*. Cambridge: Cambridge University Press, 1993.

———. *David Hume: Common-Sense Moralist, Sceptical Metaphysician*. Princeton: Princeton University Press, 1982.

———. "The Foundations of Morality in Hume's *Treatise*." In *The Cambridge Companion to Hume*, 2nd ed., edited by David Fate Norton and Jacqueline Taylor, 270–310. Cambridge: Cambridge University Press, 2009.

———. "Hume's 'Philosophy of Common Life.'" *Journal of History of Philosophy* 25, no. 2 (1983): 300–302.

Norton, David Fate, Nicholas Capaldi, and Wade L. Robinson, eds. *McGill Hume Studies*. San Diego: Austin Hill Press, 1979.

Norton, David Fate, and Richard Popkin. *David Hume: Philosophical Historian*. New York: Bobbs-Merrill, 1965.

Noxon, James. "Hume's Agnosticism." In *Hume: A Collection of Critical Essays*, edited by Vere C. Chappell, 361–83. New York: Doubleday, 1966.

———. *Hume's Philosophical Development: A Study of His Methods*. Oxford: Clarendon Press, 1973.

Nussbaum, Martha. *Upheavals of Thought*. Cambridge: Cambridge University Press, 2003.

O'Connor, David. *Hume on Religion*. New York: Routledge, 2001.

Olshewsky, Thomas. "Classical Roots of Hume's Scepticism." *Journal of the History of Ideas* 52 (1991): 269–87.

Origen. *Contra Celsum*. Edited by Henry Chadwick. Cambridge: Cambridge University Press. 1953.

Owen, David. "Hume Versus Price on Miracles and Prior Probabilities: Testimony and the Bayesian Calculation." *Philosophical Quarterly* 37, no. 147 (1987): 187–202.

Passmore, John A. *Hume's Intentions*. Cambridge: Cambridge University Press, 1952.

Pears, David. *Hume's System: An Examination of the First Book of His "Treatise."* Oxford: Oxford University Press, 1990.

Penelhum, Terence. *David Hume: An Introduction to His Philosophical System*. West Lafayette: Purdue University Press, 1992.

———. *God and Skepticism: A Study in Skepticism and Fideism*. Dordrecht: Reidel, 1983.

———. "Hume on Religion: Cultural Influences." In *A Companion to Hume*, edited by Elizabeth Radcliffe. Malden: Blackwell, 2008.

———. *Hume (Philosophers in Perspective)*. London: Macmillan, 1975.

———. *Themes in Hume: The Self, the Will, Religion*. Oxford: Clarendon Press, 2003.

Peters, Curtis H. *Kant's Philosophy of Hope*. New York: Lang, 1993.

Phillips, D. Z., and Timothy Tessin, eds. *Religion and Hume's Legacy*. London: Macmillan, 1999.

Phillips, David. "Hume on Practical Reason: Normativity and Psychology in *Treatise* 2.3.3." *Hume Studies* 31, no. 2 (2005): 299–316.

Pinch, Adela. *Strange Fits of Passion: Epistemologies of Emotion, Hume to Austen*. Stanford: Stanford University Press, 1996.

Pitson, A. E. *Hume's Philosophy of the Self*. New York: Routledge, 2002.

Plantinga, Alvin. *Where the Conflict Really Lies: Science, Religion, and Naturalism*. Oxford: Oxford University Press, 2010.

Pojman, Louis. *Religious Belief and the Will*. London: Routledge and Kegan Paul, 1986.

Polanyi, Michael. *Personal Knowledge: Toward a Post-critical Philosophy*. Chicago: University of Chicago Press, 1974.

———. *The Tacit Dimension*. London: Smith, 1983.

Popkin, Richard. "David Hume: His Pyrrhonism and His Critique of Pyrrhonism." In *Hume*, edited by Vere C. Chappell, 53–98. New York: Doubleday, 1966.

Potkay, Adam. *The Passion for Happiness: Samuel Johnson and David Hume*. Ithaca: Cornell University Press, 2000.

Price, John Vladimir. *David Hume*. New York: Twayne, 1968.

———. "Sceptics in Cicero and Hume." *Journal of the History of Ideas* 25, no. 1 (1964): 97–106.

Raphael, David D., ed. *British Moralists, 1650–1800*. Indianapolis: Hackett, 1991.

Rawls, John. *Lectures on the History of Moral Philosophy*. Cambridge: Harvard University Press, 2000.

Read, Rupert, and Kenneth Richman, eds. *The New Hume Debate*. London: Routledge, 2000.

Reid, Thomas. *The Works of Thomas Reid*. Bristol: Thoemmes Press, 1994.

Richards, Glyn. "Conception of Self in Wittgenstein, Hume, and Buddhism." *Monist* 61 (1978): 326–39.

Richman, Kenneth. Introduction to Read and Richman, eds., *New Hume Debate*, 1–15.

Rivers, Isabel. *Reason, Grace, and Sentiment: A Study of the Language of Religion and Ethics in England, 1660–1780*. Vol. 1. Cambridge: Cambridge University Press, 1991.

Robinson, J. A. "Hume's Two Definitions of Cause." *Philosophical Quarterly* 12 (1962): 162–71.

Rorty, Richard. *Philosophy and Social Hope*. New York: Penguin, 1999.

Ross, Ian S. "Hutcheson on Hume's *Treatise*: An Unnoticed Letter." *Journal of the History of Philosophy* 4 (1966): 69–72.

Russell, Paul. *The Riddle of Hume's "Treatise": Skepticism, Naturalism, and Irreligion*. Oxford: Oxford University Press, 2008.

———. "Skepticism and Natural Religion in Hume's *Treatise*." *Journal of the History of Ideas* 49 (1988): 247–65.

Sabl, Andrew. *Hume's Politics: Coordination and Crisis in the "History of England."* Princeton: Princeton University Press, 2012.

Saccamano, Neil. "Aesthetically Non-dwelling: Sympathy, Property, and the House of Beauty in Hume's *Treatise*." *Journal of Scottish Philosophy* 9, no. 1 (2011): 37–58.

———. "Parting with Prejudice: Hume, Identity, and Aesthetic Universality." In Kahn, Saccamano, and Coli, eds., *Politics and the Passions*, 175–95.

Saler, Benson. "*Religio* and the Definition of Religion." *Cultural Anthropology* 2, no. 3 (1987): 395–99.

Schleiermacher, Friedrich D. E. *On Religion: Speeches to Its Cultured Despisers*. Translated by Richard Crouter. 2nd ed. Cambridge: Cambridge University Press, 1996.

Schmidt, Claudia. *David Hume: Reason in History*. University Park: Pennsylvania State University Press, 2003.

Schneewind, J. B. "Hume and the Religious Significance of Moral Rationalism." *Hume Studies* 26, no. 2 (2000): 211–23.

———. *The Invention of Autonomy*. Cambridge: Cambridge University Press, 1998.

Schott, Jeremy. "Porphyry on Christians and Others: 'Barbarian Wisdom,' Identity Politics, and Anti-Christian Polemics on the Eve of the Great Persecution." *Journal of Early Christian Studies* 13, no. 3 (2005): 277–314.

Schumacher, Bernard. *A Philosophy of Hope: Josef Pieper and the Contemporary Debate on Hope*. New York: Fordham Press, 2003.

Schwerin, Alan. *The Reluctant Revolutionary: An Essay on David Hume's Account of Necessary Connection*. New York: Lang, 1989.

Scott, William Robert. *Francis Hutcheson: His Life, Teaching, and Position in the History of Philosophy*. Cambridge: Cambridge University Press, 1900.

Selby-Bigge, Lewis A., ed. *British Moralists, Being Selections from Writers Principally of the Eighteenth Century*. 2 vols. Oxford: Clarendon Press, 1897.

Selby-Bigge, Lewis A., and Peter H. Nidditch, eds. *Enquiries Concerning Human Understanding and Concerning the Principles of Morals*. 3rd ed. Oxford: Clarendon Press, 1975.

Sessions, William Lad. *Reading Hume's "Dialogues": A Veneration for True Religion*. Bloomington: Indiana University Press, 2002.

Shade, Patrick. *Habits of Hope: A Pragmatic Theory.* Nashville: Vanderbilt University Press, 2001.

Shaftesbury, Anthony Ashley Cooper, Earl of. *Characteristicks of Men, Manners, Opinions, Times.* 1711. Edited by Douglas den Uyl. Indianapolis: Liberty Fund, 2001.

———. "Inquiry Concerning Virtue or Merit." In Selby-Bigge, eds., *British Moralists,* 1:1–67.

Shaver, Robert. "Hume's Moral Theory?" *History of Philosophy Quarterly* 12, no. 3 (1995): 317–31.

Siebert, Donald. *The Moral Animus of David Hume.* Newark: University of Delaware Press, 1990.

Simmons, Michael B. Review of *Porphyry Against the Christians,* by Robert M. Berchman. *Journal of Early Christian Studies* 16 (2008): 263–65.

Smith, Adam. *The Theory of Moral Sentiments.* 1759. Edited by David D. Raphael and Alec L. Macfie. Oxford: Clarendon Press, 1976.

Smith, Jonathan Z. "Religion, Religions, Religious." In *Critical Terms for Religious Studies,* edited by Mark C. Taylor, 269–84. Chicago: University of Chicago Press, 1998.

Smith, Michael. "The Humean Theory of Motivation." *Mind* 96 (1987): 36–61.

Smith, Wilfred Cantwell. *The Meaning and End of Religion: A New Approach to the Religious Traditions of Mankind.* New York: Macmillan, 1991.

Soles, D. Hansen. "Hume, Language, and God." *Philosophical Topics* 12, no. 3 (1981): 109–19.

Spinoza, Benedict. *Improvement of the Understanding, Ethics and Correspondence.* Translated, with an introduction, by R. H. M. Elwes. New York: Dover, 1955.

———. *A Theologico-Political Treatise and a Political Treatise.* Translated, with an introduction, by R. H. M. Elwes. New York: Dover, 1951.

Stern, George. *A Faculty Theory of Knowledge: The Aim and Scope of Hume's First Enquiry.* Lewisburg: Bucknell University Press, 1971.

Stewart, M. A. "Hume and the 'Metaphysical Argument a Priori.'" In *Philosophy, Its History and Historiography,* edited by Alan J. Holland, 243–65. Dordrecht: Reidel, 1985.

Stewart, M. A., and John P. Wright, eds. *Hume and Hume's Connexions.* University Park: Pennsylvania State University Press, 1995.

Stove, D. C. "Part IX of Hume's *Dialogues.*" *Philosophical Quarterly* 28 (1978): 300–309.

———. *Probability and Hume's Inductive Scepticism.* Oxford: Clarendon Press, 1973.

Strawson, Galen. *The Secret Connexion: Causation, Realism, and David Hume.* Oxford: Clarendon Press, 1989.

Streminger, Gerhard. "Hume's Theory of the Imagination." *Hume Studies* 6, no. 2 (1998): 91–118.

———. "Religion a Threat to Morality: An Attempt to Throw Some New Light on Hume's Philosophy of Religion." *Hume Studies* 15, no. 2 (1989): 277–93.

———. "A Reply to Ellin." *Hume Studies* 15, no. 2 (1989): 301–5.

Stroud, Barry. *Hume.* London: Routledge and Kegan Paul, 1995.

Swanton, Christine. *Virtue Ethics: A Pluralistic View.* Oxford: Oxford University Press, 2003.

Taves, Ann. *Fits, Trances, and Visions: Experiencing Religion and Explaining Experience from Wesley to James.* Princeton: Princeton University Press, 2009.

———. *Religious Experience Reconsidered: A Building-Block Approach to the Study of Religion and Other Special Things.* Princeton: Princeton University Press, 2009.

Taylor, Charles. *Sources of the Self: The Making of Modern Identity.* Cambridge: Harvard University Press, 1989.

Taylor, Jacqueline. "Justice and the Foundations of Social Morality in Hume's *Treatise.*" *Hume Studies* 24, no. 1 (1998): 5–30.

Tertullian. *The Apology of Tertullian.* Translated and annotated by William Reeve. London: Newberry House, 1889.

Tindal, Matthew. *Christianity as Old as Creation; or, The Gospel: A Republication of the Religion of Nature.* London, 1730.

Traiger, Saul. "Impressions, Ideas, and Fictions." *Hume Studies* 13, no. 2 (1987): 381–99.

Turner, Victor. *The Ritual Process.* Piscataway: Rutgers University Press, 1969.

Tweyman, Stanley. "Hume's Dialogues on Evil." *Hume Studies* 18, no. 1 (1987): 74–85.

———. *Scepticism and Belief in Hume's "Dialogues Concerning Natural Belief."* Boston: Nijhoff, 1986.

Unger, Roberto. *The Self Awakened: Pragmatism Unbound.* Cambridge: Harvard University Press, 2007.

Vickers, Brian. "Francis Bacon and the Progress of Knowledge." *Journal of the History of Ideas* 53, no. 3 (1992): 495–518.

Wand, Bernard. "Hume's Account of Obligation." *Philosophical Quarterly* 6, no. 23 (1956): 155–68.

Warburton, William. "Remarks on Mr. David Hume's *Essay on the Natural History of Religion.*" 1777. In *Hume on Natural Religion*, ed. Stanley Tweyman, 237–48. Bristol: Thoemmes Press, 1996.

———. *A Selection from Unpublished Papers.* London, 1841.

Ward, Andrew. Introduction to *Essay on the Nature and Conduct of the Passions*, by Francis Hutcheson. Manchester: Clinamen, 1999.

Warrander, Howard. *The Political Philosophy of Hobbes: His Theory of Obligation.* Oxford: Oxford University Press, 1957.

Waterworth, Jayne M. *A Philosophical Analysis of Hope.* New York: Palgrave Macmillan, 2004.

Waxman, Wayne. *Hume's Theory of Consciousness.* Cambridge: Cambridge University Press, 1994.

Webb, Mark. "The Argument of the 'Natural History.'" *Hume Studies* 17, no. 2 (1991): 138–51.

Weisenhemer, Joel. *Eighteenth-Century Hermeneutics: Philosophy of Interpretation from Locke to Burke.* New Haven: Yale University Press, 1993.

Wertz, Spencer K. "Moral Judgments in History: Hume's Position." *Hume Studies* 22, no. 2 (1996): 339–67.

West, Cornel. *The Ethical Dimensions of Marxist Thought.* New York: Monthly Review Press, 1991.

———. *Prophesy Deliverance! An Afro-American Revolutionary Christianity.* Philadelphia: Westminster Press, 1982.

———. *Restoring Hope: Conversations on the Future of Black America.* Boston: Beacon Press, 1997.

Westfall, Richard S. "Isaac Newton's *Theologiae gentilis origines philosophicae.*" In *The Secular Mind: Essays Presented to Franklin L. Baumer*, edited by W. Warren Wagar. New York: Holmes and Meier, 1982.

Wielenberg, Erik J. *God and the Reach of Reason: C. S. Lewis, David Hume, and Bertrand Russell.* Cambridge: Cambridge University Press, 2008.

Wiggins, David. "A Sensible Subjectivism." In *Foundations of Ethics: An Anthology*, edited by Russ Shafer-Landau and Terence Cuneo, 145–56. Oxford: Blackwell Press, 2007.

Wilbanks, Jan. *Hume's Theory of the Imagination.* The Hague: Nijhoff, 1968.

Williams, Bernard. "Internal and External Reasons." In *Moral Luck*, 101–13. Cambridge: Cambridge University Press, 1986.

Williams, Christopher. *A Cultivated Reason: An Essay on Hume and Humeanism.* University Park: Pennsylvania State University Press, 1999.

Williston, Byron. Introduction to *Passion and Virtue in Descartes*, edited by Byron Williston and André Gombay. Amherst: Humanity Books, 2003.

Wilson, Fred. Review of *Hume's "Philosophy of Common Life,"* by Donald Livingston. *Philosophy of Social Science* 18 (1988): 137–56.

Wood, Forrest. "Hume's Philosophy of Religion as Reflected in the *Dialogues.*" *Southwestern Journal of Philosophy* 2 (1971): 185–93.

Wooten, David. "David Hume, 'the Historian.'" In Norton, ed., *Cambridge Companion to Hume*, 447–79.

———. *Hume's "Of Miracles": Probability and Irreligion*. Oxford: Clarendon Press, 1990.

Wright, John P. "Dr. George Cheyne, Chevalier Ramsay, and Hume's 'Letter to a Physician.'" *Hume Studies* 29, no. 1 (2003): 125–41.

———. "Hume's Academic Scepticism: A Reappraisal of His Philosophy of Human Understanding." *Canadian Journal of Philosophy* 16 (1986): 407–35.

———. *The Sceptical Realism of David Hume*. Minneapolis: University of Minnesota Press, 1983.

Yandell, Keith E. *Hume's "Inexplicable Mystery": His Views on Religion*. Philadelphia: Temple University Press, 1990.

Yoder, Timothy. *Hume on God: Irony, Deism, and Genuine Theism*. London: Continuum, 2011.

Yolton, John, ed. *Philosophy, Religion, and Science in the Seventeenth and Eighteenth Centuries*. Rochester: University of Rochester Press, 1990.

# INDEX